HEGEL: A RE-EXAMINATION

HEGEL

A RE-EXAMINATION

J. N. FINDLAY

OXFORD UNIVERSITY PRESS
New York

©John Niemeyer Findlay, 1958
Library of Congress Catalogue Card Number: 76-12155
First published by George Allen & Unwin Ltd., 1958
First issued as a paperback by Collier Books, 1962
First issued as an Oxford University Press paperback,
1976, by arrangement with George Allen & Unwin Ltd.

OXFORD UNIVERSITY PRESS

London   Oxford   New York
Glasgow   Toronto   Melbourne   Wellington
Cape Town   Ibadan   Nairobi   Dar es Salaam   Lusaka   Addis Ababa
Delhi   Bombay   Calcutta   Madras   Karachi   Lahore   Dacca
Kuala Lumpur   Singapore   Hong Kong   Tokyo

Printed in the United States of America

FOREWORD

If the present work makes hardly any reference to the standard commentaries and critical works on Hegel, e.g. Stace's *Philosophy of Hegel*, Mure's *Study of Hegel's Logic*, McTaggart's *Commentary on Hegel's Logic* and *Studies in Hegelian Dialectic*, and Hyppolite's *Phénoménologie de l'Esprit de Hegel*, this does not mean that I do not greatly value these books, and that I have not been influenced and guided by them at many points. McTaggart, with whom I agree least, I also admire most, and I regard M. Hyppolite's commentary as a model of objectivity and detachment. It was, however, my aim to give as clear an exposition as I could of certain ideas which seemed to me central in Hegel, in terms of which all his doctrines become connected, and to follow these ideas throughout the system, so as to show that they really are borne out by Hegel's statements. These ideas are not sufficiently stressed in the current expositions, and they seem to me not only to provide the key to Hegel, but also to be of the most immense and permanent philosophical interest and importance. To treat Hegel in this manner seemed to me a more worthwhile contribution to Hegelian studies than to argue with other interpreters.

References to Hegel's German text in this book are all to the Jubilee Edition of his works (edited by H. Glockner, Stuttgart). References have also been made throughout to Wallace's (W.) translations of the *Logic of Hegel* (the Lesser Logic) and the *Philosophy of Mind* (though Wallace's unfortunate omission of the invaluable editorial *Zusätze* to the latter work means that I cannot always refer to him); to J. B. Baillie's (B.) translation of the *Phenomenology of Mind*, and to the translation of the *Science of Logic* of W. H. Johnston and L. G. Struthers (J. and S.). But my quoted passages have in almost all cases been translated afresh, and I have tried to use verbal and sentence-structures resembling the German, and employing hyphenated Saxon compounds. I do not myself feel that Hegelianism accords lucidly with Latinity. I have made a great deal of use of capitals in the case of terms used technically by Hegel or involved in special discussions, but I have not found it feasible to be quite consistent in their use.

I should like in conclusion to thank my colleagues in the University of London, Professor A. J. Ayer and Professor H. D. Lewis, for their suggestions and criticisms, and to Professor Ayer for encouraging me to write this book in the first instance. He has made me spend over two years in the close and constant company of one of the greatest and least understood of philosophical minds.

J. N. FINDLAY

London, November 1957

Postscript to Foreword

This book has been found useful by many over the past two decades, and has even been translated into Spanish and Italian. I now find it too Wittgensteinian, too inclined to treat philosophical conceptions as ways of regarding things or talking about them, rather than as metaphysical essentialities culminating in a supreme, all-explanatory Idea. But, as there are many ways to approach Hegel, I am letting my previous utterances stand. One misunderstanding caused by a statement in the foregoing Foreword must be corrected: Professor Ayer was not the first influence who directed my intellectual gaze toward Hegel. Hegel's Lesser Logic was one of the first philosophical works I ever read, and my fascinated involvement in his thought goes back to 1920. Through all the changes in my philosophical persuasions I have never lost my deep interest in his unique dialectic, and have in the end, like the eternal Idea itself, returned to my beginnings. I have included references to Miller's recent translation (M.) of the *Science of Logic* in the footnotes.

J. N. FINDLAY

Boston, April 1976

CONTENTS

CONTENTS

CHAPTER ONE

INTRODUCTORY AND BIOGRAPHICAL

I HEGEL AND MODERN PRECONCEPTIONS

The aim of this book is to give a brief but rounded account of Hegel's philosophical doctrines, and to relate them to the ideas and language of our own time. Its aim is also to provide a guiding-thread through the tortuous intricacies of Hegel's principal writings, which exceed in difficulty those of any other philosopher. It will seek to capture something of the actual attitude and atmosphere of these writings, which will demand a more abundant and systematic use of quotation than is usual in expounding the views of a philosopher. Hegel's writings are at once so unique in their language, and so singular in their mode of argument, that it is not possible to represent them at all accurately in terms differing too widely from Hegel's own. Our concern will not be with those who have commented on Hegel—detailed commentaries on his writings are in fact somewhat few—nor with those who have been much influenced or greatly revulsed by his teaching —many of these have read him only superficially—but with the actual writings themselves, and with the doctrine that they embody. We shall seek to sketch and assess the contents of *The Phenomenology of Spirit* and of the three parts of the *Encyclopaedia of the Philosophical Sciences*.

There are several reasons why such a general restatement and reassessment of Hegel should be attempted. It would be worth doing even if only on account of the vastness of Hegel's influence, both in the past century and the present one. It is worth while sketching and sizing up a system which has provoked so huge a literature, which has excited such extremes of admiration and denigration, which has been so variously interpreted and criticized, and which has given birth to so many movements and counter-movements ever since it was promulgated. During that period Hegel's native Germany has at no time been free from his influence: if it deified him during his lifetime, developed his views in conflicting 'rightward' and 'leftward' directions after his death in 1831, and allowed the dust to gather on his works during the long ascendancy of positivism in the Bismarckian age, it has at length fitted him into an uncontested, 'classical' place in the façade of its historic culture, high in the centre with Kant and above all faction and party; it has also very largely gone back, to philosophizing in a manner reminiscent of Hegel's own *Phenomenology of Spirit*. Our own Anglo-Saxon world fell likewise under the spell of Hegel during the last half of the previous century, and the first quarter of the present one. We produced several highly original thinkers, e.g. Royce in America and Bradley in England, in a tradition which owed much of its inspiration to Hegel, and we spent much of the opening years of this century in elaborately abandoning and disowning Hegelian positions we had previously held. Now at length it is feasible for us to dissect and value Hegel with the detached appreciation possible in the case of other great philosophers. Italy, too, has produced several great original Hegelians (e.g. Croce and Gentile), and France, after producing much inspired Hegelian scholarship, has in our own age excelled all previous Hegelian studies in the objectivity, the scholarship and the illumination of M. Jean Hyppolite's excellent translation and commentary (on *The Phenomenology of Spirit*). Hegel has also had an immense, left-handed influence on thought through the reaction he inspired in the wilfully narrow, passionately perverse, religious soul of the mid-century Dane Kierkegaard, whose views, despite their condemnation of Hegel, might have come straight from one of Hegel's own phenomenological studies, and whose works, like the works of those he has influenced, are soaked in an Hegelian method and spirit. Hegel has further had an unassessable influence on the thought of India and the Far East. And he has been responsible (though not through his fault or merit) for the extraordinary transformation of parts of his method and doctrine which we owe to Karl Marx, a transformation involving both social penetration and much philosophical confusion. This has created a comprehensive background and mould of thought for millions of our contemporaries; in it, in fact, a whole new world of historic culture is growing up. No other philosopher can claim to have achieved anything so considerable.

It is not, however, on account of his mere influence that Hegel deserves a restatement and reassessment. He deserves it on account of the originality and permanent interest of his ideas, and on account of the extent to which these ideas have been overlaid by prejudiced misconceptions, due largely to the extreme difficulty and wanton obscurity of the language in which they were stated. Hegel only acquired a tolerably lucid style after he had been lecturing for some years at Heidelberg and Berlin, and by then his two greatest philosophical works—*The Phenomenology of Spirit* and the *Science of Logic*—had been written. In this chapter we shall merely prepare the way for an understanding of Hegel by mentioning a few of the deep-rooted prevailing misconceptions which obstruct the comprehension and remove the interest of his writings, and by trying, in dogmatic, preliminary fashion, to replace them by truer views. That they *are* misconceptions, largely underived from anything that Hegel says, and sometimes flatly opposed to his statements, can be shown only as we go systematically through his writings.

We shall say at this point that Hegel is misconceived, first of all, as being a *transcendent metaphysician*, one who deals with objects or matters lying beyond our empirical ken, or who fits together or transforms what we know or experience into some total view going beyond any individual person's knowledge or experience. We shall likewise hold him to be misconceived as some sort of *subjectivist*, one who thinks the realm of nature or history exists only *in* or *for* someone's consciousness, whether this be the consciousness of a mind like ours, or of some cosmic or supercosmic mind. We shall likewise rebut the stronger charge that Hegel thought that our mind (or the mind of God) *made* up the world in some witting or unwitting fashion. We shall hold, thirdly, that Hegel is misconceived as being some sort of manic *rationalist*, one who seeks to *deduce* or to *foresee* the detail of nature and experience from the abstract demands of certain notions, who tries to do *a priori* what we now hold can only be done *a posteriori*. We shall contend further that the extraordinary language in which he expresses his thought is not wholly devoid of illumination and justification, and that the chain of thought by which he advances from one thought-phase to the next is not rendered unworthy of study because it violates essential logical principles. We shall deny, further, the extraneous but highly prejudicial charge that Hegel was a thoroughgoing political reactionary, responsible ancestrally for the atrocities of Hitlerism: we shall deny the absurdly stronger charge that his whole system is merely a mask for such reaction. And we shall suggest, finally, that there is nothing irrelevant nor uncontemporary in Hegel's ideas, and that he has as much to say to us as to previous generations of thinkers.

As regards the view of Hegel as a transcendent metaphysician—one who speaks of matters lying beyond the bounds of possible experience, or who welds the data of our experience into a *whole* going far beyond what any mind can embrace—a good refutation is perhaps to be had simply by glancing at the contents of Hegel's two systematic works, *The Phenomenology of Spirit* and the *Encyclopaedia of the Philosophical Sciences*. Both works start with what is 'immediate', and as far as possible removed from what is ultimate and 'absolute'—the former starts with the direct certainties of sense-experience, the latter with the abstract notion of 'being'—both works likewise end up with what is 'absolute', the former with the 'Absolute Knowing' of philosophy, the latter with the three forms of 'Absolute Spirit', Art, Religion and Philosophy. Considering these works, there can be no doubt at all that Hegel sees what is 'absolute' in nothing which lies beyond the experiences and activities of men: the Absolute, he says is 'what is entirely present' (*das durchaus Gegenwärtige*), what is 'on hand and actual', not 'something over above things or behind them' (*etwas drüben und hinten*). The Hegelian Absolute is not realized in a supramundane consciousness, nor in a timeless comprehensive vision, but in the creative activities and products of the artist, the faith and worship of the religious person, and the systematic insights of the philosopher. One might say, in fact, that there never has been a philosopher by whom the *Jenseitige*, the merely transcendent, has been more thoroughly 'done away with', more thoroughly shown to exist only *as revealed* in human experience. Hegel does indeed sometimes make use of the transcendent language of religion, speaking of 'the Idea', the abstract principle of self-consciousness, as existing like God before the creation of nature and finite spirit: he also speaks of the highest stage of philosophical vision as achieving the 'abolition' of time. He makes plain, however, that the religious language thus occasionally made use of merely says by way of imaginative representation what can be more clearly said in the notional diction of philosophy, for which the 'Idea' only exists *before* the concrete world of nature and mind in the sense of being the conceptual 'blue-print', or notional possibility of the latter. And he makes plain that the only sense in which time (and for that matter space) is ever 'overcome', is that we reach levels of thought at which it simply ceases to count at all.

That any other impression of Hegel's doctrine should be current, is due, in part, to Hegel's studied conciliation of religion, whose basic principles he regarded (without absurdity) as one with those of his own philosophy. It is due also, particularly in our Anglo-Saxon world, to a confusion between the doctrines of those who learnt much from Hegel, and who were often called 'Hegelians', and the doctrines of Hegel himself. It was Bradley, not Hegel, who believed in some Absolute Experience within which the objects of our ordinary human experience would be unbelievably fused and transformed, in which ordinary categories would be done away with without being replaced by anything that *we* can hope to understand, and concerning which we certainly do not have the 'Absolute Knowing' which Hegel thinks that we have of the Absolute, and which is, in fact, for him, identical with the Absolute's own knowledge of itself. And it was McTaggart, not Hegel, who made the Absolute into a timeless fellowship of spirits, curiously but not incorrigibly deceived into seeing themselves and their own activities as in time. The un-Hegelian character of these systems is shown too, by their imperfect use of Hegel's dialectical methods: they make use of contradictions to abolish the world of appearance and the notions of ordinary life, and then pass to a realm of truth and reality in which 'all this is altered': in Hegel, however, the apparent and false are *retained* in his final result, whose content is, in fact, no more than the clear understanding of the process which has led up to that result itself. These systems are likewise differentiated from Hegel's by their doctrine of an unlimited 'coherence', of 'internal relations' between everything and everything else: as opposed to this Hegel accords a dishonourable place to unresolved *contingency* 'on the surface of nature', and to *indeterminacy* in the caprices of the will. References to the 'Universe', the 'Whole', are likewise as rare in Hegel as they are frequent in the philosophers just mentioned. What we have said must not be construed as casting scorn on the metaphysicians in question or on transcendent metaphysicians in general. Hegel, however, is not to be numbered among them, and must be praised or condemned for his own doctrines, and not for those of others.

Having thus dealt with what we may call the 'metaphysical charge' against Hegel, we may pass on to consider the 'subjectivist charge'. Hegel, we may maintain, is no idealist in the sense of holding that to be is to be perceived, or that to be is to be conceived, or that objects exist only if there are conscious minds to consider them or to refer to them. Even less is he an idealist in the sense of thinking that the mind *imposes* its forms on the material of sense, or that it 'constructs' the world in its activities of imagination or thought. That such subjectivism should be attributed to Hegel is due to an excessive stress on his relation to Kant, of whose thought he is regarded as the 'fulfiller' (Kant in his turn being regarded as the 'fulfiller' of previous post-Renaissance thought, in which the subjectivist strain is strongly stressed). From this point of view the main merit of Hegel lay in thoroughly liquidating the 'transcendental object' or 'thing-in-itself' of Kant, the thing as it exists *apart* from thought or consciousness. For the dualistic Kantian idealism, which opposes things as they exist *for* consciousness to things as they exist in themselves, Hegel is thought to have substituted an 'objective idealism', for which things have no real being except such as they have in relation to the thinking mind. This 'objective idealism' is, however, more the position of Hegel's predecessors than of Hegel himself: to attribute it to him is to ignore the extent to which his philosophy is *Hellenic* rather than Kantian, the extent to which for him 'the Idea' is objective after the manner of Plato and Aristotle and not after the manner of Kant. The *Philosophy of Nature* makes it plain, further, that Hegel believed in the existence of natural objects long before the advent of life and consciousness in the world, and in the *Philosophy of Spirit* he makes it plain that time and space are the forms of *external things*, and not merely the forms in which the mind envisages them. And if Hegel held that the whole natural world was an 'externalization' of the 'eternal Idea', this Idea is not to be interpreted as an actual self-conscious being, but rather as the mere *notion* of that spiritual self-consciousness which it is the task of the world-process to develop. It is clear that Hegel thought that conscious spiritual beings were the *last* beings to arrive on the scene of the world, and that 'Absolute Spirit', as manifest in the highest forms of art, religion and philosophy, was the *last* stage to be reached in their experience.

Hegel, in fact, must be recognized to be an 'idealist' in a

thoroughly new sense of the word: he employs throughout the Aristotelian notion of teleology or final causation, and he holds Mind or Spirit to be the final form, the goal or 'truth' of all our notions and the world. It is implicit, *an sich*, 'in itself', at the start of an ideal or a real process, and the whole process of notional or real development merely serves to make it explicit, *für sich*, 'for itself'. Hegel's thoroughgoing teleology means, further, that nothing whatever in the world or our thought can have any meaning or function but to serve as a condition for the activities of self-conscious Spirit. In distinguishing Hegel's teleological idealism from other forms of subjective or objective idealism, we are not here attempting to criticize the latter. But the elaborate fallacies which realist criticism has found in such forms of idealism must not be attributed to Hegel, who was not an idealist in this manner. Karl Marx found it necessary to stand Hegel on his head, in order to transform his 'idealism' into Marxist 'material-ism'. There is, however, as much materialism in Hegel as in Marx, since matter is for him certainly a *stage* in the 'Idea'. (Just as there is certainly also a strong strain of teleological idealism in the supposedly scientific materialism of Marx.)

Having disposed of the 'subjectivist charge' against Hegel, we may likewise dispose of the view of him as a relentless *a priorist*, one who sought to *deduce* the detail of nature and history from the relationships of abstract concepts. Hegel certainly believed in a Systematic Science (*Wissenschaft*) in which all concepts, even those applied in science and in history, could be linked together in a continuous chain, and in which each would find its unique and necessary place. The rules of this 'Systematic Science' are, however, far from being deductive in the sense in which the rules of a syllogism or a mathematical calculus are deductive. They are rather precepts which urge us to pass from notions in which some principle is latent, to other notions in which the same principle will become manifest: they do not, like deductive principles, march on a single level of discourse, but proceed rather from one level to the next. Though Hegel frequently speaks of the 'necessity' of his moves, he is clear, too, that this is not like the necessity of deductive inferences. And as regards the application of Hegel's peculiar method to the facts of nature and history, it is plain that the fit is loose, and intended to be loose. Some of the material he ranges over is dismissed as being contingent and superficial, and is even described as 'untrue', and there is absolutely no attempt to go beyond the facts and laws offered us in the empirical sciences, nor to make extrapolations or predictions which experience might or might not fulfil. Hegel sometimes 'sides' with one scientific theory against another, as he persistently espouses Kepler and Goethe against the empiric Newton: his reasons for such espousals are, however, as much scientific as philosophical. It is plain, in fact, that Hegel's philosophical aim is not to *do* the work of history or science, nor to add to their results, but to frame concepts in terms of which these results can be philosophically grasped, can be allotted a place in the teleological frame of notions and phases of being in terms of which Hegel sees the world. That such a re-conceiving of historical and scientific fact can be valuable and illuminating, as that it can also be arbitrary and absurd, will become plain when we consider actual instances. Hegel's genuine empiricism and freedom from *a priori* presuppositions is, however, much more definite than that of a philosopher like Herbert Spencer, whose *First Principles* attempts to prove much more about the physical universe, and to prove it more rigorously, than Hegel would ever have dreamt of doing. Hegel describes the facts of nature in much queer, old-fashioned language: a philosopher like Herbert Spencer makes many queer, old-fashioned misstatements of fact.

If Hegel is not to be regarded as a rationalist gone mad, he is also not to be regarded as a merely bogus reasoner, one whose words depend for an effect of meaning on a mere accumulation of pictures and suggestions, and whose thought-transitions are either non-logical and associative, or involve definite violations of logical rules. That these charges are somewhat hard to rebut can be shown by a single, brief quotation from Hegel, by no means unusual or untypical. Hegel writes: 'For the reality in itself, the general outcome of the relation of the Understanding to the inner nature of things, is the distinguishing of what cannot be distinguished, or is the unity of what is distinguished. This unity is, however, as we saw, just as much the recoil from itself, and this conception breaks asunder into the opposition of self-consciousness and life: the former is the unity *for which* the absolute unity of difference exists, the latter, however, *is* only this unity itself, so that the unity is at the same time *for* itself.'[1]

[1] *Phenomenology*, p. 142.

Passages like the foregoing certainly daunt the Hegelian student and apologist, and require much exegesis before the smallest illumination can be discovered in them.

That Hegel's use of language is in every way defensible can certainly not be maintained: it is, however, less indefensible than is usually supposed. For the purpose of Hegel is to explore notions from a peculiar angle, to see them as embodying half-formed *tendencies*, sometimes conflicting, which other notions will bring out into the open, and to explore *such* relations among notions certainly requires a new vocabulary. If we wish to say, e.g., that the notion of mechanism involves a covert mutual fittingness among interacting objects, which is more plainly brought out in a chemical or a teleological relation, we are talking of a relation among notions for which no brief expression is appropriate. Hegel is, therefore, within his rights in resorting to metaphor. And since the relations dealt with are relations of *tendency*, which would be misdescribed if given too clear-cut an outline, Hegel is justified in using metaphors which are nebulous and shifting. That this excuses *all* Hegel's obscurities is of course not arguable. To read Hegel is often to undergo an intellectual crucifixion: his greatness is shown in the fact that one seldom feels that such a crucifixion has not been worth while.

As regards the contradictory element in Hegel's language, it must be remembered that the test of self-contradiction, in the sense of what is self-nullifying and self-stultifying, does not lie in the mere combination of an expression with its verbal negative —to say 'It is and it isn't' *needn't* be nonsense at all—it lies solely in the *use* to which such a combination is put, i.e. if a man really *wants* to take back what he has just put forward, so as to leave nothing standing. If expressions like 'distinguishing what is not distinguishable' are successfully used to throw light on natural or social facts, or on the relationships between ideas, then they are *not* contradictory in the sense of being nugatory or self-stultifying. Religious discourse has in all ages said important things in superficially contradictory language, and there is no reason why a philosopher should not do likewise. Contradictions must moreover arise in developing tendencies latent in ordinary speech, or in combining various forms of discourse: to recognize such contradictions is in a sense to have gone beyond them, or to have laid the foundation for new accommodations. A full treatment of the contradictory element in Hegelianism cannot, however, be attempted here: we can only call for an initial logical charity till Hegel's actual discourse has been examined.

It is more or less irrelevant, in discussing the views of a philosophical thinker, to enter into the 'progressive' or 'reactionary' character of his political opinions. We raise the issue here only because some people think that there is a very close relation between a man's politics and his philosophy, and because the supposedly 'reactionary' character of Hegel's views has made some people wish to ignore his philosophy. He used to be regarded as a forebear of 'Prussianism', and is now thought by some to have been a forebear of National Socialism. It may be said that Hegel's political views are much more balanced and many-sided than has generally been allowed, and that he explicitly maintains that an unbounded respect for persons, overriding all racial, credal and other differences, should be the foundation of the State, a belief of which Hitler's Fascism represents the direct negation. Nor is Hegelianism without its deep relations to revolutionary movements of a 'progressive' sort, however much it may deplore their one-sided, 'inorganic' excesses. The main merits of Hegel's thought are, however, independent of his political leanings, and no attempt will be made in this book either to whitewash or emphasize the latter.

We may say, finally, that Hegel is worth restating and reassessing on account of the great contemporary relevance of many aspects of his thought. A great philosopher has a side to show to every age: if the German Romantic period valued him for one set of virtues, and our own Victorian and Edwardian ages for another, our present period may also find something to suit itself in his doctrines. Here it will merely be suggested that the main contemporary importance of Hegel lies in his recognition of the 'open texture', the unclear corners of all living notions, the fact that they *imply* more than they clearly cover, and in the further fact that it is natural for them to move or develop in certain ways as soon as they are subjected to unwonted pressures. Our ideas of time, of matter, of infinity, of knowledge, of being and so forth, are all poised, as it were, in unstable equilibrium, and the slightest push given by unusual examples will suffice to set them rolling. That our ideas and verbal usages are 'dialectical' in this manner is certainly something of which contemporary thought is aware, even if it tends rather to arrest than to promote this 'rolling' of our notions. Hegel also shares with contemporary thought the view that it is our desire to develop thought and language in one-sided ways, to exaggerate and to fix tendencies implicit in current usage, which gives rise to philosophical puzzles and contradictions. Only while modern thought ascribes this freezing, exaggerating action to the *mis*understanding by philosophers of the fluid forms of our language, Hegel ascribes it to the 'Understanding', the faculty of 'hard-and-fast' abstract thought, which he opposes to 'Reason', the more fluid and accommodating thought-faculty. Wittgenstein says: 'Philosophy is a battle against the bewitchment of our understanding through the instruments of our speech.' Hegel says in highly similar language: 'The battle of Reason consists in this, to overcome the rigidity which the Understanding has brought in.'[1] In both thinkers there is a belief in a 'trans-figured ordinariness' of thought and speech into which philoso-phical exaggerations will have 'gone back', much as the various colours vanish and annul each other in the integrity of white light. (This simile would not have recommended itself to Hegel who was quite opposed to Newton's theory of colour.) Only while for Wittgenstein philosophical exaggerations disappear in this final ordinariness, and need not, except for a confusion, have emerged at all, for Hegel their emergence is essential to the final result, and is in some sense 'preserved' in it. Hegel is also akin to contemporary thought in the great stress which he lays on the unity of thought and language, in seeing thought as much as an 'interiorization' of symbols, as in seeing symbols as an 'externaliza-tion' of thought. And he is akin to it in the stress that he lays on the profound 'wisdom' or intelligence inherent in ordinary usage, which sometimes prevents us from uttering some piece of philo-sophical nonsense to which we should otherwise feel prone. The contemporary and uncontemporary aspects of Hegel will, however, become plainer as our treatment proceeds.

II HEGEL'S LIFE AND WRITINGS

We may end this introductory chapter with a brief account of Hegel's life. Georg Wilhelm Friedrich Hegel—to give him his

---

[1] Wittgenstein, *Philosophical Investigations*, I, 109; Hegel, *L. Log.* p. 107, (W., p. 67).

full name—was born at Stuttgart, in the Duchy of Württemberg, in the year 1770, the very year in which Kant inaugurated his professorship at Königsberg with the famous dissertation on *The Form and Principles of the Sensible and Intelligible World*, a dissertation which marked the inception of the Critical Philosophy. It is common to connect Hegel with Prussia, both because he spent his later years in Berlin, and because he came to give the Prussian constitution an exaggerated philosophical endorsement: it is important, however, to remember that he was a Swabian, a South German, and that he started life with no great fondness for anything Prussian. Hegel claimed descent from one of the many refugee Protestant families which had fled from Austria to Württemberg during the persecutions of the Counter-Reformation. His father was a minor fiscal official in ducal employ: he had a mother and a sister to whom he was devoted—there is a strange glorification of sisters in his *Phenomenology of Spirit*— as well as a brother younger than himself, who took up soldiering. The family atmosphere comes out well in the various highly abstract sections on the Family in Hegel's philosophical writings, in which there are idealized portraits of its various members. It seems to have been an affectionate, simple group, earnest both in the pursuit of the intellectual and spiritual, as of the burgherly virtues: one understands why Hegel called the Family 'the immediate Ethical Substance'. Hegel had his schooling at the Stuttgart Gymnasium, where he consolidated his possession of contemporary learning and 'enlightenment' by an elaborate system of notes and extracts. An immense capacity for silent absorption seems to have characterized him at all times and explains the almost Aristotelian range of his knowledge. It explains also the way in which Greek thought, and literature, at this time mainly represented by Sophocles and the Socratic dialogues, came to permeate his mind. Of all great modern philosophers Hegel is the most thoroughly soaked and steeped in things Greek.

In 1788, at the age of eighteen, Hegel left the Stuttgart Gymnasium for the Theological Institute at Tübingen University, where he was a student for five years. Here he formed two major friendships, one with the poet Hölderlin, who shared his passion for the Greeks, and one with the philosopher Schelling, who only came to Tübingen in 1790 at the age of sixteen, but who was to work out a complete system of Absolute Idealism before the age of twenty-six. The theology taught at the Institute repelled the young men: its rationalistic theistic proofs, with their minimal injection of supernaturalism into an eighteenth-century 'enlightened' world-view, depressed their soaring spirits. Hegel was afterwards to characterize their doctrine as a theology of the 'Understanding', one which dealt in rigidly opposed, mutually exclusive abstractions as opposed to a theology of 'Reason', in which there should be something of the 'breaking down of barriers' characteristic of mystical religion.

Hegel's stay at Tübingen was enlivened by the outbreak of the French Revolution : the young men sang the *Marseillaise*, made seditious speeches, and alarmed the ducal officials. At a later stage of his life Hegel reacted strongly against the negative, merely abstract ideals of the Revolution, devoted only to levelling and liquidating, as he did to many of the Faustian aspirations and formless enthusiasms of his time. He came to see a logical necessity in the transition from an extreme of abstract freedom to one of terror. 'Universal freedom', he says in *The Phenomenology of Spirit*, 'can produce neither a positive achievement nor a deed . . . it is merely the rage and fury of disappearance and destruction.' True freedom, he came more and more to think, can be found only in the laws and usages of some concrete community, in which the individual can 'find himself'. All this must not be taken to mean that Hegel ever turned his back on the French Revolution and its 'values', or that he ceased to regard it as a supreme crisis in man's spiritual development. A careful study of his political writings will show that, whatever objectionable features he may have incorporated into his final picture of the political community, he still always regarded it as the expression of free, self-conscious individuals, who recognize and respect the same free self-consciousness in others.

During the years from 1793 to 1800 Hegel first began to develop his own ideas: at Tübingen he had merely moved in a ferment of current notions. He held two tutorial positions, the first, somewhat unhappily, with an aristocratic Bernese family, the second, more happily, in the household of a Frankfurt merchant. He immersed himself in the study of Kant's ethical writings and of his *Religion within the Bounds of Mere Reason*: he digested Fichte's early writings on 'theory of knowledge' and 'theory of morals' which coincided with the latter's Jena professorship. Hegel also read Schelling's early essays on the Philosophy of Nature (1797) and his *System of Transcendental Idealism* (1800), and corresponded frequently and lengthily with Schelling throughout this period. Like all philosophers of the time he was also much influenced by Spinoza, whose views had been brought into the forefront of discussion by the publication of Jacobi's *Letters on Spinoza* in 1789.

As Hegel's views formed themselves he expressed them, not only in his correspondence, but in several long articles and treatises, most of which only saw the light in 1907. From these it is clear that Hegel developed his ideas, not so much in reaction to the opinions of philosophers, as in deep ponderings on the meaning of that Christian religion which had been so inadequately presented to him at Tübingen. If Fichte approached his Absolute through morality, and Schelling his through art, Hegel certainly approached his Absolute through religion. Hegel started by assuming that the 'message' of Christianity must have been in essence one with the moral law as set forth by Kant. He therefore came to agonize over what he called the 'positivity' of Christianity, its attachment to unique historical events, and to a personal Saviour. Like many later thinkers, Hegel was unwilling to ascribe this 'positivity' to the founder of Christianity: it must, he thought, have been due to the restricted horizons of the time, to the crassness of the Jews. It is interesting to see how Hegel, starting with this merely 'enlightened', moralistic attitude to the Christian faïth, succumbs progressively to its fascination, how it becomes for him a figure of the highest mystical and rational truth. In the Christian story of the Incarnation, Passion and Resurrection of Christ, Hegel comes to see a pictorial expression of his central thesis: that what is absolute and spiritual can emerge only in painful triumph over what seems alien and resistant. One cannot, for instance, doubt that a Christian inspiration lies behind passages like the following (by no means untypical): 'But the life of Spirit is not one that shuns death and keeps clear of destruction; it endures its death, and in death maintains its being.' Hegel may, in fact, be said to have used the notions of Christianity in the very texture of his arguments, and to be almost the only philosopher to have done so. At the end of this Frankfurt period Hegel produced a first outline of his system, which already contains the three divisions of the subsequent *Encyclopaedia*: a Logic, a Philosophy of Nature and a Philosophy of Spirit.

At the beginning of 1801 Hegel was delivered from the need of tutoring by a small legacy. He joined his brilliant younger friend Schelling at Jena, who was then engaged in 'giving physics wings', i.e. in freeing its notions from too close a connection with the mere results of experimentation. Hegel 'habilitated' himself at Jena by a thesis on the orbits of the planets, in which he defended the profound Kepler against the empiric Newton. This thesis is in some respects more empirical, in the light of contemporary knowledge, than the Newtonian orthodoxy that it controverted. Hegel associated himself with Schelling in an important essay on 'The Difference between the Fichtean and the Schellingian Systems of Philosophy' (1801), as well as in the writing and editing of the *Critical Journal of Philosophy*, which ran for six numbers during 1802 and 1803. Five long articles in this journal are known to be Hegel's, of which the most interesting is the withering assault on the philosopher Krug, who had challenged the 'new philosophy' to 'deduce' the pen he wrote with.

In the next four years Hegel became progressively more and more dissatisfied with the position and methods of Schelling, with his friend's formless romanticism, his preoccupation with the queer and mysterious in science, and his vague belief in an 'Absolute Identity' underlying both the natural and the subjective orders. He objected also to Schelling's exaltation of aesthetic experience as the supreme mode of access to the Absolute, and to his merely negative attitude to the Understanding, the faculty which delights in clear distinctions and in precise and orderly reasonings. During this period Hegel became less and less willing to hold that the crowning insights of philosophy could be arrived at by 'intuition', 'feeling' or suchlike immediate modes of experience: they must, he felt, emerge by a rational and necessary process, to which he now gave the time-honoured name of 'Dialectic'.

Hegel's new views and attitudes in philosophy were expressed in his first major published work *The Phenomenology of Spirit* (1807), certainly one of the most brilliant and original, but probably also the most difficult of all philosophical works. Here, in a famous, exquisitely written *Preface*, he subjects the views of Schelling to a thorough criticism, and then passes on, in the ensuing *Introduction*, to describe the 'highway of despair' which will be traversed in the body of the work. This highway has certainly been a highway of despair for very many of its readers. Starting from the delusive certainties of sense, it moves through a kaleidoscope of cognitive and cultural phases, until at length it reaches its term in absolute or philosophical knowledge.

The battle of Jena, which occurred while the *Phenomenology* was being completed, may have given Hegel the satisfaction of seeing Napoleon, that 'world-soul' on horseback: it also deprived him of his livelihood. For a year he edited a newspaper in Bamberg, then held for eight years (1808–16) the rectorship of a gymnasium at Nuremberg, where he instructed the boys in a 'potted' version of his system, and discoursed (in a rectorial address on the value of a classical education) in a manner that would have graced an English public school. During this period he also found time to marry, and wrote his second great work, *The Science of Logic*, which was published in 1817.

Hegel now returned to the university. He held a Chair of Philosophy at Heidelberg from 1816 to 1818, and one at Berlin from 1818 up to his death in 1831. In the latter position he became a schoolmaster, not only to Berlin and Prussia, but to the whole German world. In 1817, at Heidelberg, he had published his *Encyclopaedia of the Philosophical Sciences*, which carries out the scheme, propounded in 1801, of a tripartite system containing a Logic, a Philosophy of Nature and a Philosophy of Spirit. The first part was a shortened version of the Heidelberg *Science of Logic*, the second salvages and refurbishes the thought-material of Hegel's Jena period, and also shows his astonishing knowledge of empirical science, the last covers most of the themes of the *Phenomenology*, but in an ontological rather than an experiential perspective. The work is written in desiccated paragraphs to which additions (*Zusätze*) from notes of students lend lucidity and life. Hegel also published, in 1820, his *Outlines of the Philosophy of Right*, an elaboration of the second part of the *Philosophy of Spirit*, containing his ethics and his theory of the State. But by far his most inspired production at this time were the courses of lectures given by him year after year on the Philosophy of Religion, the Philosophy of History, the Philosophy of Fine Art and the History of Philosophy: these were published after Hegel's death in 1831. Posterity owes a debt to the students on whose notes the published lectures are based: they show us Hegel untrammelled by the formidable casings of his written style. There are vivid accounts of Hegel's strange, broken, halting delivery, in which advances of thought seemed to mature beneath a surface of immobility and arrest. His dialectic was undoubtedly a living performance, like the dialectic of Socrates.

The latter years of Hegel's life are somewhat marred for us by his increasing association with forces that may be fairly called 'reactionary', as by the part he played in certain disedifying episodes. Hegel's personality was by no means unattractive. In an age given over to the exaggerated cultivation of sensibility, it was characterized by an almost English sobriety and good sense. Hegel died in 1831 as the result of an extremely swift attack of cholera, then epidemic in Berlin.

SUPPLEMENTARY NOTE

I attach little importance to the foregoing biographical section because, unlike many exponents of Hegel, I have not found that the study of Hegel's youthful development or of his pre-pheno-menological writings throws a vast amount of light on his later notions and methods. Hegel thought that the forms of life emerged full-fledged from inorganic Nature like Pallas from the brow of Jove: the like seems to me largely true of Hegel's own mature philosophy. It is a dateless, inexplicable product of genius, not led up to quite understandably by the past of philosophy or by Hegel's own past. It is as vain to seek to throw great light on it by rummaging in its temporal antecedents as it would be to try to understand the style of Wagner's *Ring* by making a close study of *Rienzi*. Whether this should be so on Hegelian principles I shall not ask: on my view it is the case.

CHAPTER TWO

THE NOTION OF SPIRIT

I WHAT HEGEL SAYS ABOUT 'SPIRIT'

It is characteristic of Hegel to object to stating his philosophical principles *at the beginning*: he refuses to rest his thought upon fixed assumptions or initial presuppositions. The principles of his philosophy must, he holds, emerge in its systematic development: they must be its outcome rather than its foundation. 'Any so-called fundamental proposition or first principle of philosophy,' Hegel remarks, 'even if it is true, is yet none the less false, just because and in so far as it is merely a fundamental principle, merely a first principle.'[1] Hegel's dislike of preliminary statements is to this extent justified: one could not hope to understand or assess the worth of his philosophical principles without seeing them at work in his system, without seeing Hegel applying them to materials as diverse as logical categories, natural forms, historical movements and philosophical systems.

On the other hand, there is something a little tedious in the initial darkness in which Hegel likes to place us, like children about to watch a magic-lantern show, with none but the sketchiest and most mystifying programme to guide our expectations. This absence of initial preparedness explains the distress which overwhelms many students of Hegel, a distress not unlike that felt by Descartes in connection with geometrical demonstrations, where it is possible to follow the argument from step to step, without being clear as to *how* the conclusion was first hit upon or the proof constructed. In the case of Hegel this distress is much worse, since without *some* initial knowledge of the direction and goal of his reasonings, it is not readily possible to follow them from step to step. To be lost in the great wastes of Hegel's repetitive explanations is no pleasant experience, and it is one from which the student must, if possible, be delivered.

The best way to approach Hegel is in fact *not* to take him at his word, but to give just that preliminary account of the central idea and principle of his system which he has discouraged us from

[1] *Phen.*, p. 27 (B., p. 85).

seeking. While the full sense of this central idea can no doubt appear only in the working out of the system, we may at least hope to have the same sort of initial grasp of it that a child might have of a religious creed whose full grasp requires a lifetime of experience. (This comparison is Hegel's own.) We shall, in this chapter, take up Hegel's notion of *Geist*, sometimes translated as 'Mind', but better translated as 'Spirit', as the central notion in terms of which his system may be understood. We shall try to show that while it is by no means an ordinary notion, it is not essentially obscure, that it has been used by other philosophers before Hegel, and that it has its roots as much in certain mystical needs and experiences, as in reflection and philosophy. In terms of this notion many of Hegel's most obscure transitions will become lucid: we shall see their point when we realize them to be turns on the path leading up to Spirit. And some of Hegel's oddest notions, e.g. in the *Philosophy of Nature*, will become significant when we see them as anticipating on a lower level what can be fully carried out only at the level of Spirit. In so far as Hegel gives a name to the central notion of his system, he more often refers to it as 'the Idea', or 'the Absolute Idea', than as 'Spirit'. He makes plain, however, that the Idea is no more than the mere category or notion of which Spirit is the full-blooded realization. 'The knowing involved in the simple logical Idea', he tells us, 'is merely the notion of knowing as thought by us, not the knowing which is present for itself, not actual Spirit, but only its possibility.'[1] That the idea of Spirit is the key to Hegel's philosophy is, of course, no novel discovery: it is repeatedly stated by Hegel in so many words. Such clear pronouncements may however be ignored in the interest aroused by Hegel's dialectical method—which is, in fact, unintelligible without the notion of Spirit—or by the inspired modern 'interpretations' of Hegel which depart far from his actual statements.

We shall begin our study of the notion of *Geist* with a few citations from Hegel's actual writings. We shall select these from the *Preface* to *The Phenomenology of Spirit*, and from the *Lesser Logic* and *The Philosophy of Spirit*, the first and third parts of the *Encyclopaedia*. These quotations, more than any formal exposition, will reveal the manner in which Hegel approaches the concept, as well as its actual content. We shall then expound

[1] *Phil. of Spirit*, § 381, p. 20, *Zus.*

the notion more formally, consider its origins and assess its worth.

Hegel says of Spirit in the *Phenomenology*: 'The spiritual alone is the real. It is the essence, what exists in itself. It contains itself and becomes determinate, it becomes other-being and being-for-self, and, in all this determinateness and externality to self, it remains in itself. It is in and for itself. This being-in-and-for-itself is at first merely *for us*, or in itself: it is merely Spiritual Substance. But it must also become this *for* itself. In other words, it must become an object to itself, but one also in which this objectivity is forthwith overcome, and reflected into itself.'[1] Or again: 'The living Substance is that being which is truly Subject, or, what is the same, which only is truly real in so far as it is the movement of positing itself, or in mediating between becoming-other-than-self and itself. It is, as Subject, that pure and simple Negativity, which splits up what is simple, and duplicates and opposes things to one another, but which at the same time also negates this indifferent diversity and opposition. True Being is nothing but this Self-restoring Identity, this reflection-into-self-in-other-being: it is not an original unity as such, not immediate as such. It is its own becoming, the circle which presupposes its end as its purpose and its beginning, and which is only actual in the end, in being carried out.' Or again: '*In itself* the divine life is no doubt undisturbed identity and unity with itself, which does not take seriously either other-being or alienation, or the overcoming of either. But this only is the case from an abstractedly universal standpoint, which forgets that the nature of this life is to be *for itself*, and which therefore ignores the self-movement inherent in its form.' Or again: 'The True is the Whole. The Whole, however, is merely the essence which completes itself through its own process of development. Of the Absolute one must say that it is essentially a result, that it first becomes what it truly is at the end. Herein consists its nature: to be actual, Subject, the becoming of itself.' Or lastly: 'It is of supreme importance in my view (which only the full setting forth of my system can establish) that the True should not merely be con-ceived and expressed as Substance, but as Subject as well.'[2]

Likewise in the *Lesser Logic* we find the following passages: 'The Life of Spirit in its immediacy appears as innocence and

---

[1] *Phen.*, pp. 27–8 (B., p. 86).   [2] *Phen.*, pp. 22–4 (B., pp. 80–2).

naïve confidence, but the very essence of Spirit implies that this immediate condition should be superseded. For spiritual life is distinguished from natural, and particularly from animal, life in this, that it does not merely remain *in itself*, but is *for itself*. This standpoint of severance must, however, itself be overcome: Spirit must, through its own act, return to a unified state. . . . Thought it is that inflicts the wounds and that heals them too.'[1] Or again: 'Nature is by no means something fixed and finished for itself, which could also exist without Spirit: rather does it first reach its aim and truth in Spirit. Just so Spirit on its part is not merely something abstractly beyond nature, but exists truly and shows itself to be Spirit, in so far as it contains nature as subjugated in itself.'[2] Or again: 'The determinations of thought, in so far as they present themselves separately and immediately, are *finite* determinations. The True is, however, the Infinite-in-itself which cannot be expressed or brought to mind through anything finite. . . . Thought is, in fact, by its very nature, infinite in itself. . . . In so far as I make some thought my object, I am with myself. I, Thought, am therefore infinite, since I relate myself in thought to an object which is myself.'[3] Or again: 'Thought or the Ego is the absolute antithesis of the mutual exclusiveness and externality to self of the sensuous: it is the original identity, at one with itself, and entirely with itself. The word "I" expresses an abstract reference to self, and whatever is placed in this unity is affected by it and transformed into it. The I is thus as it were the crucible and the fire, whereby the indifferent plurality (of sense) is consumed and reduced to unity. . . . We must, however, note that it is no subjective activity of self-consciousness which imports absolute unity into the manifold. This identity is rather what is absolute and true.'[4] Or again: 'To think the neces sary is to resolve its hardness, it is the encountering of one's own in the other. . . . As something existing for self this liberation may be called "I", as completely developed it may be called Free Spirit, as experience Love, as enjoyment Blessedness.'[5] Or again: 'The movement of the Notion must be treated as if it were a game: the other that it postulates is in reality not another.'[6] Or again: 'The Idea in its process itself creates that illusion and

[1] *L. Log.*, p. 93 (W., pp. 54–5).   [2] *L. Log.*, p. 228 (W., p. 180).
[3] *L. Log.*, p. 101 (W., p. 62).   [4] *L. Log.*, pp. 129–30 (W., pp. 88–9).
[5] *L. Log.*, p. 351 (W., p. 285).   [6] *L. Log.*, p. 356 (W., p. 289).

sets up another over against itself: its activity consists in overcoming that illusion. Only out of this error can truth be brought forth, and herein lies its reconciliation with error and with finitude.'[1] Or lastly: 'The Idea is the eternal seeing of itself in the other, the notion that has carried itself out into objectivity, the object whose inner purposiveness is essential subjectivity.'[2]

Likewise in the *Philosophy of Spirit* we read the following: 'For us Spirit has Nature as its presupposition, whose Truth, and absolute *Prius* it therefore is. In this Truth Nature has vanished, and Spirit has revealed itself as the Idea brought to its Being-for-self, whose Object as much as the Subject is the Notion. This identity is absolute negativity, because the Notion has its complete outward objectivity in Nature, but this its externalization is done away with, and it has become identical with self in the latter. But it is only this identity in so far as it has come back out of Nature.'[3] Or again: 'The essence of Spirit is for this reason formally Freedom, the absolute negativity of the Notion as identity with self. According to this formal determination it *can* abstract from everything external including its own externality, its existence. It can endure the negation of its individual immediacy, the infinite anguish, i.e. it can preserve itself affirmatively in this negativity, and be identical with self. This possibility is its abstract universality as it is for itself.'[4] Or again: 'Spirit is the infinite Idea, and finitude has there the meaning of the inadequacy of the concept and reality, with the added determination that it is an appearance within itself—an appearance which Spirit implicitly sets before itself as a barrier, in order that, by removing the latter, it may have and know freedom *for itself* as its own essence.'[5]

In all these passages we have the same picture of what can only be called a mystical game. Spirit *is* infinite, but it must pretend to itself to be finite, in order to overcome this pretence, to distinguish itself from everything finite, to become fully aware of its own infinity. Spirit is the only reality, but it must confront itself with something seemingly alien, in order to see through its own self-deception, to become aware that it *is* the only reality. And the creation and setting aside of this strange deception is

---

[1] *L. Log.*, p. 422 (W., p. 352).   [2] *L. Log.*, p. 427 (W., p. 356).
[3] *Phil. of Spirit*, pp. 19–20 (W., p. 163).
[4] Ibid., pp. 30–1 (W., p. 163).   [5] Ibid., pp. 41–2 (W., p. 165).

moreover *necessary* to Spirit, which could have no being without it: Spirit is in fact not merely the goal of its own game, but is indistinguishable from that game itself. These propositions are familiar enough in mystical literature, but one does not expect to find them on the pages of a sober philosopher, constituting, in fact, *the* propositions without which his system does not make sense.

II WHAT HEGEL MEANS BY 'SPIRIT'

We have assembled a number of passages, as difficult as they are interesting and brilliant, in which Hegel has set forth his paradoxical concept of Spirit. We must now give a more systematic account of the notion, in a manner which does not at first depart too far from Hegel's own. We shall then go on to explore the historic roots of the notion, and to raise a few questions regarding its internal consistency, and its philosophical legitimacy and fruitfulness.

We may say, first of all, that 'Spirit' means for Hegel both the object and the subject of 'self-consciousness'. It is what exists when there are not merely objects of varying types—embodying in externalized form notions of which they are unconscious—but in which there are also conscious experiences and references directed to such objects, and which exists in even more explicit form when there not only *are* such conscious references, but also the reflex sense of the sort of activity and the 'self' which pervades them all—and which also, according to Hegel, lies behind their objects—when this activity and this 'self' are not merely behind the scenes or *in* themselves, but also become manifest or *for* themselves. Spirit, for Hegel, is what I refer to by the pronoun 'I', what I am aware of when I 'enter most intimately into myself', when I am not merely absorbed in my commerce with definite objects, but am also aware of myself as active in dealing with them.

Hegel holds, however, that the 'I' or 'self' which is conscious, and which we deal with in self-consciousness, is no merely determinate, particular being. I am no doubt a particular person— e.g. Marcus Aurelius, son of Antoninus Pius, Princeps of the Roman Empire, etc. etc.—I am endowed with definite 'determinations' and occupy a definite position in space and in world-history, and am surrounded by other things and persons similarly

circumstanced. The 'I' of which I am conscious in self-consciousness is not, however, *tied down* to any such single position or set of
determinations: whatever or wherever it is, it *could* always have
been elsewhere or otherwise. This 'I' has what Hegel calls 'the
absolute negativity of the notion', the 'power to abstract from
everything external, including its own externality, its existence'.
'It can', says Hegel, 'endure the negation of its individual immediacy, the infinite anguish, i.e. it can preserve itself affirmatively
in this negativity and be identical with self.'[1] There is, in short,
nothing that I cannot set before myself in thought, no situation
or set of properties into which I cannot think myself, without
needing to sacrifice my identity. It is, in fact, *through* this power
to take on, or to lay aside, any and every thinkable determination that my spiritual identity is established. Hegel refers in this
connection to the implicitly universal meaning of the pronoun
'I'. I may *intend* to use it to single out what is peculiar to my single
self, but the 'divine' nature of language, whose essence is universality, frustrates this intention. *Everyone* necessarily speaks of
himself as 'I', and there is nothing distinctive in *my* experience
that could not in principle be in anyone's, nor anything in anyone's experience that could not in principle be in mine.

The 'I' revealed in self-consciousness is not, however, for
Hegel, some mysterious *Substance*, which lies behind all my conscious activities, and can with difficulty be discerned beneath
them. Hegel is quite free from the neo-realist picture of conscious
life as a system of 'searchlights', of which certain primary ones
are trained upon objects, while other secondary beams are trained
on these primary beams, and can perhaps succeed in lighting up
their *source* as well. For Hegel the spiritual 'I' of self-consciousness must be conceived, not as a Substance, but as a *Subject*, by
which he means that it must not be looked on as something
antecedently there, from which certain activities spring, and on
which these activities may throw light. It cannot, in fact, be separated from its conscious and self-conscious activities: it may,
paradoxically, be said to 'constitute' or to 'posit' itself in them.
Hegel often seems to espouse the nonsensical idea of a being which
conjures itself into existence by the mere process of asserting or
believing itself to be there.

This paradoxical idea (which Hegel inherited from Fichte)

[1] *Phil. of Spirit*, § 382, pp. 30–1 (W., p. 163).

will become more acceptable if we now state what Hegel *did* mean by the 'consciousness' of which Spirit is the subject. It is not, as we said, the illumination of an unchanged object by a metaphorical searchlight trained on it *ab extra*: it is rather a process in which an object yields up *a universal meaning* or *unifying pattern* of which it is an instance. Such universals or patterns exist *in* natural objects in an unconscious 'petrified' form: their disengagement, and the ranging of objects under them, is, however, an affair of 'consciousness', and consciousness is, in fact, no more for Hegel than *just* the disengagement of such universals and patterns. For there to be the consciousness of something, that thing must to some extent depart from the mutual externality (*Ausser-einander*) of existence in time and space, and from the hard definiteness of sense. It must declare itself as a case of some general kind, of which no case is perhaps an adequate embodiment: it must align itself with other objects in a connected picture governed by some unifying rule. And while, in the lower forms of consciousness, there will remain a tincture of what is sensuous and mutually external, in the higher forms of pure thought there will be no other particularity than what is implied in the abstract applicability of our notions. Consciousness for Hegel may therefore fitly be described as the 'self-activating Universal' or as the 'Universal in action' (*das sich bethätigende Allgemeine* or *das thätige Allgemeine*):[1] it is the activity which disengages universality and unity from particularity and plurality, and which interprets the latter through the former.

The 'self', the Subject, which *is* conscious, seems to mean no more for Hegel than this same universalizing or unifying activity, described by a somewhat misleading substantival locution. To say that *I* exist, or that *I* think, is therefore simply to say that varying items are brought together as in a single conscious focus or crucible—the latter image is Hegel's own—and that as so brought together they lose their hard outlines and their random diversity, and become instances of a kind, or elements in a unified pattern. The pronoun 'I' has therefore its root meaning for Hegel in the unity and universality characteristic of all conscious experience. To say that I am *self*-conscious is accordingly to say no more than that this active universality is itself disengaged, through its own activity, from the specific activities in which it is operative,

[1] *L. Log.*, p. 72 (W., p. 36).

and becomes manifest as the Universal it is, that it ceases to operate obscurely *in* other experiences, but becomes explicit, *for* itself. I cease, that is, to make sense of *other* things by seeing universals in them: instead I see the universal sense-making activity present in all such acts of sense-making. Strange as it may sound to ears otherwise attuned, self-consciousness is therefore no more than the supreme expression of the 'Universal in action', it is the conscious emergence of the universality common to all universalizing activities. All this renders it more intelligible how Hegel (with Fichte) could maintain that Spirit exists only to the extent that it 'posits' itself, and that its being is in a sense the product of its own 'positing'. In disengaging universality from anything, Spirit is in a sense disengaging 'itself' from such a thing, and accomplished spiritual self-consciousness is merely a more explicit form of the same process. This doctrine, that would be nonsense on most accepted models of 'consciousness', is not nonsense on Hegel's extraordinary view of the matter.

The nature of Spirit as the self-active Universal makes it reasonable for Hegel to call it 'infinite'. He calls it this, not as being capable of indefinite extension—to be thus is to be infinite in a 'false' or 'bad' manner—but in the special Hegelian sense of being self-contained and complete, and 'at home with itself (*bei sich*) in its other'. It has this infinity because it can deal with nothing without eliciting a universal or pattern from it (or imposing one on it), i.e. without assimilating it to itself. It has also this infinity because it can come into contact with nothing that is not a condition of its own activity and of its own self-awareness. And it has infinity by virtue of the 'absolute negativity' previously mentioned, its power to differentiate itself from any particular content with which it may be connected. And, having this infinity, this 'absolute negativity', Spirit is also by its nature impersonal or suprapersonal. It is not *my* exclusive Spirit or *your* exclusive Spirit, but something which by its nature transcends the distinction of persons. As said before, I may try to use the pronoun 'I' to stand for my single self, but I cannot *succeed* in meaning by it anything not shareable and public. Our most absolute privacy is most essentially what everyone shares, and our first-person autobiographies narrate the story of Everyman in a language intelligible to everyone. Spirit, for Hegel, is in fact most fully manifest in the various *intersubjective* norms which raise conscious experience above what is merely personal and finite, in the categories and canons of logic and science, the rules of legal and moral behaviour, of aesthetic taste. Hegel thinks further that the whole content of these norms follows from the 'infinity' and the freedom of Spirit. In Logic, he says, the mind is 'in its own home element and therefore free', such freedom meaning that it 'never leaves its own ground, but gives the law to itself', but in which it also 'renounces its selfish and particular being, and sinks itself in the thing'.[1] In the same way the whole content of morality and legality springs from the unlimited freedom of the pure 'self'.[2] In all these norms there is an attempt to reach a position which takes account of *everyone's* experience or attitude, and which therefore accords no special privileges to *anyone*. Such norms are for Hegel fit expressions of the 'Universal in action'.

But though Spirit must thus be regarded as 'infinite', entirely 'free' and suprapersonal, it must also, from another point of view, be regarded as finite, bounded and personal. There is, in fact, a logical connection between its having the former properties and its having the latter. This lies in the fact that the universality and unity of Spirit is essentially *active* and *conscious*: being active it must have something to act upon, and being conscious it must have something by contrast with which it can be conscious of what it is. The 'absolute negativity' of Spirit would be nothing if there were nothing for it to negate, nor could it be suprapersonal if there were no personal differences for it to transcend. It is *as* essential, therefore, for Spirit to be wedded to particular finite contents and to determinate places in the world, as it is for it to be freely ranging and 'infinite', since it is only by being the former that it can be the latter. And it is *as* essential for Spirit to assume the form of particular persons, identified with private interests and points of view, as it is for it to be impersonal, disinterested and 'public'. Superficially this may appear as a contradiction, but quite obviously it is not, since we are dealing with different 'aspects' of the same reality. Spirit may therefore perhaps better be described as what is infinite-in-finitude, or impersonal-in-being-personal, than as what is merely infinite and impersonal. (The affinity of these notions to various Christian formulations will be obvious.) Hegel therefore gives a place to the ordinary use of 'I' as referring to the particular finite person, who is certainly

---

[1] *L. Log.*, p. 87 (W., p. 49). [2] *Phil. of Spirit*, §§ 483–6.

not an impersonal 'World-spirit'. Only for him it is not owing to the mere looseness of a contextual expression that the pronoun 'I' applies to other persons, and in fact to all persons. In referring to one definite person, it also implicitly refers to all others, and to what is common to them all.

It is clear, further, that it is part and parcel of Hegel's notion of Spirit that it should always have the particularity of sense-experience, of the immediately 'given', in which it can discern, or on which it can impose, its various sense-making universals. This necessity constitutes the ineliminable element of empiricism in Hegel's philosophy. It is true, no doubt, that the 'given' of sense is there only to be 'negated', to yield up its treasure of universal meanings. It is true also that what we feel to be unrepeatable and particular in the given, is also vanishing and unseizable, opaque to thought and unsayable in words. It is a point greatly stressed by Hegel that words like 'This', 'Now', 'Here', and 'I' are implicitly universal: one may seek by their means to pick out what is unrepeatable and individual, but they remain instruments of general use, applicable by their nature to ever different contexts.[1] But though all this may be clear, it remains the case that, without a beginning in sense, the activities of thought would have nothing to sublimate or to universalize, and hence could not *be* at all. The existence of an ever fresh stock of raw experience is therefore essential to Hegel's notion of Spirit. And if Spirit requires the particularity of sense, it likewise requires the particularity of feeling and impulse: without the latter to control and organize, it can never rise to the rationality of the 'will'. For Hegel the presuppositions of Spirit are part of its notion, and therefore both the empirical and the contingently impulsive enter into its essence.

It is likewise part and parcel of Hegel's notion of Spirit that Spirit should find itself encompassed and encircled by *objects*, things to which it cannot help attributing other-being, a being distinct from, and opposed to, its own. If the nature of Spirit lies in the emergence of universality and unity, the nature of other-being seems to lie in obstructing, or in limiting, this emergence, in being merely thus and not otherwise, here and not there, lying outside of, or coming before and after, other instances of the same kind. Hegel does not regard the existence of such an

[1] *Phen.*, p. 83 *et seq.* (B., p. 151 *et seq.*).

encircling world of objects as an illusion dreamt up by the individual, in order to bemuse himself: he is not an idealist after the pattern of Kant, or even of Fichte. For him the realm of nature, which consists of just such alien objects, antedated the emergence of the individual mind in time. But the opposition between Spirit and the others confronting it is to *this* extent an illusion: that Spirit must and *can* overcome the otherness of such others by ranging them theoretically under ideal laws or patterns, or by remoulding them practically to fit various ideal requirements. By pursuing this course Spirit will at length have in these objects only the mirror-image of itself. The opposition between Spirit and others is also to this extent an illusion, that the action of Spirit upon them is not really the imposition of an alien order on them, but the bringing out of what they implicitly are, or of what they have it in them to become.[1] And, lastly, the opposition between self-conscious Spirit and its objects may also be regarded as illusory in that it is essential to self-conscious Spirit that there *should* be such others opposed to it, on which it can exert, and in exerting enjoy, its various unifying and universalizing activities. It is even essential, if such activities are to be vigorous, and the enjoyment of them vivid, that the opposition put up by such objects should be severe and difficult: Spirit for Hegel requires 'the seriousness, the suffering, the patience and the labour of the negative'. Though removable in principle, or in the particular case, such opposition must further be *permanent*, since without it spiritual self-consciousness would be impossible. But in being confronted with such other-being, and in experiencing the difficulties that its conquest involves, Spirit is only dealing with something involved in, and necessary to, its own being. It is therefore, in a sense, only dealing with itself.

This situation is at its clearest when the 'others' that Spirit has to deal with are other *Spirits*, or when the object has become a subject. It is only because there are other persons, mirroring myself as regards unity and universality, but differing as regards precise content and position, that I can come to distinguish between my universal 'spiritual' properties, and my merely personal ones. It is only because I live in a society of persons that I can rise to an acceptance of the common norms and enterprises with which I, as the self-active Universal, must necessarily

---

[1] *L. Log.*, p. 82 (W., p. 45).

identify myself. This distinction of persons can be done away with, only in the sense that it can be transcended in the enterprises in question, and that it can further be seen to be essential to the existence of spiritual self-consciousness.[1]

It is further characteristic of Hegel's notion of Spirit that it is impossible to separate the *activity* or *process* of subduing the various forms of other-being, from the self-consciousness which *results* from this process. The self-consciousness of Spirit is a result of the subjugation of otherness in the sense of having the latter as a necessary condition: it is not a result in the sense that it exists *after* this subjugation. Only as long as I continue to fight against the limitations of my finite personal being can I achieve a state of spiritual self-consciousness; the one is necessarily concurrent with the other. The life of Spirit must therefore always exhibit a curious synthesis between uneasy painful struggle and blessed tranquil repose, between a battle to which no term can be set, and a continuously emerging, ever deepening self-consciousness.

The crowning point in the notion of Spirit is that it is, in a sense, the *only* or the *absolute* reality, that it is what Hegel calls 'the True', or the 'Truth' of everything. By this Hegel means that one can only understand anything adequately in so far as it is seen as a stage towards, or as a condition of, the emergence of self-conscious Spirit. It is *in order* that the self-activating Universal should be manifest *as* the self-activating Universal that it is, that finite persons like ourselves exist, and are surrounded by other finite persons, that the senses assault and afflict us, that natural objects stand over against us and resist us, that such objects have existed in the past, long before there was any consciousness, that our individual minds have developed as they have developed, and that the collective mind of humanity has likewise developed as it *has* done in the long course of past history. Just as limited universals enable us to understand and explain various particular objects and phases of history, so does Spirit, the Universal involved in all cases of universality, yield us the ultimate understanding and explanation of everything. Such explanation involves a supreme application of the Aristotelian idea of final causation, spiritual self-consciousness being regarded as the *end* towards which all things strive. (Such final causation is,

---

[1] See, e.g., *Sc. of Log.* II, p. 327 (J. & S., II, p. 466; M., p. 824).

however, sometimes seemingly supplemented by efficient causation as where Hegel speaks of Spirit as *setting* up another to oppose itself, *creating* an illusion which it afterwards does away with, and creating itself to boot in the process of doing away with this illusion. It is plain that all such talk is metaphorical and mythic, and intended by Hegel to be such. For if Spirit could consciously plan and carry out its own self-deception by 'otherness', it would already possess the self-consciousness of which the subduing of the 'other' is a necessary condition. It follows, too, that the final causation involved in Hegel's notion of Spirit is an unconscious rather than a conscious finalism. Only *retrospectively* can Spirit regard the various alien but necessary conditions of its own self-realization as a *means* to the latter.)

The highest stage in the self-consciousness of Spirit is the simple realization that it *is* the 'truth' of everything. This stage of self-consciousness, abstractly conceived, is called by Hegel the 'Absolute Idea', and is described by him, as quoted above, as 'the eternal seeing of itself in the other, the notion that has carried itself out into objectivity, the object whose inner purposiveness is essential subjectivity'. Concretely it is achieved in certain experiences of aesthetic creation, of religious devotion and of philosophical illumination, in which the barrier of otherness is broken down, the hardness of necessity resolved, and in which whatever exists is intuitively felt, or devoutly believed, or abstractly seen, to have its *raison d'être* in Spirit. In this Absolute Idea (or in this stage of Absolute Spirit) error and finitude do not vanish: they are merely 'overcome'. And this 'overcoming' means that they are seen to be *necessary* to the self-consciousness of Spirit, and are for that reason rendered acceptable. As Hegel says in the passage quoted above, the Idea in its process 'sets up another over against itself, and its activity consists in overcoming that illusion. Only out of this error can truth be brought forth, and herein lies its reconciliation with error and with finitude'. By being seen to be necessary to the self-consciousness of Spirit, the various phases of finitude, etc., are at once 'done away with' and at the same time 'preserved'. (Both meanings are covered by the single German verb *aufheben*.)

III HISTORICAL ROOTS OF THE CONCEPTION OF SPIRIT

We have outlined Hegel's complex, highly paradoxical notion of Spirit: before proceeding to criticism and evaluation, we shall say something about its historical roots in previous philosophy. That it has many such roots is of course obvious. It has affinities with the early thought of the Greeks, with their stress on the war of the 'opposites' and their belief in a unity pervading them all: that there are such affinities shows, in fact, the primitive character of much of Hegel's inspiration. There are, in particular, many often recognized resemblances between Hegelianism and the thought of Heraclitus. To look on the world as an 'ever-living fire' which is at once 'want and surfeit', which can only burn by generating the products which must ultimately serve as its own fuel, is certainly to frame a material analogue of Hegel's Spirit: so too does the Heraclitean notion of a constancy which depends on flux, and of a harmony which depends on opposing tensions. It is also obvious that the Hegelian notion of self-consciousness has many connections with Aristotle's account of thinking. Aristotle, too, may be said to have regarded thinking as in some sense an 'overcoming' of the 'otherness of the other', an incorporation of the essences of things into our own thinking being, in which incorporation we can no longer distinguish between the essence thought of and the activity by means of which we think of it. There is in fact no page from past philosophy on which Hegel sets so much store as on Aristotle's account of the divine thought as a νόησις νοήσεως or thinking on thinking: it is quoted at length at the end of the *Encyclopaedia*.

Hegel's doctrine of Spirit also has an obvious parentage in the glorious mysticism of mediaeval and renaissance Germany, in the equivocal depth of Meister Eckhart, the paradoxes of Angelus Silesius, the illiterate, vivid symbolism of Jakob Boehme. In all these systems there is that approximation of the finite to the infinite Spirit which fits in with Hegel's notions: there is also that profound, theologically heretical stress on the *necessity* to the infinite Spirit of a world of Nature and created Spirit, which, by enabling him to exercise His creative energies and redemptive love, also enable Him to know and be Himself. Hegel quotes with approval the following sayings of Meister Eckhart: 'The eye with which God sees me, is the eye with which I see Him, my eye and His eye are one. In the meting out of justice I am weighed in God and He in me. If God were not, I should not be, and if I were not, He too would not be.'[1] Passages like the above show the religious character of Hegel's inspiration: they also almost justify a view of him as being merely a nineteenth-century representative of some *philosophia Germanica perennis*.

The direct roots of Hegel's doctrine of Spirit lie, however, much closer to him in time. They are to be found in Kant's doctrine of 'transcendental apperception' or 'transcendental self-consciousness' as set forth in the *Critique of Pure Reason*, and in Fichte's doctrine of the self-positing Ego as set forth in his Jena lectures and in his *Groundwork of the Complete Theory of Knowledge* (published in 1794). Kant in the *Critique of Pure Reason* held that it must be *possible* for an 'I think', a consciousness of self, to accompany all my other thoughts and ideas. Only in so far as I can be conscious of *myself* as the single central, co-ordinating point from which all objects are viewed, is it also possible for such objects to be objects for *me*, to be items in a single consciousness. This unification of items in a single conscious focus, and this reference of them all to the single central notion of 'myself', was called by Kant the 'transcendental unity of apperception', or the 'transcendental unity of self-consciousness'. For Kant, as for Hegel, this unity of self-consciousness was no external container into which empirical material could be indifferently cast: it differentiated itself into the 'categories', the various general forms of objectivity, which, in conjunction with empirical material, generated the various quantitative, qualitative, substantial and causal concepts in terms of which phenomenal reality must be understood. The Kantian self-consciousness is undoubtedly an ancestor of the Hegelian 'Universal in action'. For Kant, too, the 'self', to which all our thinking acts are referred, has no content whatever beyond the unifying, categorizing functions present in all thinking. It has no *further* discriminable properties, nothing that would entitle us to call it a 'substance'. In this respect Hegel's 'Spirit' follows the pattern of the Kantian 'I': it has being only as present and postulated in self-consciousness, is without particularity or specific empirical content, and can therefore not rightly be denominated a 'substance'.

It is, however, from Fichte's philosophy of the Ego that Hegel's

[1] *Phil. of Rel.*, Vol. I, p. 228.

notion of Spirit principally derives. It was Fichte who first plainly formulated the notion of an Ego or Subject as a being constituted by the very act in which it asserts its own being, as one incapable of existing except as self-conscious. He may be said to have taken over Kant's doctrine of the non-substantiality, the purely 'posited' character of the Ego, but while Kant saw these features as in some manner derogating from its status, Fichte rather saw them as a stigma of its greatness, as the signs of an ontological status higher than the merely substantial. The main problem for Fichte was, however, to find a ground, within the nature of such a self-positing, self-posited Ego, as to *why* it should posit anything other than itself, and as to why, above all, it should posit such another as confines, bounds, vexes and bewilders it.

The answer to this puzzle was given by Fichte in a remarkable myth, whose mythic character became apparent only at the end of his whole exposition. It is a myth which often colours Hegel's exposition as much as his own. Fichte pictures the Ego as the source of some boundless energy or activity, which streams forth from it *centrifugally* towards infinity. Part of this radiating energy impinges on a barrier, a resistance (*Anstoss*), from which it is reflected back *centripetally* towards the Ego. This reflected energy, encountering the Ego's centrifugal energy, appears to come from some source external to the Ego, to be the expression of some alien reality. Along the boundary where the Ego's centrifugal and centripetal energies meet, a faculty called by the Kantian title of the Productive Imagination now takes its stance: through its work our changing sensuous picture of an outside reality is built up, and is subsequently 'fixed' by another faculty called the 'Understanding'. The empirical world is accordingly a product of our own imaginative and thinking activities, though provoked by an external resistance. It is like some elaborate, orderly dream-structure built about a noise or a touch which disturbs us from without.

The activity which builds up this picture of the external world is called by Fichte the 'objective activity' of the Ego, since it surrounds the Ego with *objects* which limit it and which hem it in. It may also be called the theoretical activity of the Ego, since it seems to know and interpret what is independently there. The Ego has, however, another *absolute* activity, which is not reflected from any barrier, but which presses on beyond all barriers towards infinity. This absolute activity is the one with which the Ego posits its own being, unlimited and unlessened by anything objective. Since it is not an objective activity, it cannot posit itself, the Ego, as anything fixed and definite. It must therefore be for itself no more than the goal of an infinite *endeavour*, something towards which it can press forward indefinitely, but which it can never hope to encounter face to face. Fichte identifies this absolute, endlessly striving activity of the Ego with its *practical* activity, an activity which seeks not to know the world, but to change it. It represents its unending, necessarily unsuccessful attempt to produce something which shall perfectly mirror and be itself. Fichte sees the highest form of this endeavour in the unconditional imperatives of morality, which are all attempts to abolish the otherness of things and persons, and to establish a practical identity between them and ourselves.

Hardly, however, has Fichte completed this strange story, than he proceeds to retract it. He drops the myth of a barrier: the existence of the Ego's object-positing activity cannot be explained by an impact or a resistance, but must be a consequence of the Ego's own absolute activity. That it is such a consequence can be shown when we reflect that the striving beyond any and every object or limit (which we saw to be essential to the Ego's self-awareness) is one that can only exist *if there are objects to strive against*. The unlimited cannot be conscious of itself as unlimited, unless there are also an unending series of objects which block it, and which it can endlessly subdue and push back. In other words, the Ego posits a resistant environment precisely because it *requires* such an environment to elicit its own activities, and to bring them to consciousness. Fichte's strenuous spirit demands further that this environment should be the *worst*, the most thwarting of all possible environments, and that the Ego's struggle with it should be *endless*, and should continue beyond the limits of our present life.

Fichte does not, however, think, like Hegel, that insight into the *necessary connection* between the positing of such alien realities and the Ego's own self-positing, can in any degree 'do away' with their difference, that the non-Ego can be thereby shown to be not alien at all. There can for him be no respite from the endless moral battle against the 'other': we cannot annul the latter in the creativity of art, in the devotions of religion or the insight of philosophy. Hegel's verdict on Fichte's doctrine is terse: 'Fichte never achieves the Idea of Reason, as the complete real unity of Subject and Object, of Ego and non-Ego. It is for him merely an "ought", an aim, a matter of faith, that both are in themselves one, but an aim whose achievement involves the same contradiction as in the doctrine of Kant, never becomes a present reality. Fichte sticks fast in an ought (*Fichte bleibt beim Sollen stehen*).'[1]

But however much Hegel may be critical of Fichte, the fact remains that the principles of his system are at work in Fichte's teaching, and that there is but a nuance of difference, a subtle shift of perspective, between Fichte's final position and his own. If Hegel 'demythologizes' Fichte, Fichte has already demythologized himself. Hegel's vocabulary is further honeycombed with Fichtean metaphors, of forces which are 'centrifugal' or 'centripetal', and of 'reflections' into another or into oneself.

IV MITIGATION OF OBJECTIONS TO THE CONCEPT OF SPIRIT

We shall not, in the present chapter, attempt a justification of Hegel's concept of Spirit: this would be feasible only when we had seen the notion at work in the whole system. We shall, however, seek to remove some initial objections to it, which would otherwise effectively kill all serious modern interest in it. We may ask ourselves, first of all, whether the notion of Spirit does not rest on a simple misunderstanding of the ordinary use of the pronoun 'I', whose supposed referent 'Spirit' is thought to be. Perhaps it is because that pronoun can be used by *different* people to refer to themselves, and because it does not imply the possession of definite personal properties, that Hegel takes it to be the name of some mysterious, suprapersonal entity, active in all persons, without being identical with any. We may ask ourselves, also, whether he has not thoroughly misunderstood and gravely simplified the actual meaning of words like 'conscious' and 'self-conscious', which, instead of being recognized to be the loose, blanket words that they actually are, are thought to refer to some unique, single type of ghostly activity, connected with the emergence of what is universal and unitary. We may also look into the

[1] *Hist. of Phil.*, III, p. 635.

question whether there is any close connection between being 'conscious' or 'self-conscious', as these terms are normally understood, and the emergence of unity and universality, and whether *either* consciousness and self-consciousness *or* the emergence of universality and unity, are at all closely connected with the various rational norms of thought and behaviour, all of which a vaguely edifying word like 'spiritual' tends to bring together. Lastly, we may inquire into the possible sense that one might give to Hegel's idealistic doctrine of Spirit as the 'truth' of everything, and also, tentatively, into the *value* of such a comprehensive idealism.

We may admit, first of all, that Hegel's notion of Spirit does not provide a particularly happy elucidation of the normal meaning of the pronoun 'I', or of words like 'self' which are closely connected with it. Hegel is wrong in supposing that the word 'I' has some covertly universal meaning, that though we may *try* to use it to refer to our single, momentary selves, the 'divine' nature of language frustrates this intention, and forces us to mean something suprapersonal and universal. The pronoun 'I', together with expressions like 'you', 'it', 'this', 'here', 'now', etc., belongs to a class of expressions which may be called 'referential', and 'contextual'. Their function is to refer to, to pick out some definite object, either contained in the immediate situation or recently referred to, and to do so without by their use implying what *sort* of object is thus being referred to—except perhaps in certain general respects—and further to be tied up with a particular 'referent' (or object referred to) by the *context* in which they are used, so that we cannot determine *what* thing is being referred to *apart* from this context, and so that the same expression may refer to *different* things in different contexts. Obviously the pronoun 'I' usually serves to single out some person who is speaking, but its mere use does not tell us what kind of person is speaking (though it does tell us that he is a person), and the person whom it refers to also varies with the speaker using it. Wittgenstein says that the use of the pronoun 'I' is like putting up one's hand to show who is talking: this at least is its use in dialogue, though its use in soliloquy may raise further complexities. But the mere fact that the pronoun 'I' can be used to refer to different persons, and implies no fixed set of properties, does not mean that it stands for something mystically common to various persons and having that sheer indeterminacy of character which Hegel calls the 'absolute negativity' of Spirit.

One may likewise admit that Hegel has not really elucidated the ordinary meaning of 'being conscious' by identifying it so closely with universality and system. To be conscious, to be in a state of consciousness, obviously covers every live, waking state: it is not confined to states characterized by the reference to objects, nor to states characterized by close attention or discrimination, nor to states in which characters are emphasized and connections seen, nor yet to states in which our minds work in deep obedience to categories or norms. The use of the term 'self-conscious' by Hegel is likewise remote from ordinary uses, where the 'self' of which we are conscious is as much bodily as spiritual, as much a superficial social self as one that is deep and permanent, and as much characterized by what is peculiar and irrational as by what is universal and reasonable. Certainly no ordinary use of the term extends to cover the case where we recognize in objects something akin to ourselves, or something fulfilling universal rational demands.

But though Hegel's notion of Spirit may not have provided us with a satisfactory analysis of what we mean by using the pronoun 'I', or by speaking about being 'conscious' or 'self-conscious', it does not follow that it has not isolated and properly characterized a most important and pivotal aspect of our mental life. Though we may indeed be conscious in many blunted and uninteresting ways, reminiscent of the inert piling up of material masses without mutual interaction or relevance, yet our conscious life does regularly tend to sharpen itself into just that perceptive, intelligent state, analytic yet synoptic, in which characters are disengaged, relations and likenesses made to flash out, and the results of quite elaborate surveys resumed in the deeply felt grasp of a whole. Such sharpenings are of course as much evident in our inward experience as in our outward behaviour, and in the field of observation and theory as much as in the field of practice. Such self-collection out of random inconsequence and dispersed unrelation is certainly a fundamental, if wholly familiar, sort of mental transition which occurs on every critical occasion. It is not therefore absurd to say that we are *par excellence* conscious in such collected states, and that our consciousness is blurred, dim, obscure or imperfect to the extent that we depart from them. And there can be no doubt that even in the most rudimentary rises to such collection, there is to some extent that detachment from single points of view or from immediate feelings and impulses which occurs at a much higher level in the activities of the scientist or of the practical planner. The most simple manipulative examination of a new object shows something of the experimental procedures of advanced science, and the simple negotiation of an immediate obstacle something of the most advanced and organized practice. It is likewise clear that the rise to a consideration of the points of view and interests of other persons, and to co-operative work with them, is no more than a natural extension of the same organizing self-collection of thought and behaviour which occurs in the simplest exercises of intelligence. We have therefore reason to say that conscious life, to the extent that it sharpens itself into intelligence, will show some tendency to move towards the rigorous intersubjective canons of science, the impartial directives of morality, the detached appreciations of art and the 'self-naughting' surrenders of mystical religion. It seems plain, in fact, that the source of our various impersonal norms and values is to be found in the universalizing tendencies native to the human mind, and that the impotence of recent thought to give a plausible account of them lies in its determined ignoring of this simple source. To give the name 'Spirit' or 'the spiritual' to this whole constant side of our mental life is to single out and tie facts together which deserve to be singled out and tied together. If the names used are both edifying and familiar, the facts that they cover are also quite familiar and extremely edifying. And while our 'spiritual' tendencies are by no means *all* that we regard as belonging to ourselves—and while we may have reason to speak of them in quasi-religious self-abasement—yet they certainly are our own and not forced on us *ab extra*, and so may reasonably be incorporated into our own self-consciousness.

Hegel is further right in acknowledging the dependence of such 'spirituality' on the element of 'otherness', of resistance and conflict, in which it arises. In acknowledging this, he is, in fact, acknowledging Spirit to be a natural product—this need not, of course, be *all* that it is—born out of the struggle of the self-centred semi-animal human being with its confused environment of things and other persons. Obviously it is true that, in the absence of an empirical situation which presents difficulties for understanding or for manipulative mastery, and in the absence of many deep conflicts within ourselves, or between ourselves and others, the supreme spiritual achievements of science, art, religion, politics and morality would be impossible. It is also plainly true that these achievements are remarkable and glorious in proportion to the variety, the intensity and the disorganized deadness of the resistances that they overcome. Within limits it is plain that we should not wish the 'other' away, nor wish it profoundly different.

* We may now pass to our last, most difficult question, which we can here answer only by anticipation. What sense may we give to the Hegelian doctrine that Spirit is the 'truth' of everything, even of what seems most obviously and most blatantly unspiritual? As we have hinted, this view is in some sense, teleological: it is not merely a theory of the epistemological dependence of the world upon conscious Spirit, since Hegel acknowledges Spirit to be merely 'implicit' in many parts and phases of the world, and since it is fully 'explicit' only in a few philosophers. Nor is it to be interpreted as some metaphysical theory of origins or purposive construction, even though Hegel frequently uses such language, both in speaking of self-conscious Spirit, and of its abstract deputy 'the Idea'. Spirit is sometimes said to posit an illusory 'other', in order thereby to achieve its own self-consciousness: sometimes, more daringly, it is said to posit *itself*, and to be the result of its own activity. As said before, these accounts are as intentionally mythic as are those of the Platonic *Timaeus*. If Spirit could launch itself or the world into being through a conscious process, the existence of that world would be gratuitous: Spirit would already enjoy the full reality and the full self-consciousness which it is the function of the world-process to elicit. Equally plainly, Hegel's view is not merely a high-level empirical hypothesis to the effect that unspiritual states tend to pass over into more spiritual ones, though this, we shall see, is *part* of what the doctrine means in certain fields.

Here we may hold that Hegel's view is in principle a *philosophical way* of regarding the world, which depends for its acceptability on conceptual rather than factual considerations, though it can be used to illuminate fact, and though it is more applicable to certain sorts of fact than others. This is why it becomes true and explicit only in so far as men practise philosophy, which is the supreme form of Spirit, and why it adds no more than a last crowning nuance to the facts and notions that have led up to it.

Spirit, the principle of unity and universality, can only *fully* understand the world by regarding that world as being no more than the material for its own activity, as being opaque to such activity merely to the extent that such opacity is a necessary condition for the process of removing it, of rendering the world transparent. And it can find no *complete* satisfaction in any other way of viewing the world; it cannot, e.g., be content to regard it as a concourse of atoms casually associated with consciousness. It will find, finally, that the partial satisfaction it gains by viewing the world in alternative ways, breaks down on examination and involves its thought in conflict and intellectual frustration. Whereas in the understanding of itself, Spirit, as the 'truth' of everything, all these other partial ways of understanding the world will be brought together and harmonized.

What reason can we have for embracing this view? We may at least give it a provisional justification by holding it to be involved in all our rational procedures. Since our rationality makes us look in the data of experience for what is universal, unifying and inter-subjective, we must proceed *as if* such universality, unity and inter-subjectivity were there to be found, as if the facts could be brought under simple formulae which could be verified and applied by all. Since the same rationality draws us beyond the exclusiveness of personal interest, we must proceed *as if* personal barriers are such as to yield progressively to the advances of understanding and co-operative enterprise. And we must proceed *as if* the set-backs, the difficulties and the frustrations which meet us on these courses are such as either to pass away altogether, or to add richness to the final result. To proceed in this way is certainly to proceed as an Hegelian Idealist, to treat the world as if its 'truth' lay in self-conscious Spirit. Hegel thinks, however, that there is no *other* satisfactory way of viewing the world than the one just mentioned, and that every other way of looking on that world must lead us, on pain of conflict or intellectual frustration, to the view in question. This doctrine we shall only be able fully to evaluate when we have discussed Hegel's dialectical method, in which the breakdown of alternative ways of looking at things will be exhibited. We must consider whether this method really does establish the primacy of Spirit, or whether it does not rather presuppose it.

CHAPTER THREE

THE DIALECTICAL METHOD

I WHAT HEGEL SAYS ABOUT DIALECTIC AND ITS RELATIONS TO UNDERSTANDING AND SPECULATIVE REASON

Hegel, it is well known, practised a philosophical technique called 'Dialectic', and his philosophy may be called a dialectical philosophy. Exactly what is meant by calling his philosophy 'dialectical' is, however, far from clear, nor whether it is a good or a bad manner of philosophizing. The meaning and worth of the Hegelian Dialectic is, in fact, teasingly obscure even to those who have studied Hegel longest and most sympathetically, who have brooded deeply over the discrepant accounts that he gives of his method, and on the Protean tricks through which he operates it. If one starts by thinking Dialectic easy to characterize, one often ends by doubting whether it is a method at all, whether any general account can be given of it, whether it is not simply a name covering any and every of the ways in which Hegel argues. And if one tries to distinguish between the way in which the method *should* be used, and the way in which Hegel actually uses it, one soon finds that his practice provides no standards by means of which its detailed working can be tested. Clearness is not helped by the cross-lights thrown by the use of dialectical ideas and methods by the Marxists, who try to operate Hegelian machinery with a quite alien and unsuitable fuel. Nor is it helped by the unbounded prejudice of those who, often without the smallest direct knowledge of Hegel, condemn him for violating elementary logical rules. Our task in this chapter will be, in the first place, to expound what Hegel actually *said* about his Dialectic, then to consider, in a general way, how he actually uses it, and lastly to examine certain serious initial objections to it. All this will be preliminary to studying the Dialectic actually at work in Hegel's writings, in which alone it can be profitably examined.

We may begin our account of Dialectic by first saying what it plainly is not, and what it does not attempt to be. It is not a method which seeks to build up a deductive system, such as Hegel knew in the various branches of mathematics, and such as *we* know in our systems of symbolic logic. It does not proceed, that is, by framing a few simple undefined concepts, whose content is clear at the edges and without tendency to shift, and then defining the more complex concepts of the system in terms of such primitive notions, such definitions expressing uses which are to remain fixed throughout the development of the system. Nor does it proceed by fitting these original concepts into a few axioms or primitive presuppositions, from which all the other propositions of the system are deduced, according to definite and unchanging rules. Hegel discusses this sort of constructive, deductive method in his account of the 'analytic' method of arithmetic and of the 'synthetic' method of geometry.[1] He says that such methods, though essential and brilliantly successful in their own fields, are quite useless for philosophical cognition. They are successful in mathematics, since mathematics is such an extremely abstract science, one that deals with things merely as units, merely as externally ordered and assembled, and not as having any deeper affinities or relations with one another. Because its concepts have been artificially arrested, and purged of anything half-thought or implied, it is possible for them to achieve a hard clearness possible in no other science, and because it is only concerned with abstract equalities and identities among its concepts, it is possible for its propositions to achieve an unmodifiable and lifeless fixity. Hegel certainly does not believe that mathematics will be internally subverted as long as one remains *within* its boundaries. 'The self-evidence of this defective mode of knowledge', Hegel tells us in the *Phenomenology*, 'on which mathematics plumes itself before philosophy, rests only on the poverty of its aim and the defectiveness of its material, and is, accordingly, a sort of knowledge that the philosopher must entirely despise.'[2] Hegel, it may be noted, was clear (as Kant was not) that the truth of such propositions as $7 + 5 = 12$ was a tautologous consequence of the definitions and rules of the number system: he says even that it might have been established by a machine.[3] It is not into such propositions that Dialectic enters. It is only on its fringes that mathematics becomes dialectical, where, passing beyond the situations with which it is adapted to deal, and becoming involved in contradiction and conflict, it is forced to frame wholly new

[1] *Sc. of Log.*, II, pp. 278–319; *L. Log.*, §§ 227–32.   [2] *Phen.*, p. 42 (B., p. 102).
[3] *Sc. of Log.* I, p. 261 (J. & S., I, p. 232; M., pp. 216–17).

concepts of the infinite, of the infinitesimal and the incommensurable.

The kind of thought characteristic of a formal deductive system is called by Hegel the thought of the Understanding, a thought characterized by great fixity and definiteness of notions, presuppositions and deductive procedures, as well as by an extreme stress on the distinctness and independence of one notion or principle from another. The Understanding, we may say, cuts off the corners of our ideas, all the fine penumbra by which they shade into other ideas, or imply them without plainly including them: it also checks the tendency of our ideas and principles to shift and transform themselves into other ideas and principles when faced with unwonted cases or questions. Having cut out our ideas in this manner, it proceeds to play various neat games with them, which are entirely successful just because their counters are of standard shapes, and fit perfectly into each other. This use of the term 'Understanding', with its faint flavour of depreciation, to stand for a somewhat hidebound, philosophically inadequate form of thinking, is common to all the German idealists. It goes back to Kant, who opposed Understanding, as a faculty content to apply categories and principles to the wonted material of finite experience, to 'Reason' which attempted an 'unconditioned synthesis', and which tried to apply the same categories and principles on and beyond the very horizons of experience. Only while Kant saw merit in the pedestrian ways of the Understanding, as opposed to the soaring, dangerous ways of Reason, the latter idealists reversed this preference. For them Reason was the higher mode of cognition, which emerged out of Understanding through Dialectic.

For Hegel Understanding is at work, not merely in mathematics, but wherever ideas and procedures are given a quasi-mathematical definiteness, and are kept apart from other ideas and procedures, into which, however, they naturally shade, and without which they can have no significant application. The sciences and practical arts all involve Understanding in their initial abstractions, and would be impossible without it. They must deal with their subject-matter from a peculiar, single standpoint, and must dismiss all other standpoints and considerations as irrelevant. It is, in fact, only by such one-pointed attention to single aspects of a matter on hand, that anything can be efficiently mastered or achieved. Understanding is for Hegel the principle of all bourgeois virtue, the quality that makes a man stick to the duties of his calling. 'There are', he says, 'many interesting things in the world, Spanish poetry, chemistry, politics, music . . . and one cannot blame a man for concerning himself with them. But in order to achieve anything as an individual fixed in a definite station, one must stick to something definite and not spread one's power into many directions. . . . In this manner the judge must stick to the law and give his judgment in accordance with it, not allowing himself to be held up by this or that, not permitting excuses, not looking to right or left. In the same way, Understanding is an essential element in cultivation. The cultivated man is not satisfied with anything nebulous and indefinite, but seizes on objects in their definiteness, whereas the uncultivated man vacillates hither and yon, and it is often hard to achieve an understanding with him on the precise point at issue.'[1]

There is a passage in which Hegel even waxes lyrical in praise of the Understanding. It is said, in respect of its power to separate off the abstract aspects of things, to be 'the most marvellous and mighty, or rather the absolute power. The circle which remains locked in itself, containing all its aspects, is the immediate and therefore not marvellous relationship. But that the *merely accidental* which is real only as bound up in close connection with other things, should be severed from this context, and should achieve a free and separate being of its own: this is the amazing power of the negative, it is the energy of thought, of the pure Ego. Death, as we may call that unreality, is the most terrible of things, and to hold fast to what is thus dead requires the greatest of powers. Impotent beauty hates Understanding since it demands of her what she cannot perform. But the life of Spirit is not one that fears death or preserves itself untouched by ruin: it is one that submits to death, and in death maintains itself.'[2] For Hegel Understanding is the *beginning* of philosophy: only when various mutually complementary, often antithetical abstractions have been clearly developed, will it be possible to integrate them into a richly analysed, living view. For Hegel philosophy must be able to use and absorb the work of the Understanding, as the intuitive or aesthetic philosophy of some of his contemporaries (e.g. Jacobi or Schelling) was not.

[1] *L. Log.*, § 80, *Zus.*, p. 187 (W., p. 145).   [2] *Phen.*, pp. 33, 34 (B., p. 93).

But however much Understanding may be the foundation of the sciences and of practical life, and must serve as a beginning to philosophy, it will none the less lead to thwarted and arrested development if it is allowed to dominate philosophical thinking. For philosophy, having separated off aspects from the continuum of the unanalysed, must again allow these aspects to 'pass over into one another', if it is to reinstate and understand this continuum, and not merely to reduce it to senselessness. Such arrested thought, Hegel holds, occurred in pre-Kantian metaphysic, particularly in the Wolffian scholasticism, a thought which had no sense 'of the internal opposition of thought to itself'.[1] In this hard-and-fast, pre-Kantian metaphysic various terms such as 'existence', 'infinity', 'simplicity', etc., were treated as having a single, definite meaning in abstraction from their context, and were then applied beyond their normal use to various objects of Reason which were not matters of common experience. It was thought, e.g., that the question of the existence or the non-existence of God was as plain and as unambiguously answerable as the question of the existence or non-existence of a finite empirical object, that one could decide, in like manner, whether the whole world was finite or infinite, or whether the Soul was a simple entity or one compounded out of other entities, etc. It was likewise assumed that the notion one formed of these matters in popular discourse was definite and without internal inconsistency, and could be sustained throughout philosophical investigation, that one would be able to conceive God in the same manner at the end of one's philosophizing as one had at the beginning. Whereas, according to Hegel, the subject of a philosophical proposition only acquires a definite content as we go on to predicate notions of it in thought, in which process we may find ourselves wanting to distort the normal use of our predicates, and to say, for example, that the Soul is both finite and infinite, or again that it is neither.

Understanding is not, of course, limited to systematic metaphysic: it is present in the less systematic reasonings of empiricist philosophers, or in the disjoined dogmas of a philosophy of common sense, of the sound human understanding. It seems plain that Hegel would have regarded practically all British realism, empiricism and analytic philosophy in the present century as a

[1] L. Log., § 26, p. 99 (W., p. 60).

philosophy of the Understanding, and would probably have admired it for being uncompromisingly so. Perhaps, too, he would have seen in the thought of Wittgenstein its inevitable dialectical 'overcoming'. Moore's emphatic quotation from Butler, 'Everything is what it is and not another thing'—propounded to put an end to the 'identities in difference' and the 'organic unities' of the British idealists—is a typical expression of Understanding. On the other hand, several philosophers who have tried to use a rigorously deductive method are not, for Hegel, philosophers of Understanding. Thus he holds Spinoza's thought to be through and through a product of speculative Reason, however much it may be tricked out in a misleading geometrico-deductive form.

It is to the hard and fast, isolated notions and axioms and rules of the Understanding that Dialectic, the second characteristic 'moment' in philosophical thinking, stands opposed. The dialectical aspect of thought is said by Hegel to be 'the self-supersession of the finite determinations of the Understanding', it is, 'their indwelling tendency to go out of themselves', whereby their 'one-sidedness and their limitation shows itself for what it is, namely their own negation. For this is just what it is to be finite, to set oneself aside'.[1] In Dialectic one-sided abstractions demand to be complemented by alternative abstractions, which are often as much antithetical as complementary, and this demand may express itself by a sheer breakdown into senselessness, or by the sheer passage to the demanded complement or antithesis, which may be just as one-sided and abstract as the original notion, and may merely supersede it. At higher stages, however, Dialectic becomes a reflective shuttling to and fro between notions known to be interdependent and correlative, and at a yet higher level it becomes a simple *development* of our notions, the more narrowly abstract merely growing into the more 'concrete' or rich in 'sides'.[2] In all these processes *contradiction* is most evident: it is implicitly present in the original products of Understanding, it becomes explicit when these products break down, and start passing into their complements, or being referred to their correlatives, or growing into more 'concrete' forms, and it is 'preserved' in the result of all such processes.

Hegel is eager to stress that this Dialectic, together with its

---

[1] L. Log., § 81, p. 190 (W., p. 147).
[2] L. Log., pp. 259–60, 355 (W., pp. 206, 289).

contradictions, is nothing accidental and subjective, begotten out of the misunderstanding or abuse of concepts fundamentally sound, and which can readily be put right. He would agree with Wittgenstein as to the 'deep-seated' character of our philosophical perplexities, and their source in profound conceptual needs which lead us to feel a kind of mental cramp when we adhere to too rigid a way of conceiving and talking. Hegel emphasizes that the corrosive philosophical doubts, which are characteristic alike of the destructive modern and the 'noble' ancient scepticism, are deep forms of cognitive despair which are not to be appeased by an ordinary proffer of information: in ancient scepticism they led to the transcendence of the Understanding and its fixed ways, and to a consequent imperturbable intellectual peace. Nor is Dialectic to be identified with sophistry, the arbitrary and tendentious seeing of facts from points of view which lead to distorted conclusions. Hegel is therefore deeply opposed to any view which makes the contradictions of Dialectic *merely apparent*, something that will vanish once Systematic Science has been achieved. To think of them in this manner is to turn Systematic Science itself into a restored discipline of the Understanding, from which contradiction and movement have been eliminated. 'The dialectical', says Hegel, 'therefore constitutes the moving soul of scientific progress,' and is 'the principle through which alone *immanent connection and necessity* enters into the content of Science, just as it contains the true and not merely external elevation above the finite.'[1] It is the determined refusal to accept the full implications of statements like the above which makes the idealism of philosophers like Bradley or McTaggart so very different from that of Hegel.

Hegel recognizes the presence of his Dialectic in the ancient modes of argument that went by the same name: the arguments of the Eleatics against motion, the Socratic 'irony' with its universal levelling of pretended definitions, the Platonic development of ideas in dialogues like the *Parmenides*, in which Hegel (like the Neoplatonists) sees 'the true uncovering and positive expression of the Divine Life'.[2] It is, however, in the Kantian antinomies that Hegel sees the most explicit modern expression of Dialectic. Kant is praised, not only for showing that our notions of time, space, and causal dependence can be

---

[1] *L. Log.*, § 81, p. 190 (W., pp. 147–8).   [2] *Phen.*, p. 65 (B., p. 129).

developed in contradictory ways, but in showing further that such contradictions are 'essential and necessary', that they do not spring from a casual error or conceptual mistake as previous philosophers had supposed. It is true that Kant holds that his antinomies are merely afflictions of our Understanding, that they have no application to 'things in themselves'. In holding this view Kant shows (Hegel thinks) a misplaced tenderness for the 'things in the world', an unwillingness to see contradictions in *them*, and a greater readiness to see them in Thought or Reason or Spirit. This Hegel regards as perverse: he sees no reason why 'things' should not, as much as Spirit and Reason, involve contradictions. He further criticizes Kant for confining his antinomies to a limited set of cosmological ideas: he should, on Hegel's view, have recognized their presence in objects of *all* types, and in *all* notions and ideas.[1]

It will be plain from what we have said that Hegel has no merely subjective, no merely linguistic or conceptual view of the contradictions involved in Dialectic. He does not limit contradictions to misapplied or misguided notions or principles: he goes further, and attributes them to 'the world'. This further extension is, of course, one of the most disturbing, most bitterly assailed of Hegel's doctrines; it is important, for the sake of establishing the sense of his key-term 'contradiction', to be clear that he really does do this. 'Dialectic', says Hegel, 'is the principle of all the movement and of all the activity we find in reality. . . . Everything that surrounds us can be treated as an instance of Dialectic. We know how all that is finite, instead of being stable and ultimate, is rather changeable and transitory: this is no other than the Dialectic of the finite whereby it, being implicitly other than itself, is driven beyond what it immediately is, and turns into its opposite.' Such Dialectic is manifest in the motions of the heavenly bodies, in political revolutions from anarchy to despotism, and in the paradoxical shifts and switches of emotional mood and expression.[2] Everything in the world is said by Hegel to involve opposed and contradictory aspects: he maintains in fact that contradiction is the motive force of the world, that it is absurd to say that contradictions are unthinkable.[3] The experience

---

[1] *L. Log.*, § 48, p. 141 (W., p. 99).

[2] *L. Log.*, § 81, pp. 190–3 (W., pp. 148–50).

[3] *L. Log.*, § 119, *Zus.* 2, p. 280 (W., p. 223).

of pain is in one context said to be an actually realized contradiction.[1] And there is a peculiar contradiction involved in certain actual objects which Hegel calls 'untrue', a contradiction between the notion of those objects and their actual existence. A bad state and a diseased person are contradictory and 'untrue' in this sense, as not living up to their concepts. [Hegel is careful to say that such contradictory 'untruth' has nothing to do with the *correctness* of the judgements describing the corrupt condition of such objects. The conformity of *our* notion to the object (correctness) is quite different from the conformity of the object to *its own* notion ('truth'). Here it is plain that Hegel is using the predicates 'contradictory' and 'untrue' in a manner quite different from other logicians and philosophers.[2]]

Dialectic is not, however, for Hegel the end of philosophizing: it is only a 'moment', an aspect in philosophical thinking. If it overcomes the hard-and-fast notions and fixed presuppositions of the Understanding, it must itself be overcome in the higher thought of Reason, or, as Hegel also calls it, Speculative Thought. The characteristic of Reason or Speculation, as opposed to Dialectic, is that it succeeds in *uniting* or *reconciling* opposed characteristics, so that the unalloyed contradiction marking the dialectical stage, which is responsible for its unease, passes over into a state which is also one of harmony and peace. If the action of Understanding has, e.g., been to separate off, and to oppose blankly, such pairs of concepts as 'what appears to the senses' and 'what exists in reality', 'what pertains to something intrinsically' and 'what pertains to something only in relation to other things', 'what is a free expression of a thing's nature' and 'what is forced on a thing by the action of outside things'—and if Dialectic has shown that concepts so opposed either break down into senselessness or simply pass over into one another—then the function of Reason is to integrate such notions into new unities, where they will be shown to require each other and to be necessary conditions of each other. Thus Reason would lead one, e.g., to form the notion of an underlying reality which reveals itself more and more fully the more we probe it with our senses, or of an intrinsic nature shown up in the interactions of things with other things, or of a freedom which entails necessity, etc. etc.

---

[1] *Phil. of Spirit.*, § 472, p. 370 (W., p. 233).
[2] *L. Log.*, § 24, *Zus.* 2, p. 90 (W., p. 52).

The speculative or reasonable attitude in philosophy, **according to Hegel,** marks a thinking return to the unthinking reasonableness of ordinary thought and speech, as this had been *before* it was disrupted and fixed by the action of the Understanding. 'As far as its content goes,' Hegel tells us, 'the reasonable is so little the exclusive property of philosophy, that it is rather present in all human beings, at whatever level of cultivation and spiritual development they may find themselves, for which reason man was of old called a rational being.'[1] Speculative Reason involves the same flexible compromise between varying approaches and points of view that is characteristic of ordinary thought, which never applies a notion unsuitably nor sharpens it to excess. But in Speculative Thought are also contained all the abstractions that the Understanding has fabricated: these will release and distinguish themselves as soon as the dialectical and reasonable element is omitted. And it will also contain the dialectical element, together with its contradictions: these too will persist and be preserved in the results of Reason.

It is therefore all-important to stress that Hegel does *not* think that the harmonies of Reason involve any mere rejection of the disharmonies and contradictions of dialectical thought. These disharmonies may be 'overcome' but their overcoming is also their perpetual preservation. For they are overcome only in the sense that they are seen to be necessary conditions of a reasonable result, and so, in a sense, *not* overcome at all. One may, in fact, say, with some exaggeration, that for Hegel the overcoming of contradictions and irrationality consists really in their permanent acceptance, since they are seen to be essential to, and therefore part of, the final rational outcome. As Hegel himself puts it: 'A speculative content cannot express itself in any one-sided proposition. If we say, e.g., that the Absolute is the unity of the subjective and the objective, this is indeed the case, but is to this extent one-sided, in that here only the *unity* is pronounced and stressed, while in actual fact the subjective and the objective are not only identical, but also different.'[2] From the point of view of the Understanding, Hegel insists, the results of Reason cannot be anything but self-contradictory, since they combine conflicting aspects. To this charge of contradiction Reason retorts by showing

---

[1] *L. Log.*, § 82, *Zus.*, p. 196 (W., pp. 152–3).
[2] *L. Log.*, § 82, p. 197 (W., p. 154).

that the clarity of the Understanding—'the subjective which is to be subjective only, the finite which would be finite only', etc.— is itself contradictory and dialectically productive of its opposite, so that the 'very transition and the resultant unity of superseded, apparent aspects' is established as ultimately true.[1] The stability of the reasonable result, as opposed to the unrest of the dialectical phase, lies further in the fact that one of its aspects overreaches (*übergreift*) the other, and demotes it to a mere condition of itself —the infinite, e.g., overreaches the finite, the subjective the objective, etc. We are reminded in these accounts of those photographs in which several successive ballet-positions are projected on the same film: Reason sees together what in Dialectic are separate and incompatible.

Hegel's conception of the reasonable being what it is, it is not hard to see why he should liken it to the mystical in religion. The mystics are precisely the people who tolerate a species of near-contradiction in reporting their experiences, and who reject those firm oppositions between God and the soul, the infinite and the finite, eternity and the passing moment, on which ordinary piety and theology lay such stress. As against theological metaphysicians who locate God beyond the universe of experience, and who deck Him out in magnified predicates of the Understanding, they are prepared, with Jakob Boehme, to see Him in the reflected sunlight in some kitchen pot. This is at least the case with the 'immanent mystics' to whom Hegel plainly belongs: it is not the case with the 'transcendent mystics' (among whom both Bradley and McTaggart must be reckoned) who are ready to give precisely the one-sided interpretation which Hegel repudiates, and to believe in some unity of Reason in which oppositions and contradictions vanish altogether. Such a unity passes our comprehension, and must involve elements which are permanently mysterious. Whereas for Hegel it is not thought in general, but only a particular class of thought, to which a reasonable solution seems opaque.

From what has been said it will be easily grasped how Hegel came to connect Dialectic with the *triad*, or with *triplicity*. A dialectical rhythm essentially involves a triplicity of stages, though there is more than one sense in which this will be so. There will be three stages in such a rhythm in so far as there is a movement

[1] *L. Log.*, 214, p. 426 (W., p. 355).

from an initial stage of positiveness and stability, characteristic of the Understanding, through a stage of contradictory, sceptical malaise, characteristic of Dialectic proper, to a stage of accommodation which will reinstate stability and positiveness at a higher level, and will therefore be typical of Reason. (It may, however, represent Understanding from the standpoint of a new dialectical rhythm.) The Dialectic can further be regarded as triplex in so far as two opposed, but complementary abstractions are developed more or less concurrently, are shown to be senseless apart from one another, and are then fitted into a reasonable synthesis. In this second type of triplicity the contradictory breakdown does not count as one of the stages, but merely as a transition between them. Plainly the second type of triplicity could readily have been expanded into a quadruplicity, a quintuplicity and so forth: there is no reason why *any* number of abstractions should not be concurrently evolved, shown to possess no genuine independence, and then fitted into a single synthesis. As we shall see, Hegel's practice sometimes conforms to such patterns.

Hegel ascribes an honourable lineage to the threefold pattern of his Dialectic: he attributes it to the Pythagoreans, to the Neoplatonists and to early Christian thought. He thinks it was one of the main merits of Kant to have rediscovered this ancient triplicity, and to have used it in drawing up his list of categories. (These occur in groups of three, the third category being in a sense a combination of the two previous ones, e.g. 'Limitation' combines 'Reality' and 'Negation'.) Hegel holds, however, that Kant's discovery was merely 'instinctive' and that he applied the triplicity in an uncomprehending and lifeless manner. But, quite obviously, Hegel did not really borrow his triadic scheme from Kant: it had already been read into Kant by Fichte, who had grounded the Kantian categories in the relations of the Ego to the non-Ego, and who had also treated these relations in a series of threefold movements, a *thesis* being confronted by a contradictory *antithesis*, and both being combined in a *synthesis*, which in its turn becomes the starting-point for a new triadic movement. [Thus the Ego's positing of itself (Reality), was balanced by a positing of the non-Ego (Negation), and both were harmonized in the positing of Ego and non-Ego as limiting each other, the source of the category of Limitation.] The terms 'thesis', 'antithesis' and 'synthesis', so often used in expositions of Hegel's doctrine, are in fact not frequently used by Hegel: they are much more characteristic of Fichte.

If Hegel says little about the debt of his Dialectic to Fichte, he says much, on the other hand, about the abuse of the triadic pattern by his friend and predecessor Schelling. Schelling, he maintains, used the Dialectic on varied materials in a wholly external and formal manner. Having found three fundamental 'potencies'—the magnetic, the electrical and the chemical—in the inorganic realm, and having found three similar 'potencies'— the sensible, the irritable and the reproductive—in the organic realm, he without more ado established a correlation between the members of the first triad and those of the second. In all this, Hegel suggests, Schelling did no more than violently *fit* material drawn from external sources into an arbitrarily chosen dialectical schema: he did not allow his notions to develop in their own necessary, non-arbitrary way.

In regard to a genuine Dialectic, Hegel holds that its various stages should arise out of each other in a *necessary* manner. It is not *we* who must determine its course: it must determine this itself. Though a dialectical system may not have the lifeless necessity of a mathematico-deductive system, it will have, none the less, its own species of necessity. As a method, Dialectic is the 'moving soul' of all Science. Hegel assumes, further, that a dialectical system is in a sense *more* rigorous than a mathematical system. For whilst in the latter there are many starting-points and many alternative directions that proof may take, in a dialectical system there are both unique starting-points and a single line of proof. Each stage, Hegel tells us, is precisely the 'nullity' of the immediately previous stages, the full 'experience' of just what these previous stages were attempting and failing to do:[1] it has no further content than this, and could not therefore be different in any respect whatever. In developing a dialectical system Hegel admits that much may be derived from instances offered us by experience: these may illustrate notions previously arrived at dialectically, or may prompt us to form such notions. All such empirical borrowings must, however, be transformed in a dialectical treatment, and must acquire a necessary connection that they did not seem to possess. Hegel holds, further, that his unilineal

[1] *Phen.*, pp. 78–9 (B., pp. 142–3).

dialectical chain will twist round in a circle, that it will, after many windings, return to its point of origin. And he thinks that it will provide us with a *proof* of his idealism, of the primacy of self-conscious Spirit, all other notions and phases of being having been shown to break down dialectically until reconstituted in the Idea of Self-conscious Spirit. The idea of Spirit will explain and resume *them*, as they do not explain and resume *it*. In this way the implicit origin of the whole Dialectic will be made its explicit result.

II HOW HEGEL ACTUALLY USES HIS DIALECTIC

Having so far dealt with what Hegel *says* about his Dialectic, we may now consider what he *does* with it, how it actually works in practice. One way in which this working is revealed is in the triadic structure of Hegel's writings: this is alike characteristic of *The Phenomenology of Spirit* and of the *Encyclopaedia of the Philosophical Sciences*. Each of these works consists of a main triad, which is divided into subordinate triads, and so on for a fair number of stages.[1]

Thus the *Phenomenology* has a main triad whose members are (A) *Consciousness*, (B) *Self-consciousness* and (C) *Reason*. *Consciousness* is subdivided into (a) *Sensous certainty*, (b) *Perception*, and (c) *Understanding*. *Self-consciousness* has, however, only *two* main headings: (a) *Independence and Dependence of Self-consciousness*, and (b) *Freedom of Self-consciousness*, though the last subdivision is triply subdivided into *Stoicism*, *Scepticism* and *The Unhappy Consciousness*. *Reason*, which occupies the rest of the book, has a complex *fourfold* subdivision. Its first subdivision, entitled *Certainty and Truth of Reason*, has three main subdivisions, concerned, respectively, with *Observational Reason*, Practical Reason and *The Individuality which is real in and for self*. Its second subdivision, entitled *Spirit*, has three subdivisions concerned, respectively, with *The true Spirit* (*Ethical life*), *The self-alienated Spirit* (*Culture*), and *The self-assured Spirit* (*Morality*). Its third subdivision, entitled *Religion*, deals with *Natural Religion*, *The Religion of Art* and *Revealed Religion*, and its final subdivision, entitled *Absolute Knowledge*, deals undividedly with Philosophy. Through this series of dialectical spirals Hegel pro-

---

[1] See the *Appendix* to this work.

fesses to prove that the self-consciousness which Spirit achieves in philosophy is the supreme phase of conscious experience, to which all other types of experience inevitably lead.

In the *Encyclopaedia* the triadic division follows a simpler and more intelligible course. The principal triad consists of the *Science of Logic*, which studies the Idea in the abstract medium of thought, the *Philosophy of Nature*, which deals with the same Idea in its self-alienation and self-externalization, and the *Philosophy of Spirit*, which studies the Idea in its return to itself from self-alienation. Each of the members of this main triad is in its turn triadic. The *Logic* divides into (A) *The Doctrine of Being*, a study of sturdily independent ontological categories, grouped under the three headings of *Quality*, *Quantity* and *Measure*; (B) *The Doctrine of Essence*, a study of subtle relational categories, grouped under the three headings of *Essence*, *Appearance* and *Actuality*, and (C) *The Doctrine of the Notion*, a study of various non-rigid, self-developing categories grouped under the three headings of *The Subjective Notion*, *The Object* and *The Idea*. In the *Philosophy of Nature* we have likewise a main triad of *Mechanics*, *Physics* and *Organics*, while in the *Philosophy of Spirit* the main triad is that of *Subjective Spirit* (Psychology), *Objective Spirit* (Law, Morality and Politics) and *Absolute Spirit* (a study of Art, Religion and Philosophy). The triadic division is carried much further than we have indicated, though the extent to which it is thus carried differs from case to case. The sense of this elaborate series of spirals is to offer *two* proofs of the primacy of self-conscious Spirit, once abstractly in the *Logic*, and again, more concretely, in the *Philosophy of Nature* and the *Philosophy of Spirit*.

It may now be said (though a full justification must await our complete study of the system) that the triads of Hegel's system vary vastly in their make-up. In some the second member of the triad is the direct and obvious contrary of the first, as where Being is opposed to mere Nothing, or Essence to Appearance. In others the opposition is of a much less extreme character (as where, for instance, the notion of a Whole and its Parts is superseded by the very similar notion of a Force and its Manifestations). In some triads the third member is an *obvious* choice as mediating between the other two—as where Spirit mediates between the Logical Idea and Nature, or as where Measure synthetizes Quality and

Quantity. In other cases, the third member of the triad is merely *one* of the things in which the first two members *could* be united, as where the notion of Ground is said to mediate Identity with Difference. In yet other cases the reconciling functions of the third member are not at all obvious, as where Teleology reconciles the Mechanical and the Chemical, or an Unhappy Other-worldliness emerges out of Stoicism and Scepticism. There are many more triads in which the third member emerges out of the second member *alone*, than triads in which it emerges out of the two previous members conjointly.

The dialectical *transitions* from one notion or phase of being to the next also differ vastly from case to case. Sometimes a term plainly involves an inner *absurdity* or *contradiction* which only the next term can remove, as where the absurd notion of an inner Essence which is indifferent to outward manifestation, yields to the more reasonable notion of an actuality in which inner and outer match each other precisely. In other cases a term merely involves an *incompleteness* of which the next term furnishes the required complement, as where a Subjective End leads on to the Means by which it may be realized. In yet other cases a subsequent phase merely represents a more explicit version of some character obscurely manifested by its predecessor, as where conscious Cognition and Volition represent a more explicit version of the self-adjusting purposive unity of life. In yet other cases the transition resembles the passage from talk which obeys certain rules, to metalinguistic talk *about* that talk and about its rules, as where the dialectical transition from Being to Nothing is itself recognized as being the *transition* it is, and is therefore made the basis of the new category of Becoming. In yet other cases the transition is really a philosophical joke, reminiscent of the profound jokes in the Platonic dialogues, as where the phrenological doctrine which reduces everything spiritual to a configuration of the skull-bones, is astonishingly twisted round to reveal suddenly that skull-bones (and therefore everything gross) are entirely spiritual. The devices by which the Dialectic is made to work are, in fact, inexhaustible in their subtlety and variety. Hegel admits that they change systematically from one section of the Dialectic to another, but the change is much greater and less systematic than he ever admits. McTaggart, in the brilliant fourth chapter of his *Studies in Hegelian Dialectic*, has gone further in systematizing them than has any other writer on Hegel, and if *he* has failed to reduce them completely to order, it would be vain for anyone else to hope to succeed.

A study of Hegel's dialectical practice will show, further, that in spite of anything he may *say* regarding their necessary, scientific character, his transitions are only necessary and inevitable in the rather indefinite sense in which there is necessity and inevitability in a work of art. His dialectical triads certainly reveal a community of style, but this community breaks up, on examination, into a number of distinct resemblances all of which are not present in every case. This community of style means that, at any point in the development, only *certain* continuations would seem natural and fitting. There is not, however, *one* continuation which alone seems obligatory, but rather a number of permissible continuations, some of which seem more fitting than others. Thus the Stoic indifference to external circumstances passes over dialectically into the Sceptical consciousness of their nullity, and the divided consciousness involved in Scepticism passes over dialectically into the explicitly dualistic, two-world consciousness of mediaeval Catholicism. Can anyone doubt that the profound connections here brought out could not have been paralleled by equally interesting and important connections tending in quite different directions? To look for absolute rigour in the Dialectic is to ignore the illumination it *has* for the sake of some quasi-mathematical interconnection which it does not and cannot possess.

We may note, further, that in the actual working of the Dialectic there is a recourse to experience which is simply a recourse to experience, and which is not based on the demand of abstract argument. Hegel in fact sometimes simply admits that it is hard to place certain natural phenomena in the Dialectic, but that a place *has* to be found for them in it, since they undoubtedly exist. The old charge of Trendelenburg, that Hegel merely undoes his initial abstractions by importing many distinctions from experience, must simply be conceded. The precise content, even the form, of the Dialectic largely depends on the material, drawn from common experience, history, biography, literature and natural science, which it enables us to organize, and from which it cannot well be separated. In casting about for something that will serve as an opposite, a complement or a reconciling unity of certain phases, Hegel has constant recourse to nature and history: he introduces forms that would never have been arrived at through the abstract development of concepts. It is in his power to introduce such forms, and to illuminate them surprisingly by philosophical concepts, that Hegel's unique genius consists. No other philosopher has shown a like blend of factual knowledge and conceptual skill. Thus the *Phenomenology* deals with such phases of civilized experience as Stoicism, Scepticism, Mediaeval Otherworldliness, the moral issues posed by Greek tragedy, the eighteenth-century Enlightenment, the revolutionary terror in France, the romantic cult of 'Beautiful Souls', etc. etc. In the same way, in his brilliant and informed *Philosophy of Nature* Hegel is concerned to make philosophical sense of the findings, problems and theories of contemporary science: these he neither seeks to modify nor to demonstrate, but merely to put into what he regards as satisfactory conceptual frames. In the same way, in his theodicistic philosophy of history, he bases himself on ordinary sources and documents, on actual works and products, on the researches of scholars, and on the work of reflective but non-philosophical historians and critics. The owl of Minerva only wings its interpretative flight—to modify one of Hegel's most famous statements[1]— when all this common-or-garden spade-work has been completed. And even the *Logic*, which professes to study concepts in the medium of pure thought, is full of notions employed in the empirical science of Hegel's own day. If one is to judge the value of the dialectical method, one must judge it for what it is, and not for what, on a one-sided interpretation of certain of Hegel's claims in regard to it, one thinks it ought to be. Otherwise we shall find ourselves in the position of McTaggart who, after being led to interpret the *Logic* in a manner flatly at variance with Hegel's statements, is then forced to jettison the whole of the remaining system as being the sort of semi-empirical venture which is not dialectically admissible.

We may note, finally, that though Hegel has offered three dialectical demonstrations of the primacy of self-conscious Spirit—one in the medium of individual culture and experience, one in the abstract medium of concepts, and one in the concrete medium of nature and social mind—it is not clear that these demonstrations would carry persuasion to anyone who had not already—at least in temperament or attitude—embraced their

[1] *Phil. of Right*, Preface, p. 37.

outcome. The lower categories and forms of being really break down because they are felt to be inadequate approximations to the sort of self-differentiating unity which is to be found only in self-conscious Spirit. This is the secret standard by which all ideas and performances are judged, and the lubricant without whose secretly applied unction the dialectical wheels and cranks would not turn at all. Anyone who does not feel impelled to think in terms of this sort of self-differentiating unity, will *not* find his inferior categories breaking down, nor leading him on to Hegelian results. And anyone who tries to operate the Dialectic without this key-notion, and to prove by its means the future emergence of a classless society, or of some similar outcome, must either be thinking in a wholly confused manner, or be endowing his outcome with many of the self-explanatory properties of Hegel's Spirit.

III MITIGATION OF OBJECTIONS TO HEGEL'S DIALECTIC

We may now turn to consider a few serious criticisms and difficulties in regard to Hegel's notion and use of 'Dialectic'. There are, in the first place, the many difficulties connected with his use of contradiction, with his doctrine that it enters into *all* our notions and ideas, even those that are most securely founded and in most constant use, that it also enters into all the *things* in the world, that it is the moving soul of scientific method and the one motive force behind all change, that it causes finite notions and objects to 'break down' and to 'set themselves aside', and that it also *persists* in the reasonable outcomes which issue from this breakdown. All these doctrines are extremely hard to stomach, since a contradiction is, for the majority of logical thinkers, a self-nullifying utterance, one that puts forward an assertion and then takes it back in the same breath, and so really says nothing. And it can be readily shown that a language-system which admits even *one* contradiction among its sentences, is also a system in which *anything whatever* can be proved, so that the *whole* of such a system becomes self-nullifying, and infected with contradiction.

It seems hard, further, to believe that contradictions infest our most ordinary notions and categories. If, e.g., Hegel is right in holding there to be a contradiction in every ordinary subject-predicate assertion (since the subject and the predicate are plainly not the same thing), then it would seem that we must be condemned to wholesale dumbness on all topics whatever, whether ordinary or philosophical. And if there is a contradiction in so common a concept as that of a *cause*, then practically all ordinary and scientific discourse must be cast forth as worthless. And it seems especially absurd to hold that contradiction not only exists in thought and language but also in 'the world', since it is the very mark of a self-contradictory utterance that it describes nothing whatever. And it is supremely uncomfortable to believe in the presence of contradictions as 'preserved' permanently in the highest forms of reality and truth. There, at least, one may cry with thinkers like McTaggart or Bradley, they should be banished altogether.

Hegel further emphasizes that he is not talking of 'contradiction' in some half-hearted or equivocal manner: he is not saying that X is A in one sense, but not A in another, that it is A from one point of view but not from another, that it is A *in so far as it is X* but not in so far as it is something else. All these devices for avoiding contradiction are explicitly disowned by Hegel: they are seen as the eternal ruses of the Understanding, which, however much baffled and harried, always rallies and returns to its vomit. Hegel makes it as plain as possible, that it is not some watered-down, equivocal brand of contradiction, but straightforward, head-on contradiction, that he believes to exist in thought and the world, and to be an ineliminable component in self-conscious spiritual reality.

We may, however, maintain that, whatever Hegel may *say* in regard to the presence of contradictions in thought and reality, the sense in which he admits such contradictions is determined by his *use* of the concept, and not by what he says about it. And since he uses 'contradiction' to illuminate the workings of ordinary notions, and things in the world, and not to cast doubt on their meaning or reality, it is plain that he cannot be using it in the self-cancelling manner that might at first seem plausible. By the presence of 'contradictions' in thought or reality, Hegel plainly means the presence of opposed, antithetical *tendencies*, tendencies which work in contrary directions, which each aim at dominating the whole field and worsting their opponents, but which each also require these opponents in order to be what they are, and to have something to struggle with. Such 'contradiction' exists in an easy form in the unthinking reasonableness of ordinary life, where antithetical modes of conception are applied side by side, where their vague mutually exclusive tendency has not yet been developed into rigid mutual exclusion, and where any head-on conflict is met by an evasive appeal to 'different points of view'. (The 'contradiction' between our ever-shifting concept of what is 'essential' to something, and what merely 'accidental' to it, are a case in point.) This happy condition of unreflective reasonableness tends, however, to vanish as soon as Understanding enters on the scene, when it seeks to give to each of such notions its distinct empire, or when it sharpens or exaggerates either so as to dominate the whole field and to eliminate its rival. (Thus one might form the notion of some pure Essence which excludes all determinations, or of a cluster of accidents without relation to anything essential.) The opposition suppressed by the Understanding now vents itself in Dialectic: the separated concepts are found to have lost their sense, to demand completion by their antitheses, or even to have become mutually indistinguishable. All this can only be righted by a return at a higher level to the reasonableness out of which all these difficulties developed. This will, however, be a richer reasonableness than the first, since its antithetical basis will be apparent, and since the internal opposition of its aspects will be seen to be necessary to their significance.

If this is an account of what contradiction means in the realm of thought, a precisely parallel account will apply to the meaning of its presence in objective reality. There too there may be various antithetical tendencies, each set on ousting its rivals from the field, and capable of producing various circumscribed, one-sided forms of being. The formation of such one-sided forms may, however, release forces which will restore the balance, and the whole process may very well lead on to ever-richer states of equilibrium. If there is much dangerous metaphor in conceiving changes in the world as if they were arguments among philosophers, it is at any rate not without illumination; it at least brings out the continuity of the struggle involved in thought with the wider struggle involved in existence and life.

We may note, further, that Hegel's doctrine of contradiction as present in all our concepts does not mean that such contradiction will impede their working in ordinary contexts, or in the well-drilled precision of deductive systems. Hegel is no philosophical anarchist concerned to disrupt orderly processions by hurling dialectical bombs. Ordinary thought steers clear of contradiction by refusing to apply its concepts in unwonted cases, and a deductive system avoids them by the sheer precision of its abstractions, in which all factors that might lead to hesitation or conflict have been deliberately excluded. Contradiction will not arise as long as one remains resolutely at a single level of discourse, which one does not seek to connect, nor to see in relation, with other forms of discourse. It arises only when one tires of the deadness and sheer senselessness of such one-level discourse, and tries to pass on to something deeper: its point of emergence is not *within* smoothly functioning patterns of discourse, so much as *between* them. Hence the hesitation, the conflict it involves does not lead to the demoralizing paralysis it would engender were it injected into a well-oiled conceptual system, but it provides the spur to that deepening of our conceptual grasp which is the essence of philosophy. The contradictions in ordinary concepts are, in fact, only contradictions to those concerned to see the facts completely and from *every* conceptual angle, who believe with Hegel that 'the truth is the whole'.

We may hold, in fact, that Hegel's notion and use of contradiction, confusing as it in many ways is, none the less embodies one of the most important of philosophical discoveries, whose full depth has not even yet been properly assessed. Whatever one may think of the detailed application of his Dialectic, he has certainly made plain that our notions do carry with them a certain natural shading into other notions, a natural implication of such notions, and a natural favourableness and unfavourableness to other notions, which it is not in our power to create or alter, but which may be said to rest solely on their affinity of content. And with this affinity of content goes a natural tendency of our notions to slide over into other notions, to alter and develop in certain ways (many of them contrary), which tendency again we can neither make nor unmake, but can only yield to, or suppress. Our notions and modes of speech have, in fact, not merely a 'logical geography', to use a widely current contemporary phrase: they also have a 'logical dynamic' which determines them to move forward in certain directions when pushed in unwonted ways. Thus it is part of the logical dynamic of the notion of 'appearance' to be applied more and more widely as we consider such circumstances as perspectival variation, illusion, hallucination, influence of media, etc. etc., until in the end it almost ousts the correlative notion of 'essential underlying reality' from the field, thereupon probably setting up a counter-movement in the opposite direction. What we can do in regard to our notions is not to cut off their 'logical halo' of implications but only to ignore it: what we can do in regard to their 'logical dynamic' is only to arrest it artificially. This we do when we define our terms, when we consider only what they entail and not what they favour or fail to favour, when we lay down necessary or sufficient conditions for their use, and endeavour to keep these constant. But, however much we may fix our usages in this way, we cannot get rid of the various deep needs which prompt us to change them in various directions, to bring out affinities or profound differences which current concepts mask or conceal. And where Hegel makes his supreme contribution is in holding that *all* these dialectical tendencies need to be made fully explicit before we can achieve the reasonable, the philosophical result.

Hegel may in fact be said not merely to have anticipated many of the views that we now associate with the name of Wittgenstein, but even to have gone beyond these. Wittgenstein recognizes that philosophers suffer from a 'mental cramp' engendered by the rigidities of ordinary language, and experience various 'deeply rooted needs of the greatest variety', which *may* lead them, e.g., towards notations which stress *differences* more strongly than does ordinary speech, or which employ more closely *similar* expressions than ordinary speech does. He also often recognizes that it is a worth-while thing, and not a mere product of confusion, to work out these extraordinary philosophical notations. But in the main he chooses to stress that philosophical novelties are due to the 'fascination' exerted by misleading linguistic analogies, to the 'discomfort' caused by our incomprehension of the 'grammar' of ordinary expressions, and to the lure of a false ideal of exactness. He talks often as if the whole task of philosophy were to dispose of these linguistic snares—to 'show the flies the way out of the fly-bottle'—after which we can revert with perfect comfort and added insight to our original speech-forms. Whereas in Hegel there is no mere liquidation or abandonment of the various one-sided exaggerations which spring from the action of Understanding: they are all incorporated into our final mode of speaking, and add to its richness. Hegel's last form of reasonableness is quite different from his first.

Having considered the objections to the Dialectic on the score of its tolerance of contradictions, we may briefly consider other objections, themselves somewhat contradictory, concerned with his alleged attempt to *construe* the world in *a priori* fashion, with the *arbitrary* manner in which this construction proceeds, and with its frequent, though covert, reliance on *experience*. Ever since Krug demanded a philosophical deduction of his quill pen, it has been thought that Hegel was committed to deduce all ideas and all reality out of a few abstract philosophical notions and principles. It has then been objected that, the aims and claims of the method being what they are, Hegel's performance has fallen infinitely far short of them, that he has arbitrarily fitted empirical borrowings into a ready-made dialectical schema, and that the faults that he attributes to Schelling are, in fact, his own.

Here we may merely maintain that Hegel's main mistake, both in what he *says* about his Dialectic and in what he tries to do with it, lies in his assumption that it has *a kind of deductive necessity*, different from, but akin to, that of a mathematical system, whereby we shall find ourselves forced along a *single* line of reasoning, culminating in 'the Idea', and then leading back to our point of origin. Whereas, quite obviously, since dialectical development only proceeds by the undoing of one-sided abstractions, and by the provision for them of their appropriate complements, it is impossible that the steps it takes should *follow* from the one-sidedness and from the contradictions that lead up to them: they must represent a new departure, a 'transformation' of the position, a rise to a more 'concrete' level of thinking. From the point of view of this new level of thought what went before may seem a confused preamble to itself: this cannot, however, be obvious at the lower level. There may be a felt gap and an inward unease in a conceptual situation which brings about its own filling and appeasement, but this 'bringing about', since it involves new features, and an altered way of looking at things, cannot be regarded as a case of logical entailment. The abstractions of the Understanding can, in fact, only entail *themselves* and the contradictions in which they break down can only entail further contradictions. This Hegel himself recognizes when he stresses the *self-mediated* character of his results, despite their *appearance* of being mediated by something else, and when he talks of the 'elevation of thought' necessary to lead us from the finite world to God, which is misrepresented in the Cosmological Proof. It is therefore by no means unreasonable that Hegel should undo the unreasonable abstractions of the Understanding by bringing in what we *already know* to be their actual complement, and that he should do so by appealing to a wider experience. And if the undoing of such abstractions *could* have followed a variety of routes, and not merely the one route followed by Hegel, this is no objection to the dialectical method as such, but only to an inadmissibly rigorous conception of it. Hegel in fact admits that much of the detail of the world is contingent and dialectically indeducible: he should have gone further, in conformity with his actual practice, and have admitted that even its broader features admit of no precise deduction, but merely of an illuminating treatment. We can show, that is, how things and notions can be regarded as making contributions to the self-consciousness of Spirit: we cannot show that the same contributions could not have been otherwise made.

We may note, lastly, that the notion of Spirit, in which the Dialectic culminates, is such as to *forbid* that the Dialectic should be anything like a deductive system, in which unique conclusions follow rigorously upon definite premisses. For Spirit can only exist as Spirit in so far as it is confronted by an other which it cannot render completely transparent. Its overcoming of this other does not consist in understanding it completely nor in dominating it exhaustively—either would involve the finitude and the ruin of Spirit—but in realizing the opacity of the other to be the necessary condition for its own self-consciousness. Such being the case, an arbitrary and an empirical element are essential to the being of self-consciousness, and are therefore rightly present in the Hegelian Dialectic. But that the Dialectic both permits and demands this arbitrary and empirical element is not plainly stated by Hegel: it appears only in his practice. It seems better to judge Hegel's remarkable performance in the light of the reasonable aims which appear in his practice, than in the light of the unreasonable aims which may be read into his less careful statements by his admirers or his detractors.

CHAPTER FOUR

THE PHENOMENOLOGY OF SPIRIT—I
Consciousness, Self-consciousness and Reason

I THE PREFACE AND INTRODUCTION
TO THE PHENOMENOLOGY

Having removed some of the main sources of prejudice against Hegel, and having sketched the principles and charted the course of his dialectical navigation, it is time to turn to his actual works. We shall, in this chapter and the next, deal with *The Phenomenology of Spirit*, the earliest, the most difficult and (in the opinion of many) the greatest of Hegel's mature works. In it the themes are all sounded that will be worked out in detail in the later system. But they are stated in an inspired, fragmentary, allusive manner, which imposes much greater strain on the reader's interpretative effort than does the later encylopaedic exposition. The age, the social and cultural group that could read the *Phenomenology* with ease and pleasure has now passed utterly away: to fill in its gaps, to puzzle out its allusions and follow out its hints, involves for us an agonizing effort, a major archaeological and philosophical reconstruction. In the next two chapters we shall do little beyond giving the pertinacious reader a thread to guide him through the windings of the work, and a reassurance that this way of the cross is also a road to the highest intellectual glories. For more detailed interpretation he may be referred to M. Hyppolite's admirable commentary.

The *Phenomenology* is preceded by a remarkable *Preface*, which is a literary as well as a philosophical masterpiece. We have quoted from it so often in previous chapters, that a fairly brief treatment will suffice now. This *Preface* is followed by an almost equally interesting *Introduction*, which is more closely connected with the themes of the ensuing work. It seems likely that the *Preface* was written *after* the *Phenomenology* had been completed, since in a sense it sums it up and rounds it off, whereas the *Introduction* was written before it, and genuinely introduces it.

In the *Preface* Hegel begins by setting forth his notion of *Wissenschaft* or Systematic Science as the goal of all *Wissen* or knowledge. It is only, he holds, in a single, coherent, developing system, in which every term is a notion divested of anything concrete or particular, and in which each term grows out of preceding terms in a necessary fashion, that 'truth', in the peculiar sense in which Hegel uses it, can exist. 'The true shape in which truth exists', he tells us, 'can be no other than the scientific system of the same. . . . The inner necessity that knowledge should be Science, lies in its very nature, and the only satisfactory explanation of this fact is in the exposition of philosophy itself.'[1] Hegel believes that the time is exactly ripe for the birth of this Systematic Science. This birth has been prepared for by a long, winding and difficult course of development, and has been led up to by countless forms of culture. It has had its immediate forerunners in the intuitionism of Jacobi, and in the mechanical dialectics and absolutism of Schelling, but its advent, like that of the Redeemer in Christianity, remains a momentous and decisive happening. 'Spirit', says Hegel, 'has broken with the previous world of its being and thinking, has in mind to let it sink into the past and is active in reshaping it. It is never at rest, but always moving forwards. But, as in the case of a child, after a long period of silent nurturing, there is a qualitative leap: the first breath puts an end to the continuous process of mere growth, and the child is born.'[2]

Hegel then proceeds to give a magnificent account of the content to be worked out in Systematic Science, the doctrine (expounded by us in Chapter II) that 'the true' should not 'merely be thought of and spoken of as Substance but also as Subject',[3] that it should be envisaged as a living, spiritual reality, which can exist only in the vivid consciousness and affirmation of itself, and which can only rise to such active self-consciousness by being first embodied in a long series of distinct and opposed forms, in all of which it can come to see itself. This procession of forms in which spiritual reality has expressed itself *before* rising to Systematic Science extends far beyond the individual's experience: it covers the whole past range of human experience, as well as the whole ascending ladder of natural forms. If Systematic Science is to arise in the individual, he must recapitulate, relive and appropriate this procession of forms in his own experience: he must submit to a personal preparation for Systematic Science which is

---

[1] *Phen.*, p. 14.   [2] *Phen.*, p. 18.   [3] *Phen.*, p. 22.

precisely parallel to the cosmic preparation which has gone on in nature and history.

Hegel further holds that, for Systematic Science to be fully completed, the process that leads up to it must itself be made part of it, that Systematic Science must include in itself a prelude, framed in its own systematic manner and language, which will set forth the whole genetic process that has led up to Systematic Science itself. Systematic Science will contain other more central, less educationally concerned parts—parts which deal with the abstract logical evolution of concepts or with the more concrete evolution of natural and spiritual forms: all these must, however, be completed by a systematic restatement of the *educational history* that has led up to them, and that has rendered them possible. This systematic restatement will not be the idealized biography of some particular individual or type of individual: it will not sketch the spiritual history of an Aristotle, a Goethe or a G. W. F. Hegel. It will rather set forth, in abstract notional terms, how *any* individual must advance to Systematic Science. This universalized biography or transcendental propaedeutic, which only actual elaboration can show to be possible, is called by Hegel the 'Phenomenology of Spirit'. 'Science', he tells us, 'must present the pattern of this whole developmental movement in its complete detail and necessity, as something which has already sunk down and become an aspect and possession of Spirit. Its end is Spirit's insight into the nature of knowledge. Impatience demands the impossible, the achievement of this end without the means. . . . But because the substance of the individual, and even the World Spirit, has had the patience to go through these forms in the long stretches of past time, and through the colossal labour of world history . . . and because it could not with less labour have reached the consciousness of itself, so obviously the individual mind cannot hope to grasp its own substance with less labour.'[1] We may note how Hegel unquestioningly assumes that there can be but a *single* experiential route leading up to Systematic Science, the trail actually blazed by the 'World Spirit' in the past and recapitulated in each individual's educational experience, a route in which there are absolutely no arbitrary steps nor the smallest possibility of deviation. It would have been better, and more in agreement with his own central ideas, had Hegel recognized an

[1] *Phen.*, pp. 31-2 (B., pp. 90-1).

indefinite plurality of such routes, and had he looked on his own *Phenomenology* as being (what it actually is) a single paradigmatic instance.

For the rest the *Preface* deals with the method of Phenomenology and of Systematic Science in general, which it opposes to various contemporary alternatives. The method of Science, Hegel tells us, is a method which deals only in universal types or notions, which completely excludes all forms of picture-thinking. It may be 'concrete' in the sense of dealing with notions that are many-sided and developing: it is not concrete in the sense of dealing with anything sensuous. Hegel holds, however, that the systematic scientist will be largely exempt from the painful task of *abstracting* notions or types from empirical instances: this task has been, for the most part, performed in previous phases of thought and existence. The systematic scientist has rather to weave types and universals into a continuous pattern, than to tease them out of empirical contexts. 'Our task', says Hegel, 'is not now to purify the individual from the immediate mode of sense, and to make him something that thinks and is thought, but on the contrary to realize and animate the universal by the overcoming of fixed and definite thoughts.'[1] It will be noted how the terms of Hegelian Science are almost always notions or concepts, not propositions into which such concepts enter: in Science we progress to ever more adequate modes of *conceiving*, not to new truths deductively entailed by previous truths.

The method of Science is, further, the dialectical method, the living, triadic form of development, well known to the ancients, brought back into philosophical currency by Kant, and appearing in degraded, formalized guise in the thought of Schelling. It is a method, Hegel insists, which involves no personal pushing or interference: the dialectician, like some quietist saint, must simply wait upon, or surrender himself to the 'immanent rhythm' of his notions. This dialectical method is opposed to the romantic intuitionism of Jacobi, who was led through his study of Kant and Spinoza to distrust all forms of conceptual thinking, and to seek to approach the Infinite and the Divine through direct 'feeling' or 'intuition'. Of this affective-intuitional approach Hegel pithily remarks: 'Just as there is a breadth which is empty, so there is a depth which is empty too. . . . These people imagine

[1] *Phen.*, p. 35 (B., p. 94).

that by clouding self-consciousness and renouncing understanding they will become those beloved ones to whom God gives His wisdom in sleep. . . . What they do in fact receive and bring forth from this sleep are accordingly dreams.'[1] Equal criticism is directed to Schelling's violent forcing of external triplicities on to any and every material, and to his monotonously repeated, Bradleian asseveration that while we may indeed *say* that this or that form of being exists, 'in the Absolute, the A = A, there is no such thing, for there everything is one'. Hegel also opposes the living dialectical evolution of content to the lifeless procedure of the ordinary empirical and mathematical sciences. In all these there is a fixed opposition, begotten of unbending notions, between the true and the false: what is taken for true is retained in the science, while what has been proved false, is cast forth from it. Whereas in dialectical thought the false must always be in a sense preserved in the truth, not indeed *qua* false, but as overcome in this truth.

Having done no more than sample a few of the points in the 'Bacchanalian riot' of the famous *Preface*, we pass on to deal with the less tangled *Introduction*. Here Hegel seeks to sketch the nature of that 'Absolute Knowledge' at which Systematic Science must aim, and to differentiate it from the 'common view of things', and from various states of 'unreal consciousness'. Hegel is here mainly concerned to reject the notion of there being some absolute *criterion*, other than one immanent and inherent in conscious experience, by means of which the genuine knowledge of an absolute reality can be distinguished from forms of consciousness that are 'unreal' or spurious. 'Consciousness', says Hegel, 'is on the one hand consciousness of the object, on the other hand consciousness of itself: consciousness of that which is for it the True, and consciousness of its own knowledge of this. Inasmuch as both are there for the same consciousness, it is itself their comparison; it is a fact *for* consciousness whether its knowledge of the object corresponds to it or not.'[2] Hegel is here saying, most persuasively and acceptably, that it is senseless to talk of an 'absolute' or 'objective' reality without connecting it with the procedures through which such a reality could be established as real by us. As long as there is some discoverable inadequacy or discrepancy in the notions we form of some object, there is sense

[1] *Phen.*, p. 18 (B., pp. 74–5).   [2] *Phen.*, p. 77 (B., p. 141).

in opposing this object as it is *for us*, to the same object as it is *in itself*. When, however, all such inadequacies and discrepancies have been removed, there is no longer sense in drawing this distinction. An object that has passed every validating test may be properly called an absolute reality.

It is from this point of view that Hegel vehemently rejects all Lockean attempts to *scrutinize* the faculty of knowledge, to discover whether it is or is not capable of knowing absolute reality. Such seemingly modest attempts Hegel holds to be both arrogant and absurd. They assume without question that the relations between what is real, and the conscious processes which establish its reality, are wholly external and accidental, an assumption destructive *ab initio* of the very possibility of knowledge. Hegel also rejects any *mere* opposition of absolute knowledge to the affirmations of the 'natural consciousness' or to the 'common view of things'. To range two such modes of consciousness side by side, as merely differing in the *kind* of consciousness they involve, is to remove all ground for preferring one to the other, is to do no more than accept the 'dry assurance' of one in preference to that of the other. The only way in which we can *show* the difference between an absolute knowledge, and a consciousness which is inadequate, is the dialectical method: we must allow the latter to develop into the former. Each inadequate form of consciousness must be given enough rope to hang itself: it must be allowed to ruin itself in doubt, and to break down in utter despair. Its view of the object, which seemed identical with the object as it is *in itself*, must be shown to be no more than the object as it is *for us*. It must yield place to another phase of consciousness, which takes another view of the object as it is *in itself*, and which must in its turn be permitted to break down in the same fashion. Consciousness will thus be made to traverse a series of forms in what Hegel holds to be an invariable and inevitable order—an assumption we have held to be untrue in itself and false to Hegel's own practice —until at length a stage has been reached where the immanent criteria of consciousness have all been satisfied, where it is perfectly appeased, where there is no longer any opposition between the object as it is *for us* and the object as it is *in itself*. Hegel will show that the object of such absolute knowledge is simply absolute knowledge itself, and that this absolute knowledge is accordingly *self*-consciousness. In this final view we shall at once possess absolute knowledge, and shall also know how our previous states of consciousness fell short of it.

Hegel makes use of the word 'experience' in a curious phenomenological sense in reference to the way in which earlier, more naïve views of absolute reality are incorporated into later, more developed ones: the objects of later views are said to be the 'experience' of the earlier ones.[1] It is by *having had* the earlier views that we are able to have the later: the objects of the later views are accordingly said to be our 'experience' of the former. The assumption is that there will be nothing in a later dialectical phase than what is involved in a higher-level description of what is contained in its predecessor. Hegel further maintains that the full inevitability of the process which leads consciousness on from one inadequate view of things to another more adequate, must in a measure be hidden from consciousness: it will go on 'behind the back of consciousness', and will be evident only to the phenomenological observer, or in the phenomenological retrospect.[2] (In a meta-language, we should say, one can say things about a given language which that language is unable to say of itself.) Thus the scientist will be led on from the things of sense-perception to the non-sensuous things of the scientific understanding, but he will not know exactly why he is thus led. It is we, the phenomenological observers, practising our external reflection, who can understand the whole transition. What is for him merely a factual discovery can be seen by us to be an inevitable revolution in consciousness. We shall not here discuss these profoundly suggestive and obviously illuminating contentions, but shall pass on to illustrate them in the dialectical developments which follow.

II SENSE-CERTAINTY, PERCEPTION AND SCIENTIFIC UNDERSTANDING

The first section of the *Phenomenology* has the heading 'Consciousness': it studies the ordinary, naïve consciousness of an 'outer' world, which is at first taken to be independent of, and wholly indifferent to, the manner in which we are conscious of it. As the Dialectic proceeds, this indifference and this independence

[1] *Phen.*, p. 78 (B., p. 143).   [2] *Phen.*, pp. 79–80 (B., p. 144).

break down: the external world is shown to be such as to meet at all points the requirements of consciousness. Hegel begins by dealing with *Sense-certainty*, the state of mind in which, in Russellian terms, we enjoy a direct acquaintance with some object, which we *app*rehend without seeking either to *comp*rehend or describe. The content of such sensuous apprehension seems to common thought indefinitely rich—all comprehension seems merely to select from it or to abridge it—it also seems to be the most solidly *true* element in our knowledge, all other knowledge being based upon it, or confirmed by it. Hegel maintains, however, that such Sense-certainty is the most emptily abstract of consciousnesses: its whole content can be covered by such bald phrases as 'There is this' or simply 'It is'. To say anything *more* about what confronts us in Sense-awareness is at once to pass beyond it, to dissolve it into a series of concepts or universals, with which step the solidity of our knowledge will at once suffer an attenuation. We can of course point to, or pick out, some object present to sense: we can pin it down by an ostensive gesture accompanied by a demonstrative word like 'this' or 'here' or 'now'. This mode of pinning down is, however, entirely evanescent: a moment later we shall be confronted by another sensuously given object, and it is to *this* that our demonstrative words will apply. Hegel describes the situation in these terms: 'To the question "What is there now?" we may answer "Now it is night". A simple investigation will suffice to test this piece of Sense-certainty. Let us write this truth down: a truth can't lose anything by being written down, any more than by being stored away. Let us now look at this written-down truth at this moment of noon, and we shall have to confess that it has become stale.'[1]

Hegel maintains further that, despite our wishes, it is *impossible* to give words like 'here', 'this' and 'now' a genuinely particular meaning. Their meaning, in so far as they have any, remains obstinately universal: it is that of a something-or-other, a being and another being, etc. etc. It is this universality of their meaning which enables us to apply demonstratives to ever new things and situations. We may *want* our words to mean something quite particular, we may *intend* (*meinen*) something wholly particular by them, but the 'divine nature' of language frustrates this intention, and turns it upside down. Our words must necessarily mean some-

[1] *Phen.*, p. 83 (B., p. 151).

thing abstract and universal, since the particulars of sense cannot be reached by language at all.

Sense-certainty therefore breaks down as the proud base of all knowledge. It is only knowledge implicit, and to yield explicit knowledge it must pass over into the Perceptual Consciousness, in which the object confronting us will cease to be a mere 'this', and will become a *Thing* characterized by a number of distinct universals or properties. It may, e.g., be a lump of salt, which is perceived as sharp, white, cubical and so on. Hegel says that the wealth of distinctions commonly credited to Sense-awareness really belongs to this Perceptual Consciousness. The Thing is pinned down and identified as the seat, the *medium* of a characteristic pattern of properties, which remain constant and self-same —where drastic alterations occur, we ascribe the irregularity to ourselves, and regard them as 'illusory'. It is also pinned down by its exclusive, unitary character: it stands apart from things different in character, and its properties are likewise opposed to various contrary properties.

Hegel now goes on to show how this Perceptual Consciousness likewise breaks down, as a consciousness claiming to give us knowledge of an absolute reality. It is impossible to reconcile the unity and exclusive character of the *Thing* of Perception with the presence in it of several *mutually distinct* sense-qualities, which are likewise present in *other* similar Things. If the distinctness and universality of the properties be stressed, the Thing's unity and separateness become shadowy: this unity deteriorates into a mere 'also' in which the properties are externally related. But if, on the other hand, the unity and separateness of the Thing are emphasized, the mutual distinctness of its properties, as well as their genuine universality, falls into jeopardy. They can be referred to only by a mere 'in so far', and cannot be clearly and independently meant. (The fit of the above exposition to the difficult text is designedly loose: to come closer would be to sacrifice intelligibility without a certain gain in accuracy.)

We are now impelled to have recourse to an idea which will be strengthened by the inconsistencies and inconstancies of Sense-perception, to the effect that the thing's multiplicity of properties, of discriminable sensuous aspects, has existence only *in us*, and is without foundation in external reality. Equally well we may be led to hold that external Things are merely a *congeries* of properties or aspects, which *we*, as subjects, have externally colligated. But such excursions into subjectivity soon betray their vanity, since the reconciliation of concrete unity with the diversity of sensuous aspects, remains precisely the same issue whether it be attempted in the *Thing* or be carried out in *us*. We are, therefore, forced to draw a last-ditch distinction between what the thing may be *in itself*, its simple, unchanging core of essential properties, and the multitude of unessential, changeable characters which it assumes in its intercourse with other things. But this distinction, too, soon proves itself invalid. The changing aspects of the Thing must have *some* root in its unchanging essence, and this unchanging essence must itself be compared, and therefore *connected*, with external Things.

The collapse of every attempt to reconcile the Thing's unity with a diversity of aspects on a merely sensuous plane, now pushes us on to deal with our difficulties in a *two-world* manner. The diversity of aspects or properties of the *Thing* is held to belong to the world of sensory appearance, but to have a backing in a reality or realities which lie behind the scenes at some *deeper* or *inner* level. We therefore leave the stage of the Perceptual Consciousness and pass on to the realm of the Scientific Understanding, whose typical ruse it is to postulate *unobservable* entities to explain the phenomena offered us by our senses. These explanatory entities are of course pure notions, 'unconditioned universals', but they are not so *for* the Scientific Understanding, to it they seem non-phenomenal *objects* or realities.[1]

The first type of explanatory entity now introduced by Hegel is that of a Force or a Power: this must, on the one hand, be credited with an unmanifest withdrawn existence of its own, which can be withheld from sensuous expression, but, on the other hand, it must also be credited with a diversity of external sensuous Manifestations or Expressions, in which the withdrawn nature can from time to time be manifest. These two aspects of Force seem at first to be quite *independent* in their existence. Force exists as an unmanifest reality, and its outward Manifestations exist also, and the former explains the latter. But such an independence soon shows itself up as identical with the extremest *dependence*: the Manifestations of Force are essentially such as to *require* that Force for their explanation, as the Force is essentially such

---

[1] *Phen.*, p. 108 (B., p. 180).

as to express itself in certain sorts of Manifestation.[1] Hegel dwells with great subtlety on the relation between a Force and other Forces which provoke or *solicit* it into manifestation, or which likewise *inhibit* it from manifesting itself. Plainly it is part of the notion of a Force to require such external solicitation: it cannot pass out of its unmanifest state, or withdraw again into it, unless some external agency 'touches it off'. But since it *is* part of the notion of a Force to require this outward solicitation, and since the provoking Force itself requires the provocation of the Force it provokes to touch off its own provocative efficacy, the provoked Force may be said in a deep sense to provoke or solicit *itself*.[2] (This passage is very instructive: we see how, for Hegel, a thing's *self* includes whatever it may presuppose or require. It is in this sense that Spirit includes Nature, the necessary the contingent, and the rational the irrational.)

What emerges from this Dialectic is that we cease to regard the supersensible background of phenomena as consisting of several distinct Forces, each provoked by, and provoking, others. We see it rather as a realm of *Laws* which connect various types of phenomena, and which are explanatory of their changes. Hegel speaks of this realm as the 'stable image of unstable appearances', 'the quiet model of the perceived world', the 'tranquil Kingdom of Laws'. These Laws are not here to be regarded as mere *concepts* through which phenomena must be understood—which is of course what *we* know them really to be—but rather as some sort of non-phenomenal framework of tracks along which phenomena necessarily take their course.

The Dialectic now shows that this notion of Law, like that of its predecessor Force, becomes, if developed, less and less able to perform the explanatory work that the Understanding wants it to do. The most general laws of nature, that of gravitation for instance, are held by Hegel (quite absurdly, no doubt) to have no empirical content whatsoever, and to say no more than that everything makes a constant difference to everything else.[3] More particular laws, on the other hand, merely state some general pattern involved in what is found to happen empirically: they do not, in the manner desired by the Understanding, really *explain* phenomena. Thus a case of lightning may be explained by

---

[1] *Phen.*, pp. 111–12 (B., p. 184).
[2] *Phen.*, p. 114 (B., p. 187).
[3] *Phen.*, p. 123 (B., p. 196).

means of electrical forces and the laws governing such forces. But, says Hegel, 'this force is so constituted that, when it manifests itself, opposing electricities manifest themselves, which again vanish into each other. . . . In this tautological motion the Understanding can be shown to stick merely to the tranquil unity of its object, and the movement is an explanation that not only explains nothing, but is so clear that, while it pretends to say something new, it merely repeats itself'.[1] Scientific laws, in short, merely provide us with an orderly *redescription* of the phenomena we wish them to explain, a conclusion platitudinous to us, but not so to the contemporaries of Hegel.

At this point Hegel turns to the extremely queer, arbitrary fantasy of an inverted, or topsy-turvy (*verkehrte*) supersensible world, a world that does not copy or correspond to the perceived order, but which at every point runs *counter* to it. In such an inverted world the sweet will be sour, the north pole of a magnet identical with its south pole, and so forth. Hegel also adds for good measure a few ethical examples with a strong New Testament flavour, e.g. the punishment which disgraces us in *this* world, is in the *other* world an exercise of pardon.[2] The point of this grotesque fable would seem to be that the inversion in question makes no difference at all: it does not in fact matter *what* sort of explanatory entities we locate behind the curtain—Hegel speaks of a curtain though not of an iron one—provided they do the universalizing, conceptual work we require. He is also making much the same point as do Russell and Carnap, when they stress the importance and the communicability of *structure* and the unimportance of *content*. At this stage of the discussion the Scientific Understanding, with its transcendent realism, breaks down altogether. It becomes plain that its ruse was a ruse, that the non-phenomenal order is merely a product of the Understanding, that its whole content is purely notional. Consciousness accordingly becomes aware of *itself* as the one reality lying behind the curtain. We have, therefore, passed out of the sphere of Consciousness into that of *Self*-consciousness.

It will be plain that, despite the difficulty and complexity of the foregoing treatment (which we have only faintly indicated), Hegel has worked out a genuine dialectical path that has often been traversed by thought, and that he has said several things of

---

[1] *Phen.*, p. 127 (B., p. 201).   [2] *Phen.*, p. 131 (B., pp. 204–5).

very great importance. His treatment of 'direct apprehension', and the incorrigible judgements based on such apprehension, is both pertinent and penetrating: it could be applied in criticism of many contemporary views. His view of demonstrative words like 'here', 'now', 'this', etc., as being purely universal in meaning, may be open to criticism, but it is superior to Russell's view of them as 'logically proper names'. The whole subsequent development of thought out of Sense-awareness, through the many-sidedness and deceptiveness of Perception, to the acceptance of non-phenomenal, explanatory entities lying behind the data of sense, is not unlike the course taken by Russell's thought in such a work as *The Problems of Philosophy*. The familiarity of the argument is in fact obscured by the wilfully baroque exuberance and difficult detail of Hegel's writing. Hegel even goes a step beyond Russell in asserting the purely constructive, conceptual character of the explanatory entities located behind our sense-data. Hegel is, of course, wholly wrong if he thinks that the particular dialectical trail that he blazes is the *only* one that thought can follow: quite obviously his embarrassments could have been developed in different ways at every point. It is also obvious that there must be many *easier* ways through the dialectical jungle than one which takes the amazed reader, like some traveller in an Indo-Chinese forest, through the strange ruin of an inverted non-phenomenal world. The effort to see the wood for the arbitrary trees is, in the case of Hegel, often superhuman; it becomes easier when one realizes that the trees *are* disposed in an arbitrary manner.

III   SOCIAL SELF-CONSCIOUSNESS:
MASTERSHIP AND SLAVERY, STOICISM, SCEPTICISM AND UNHAPPY OTHER-WORLDLINESS

Having reached the stage of Self-consciousness along the epistemological route followed in Section *A* of the *Phenomenology*, the Dialectic suddenly swings over into the social sphere. Hegel becomes much more lucid and illuminating when he has to deal with such concrete and congenial notions as Mastership and Slavery, Stoicism, Scepticism and the 'Unhappy' Religious Consciousness. The transition to these topics is fairly straight-forward. The consciousness of *Self* as the reality responsible for non-phenomenal constructions, and, therefore, lying behind external phenomena, has a more adequate exemplification in the state of Desire (*Begierde*), the attitude which seeks to *make* external things conform to our requirements, instead of merely seeking to *discover* that they do so. It has also a more adequate exemplification where a phenomenal object is *living*: a living thing has something of the perpetual direction towards self which is characteristic of the self-conscious subject, and, therefore, serves to mirror the latter.[1] Practical intercourse with living things develops in *explicit* form the dependence of the external world on the self which was *implicit* at the epistemological level. The Dialectic, on the general principle of making the implicit explicit, therefore 'moves' from the epistemological to the practical, social level. Here, as elsewhere, Hegel's transition is in a queer way 'logical', though it shows not a trace of anything that one could call 'rigour'.

Hegel devotes some space, at this point, to a somewhat exuberant characterization of life. Its essence is said to be 'infinity as the supersession of all difference, the pure rotation on a thing's own axis, the peace involved in its own restless infinitude, the very self-sufficiency in which the differences of movement are dissolved, the simple essence of time which, in its equality with self has the solid form of space'.[2] It requires patience to distil some residual sense from language so turgid. Life, in brief, is held to be fluid; its development is continuous, and it preserves its unity of pattern and purpose even when dispersed among a number of distinct organs. It also manifests itself as a *genus*, a pure type or notion, which runs through a large number of distinct individual organisms. It can serve, therefore, as a suitable mirror, or external analogue, in which the self-conscious subject can survey its own features.

A great deal is now said of which the one clear outcome is that self-consciousness cannot be adequately mirrored in an object incapable of itself 'negating' what is external, of practically remoulding objects in the way in which the subject can 'negate' and remake them itself. *Another self* is, in short, the only adequate mirror of *my* self-conscious self: the subject can only satisfactorily see itself when what it sees is another self-consciousness.[3] At this

---

[1] *Phen.*, p. 141 (B., p. 220).
[2] *Phen.*, p. 142 (B., p. 221).   [3] *Phen.*, p. 147 (B., p. 227).

point, Hegel informs us, *Spirit* for the first time makes its appearance on the dialectical stage: we meet with a self-consciousness which is dispersed among a number of distinct centres, in all of which it recognizes itself, 'an I which is a We, a We which is an I'. Hegel makes it plain beyond question that self-conscious Spirit only knows itself for what it is, when it thus rises superior to the distinction of persons. He beautifully remarks: 'Consciousness achieves its turning-point in self-consciousness, at which point it leaves the coloured seeming of the sensuous here-and-now, and the empty night of the supersensible beyond, and enters into the spiritual daylight of the present.'[1] Henceforth he will keep us in this companionable, social daylight, and we shall have only indirect dealings with unspiritual objects.

The social-spiritual sphere we have now entered is said by Hegel to repeat at a higher level the interplay of forces dealt with by the Scientific Understanding. There we had an underworld of distinct forces, mutually releasing and inhibiting one another: here, on the other hand, we have an upper world of mutually acknowledging, conscious persons, who are conscious also of their mutual acknowledgement, and who are thereby raised to the fullest self-consciousness.[2] (One is reminded of the Henry Jamesian world where the characters not only see each other, but also see each other seeing each other.) The analogy between the interplay of forces and that of persons is as interesting and as revelatory of the far-flung affinities exploited by the Dialectic as any other instance in Hegel.

Hegel begins, however, at a level where this mutual acknowledgement among persons is imperfect, where each only *fully* recognizes his *own* conscious being, and is disposed to belittle or negate any *rival* claim to self-consciousness. (This is, perhaps, what Freud calls the natural 'narcissism' of the infant, from which certain Proustian characters never successfully emerge.) We have, as a natural product of this stage of the Dialectic, the life-and-death Struggle, where each self seeks to assert his own self-consciousness at the cost of annihilating the life and self-consciousness of the other, and does so, moreover, at the risk of his own vital existence. Hegel suggests poignantly that only a being who is prepared to risk his life in this manner can be deservedly reckoned a *person*. To carry on this struggle till it

---

[1] *Phen.*, pp. 147–8 (B., p. 227).   [2] *Phen.*, p. 150 (B., p. 231).

results in the death of one of the parties will, however, remove a necessary condition of self-consciousness: self-consciousness will be more stably sustained where the relationship is one of Master and Slave, to which the Dialectic accordingly turns. This relationship has its origin in war and fear: in it one party arrogates self-consciousness to himself, and denies it to his trembling adversary, who becomes thereby degraded to a thing-like attenuation of life and self-consciousness. Hegel seems right in recognizing the Master-Slave relationship to be not only a form universal in primitive society, but also one which makes a unique contribution to human self-consciousness.

The Master-Slave relationship is now allowed to develop itself more fully, and so to lead to its own supersession. Plainly, Hegel points out, it is a relationship mediated by impersonal material objects. It is by material chains that the slave is held in check, and the master employs the slave to secure enjoyments for himself from various material objects upon which the slave must toil. The master cannot, however, achieve the fullest self-consciousness when the 'other' in whom he must view himself, has the reduced status of a slave: to be *merely* a master is to fall short of being a fully self-conscious person. Hegel holds, further, that the slave has in some respects the best of the bargain, the advantage over the master. For the 'other' in which the slave sees self-consciousness manifest, and before which his personal being dissolves in quaking terror, is a more worthy representation of self-consciousness than the one *he* sets before his master. The slave's labour is also a more genuine overcoming of material externality than the master's idle round of vanishing enjoyments. But, since for the slave all rational direction lies outside himself in the master, his self-assertion will be necessarily degraded to mere self-will (*Eigensinn*), and his intelligence to a relatively hidebound skill or aptitude (*Geschicklichkeit*).[1] It is only in an attitude that can rise *above* the whole master-slave distinction that self-consciousness can adequately be realized. The Dialectic accordingly passes to this higher attitude.

From this profound discussion, with its revolutionary social and political implications, Hegel now moves over into a quieter philosophico-religious region. The required attitude which rises above both mastership and slavery is found by him in the *Stoical*

[1] *Phen.*, p. 158 (B., p. 240).

consciousness, a phase of mind which, according to Hegel, arises only in epochs characterized by universal fear and servitude, but which have also achieved a high level of culture. The Stoical consciousness *disdains* the master-slave distinction: whether on the throne (Marcus Aurelius) or in fetters (Epictetus), the Stoic wise man withdraws his ego into the 'universality of thought'. As a thinking person, he can admit nothing to be essential, nothing to be true or good, except in so far as it renders itself acceptable to his thinking self. Hegel has, however, no difficulty in showing up the emptily abstract character of this Stoic self-sufficiency: it achieves the *idea* of freedom rather than freedom's living reality. By releasing itself from the particularity of impulse and existence, it likewise releases *these* from itself: they become something unexplained, alien, merely 'there'. Hence the Stoical Consciousness can only rise to empty platitudes and edifying tautologies when it seeks to give us a universal mark or test of truth or virtue.

From this brief, trenchant characterization of Stoicism, the dialectic passes on to Scepticism, which is said to be the explicit realization of what Stoicism is merely the implicit notion. The Stoical consciousness seeks to maintain a positive ideal of truth and virtue, while adopting a wholly negative attitude to content and relationships: the Sceptical Consciousness, on the other hand, sees that an attitude of such thoroughgoing negation must of necessity involve the renunciation of all positive affirmations. For the Sceptical Consciousness the certainties of sense, the solid objects of perception, the proven hypotheses of the Scientific Understanding, as well as the moral rules sanctioned by the ruling group (*Herrschaft*) in society, are all dissolved, leaving the self-conscious subject—this is true, at least, in the noble scepticism of antiquity—entirely untroubled, free and self-secure among this universal dissolution. There will, however, be a necessary flaw in this abstract freedom of Scepticism. For the Sceptical consciousness will merely exist *alongside of* the natural, positive consciousness that it questions: it will not annul the latter. The sceptical subject will never cease to experience *two* consciousnesses, one sophisticated and one ordinary, and will pass continually from the one to the other. Scepticism, Hegel puts it, 'lets the unessential content in its thought dissolve, but in that very act it is the consciousness of something unessential; it pronounces a universal vanishing, but its pronouncement exists and, therefore, *is* the vanishing it has pronounced; it affirms the nullity of seeing, hearing and so forth, and must itself see, hear and so on; it affirms the nullity of essential ethical principles, and makes of them the ruling powers of its own actions. Its deeds and words always belie one another: it has in itself the twofold contradictory consciousness of its own unmodifiable equability, as well as of its total inequability and contingency.'[1] In other words, philosophical Scepticism, just because it is merely philosophical, always reinstates the dogmatism that it both requires and negates.

Scepticism is, therefore, held by Hegel to be infected with an inherent but unrecognized contradiction. It accordingly passes over, on the approved principles of the Dialectic, into a consciousness in which this inner contradiction becomes recognized and explicit, in which, in fact, inner contradiction is the central feature of consciousness. This consciousness is found by Hegel (again arbitrarily but appropriately) in the so-called 'Unhappy Consciousness', a consciousness openly rent by the conflict implicit in the Sceptic's vacillations, but also experiencing within itself the whole Slave-Master antithesis, which was overcome in merely one-sided, abstract fashion in both Stoicism and Scepticism. This Unhappy Consciousness is for Hegel the two-world consciousness of mediaeval Christendom, a consciousness in which there is always an opposition between the 'Unchangeable', the simple essential Godhead, on the one hand, and the 'Changeable', the unessential, complex 'things of this world', on the other. This Unhappy Consciousness locates itself among the things of this world, but it never ceases to stretch forth yearning hands towards the further divine shore. It cannot, however, do *more* than stretch forth its hands in this fashion, since a nearer approach would *rid* it of its essential unhappiness. Each approach to the Godhead must, therefore, be succeeded by the painful reaffirmation of its own nothingness, each positive achievement or enjoyment by an act of humble thanksgiving for Divine Grace. Much of what Hegel here says would assort better with Kierkegaard's morbid Protestant Christianity than with the positive, often joyous attitude of Mediaeval Christendom. The Unhappy Consciousness is further said by Hegel to be an attitude in which the otherness of the Godhead, and its opposition to this world, are *felt* rather than conceived. The Unhappy Consciousness devotes

[1] *Phen.*, pp. 165–6 (B., pp. 249–50).

itself to the Godhead, yearns after it with infinite longing, but never attempts to *think* it. The thought of this Unhappy Consciousness is in fact said by Hegel to be no more than 'the formless passage of the sound of bells, or the warm spread of incense, a musical thought that never rises to a notion, the only way in which the object could become immanent'.[1] Surely a strange characterization of the age that produced Aquinas.

The three persons of the Trinity now enter Hegel's argument in an obscure but unmistakable manner, as expressing different 'sides' of the Unhappy Consciousness. In God the Father we have the stern, negative judgement passed by the Unchangeable, the universal and essential, upon the changing, the unessential and singular. In God the Son we have an attempt to heal the division between the two sides of the Unhappy Consciousness, but made only in a single historic individual, quite distinct from all other individual persons. In God the Holy Spirit the same reconciliation is tentatively effected in a community of persons. Hegel lays stress on the imperfect character of the reconciliations achieved by the Unhappy Consciousness. In uniting the Unchangeable with the changeable in the single historic individual, Christ, and in failing to make it the prerogative of self-consciousness as such, the Unhappy Consciousness ends by giving a spatial and temporal remoteness to the reconciliation it so fervently believes in, a remoteness as bad as the abstract remoteness of the Unchangeable. The Crusaders sought to abridge this remoteness by the somewhat crude expedient of a movement in space, but it was only possible for them to lay hands on the abandoned *grave* of their Godhead.[2]

The most extreme, and therefore for Hegel the most logical, form of the Unhappy Consciousness is now seen in monkish asceticism, a state in which an intense opposition to this-worldliness reduces the latter to its most animal forms, and whose whole attempt to chastise and subdue the flesh succeeds only in giving it central importance.[3] (Again a strange distortion of a mode of life which must often have been orderly and happy.) The extreme division between the two sides of the Unhappy Consciousness demands some living and contemporary link: this it finds, through Hegel's selective ingenuity, in a body of men

[1] *Phen.*, p. 172 (B., p. 257).
[2] *Phen.*, p. 173 (B., p. 258).   [3] *Phen.*, p. 178 (B., pp. 263–4).

who (according to him) decide nothing, own nothing and enjoy nothing for themselves, and who are given over to the performance of (to them) senseless mummeries (Hegel's Lutheran picture of the activities of the Catholic priesthood). Men of this order mediate between invariable law and contingent sinfulness, and it is according to Hegel, in the sacramental act of *Absolution*, when carried out by them, that the Unhappy Consciousness comes closest to overcoming its inward schisms, and to uniting its changeable self with the Unchangeable.

This act of Absolution is now arbitrarily (if suitably) chosen by Hegel as an act which anticipates (though in external, mechanical fashion) the complete and satisfactory reconciliation between the Unchangeable and the changeable, the universal and the singular, the essential and the unessential, will be *explicitly* carried out by Reason. The sort of union between invariable principle and detailed contingency which the Catholic Church achieves only in symbol and show, must be carried out in sober reality in the activities of theoretical and practical Reason. It is to these that the Dialectic must accordingly turn.

The section of the *Phenomenology* just sketched has been deservedly admired: it has also exercised great influence. Hegel's analysis of the Master-Slave relationship has been much pondered on by Marxists and by other social analysts. Hegel has certainly shown the deep but subtle affinity between the various attitudes he has sketched, as well as the obscure but powerful 'logic' pushing one on from one to the other. The self-assertion of intelligent, conscious beings necessarily seeks its *first* expression in a crude mastery over other conscious beings, a mastery which would override their claims to exist, or think, or enjoy. In overriding these claims, we seek to aggrandize our own conscious being, but we only manage to do so in a reduced, exclusive, narrowly personal fashion. It is the same impulse to mastery which assumes subtler forms in the self-righteous pride of Stoicism, and the unruffled calm of Scepticism. And Hegel's insight detects the same impulse to mastery, turned upon the individual's own self, in the self-flagellations and self-humiliations of ascetic religion. The Master-Slave relation is not truly overcome even when the Godhead becomes master, and we its slaves. And clearly these inadequate forms of mastery tend to pass over into that final rational form of mastery, where neither the unifying tendencies inherent in consciousness, nor the particular tendencies and circumstances on which these work, are felt to be alien to ourselves.

IV THE OBSERVATIONAL STUDY OF NATURE AND MIND

In the varied forms of self-consciousness that we have been studying the individual has been conscious of himself only *in opposition* to other realities, other individuals, particular impulses and certainties, a natural and a supernatural order. We now pass to forms of experience that are *reasonable* or *rational*, in the peculiar sense that the relation of the conscious individual to what is other than itself becomes positive rather than negative, becomes one of *acceptance* and *acquiescence* rather than of opposition. In all the phases just gone through, the 'other' may have been involved in the being of the conscious individual, but it has always *appeared* to encroach on it, and to confront it from without. In the reasonable phases now on hand, this appearance is shown up as the mere appearance it is. The self-conscious individual becomes clear that the world is 'his oyster', the mere field of his conscious activity, that consciousness is, in a sense, *all* truth and all reality.

The phase at which consciousness has arrived is said by Hegel (in the difficult section called 'The Certainty and Truth of Reason') to be one of 'Idealism'. It is the living experience of which philosophical systems of Idealism are the empty and formal statement. The 'Idealism' of Reason means that objects are all in a deep sense *mine*—mine to understand, mine to experiment with, mine to remould and mine to find myself in—and that the categories of Reason, its varying *a priori* concepts of objects, are no more than the ways in which such objects can be made mine, in which they can make an enriching contribution to my self-consciousness.

The Idealism of Reason will not involve an *understanding* of the difficult dialectical route that has led up to it, and by which it is justified: it will show itself, rather, in the simple unwavering *confidence* with which the mind handles what the world lays before it. The scientific observer, confident of a naturalistic explanation, is, in Hegel's sense, an Idealist, and so is the practical individual confidently shaping his course in society. Philosophical Idealism, on the other hand, contents itself with the empty

Berkeleyan assertion that the things of the world are all *my* ideas
and sensations, an assertion which leaves to brute experience
the *content* of all such ideas and sensations, and can point to
nothing that *makes* them mine. Such Idealism is merely Scepticism
inverted: while the latter rejects all content indifferently, Berkeleyan Idealism indifferently swallows it all. We see from this whole
passage how little Hegel's Idealism has of the subjective, productive character commonly associated with the name. Idealism is
for him the view that the world may, with great effort and without
finality, be intellectually and practically mastered, a view which
both permits and entails much that would ordinarily be called
realism and materialism.

The content of this true Idealism is now worked out in three
long sections whose connection with each other is none of the
most obvious. The first deals with the varied *observational*
activities of Reason, the next with its *practical self-realization*,
the third with an 'individuality' which is described by Hegel
as being 'both implicitly and explicitly real to itself'. We shall
deal with the long section on Observation in our present section,
and consider Hegel's two remaining sections in the last section
of this chapter.

In the treatment of Observation which follows Hegel retraces
at a higher level some of the ground covered in his previous study
of Sense-certainty, Perception and Scientific Understanding:
then, however, he was studying a relatively passive picturing of the
object, almost unconscious of itself, whereas now he has to deal
with an attitude of searching experimentation, which is determined to find its 'self', its rationality, in the object. Self-consciousness may at first merely divine its own presence in the object
before it, but it must go on to assume complete possession of the
property assured to it: it must, says Hegel, 'plant the sign of its
sovereignty upon every height and depth'.[1] In this taking possession of objects consciousness may feel itself to be merely taking
in sense-given realities alien to itself, but its real activity belies
this impression, since it can know objects only by refining their
sensuousness into notions, i.e. by assimilating them to itself.

The most superficial form of such notional activity is the
simple act of *Description*: an object is first classified as a such-
and-such, then as a particular sort of such-and-such, and when

[1] *Phen.*, p. 191 (B., p. 281).

Reason can get no further with the thing itself, it will proceed to classify its parts or divisions. Obviously there can be no limit to this sort of descriptive activity, as long as it stays on a merely superficial level. Reason cannot, however, remain satisfied with such descriptions unless they manage to seize on important or essential properties, properties which represent how things really differentiate themselves from and maintain themselves against each other, not merely for our knowledge, but also 'in nature'. (A case of this self-differentiation occurs when we classify animals by the shape of their claws, teeth and other defensive organs, the very weapons through which they maintain their identity as a species.) Even this sorting of things into natural kinds must, however, prove unsatisfactory to Reason; there will always be transitional forms that will bring together what Reason wishes to separate, and separate what Reason wishes to unite. Reason must, therefore, pass from a merely classificatory to an *explanatory* stage: it must begin to understand things, not in terms of mere kinds, but by means of scientific laws and hypotheses. These laws, in their turn, from being mere summaries of sensuously given fact, will become ever more remote, abstract and notional. They may start by telling us of the properties of the lodestone or of glass rubbed by silk, but they will end by talking about the relations of electric charges, or of other non-showable things and processes. In the end, Hegel holds, Reason can only find satisfaction in dealing with objects which, while sensuous and observable, are none the less not bound up with any one sensuous form of being. Like laws, they must unite in themselves the possibility of quite varied characteristics, as well as the possibility of quite varied relations to other objects. Such lawfully variable objects are found by Hegel in *living organisms*. Hegel, therefore, passes with relief from his confused and uncomfortable treatment of the observation of inorganic phenomena, to a treatment of the observation of organic forms, which alone are well-pleasing to Reason.

In observing the organism, Hegel tells us, Reason constantly makes use of the category of *end* or *purpose*. This may be the external purposiveness shown in the adaptedness of organic structure to features of the environment, e.g. of fur to polar cold; it may also be the deeper, *immanent* teleology shown in the organism's preservation of its characteristic pattern among changing and opposing conditions. At the level of Observation, Hegel maintains, Reason never completely identifies the organism's self-maintenance in varying conditions with the *purpose* it uses to interpret it. If it sees purpose in the organism, it attributes this to some interfering, guiding 'soul', of whose will self-maintenance is the outward expression. Reason at this stage does not see that the inner purposiveness of the organism and its outward self-maintenance have, in the end, no difference of content, that organic purposiveness simply *is* self-maintenance and *vice versa*. (This passage is interesting as throwing light on Hegel's view of teleology.)[1]

Hegel argues, however, that biological observation will never be able to bring living creatures under peculiar laws: their behaviour is too fluid and variable to be broken up into clear-cut aspects or functions, between which definite laws can be shown to hold. All living functions *pass over* into each other, and can at a push do duty for one another. Biological theory in Hegel's day made great play with a triplicity of organic functions, Sensitivity, Irritability and Reproduction, between which various portentous laws were thought to hold. Hegel emphasizes, somewhat heavily, that it is not really possible to separate these functions, that all that can be ranged under one of them can be ranged under the others as well. Sensitivity, e.g., must show itself in discriminative *reactions* if it is not to be lifeless passivity, and reactions which are not sensitive *to* anything are not cases or organic Irritability.[2] And since both functions represent self-maintenance among everchanging conditions, both may be identified with Reproduction, which is merely self-maintenance written large. The pretended laws connecting the various functions are held by Hegel to be veiled tautologies: it is as if one said portentously that a hole grows with the diminution of the matter that fills it, or with an increase in the material that is removed from it.[3] Hegel's treatment here shows great penetration, though devoted to notions that no longer have the least interest.

In dealing with organisms we are, in fact, on Hegel's view, placed between Scylla and Charybdis. We can consider them *as* organic, in which case all will be lawless, fluid and elusive: life is a stream that can be diverted into countless courses, which

---

[1] *Phen.*, p. 208 (B., p. 301).
[2] *Phen.*, p. 211 (B., p. 308).   [3] *Phen.*, p. 212 (B., p. 306).

'does not care what sort of mills it drives'.[1] Alternatively we can study various separate *properties* of living creatures, e.g. their colour, hardness, cohesion, specific gravity and so forth: none of these will have any necessary connection with the others, and all will be found in inorganic things as well. The same random looseness of differentiation is shown, Hegel claims, in the various species of an organic genus. The genus does not break up into species by virtue of some inner principle of development: if it did, it would be conscious, not merely living. Rather does it become differentiated by fortuitous *geographical* influences: it is comically said by Hegel to suffer violence at the hands of the Universal Individual, i.e. our earth. Our understanding of such unsystematized diversity must itself remain unsystematized: it can never rise above the half-childish, arbitrary fancyings of the school of Schelling. In organic nature we can detect only rudiments of laws, vague environmental adaptednesses and influences, adumbrations of order and connection, traces of necessities and far-fetched, intriguing analogies.[2] It becomes obvious, from this argument, that Reason can at best find a cracked, blurred image of itself in the mirror of external nature: it is, therefore, driven to seek a better image of itself in the introspective sphere, in the data of consciousness itself. To this the Dialectic accordingly turns.

The first object of this inward-turned observation of Reason is found by Hegel in the logical Laws of Thought, the ill-assorted, psychologistically conceived rag-bag of principles of the formal logic of his time. To these laws Hegel characteristically objects, not that they are too formal, but rather that they represent mere matter without form. They come before us as a mere plurality of principles, which we actually follow, or try to follow: they are not shown to be 'vanishing moments' in the unity of thought. Hegel would certainly have welcomed the connectedness of modern symbolic calculi, as well as the semantics which reduces all their principles to a single tautology.

Hegel is driven further, therefore, to that observation of conscious activities which is carried on by empirical psychologists. This becomes involved in the counting up of a vast range of passions and proclivities, all thrown together into the 'soul', as

[1] *Phen.*, p. 222 (B., p. 316).
[2] *Phen.*, pp. 231-2 (B., pp. 326-7).

into some containing sack.[1] It then goes on to look for *laws* which will connect these various psychic faculties with features of the environment or the social *milieu*. Hegel gives short shrift to such an observational psychology, little dreaming of its immense future. He denies altogether that we can draw clear-cut distinctions between the environmental *influences* which act on an individual and the *individual* they act upon. The 'world' which impinges on an individual is, he says, a world refracted in terms of his peculiar individuality: the knowledge of the reactions it will provoke depends entirely on the knowledge of that individuality. Observational psychology, therefore, 'passes over', by virtue of its proven inadequacy, into various forms of psycho-physical observation, in which the inward and the outward in man are no longer seen as separate factors acting upon each other, but rather as distinct sides of one individual, the conscious side being such as to *express* itself in certain characteristic bodily manifestations.

Hegel now takes the opportunity to comment scathingly and at length on two pretentious pseudo-sciences of his time, the 'physiognomy' which had been given currency by Lavater, and the much-trumpeted 'phrenology' of Gall. The former seeks the characteristic expressions of a man's individuality in the forms and movements of his face and figure, or in the style of his speech or writing, whereas the latter looks for them in the bumps and hollows of his skull-bones. In criticism of Physiognomy Hegel emphasizes that the true externalization of a man's nature lies not in the superficialities of expressive style, but in the quality of his *acts*, whether brave, benevolent, thieving, murderous and the like. As regards Phrenology, Hegel admits that the skull and its bones are in a sense 'the immediate reality and existence of Spirit': they represent Spirit as a hard reality, as a definitely located, enduring existent. If Spirit is to be treated as a *thing*, a mere existent among other existents in nature—as much of our thought demands that we should treat it—then we may as well carry our crass identification to the limit: we may make Spirit identical with a bone.[2] This is, in fact, what Spirit *is* for mere Observation. The way in which the skull-bones represent Spirit must, however, preclude them from representing it adequately: they can never represent its *freedom*, and even the connection of

[1] *Phen.*, p. 236 (B., p. 332).   [2] *Phen.*, p. 264 (B., p. 309).

particular capacities with particular bumps and hollows must be in the last degree arbitrary and contingent.[1]

Having thus exposed the extreme arbitrariness of Phrenology, Hegel himself executes one of the most arbitrary somersaults in the whole course of his dialectic, even if (like many Socratic arguments) it combines profundity with sophistry. He points out that since Spirit, conceived as something merely existent, is a bone, a bone will be simply and indefeasibly Spirit.[2] The equation works both ways; in dragging Spirit down to the dregs of materiality, we exalt those dregs to the heights of Spirit. We have here a union of the high and the low in a single object, which Hegel, with Lutheran frankness, compares to the union of generation and micturition in a single organ. This piece of homely coarseness does as well as anything else to waft Hegel on from the now exhausted topic of the observational consciousness to the consideration of a consciousness which is at once practical and social, and which finds itself in its 'other', not by describing or explaining the latter, but by practically imposing its wishes upon it, or by recognizing self-consciousness in it. Those who seek a strict deductive necessity in Hegel's transitions will do well to ponder the above passages: in them Hegel may be said to laugh at their pains.

V THE PURSUIT OF HAPPINESS, THE LAW OF THE HEART, MORAL IDEALISM, DEDICATION TO CAUSES, MORAL LEGISLATION, MORAL CRITICISM

With a wave of the dialectical wand we are accordingly transported from phrenology to practical life in society. Reason now makes its appearance as a 'fluid general substance, as unchangeable, simple thinghood, which, like light breaking up into stars, breaks, as into countless luminous points, into numerous entirely independent beings'. These independent beings are conscious of being thus independent only in so far as 'they offer up their singularity, and this general substance becomes their soul and essence'.[3] We are dealing with individuals integrated into the life of a 'free people', whose laws and customs they accept as their

---

[1] *Phen.*, p. 251 (B., p. 257).
[2] *Phen.*, p. 270 (B., p. 371).   [3] *Phen.*, p. 273 (B., p. 376).

own, while they see each of their fellow-members as *themselves*, themselves as those fellow-members.[1] This somewhat heady introduction of the social organism occurs only by way of a fore-taste; Hegel admits that the life of a 'free people' is only an immediate, implicit, merely contingent expression of the rational order, and that Reason must in fact *break* with what is merely customary in order at a later stage to become conscious of its full dignity and importance.[2] At the stage, therefore, where we actually are, Reason takes the form of making the world conform to the individual's *wants* or *needs*, in the course of which effort he comes into collision with the similar endeavours of others. We have the typical 'free-for-all' characteristic of the pursuit of 'happiness'. (This is a stage *after* the break with corporate, merely customary life, when its lost forms are being searchingly resumed in consciousness, but *before* this corporate life has once more been accepted at the higher level of morality. Hegel tells us frankly that he is taking up the dialectical story at *this* point, because it is more in keeping with the spirit of his own time, a confession of contingent motive such as he does not often give us.)

The first form of the practical consciousness to be studied by Hegel is that of the 'man on the make', the man 'out for a good time', who has turned his back on the 'grey shadows' of custom and tradition, and who regards his life as a fruit ripe for his plucking. Hegel holds that this vague, indefinite pursuit of happi-ness necessarily becomes a *general* philosophy: it extends itself to a whole society of persons, all out to drain life to its fullest. As so extended, this cult of success, of the full life, necessarily destroys and supersedes itself: the efforts of countless happiness-hungry persons must collide with one another, and cancel each other out. Each man's pursuit of his own personal fulfilment must necessarily be the Nemesis, the *Schicksal*, of the other per-son. As in the modern American 'firing' or divorcing situation, nothing 'works out' as the parties intended, each is always having to face up to 'another one of those things'. (The foregoing repre-sents an attempt to make a viable sense out of five very sibylline pages, 279–83.)

After its disillusioning 'experience' of the life of pleasure, Reason must move on to a phase of practical experience which will accept the Law or Necessity which now frustrates it, as a

---

[1] *Phen.*, pp. 274–5 (B., p. 378).   [2] *Phen.*, p. 275 (B., p. 378).

part of itself. This Necessity will no longer be an external Necessity : it will be an inner Necessity, a Law of the individual's own Heart. It will be a necessity that the individual accepts gladly and freely, and that he does not doubt that others, could they but free themselves from enslaving laws and prejudices, would accept with equal joy and freedom. As opposed to his frivolous predecessor, the Man of Heart is high, grave and disinterested. He may flout laws and ordinances, but he will do so only for the sake of humanity, or to express his own noble nature : the laws he flouts will also seem to him senseless and oppressive. It is easy for Hegel to show that this high-minded, romantic self-fulfilment of the *homme de cœur* is as anarchic and as self-destructive as is the low-minded earthy self-fulfilment of the *homme moyen sensuel*. The pretendedly universal and impersonal dictates of a man's heart, are in fact distressingly personal and particular, and being so, they will always come into conflict with the similarly heart-felt dictates of other persons, to whom *his* dictates will seem senseless. Each man's heart will in fact be the utter heartlessness of the other person. The *homme de cœur* will find, further, that the 'soul destroying' ordinances he sees around him, are in fact not dead and heartless at all, that they are an actual law for *all* hearts, his own included. The Man of Heart will, therefore, find his heart divided, and will only be able to maintain his own perverse, private standards by denigrating as perverse the public standards which he, with all others, covertly acknowledges. 'The heart-throb for the good of humanity, therefore, passes over into the ravings of insane self-conceit, into the rage of consciousness to save itself from destruction by casting forth from itself the perversion that itself really is, and by making every effort to see it, and to speak of it, as being elsewhere.'[1] The following of the heart will lead therefore (whether the heart followed be dissident or conforming) to a savage, ruthless war of all against all, in which the conqueror will in his due turn be defeated. Reason, therefore, leaps to a stage in which it foreswears this perverse individualism of the heart, and erects itself into a pillar of the general ordinance. It now takes the form of self-conscious *Virtue*, while the warring rabble of appetites to which it is opposed are the Way or Course of the World.

Hegel now gives a sketch of a highly idealistic, *bien pensant*

[1] *Phen.*, pp. 289–90 (B., p. 397).

model of conscious Virtue, a Virtue not harshly opposed to the
Way of the World, but seeing in the latter its own raw material.
The Way of the World is not crassly unvirtuous: it involves countless misapplied but excellent capacities, gifts and powers. The
aim of Virtue is not to fight against the Course of the World, but
to overcome its perversion, to restore it to its natural and right
direction. The 'knight' of this kind of Virtue is a somewhat
narcissistic, unserious person: he needs the World and its courses
to call forth his knightly prowess, he regards everything in it as
'good at bottom'. He believes that the good will always triumph
anyway; his battle with evil he looks on, therefore, as a sham
fight before a looking-glass (*Spiegelfechterei*). He is so considerate
of the hidden excellencies of his adversaries that his one concern
is to come out of battle without blood on his sword. Virtue of
this *fainéant* type hardly exists in the present age: Hegel tells us
that it was practically defunct in his own. It is a sort of Virtue
which is *bound* to be overcome by the World: being concerned
to edify rather than really to build up, it is content with a victory
so bloodless and so verbal that the World is certain to have its
Way. Reason, therefore, passes on to a stage where there is no
longer any opposition between an ideal of pure Virtue, on the one
hand, and the Worldly Course, on the other.

Hegel now enters upon an obscurely sketched dialectical phase
which we may translate as 'the Spiritual Zoo and Humbug, or
the Affair-on-hand itself' (*Das geistige Thierreich und Betrug,
oder die Sache selbst*).[1] In this phase the whole nature of a reasonable individual becomes completely absorbed in carrying out some
task or enterprise-on-hand: it is, says Hegel, no longer possible
to draw a distinction between the individual's capacities and
attitudes, the circumstances that provoke them, the end that the
individual aims at, his personal interest in this end, and the means
he uses towards its realization. All these things are 'moments'
in a single activity, and that activity simply *is* the individual.
What emerges as alone solid and permanent is the Task, the
Enterprise, the Game, the Cause, the Matter-on-hand itself
(*die Sache selbst*), of which these factors are merely vanishing
'moments'. One can only be engaged in an enterprise *if* there are
ends, means, circumstances, interests and capacities, but the
enterprise is 'the thing' for which these factors provide merely

[1] *Phen.*, pp. 303–22 (B., pp. 419–38).

the occasion or the material. A man's consciousness achieves honesty of purpose (*Ehrlichkeit*), in so far as he sets himself to get on with the Matter-on-hand, to 'do his bit', 'play the game', to serve 'the cause'—we use random phrases to translate the untranslatable—*regardless of either failure or success*. The cult of the Matter-in-hand is, therefore, yet another case of that self-absorbed high-mindedness of which we have had instances in the case of Stoicism, Scepticism, the pursuit of Virtue and the Law of the Heart. Not only was it the typical vice of German Romanticism, but we may identify it also as the vice of the American business executive, the nineteenth-century empire builder, the disinterestedly frightful Nazi, or the pure practitioner of scholarship or research. (This last was probably most in Hegel's mind.) Hegel points out, however, that the 'truth' of all this disinterested 'honesty' is to be *not* as honest as it seems: to do something merely in order to *try* to do it, is in a sense not honestly to try to do it at all. A society of high-minded 'players of the game' is, in a sense, a society of cheats: they appear to *need* each other's help and co-operation, but are each really putting on an independent show, and are indifferent or hostile to such help. The premature arrival of the rescue-party spoils the 'last stand'. Nothing can be more petty and more venomous than the disputes of 'disinterested' scholars. There is even *self*-deceit in such a pure playing of the game, since no one is in fact satisfied with mere endeavour, but commits himself to definite deeds. As a result of these deep disappointments, Reason dialectically shifts to a position where the game to be played *ceases* to be merely individualistic, where it becomes *co-operative*, the work of a linked *team*. We have passed on from the *mere* game or Matter-on-hand, to the essentially *ethical* game or Matter-on-hand.

Reason in this ethical character appears at first as a *legislative* faculty, one that lays down laws that will be 'true' or valid for all. These are, in the first place, isolated intuitive deliverances, which seem to call for no further warrant than the mere pronouncement of healthy, natural Reason. Such are the celebrated commandments to tell the truth, love our neighbours and so forth. Hegel shows without difficulty that it is only possible to sustain such laws if they are indefinitely qualified, in which case they will soon be robbed of significance. It becomes clear, further, as we engage in the Danaan task of stopping up the leaks in our laws by an endless series of qualifications, that it is not really a work of Reason to be involved in such endless detail, that it is for Reason to lay down general *criteria* in terms of which all detailed rules can be tested. We pass, therefore, from Reason as a *legislative* faculty to Reason as a mere *critic of laws*.

We have now left the pre-Kantian stage of isolated, intuitive moral prescriptions to the Kantian stage where pure Reason demands merely that what we do or approve should be universalizable, that we should be *self-consistent* in our practical judgements and our living. Hegel easily shows that this new pose of Reason cannot take us far. As we look on a matter from one angle or another, practically any rule for action can be rendered self-consistent, or can be made to seem self-contradictory. It is vain to hope that a condition so vacuous as non-contradiction should be the source of valuable critical guidance. The upshot of these considerations is that Reason, whether considered as laying down or as criticizing laws, can guide us to no positive collective ethical enterprise. As prescribing laws, it is *insolent* in its arbitrary positiveness, while as criticizing laws it is insolent in its detached intellectual negativity. We must move, therefore, to the notion of a moral order which will have all the unwritten inerrancy and supra-individual fixity of the law mentioned by Antigone, whose life 'is not of today or yesterday, but from all time', and concerning whose first setting forth 'no man knows aught'. The content of this life, here merely adumbrated, will be the theme of the next major section of the *Phenomenology*.

We have now completed our sense-making survey of Section *AA* of the *Phenomenology* which deals with Reason. We have throughout considered phases of experience in which Consciousness 'sees itself' in its object, whether by observing or understanding it, or by modifying it practically. Under Observation we dealt with the observation of the inorganic, of the organic and then of the conscious. We then passed on to self-realizing practical attitudes of a somewhat introverted type: the Pursuit of Happiness, the Law of the Heart, the Cult of Virtue. We then passed on to attitudes of a more extraverted type: to play the game, to set up moral prescriptions, to criticize such prescriptions. We have now broken with all these piecemeal, individualistic approaches, and are about to immerse ourselves in the life of a 'free people', of an 'ethical substance', which was previously touched upon. It would be vain to pretend that the dialectical pattern of this section on Reason has anything of the inevitability commonly associated with the rational, or that it could not have been *otherwise* developed at practically every point. It is vain to pretend, further, that many of Hegel's transitions are not highly arbitrary, in some cases scandalously so. On the other hand, it would be vain to deny that Hegel's methods generally strike tinder, that in his least justifiable transitions there is not also a queer aesthetic appropriateness, an extraordinary breaking of light. There is as much hidden logic in Hegel's apparent arbitrariness as in T. S. Eliot's *Waste Land*. One only longs for the terminal glosses that would have saved the reader much blood and sweat.

CHAPTER FIVE

THE PHENOMENOLOGY OF SPIRIT—II
Spirit, Religion and Absolute Knowledge

I UNREFLECTIVE ETHICAL LIFE

In our second chapter on Hegel's *Phenomenology of Spirit* we shall deal with Section *BB* (or *D*), entitled 'Spirit', Section *CC* (or *E*), entitled 'Religion', and Section *DD* (or *F*), entitled 'Absolute Knowledge'. The numbering of the sections seems to mean that Hegel regarded all the parts of the work after the part entitled 'Self-consciousness', i.e. the four sections on 'Reason', 'Spirit', 'Religion', and 'Absolute Knowledge', as constituting the *single* third member of the main triad of his work.

The long section on Spirit that now follows has the usual triadic structure. It has a first subsection, triadically divided, entitled 'The true Spirit: the Ethical Order': in this we study the ethical life of individuals *unreflectively* engrossed in the customs and laws of a given society. In the long second subsection we study the many metamorphoses of 'The Self-estranged Spirit', a consciousness *reflectively detached* from the unreflective 'ethical substance' of the first subsection, and running through a long gamut of *cultural* phases, all expressive of sophisticated, somewhat disintegrated individuality. The third subsection is entitled 'The Spirit sure of itself: Morality': here we study Spirit reintegrated, once more confident of itself, and going back to the ethical order at the higher reflective level of Morality. (We shall, in what follows, use the word 'ethical', with its connotation of the unreflective and customary, for Hegel's term *sittlich*, while the word 'moral' will have the reflective connotation of his expression *Moralität*.)

Unreflective ethical life is said by Hegel to revolve about *two* foci, the Family and the Community: it is also said to be subject to *two* governing Laws or 'Powers', the Divine and the Human Law (or Power) respectively. The Community is said to be the Ethical Substance in the form of *conscious action*, while the Family is said to be the same Substance in the form of *immediate existence*. The deliberate conscious unity of effort found in the Community has its roots in the undeliberate, unconscious unity of effort found in the Family. The Human Law is in the same way the body of usages and publicly promulgated laws which obtain in the Community, and which are given authority by its governing elements. The Divine Law or Power, on the other hand, has its obscure roots in elemental family relationships, and, since the Family lies at the foundations of the Community, the Divine or Family Principle underlies all communal life. Alone among modern philosophers Hegel has an almost Freudian realization of the simple sexual and family foundations of organized group-life. The Divine Law has, further, one of its main points of concern in *death* and the *dead*, in the passage of individuals out of active being into a state in which they merely *have been*, but in which they none the less remain the source of important, lasting 'blood-ties'. In the act of burial the departed individual is made one with the 'nether powers', who are the appointed guardians of the Divine Law. Here again Hegel seems unique among philosophers in recognizing the importance of death and funerary practices in early ethical life.

Hegel's analysis of family life is in many ways interesting and touching: he emphasizes the close relation of the womenfolk of the family to the elemental Divine Law, and also lays peculiar stress on the unique character of the brother-sister relationship: a sister's duty to her brother is said to be of the highest, and his loss to her irreparable. This stress obviously reflects personal attitudes and experiences, as well as the deep influence of Greek tragedy. Hegel's treatment of the Community is much less interesting. In it 'justice' is said to perform an equilibrating function much in the manner of the Platonic *Republic*, while a positive ethical function is ascribed to *war*, as the factor which, by making individuals feel the power of 'their Lord and Master, Death', prevents various elements in society from hardening into separateness, and by so doing allowing the unifying social spirit to evaporate. 'By this breaking up of the fixed form of being, Spirit prevents the ethical order from lapsing into a merely natural existence, and raises up and preserves the self of which it is conscious, to freedom and to its own power.'[1] These warlike passages in Hegel seem shocking to modern sensibilities but should they really seem so? Can it be denied that the facing of death in

[1] *Phen.*, p. 347 (B., p. 474).

war *has* an ethical significance, and that it is an important, even if ultimately to be superseded, phase in moral development?

The ethical order having been thus sketched in somewhat primitive, legendary terms, it is fitting that the next phase of the dialectic should be concerned with a typical situation of Greek tragedy, the conflict between the Human and the Divine Law, the conflict which led Antigone to sprinkle dust over her brother's unburied body, and which led Creon, with equal justification, to punish her for her treasonable contumacity. Hegel here emphasizes the profound *guilt* that the individual brings upon himself by violating *either* branch of the ethical order, a guilt not removed by the plea that one acted for the best, or that one acted under orders or under some other law or edict: so too might the ghosts of those murdered at Auschwitz spurn all specious self-exculpatory pleas. The violated law may, to begin with, yield place to the law which enjoys force and publicity, but it remains rooted in the 'Nether World', in the 'mute unconscious substance of all, in the waters of forgetfulness', in the 'all-binding oath which binds a people together'.[1] It will ultimately rise up and destroy the community that has violated it. The outcome of such a fundamental conflict of laws can only be the *Doom* (*Schicksal*) in which both sides go down in ruin, as where Antigone hangs herself in her rocky tomb, and Creon is brought low by the death of both son and wife. It is plain that Hegel has nothing to learn from modern psychology as to the inexorable, unreasoning, contradictory pressures of the 'Super-Ego'. The primitive Ethical Substance therefore destroys itself dialectically through its own inherent conflicts, as by the forceful deeds and knot-cutting choices of strong-minded individuals. Its authority passes to an order which will take more account of the individual's force and right.

By a turn of his revolving stage Hegel now shifts us from the mythic age of Greece to the imperial Roman age, the period between the Antonines and Justinian, when any and every individual might have Roman citizenship, and might enjoy rights that were being ever more clearly defined by the great jurists. Here, according to Hegel, we have 'the soulless community which has ceased to be the unselfconscious substance of individuals, in which they now count as selves and substances in their own right.

[1] *Phen.*, p. 364 (B., pp. 494–5).

The universal has been split into an absolute plurality of individual atoms, and its vanished spirit has become one of *equality* between each and all, where all alike count as persons.'[1] Such juridical persons, Hegel tells us, represent in the concrete what the Stoic sage, with his complete indifference to external conditions. represents in the pure medium of thought. And just as Stoicism, with its indifferent acceptance of *all* content, passes over into the Scepticism in which all content is suspect, so too does the mere abstract assertion of personal rights pass over into the doubt or the question as to whether persons have any rights at all. The abstract notion of right leaves undecided what a man has a right *to*, and it is impossible to decide this except by pure chance or personal caprice. The world of juridical persons therefore finds its appropriate completion in a *Caesar*, a 'Lord and Master of the World', a person whose power is as perilously based upon, and girt about, by warring forces, as he is sovereign over them all. And just as Scepticism passes over into the 'Unhappy Consciousness', in which its covert conflicts become overt and explicit, so too must the covert conflicts in juridical personality pass over into the explicit conflicts of the 'self-estranged' man, who will be the theme of the next subsection. The links forged between the primitive ethic of Greek tragedy, Roman jurisprudence and Caesarism, and the self-estranged culture of the eighteenth century, may seem decidedly tenuous: they are none the less genuine and interesting. It is not the task of an expositor of Hegel to make them more substantial than they really are.

II THE 'SELF-ESTRANGED' LIFE OF CULTURE

The 'self-estranged' phase of consciousness to which the dialectic now passes is a state of mind chiefly manifest in post-Renaissance and eighteenth-century Europe, when the break-up of mediaevalism and feudalism, with their profound ethical and religious unity, had led to a more expansive, experimental, power-seeking and wealth-amassing state of society. Much of the intense obscurity of Hegel's text is here due to the concealed presence of an historical framework, to which constant allusion is made, but which is much too slightly suggested. Hegel describes the self-estranged type of consciousness as one that sets itself in

[1] *Phen.*, p. 368 (B., p. 501).

opposition to the natural and social world in which it had its origin: its essential attitude is one of alienation, divorce, distance from every sort of natural being.[1] For the variety of things and persons that occur naturally in the world or society it has only an undiscriminating contempt, much as a horticulturalist might despise the 'wild' varieties of the geranium or the rose. For it excellence is essentially something *made*, thoughtfully and deliberately constructed or cultivated: its one desire is to polish, refine and reshape itself and the world. This consciousness is also much concerned to pass *judgements* on things as *good* or *bad*, the good being what is conformable to itself, what represents the triumph of 'culture' over chance or nature, the bad whatever represents the corresponding defeat.

There are, however, Hegel tells us, *two* natural objects in which these 'values' of civilization tend principally to be incarnated: these are State Power, on the one hand, and Wealth or Resources on the other. In a 'civilized' state of society, arrangements and changes tend more and more to be made by the deliberate action of central authorities, or on the personal initiative of wealthy persons: they are not brought about in an unenterprising, half-conscious manner by persons operating smoothly along the grooves of custom. Obviously, too, the period on which Hegel's dialectical searchlight is now dwelling is one characterized by the rise of the nation-state and of more concentrated central power: it is also an age in which the wealthy burgher and merchant classes become ever more influential. The attitude of civilized man to these two main organs of control over nature and society tends always to vary: sometimes the State Power is regarded as the main organ, the fructifying power of Wealth being merely its instrument, sometimes the roles and values are reversed. Sometimes, too, the 'civilized' attitude to these instruments is high-minded, generous, disinterested, full of a desire to 'serve' or benefit society, whereas at other times it becomes low-minded and cynical, full of the spirit of exploitation and arrogant self-aggrandizement.

Hegel indicates with a light touch the transition from a rather loosely constituted state-unity, in which the nobles are 'haughty vassals', offering independent 'advice' to their sovereign, to the stage in which the whole of a brilliant, noble society flutters

[1] *Phen.*, p. 377 (B., p. 515).

intoxicated about some *Roi Soleil*, in whom all state-power is incarnated. Obviously the Dialectic is modelling itself on developments in France, and not on those in Britain. Hegel also indicates lightly how the spirit of Wealth tends from beneficent public-spiritedness to an ever-increasing domination by blind caprice, to a belief that *any* service can be demanded from anyone for a sufficient money-bribe, and to a complete blindness to the abyss of ill-will and resentment it is preparing for itself. Hegel also lays a curious stress on the part played by *language* in the centralized, wealthy type of society he is sketching. The 'service' rendered by the 'civilized' man to the State power involves less and less of a readiness to die for his sovereign, and more and more of a readiness to surround him with Byzantine flattery and incense. The same verbal self-prostration and adulation characterizes the 'civilized' attitude to Wealth. (Hegel's account reminds one of those happy gatherings where no one can conceivably be 'unimportant', and where everyone who is not a state-official is at least 'immensely rich'.)

Hegel is concerned to stress how the high-minded, disinterested attitude to state-service and expenditure is at bottom one with its low-minded, self-interested opposite, and tends to pass over into the latter. He probably means to suggest this to be a consequence of the denatured character of a 'civilized society', which lacks the inherent order and direction of an 'ethical' community. The culmination of this spirit of sheer culture and civilization is found by Hegel in the brilliant, sophisticated, precious, witty and disintegrated inhabitants of the eighteenth-century, pre-revolutionary salon, the people who made David Hume look on Paris as the most agreeable city in the universe. (Hegel describes this disintegrated, brilliant life in connection with the *nephew of Rameau*, a famous type from one of Diderot's dialogues.) In this phase of denatured culture nothing whatever, whether noble or base, is allowed to possess truth or solidity: everything is exposed, 'debunked' and shown to be one with its opposite. What emerges is a spirit 'whose very existence lies in universal talk and devastating judgement, before which all aspects, which seem to count as real and essential, and as real members of the whole, are dissolved, and which is accordingly a game of dissolution that is played with itself. The judging and talking is therefore the invincible truth, since everything else is overwhelmed by it'. Hegel follows

Diderot in comparing this kind of talk to a sort of mad music 'which mixes up thirty airs, Italian and French, tragic and comic', and 'which at one moment goes down to hell with a deep bass, then contracts its throat to a high falsetto with which it rends the upper airs, clamorous and subdued, imperious and mocking in turn'.[1] Since this type of talk is always bringing together things which to a blunt intelligence seem worlds apart, it seems always to abound in *wit*.

Hegel then points out how the reduction of all things to vanity must end by reducing *itself* to vanity, how the revelation of conflict in every sphere must end by yielding a sober, *positive* vision of Spirit. 'That in possessing them (i.e. State power and Wealth) one's self can thus stand apart from them and outside of them, this is the real point of this witty talk, which is accordingly its highest interest and the truth of the whole. In such talk one's self emerges pure, unbound by the determinations of reality and thought, something spiritual, truly universal. It is the self-rending nature of all relationships and the consciousness of their rending. Only in the rage of its self-consciousness does it know its own rent state, and in knowing it has forthwith risen above it.'[2] Spirit therefore raises itself to a new dialectical phase in which it faces two contrasted visions, one representing the simple thought or ideal of integrated unity, the other representing an attempt to carry out that unity by combining into one picture the scattered traits confusedly offered by the world of 'culture'. We have the contrast between Religious *Faith*, on the one hand, the mere *thought* of something akin to Spirit behind appearances, and Rationalistic Insight, on the other, the attempt to subordinate things to perspicuous concepts, which shall be as clear to others as they are to ourselves.

III   RELIGIOUS FAITH AND 'ENLIGHTENMENT'

Hegel's next subsection, entitled 'Faith and Pure Insight', is best regarded as a transition leading up to the treatment of the *Aufklärung*, the spirit of the 'Enlightenment', which follows. The disintegrated world of culture is here set over against the pure consciousness of an Absolute Being, something 'in and for itself . . . which *is* all and does all, but never itself makes an appearance'.[3]

---

[1] *Phen.*, pp. 401-2 (B., pp. 542-3).
[2] *Phen.*, p. 405 (B., pp. 547-8).   [3] *Phen.*, p. 412 (B., p. 556).

Religious Faith, in this disintegrated context, no longer *expects* to see its object: it only seeks by constant absorption in praise and service to produce and maintain in itself the *sense* of being at one with such a principle. As opposed to such Religious Faith, Rationalistic Insight likewise works towards a definite goal or ideal: it aspires to 'overcome every sort of independent self-existence, whether of the actual or the essence lying behind it, and to turn it into a *concept*'.[1] This programme of conceptualization is, however, essentially unrealizable: it is, and must remain, merely an *intention*. Hegel is concerned to stress that there is *really no quarrel* between the two modes of consciousness, that they are, in fact, two forms of one and the same consciousness. The absolute unity which Religious Faith obscurely thinks, is the same as the absolute unity towards which Rationalistic Insight painstakingly seeks to arrive.

The underlying unity of the religious and the rationalistic consciousness is, however, only a fact for *us*, the phenomenological reporters and observers: for the man of Insight and the man of Faith it is by no means obviously so. A conflict therefore ensues between the two modes of consciousness, which is all the more bitter because it is without substance, because it is merely a fight with one's shadow or echo, because the two contestants are incarnations of the same principle. This conflict appears historically in the fight of the eighteenth-century *philosophes*, the men of the 'Enlightenment', against the *Infâme*, the enslaving obfuscations of religion. Hegel had lived through this struggle at the university and in the period which followed: it therefore looms large in his *Phenomenology*, the Odyssey of his spirit.

The *philosophes*, the men of the Enlightenment, who disport themselves in the next subsections, are men concerned to extend the sphere of our Insight, our conscious conceptual grasp, so as to leave no room for a Faith which seeks to probe beyond appearances: for them such probings reflect only superstitions, prejudices or errors. The *philosophes* cannot, however, help placing *some* Insight behind the elaborate utterances of Faith, even if this be only the cheating Insight of priests and despots, men concerned to stupefy and manage the people. The *philosophes* do not, however, realize the *spurious* character of the combat in which they enage, how they are not really saying anything different

[1] *Phen.*, p. 412 (B., p. 557).

from their opponents, how they are in fact merely helping to purify the latter, and to bring them to a clearer consciousness of their own principles. Thus Enlightenment holds the object of religion to be merely a fabrication, a product of the believer's own consciousness: the believer may accept this impeachment, since in putting his *trust* in his deity, he is in effect putting his own self-consciousness in it. In the same way Enlightenment caricatures the content of Faith by making it a worship of wood and stone, or of consecrated wafers, or by holding it to be concerned with events remote in time and space, which are much less certain than those in the newspapers: Religious Faith is, however, unconcerned with such outward events and evidences, and the fact that it *does* sometimes worry about them, merely shows the infection of Enlightenment.[1]

Hegel then shows how Enlightenment itself indulges in metaphysical constructions which are indistinguishable from those of Religious Faith. As Deism it gives its phenomenal order the backing of an *être Suprême*, concerning whom nothing determinate can be said: this Absolute merely differs in name from the religious Absolute which is likewise 'unsearchable in all its ways and unreachable in its being.'[2] Alternatively, in the form of Materialism, it sees the backing of all sensuous differences in an invisible, inaudible, tasteless substance called Matter : this Matter is identical with the *être Suprême* just mentioned, its only difference consisting in the standpoint from which we approach it. The God who seems a folly to the tough-minded man of the Enlightenment, and the Matter which is a horror to the tender-minded man of Faith, are ways of thought which intersect in a point.[3] The only positive result of all this Enlightenment, with its constant shuttling from one pole of abstraction to the other—a shuttling which Hegel has painted so brilliantly—is now held to be the eighteenth-century notion of *Utility*. The inner being of things reduces itself to their mere serviceableness for other things. In this crassest of outcomes the Dialectic of Rationalistic Insight comes to an end.

Hegel now passes dialectically to the crowning phase of eighteenth-century culture and Enlightenment: the French Revolution with its Absolute Freedom and its Terror. The transition is not

---

[1] *Phen.*, pp. 426–7 (B., pp. 572–3).
[2] *Phen.*, p. 437 (B., p. 584).   [3] *Phen.*, p. 444 (B., p. 593).

more than usually tenuous. The notion of Utility which appears to be no more than an objective relation of one thing to another obviously conceals an implicit relation to the self which sees all things. When this is brought out, the reduction of all things to Utility is the reduction of them all to the unfettered liberty, the pure self-consciousness of the subject.

Hegel then sketches the terrifying portrait of a spirit emancipated from all social and supernatural ties, which is 'conscious of its pure personality, and therein of all spiritual reality, all reality being solely spiritual: the world is for it merely its will, and this will is universal'.[1] Such a liberated spirit raises itself without resistance to the 'throne of the world', and proceeds at once to abolish all the ranks and classes in which social life has previously organized itself. The only work in which it can realize itself must be a collective, a *total* work. Because such a liberated spirit cannot delegate its functions to particular persons or bodies of persons, because it cannot allow itself to be *represented*, it can achieve no positive result whatever: it can only reveal itself negatively in a general fury of liquidation.[2] And since, after the destruction of all social estates and positions, there is nothing positive left to liquidate, this fury can only be turned inward on itself. Free Spirit, in the abstract form of 'inflexible, cold universality' must proceed to liquidate itself in the equally abstract form of 'hard brittleness and self-willed atomicity', i.e. in the form of particular persons. There being nothing left to take from these latter beyond their mere existence, the work of Freedom will consist in depriving them of this. Its work will be death, and this death 'the coldest and dullest of deaths, with no more meaning than the chopping off of a head of cabbage or a draught of water.'[3]

An absolute Freedom which liquidates the complex, positive organization of society therefore shows itself to be self-liquidating. Its principle must be carried over into that of a freedom which develops a social order as part of itself. From being a *negative* will which impartially liquidates anyone and everyone, it must swing over into being a *positive* will which is the impartial will of all. It must rise to the freedom which is a freedom from particular interest, to the 'autonomy' of Kant's Categorical Imperative. Hegel sees in the positive impartiality of the Categorical Impera-

---

[1] *Phen.*, p. 450 (B., p. 600).
[2] *Phen.*, p. 453 (B., p. 604).
[3] *Phen.*, p. 454 (B., p. 605).

tive a mere transformation of the death-dealing negative impartiality of the guillotine.[1] We pass thereby into the third major
subdivision of the long section of Spirit. We are to deal with
Spirit as *sure* of itself, i.e. in the form of Morality.

IV PERSONAL MORALITY AND CONSCIENTIOUSNESS

Morality is dialectically dealt with by Hegel under three
headings: 'The Moral World-view', which is largely a statement
of the Kantian view of duty, 'Moral Duplicity' (*Verstellung*)
which is largely a study of the contradictions flowing from this
sort of world-view, and, lastly, 'Conscience' or 'Conscientiousness'
in which the difficulties of the two previous phases are overcome
and reconciled.

The first form of the Moral Consciousness with which Hegel
deals is one that is free, autonomous *only* in the performance of
duty, and in duty done for its own sake. Such performance of
duty presupposes a setting provided by various natural realities,
but the Moral Consciousness refuses to see itself in *them*. They
form a closed system governed by laws to which moral considerations are irrelevant, and which are likewise irrelevant from the
standpoint of morality. The Moral Consciousness is concerned
only to perform its role, to play its appointed part: the course of
nature may or may not bless its endeavours and itself. Hegel
points out, however, that the Moral Consciousness must proceed
as if the natural order is such as to permit or aid its endeavours:
it must *postulate* an ultimate harmony between this order and
itself. It must likewise postulate that the nature present *within*
itself, in the form of particular sensual impulses, will be such as
to conform to itself, and to be dominated by itself 'in the end'.
It cannot, indeed, postulate that a harmony between itself and
such impulses should be achieved in a *finite* length of time—to
demand this would be to demand the supersession and destruction of the Moral Consciousness—but rather that this harmony
should be achieved in an *infinite* time, a comfortable form of
words whose true meaning is much less comfortable. Being a
practical consciousness, the Moral Consciousness must further
differentiate itself to suit the particularity of cases: it cannot merely
lay down a general law of duty, but must prescribe many specific

[1] *Phen.*, p. 458 (B., p. 609).

duties. But, being the abstract pursuit of duty for duty's sake, it cannot deal understandingly with this opposition between the generic and the specific. It can at best deal with it in an *imaginative* or *pictorial* fashion, by postulating the existence of a Divine Moral Legislator, responsible either by His detailed edicts for the multitude of duties falling under the general law of duty, or, alternatively, responsible only for this general law, while we, as creatures involved in the specificity of impulse and situation, are responsible for its further differentiation. (Hegel holds that the Moral Consciousness will prefer the *second* imaginative form of presentation to the first. It will attribute the general law of duty to an august Divine Legislator external to itself, while it will see itself as the poor creature whose variety of sensual impulse begets that long list of duties which it also makes it incapable of fulfilling, and which can merit no happiness save as the result of a free outpouring of Divine Grace.)

So far Hegel has sketched an abstract moralistic world-view not unlike the one developed in Kant's *Critique of Practical Reason*. He now shows that this sort of Moral Consciousness is inherently dishonest, that it involves an essential shiftiness (*Verstellung*), that it is, in practical terms, a very 'nest of contradictions'. It constantly pretends to itself to take *A* in earnest, and to value *B* only for the sake of *A*; then, by an unscrupulous shift, it proceeds to regard *B* as the only thing worth bothering about, and *A* as merely worth while on account of *B*. Thus the Moral Consciousness at one moment locates its goal in a harmony between morality and existence which can only be achieved yonder (*jenseits*), in a transcendent God. At the next moment, however, it sees the only worth-while thing in its *own* endeavours to reach this harmony, while God is merely the carrot dangled before the donkey, the imaginary goal which quickens its moral endeavours. The Moral Consciousness oscillates unceasingly between the pursuit of a goal which, if realized, would soon put a term to its own life, and the desire to stave off this goal indefinitely, so that it, and its good works, may continue. The same shifts of view are apparent in relation to sensual desires: from a moral point of view they should, and again they should not, be completely wiped out. This same dishonest oscillation is to be seen in the treatment of God, the supreme moral convenience. At one moment He is brought in to specify the abstract norm of duty (though it is far from clear how a particular moral being can sanctify what the moral law has not itself sanctified), at another moment He is required to represent the concrete union of the moral and the real (though it is not clear how a being raised high above nature and sensuality can represent any such thing). Hegel suggests (what few would wish to question) that this Moral Consciousness, which would be pure both from natural impulse and environing circumstance, is a self-destroying, self-contradictory consciousness, which can be saved from ruin only by a liberal injection of myth. In the ruins of such a consciousness Hegel, however, discovers a new type of Moral Consciousness, that of Conscience (*das Gewissen*). This consciousness is neither ashamed nor unable to provide morality with a content, to make decisions valid for a particular agent, and for the particular circumstances in which he finds himself. While many philosophers have looked on this personal, oracular Conscience as a form of morality lower than the generalizing Moral Consciousness of Kantian theory, Hegel, very arguably, looks on it as higher and more concrete.

The Conscientious Consciousness is described by Hegel as 'that which is completely valid to itself in its contingency, which knows its immediate singularity as pure knowledge and action, as the true actuality and harmony'.[1] This Conscientious Consciousness does not set up an empty general standard of duty like the Kantian Categorical Imperative: it makes concrete moral decisions which are inseparable from its actions. While it may have to face distinct circumstances in coming to its decisions, it will not break up its response to them into a number of distinct duties, between which it will hover anxiously: it will be 'simple dutiful action, that does not perform this or that duty, but which knows and does what is concretely right'.[2] Being an essentially practical consciousness, it will not project its general form, or its specific content, into a Legislator external to itself: it will decide both for itself. And while it must aim at considering *all* the circumstances relevant to its decisions—circumstances, as Hegel says 'which spread back into their conditions, sideways into their setting, and forwards into their consequences'—it will not seriously try to carry out this programme: the only circumstances it *need* consider are the circumstances that it *knows* of, and that it thinks it worth its while to know. Conscience, as so depicted, is sovereign

[1] *Phen.*, p. 484 (B., p. 644).   [2] *Phen.*, p. 487 (B., pp. 647–8).

over all definite content: 'in the might of its self-certainty, it has the majesty of absolute self-sufficiency, the power to bind and loose'.[1] 'In the majesty of its elevation above particular laws and every content' (Hegel assures us) 'it can put what content it likes into its knowing and its willing. It is Moral Genius, which knows the inner voice of its immediate knowledge to be the voice of God.'[2]

Hegel emphasizes, however, that the authority of this Conscience cannot be *merely* personal: it must be acknowledged and respected by other persons as well. What a person knows to be right for *him* must be acknowledged to be right for *him* by all other conscientious persons. It must also express itself in words like 'ought' and 'right', which, however much they may wish to express something personal and individual, cannot help expressing what is universal. (They are, in this respect, in the same position as words like 'I', 'this', 'now'.) For they can be used by other persons to express *their* conscientious decisions, and what they stand for must therefore be respected and understood by all. This universality of Conscience is, however, only a universality of *form*, not of content. Whatever *you* conscientiously hold right I respect as right *for you*, but it need not coincide with what I hold right *for myself*, and what I expect you to recognize as right *for me*. Hegel in this passage would seem to have given a more accurate analysis of our normal use of the word 'conscience' than is at all common among moral philosophers. He has taken the somewhat 'English' view that conscientious decisions are, in the last resort, matters which are simply 'up to' individuals, and which may therefore differ irreconcilably from one individual to the next.

It is not, however, hard for Hegel to discover contradictions in the Conscientious Consciousness just sketched. Its devotion to duty has no other proof than its words: it arbitrarily fills in the content of that duty to suit itself as a natural person. Hence its attitude can as readily be regarded as hypocritical and evil as it can be regarded as dutiful and conscientious. Conscientiousness may moreover be as readily negative as positive, as readily queasy as robust. It may take refuge in the wholly negative conscientiousness of the 'Beautiful Soul', a phenomenon of Hegel's romantic period. This Beautiful Soul is so infinitely conscientious as to fear to commit itself to any decision: it has, says Hegel, 'lost the

[1] *Phen.*, p. 496 (B., p. 658). [2] *Phen.*, p. 501 (B., p. 663).

power of externalizing itself, the power to make itself into a thing
and to endure being. It lives in anxiety lest it should stain its
resplendent interior with action or being. In order to preserve
the purity of its heart, it flees from reality and takes refuge in
self-willed impotence.'[1] If further pressed, it will take refuge in
madness, or pine away in consumption.[2] But though infinitely
fastidious in regard to *action*, the beautiful soul is not so fastidious
when it comes to *speech* and *judgement*. It will *judge* those who have
committed themselves to action and decision, not realizing that
to judge is as much a commitment as to act. In taking it on itself
to judge others, the Beautiful Soul exposes itself to the same
charges of self-will and hypocrisy as does the guilty man of action.
It may even meet a confession of inadequacy on the part of the
man of action with 'the stiff neck of its equability, and the taci-
turnity which keeps itself to itself, and refuses to lavish itself on
another'.[3] Hegel regards such self-righteousness as the lowest
depth of immorality: it is a consciousness which 'both rejects and
is rejected by Spirit'.

The Morality of Conscience differently expressed in the hard
self-righteousness of the 'Beautiful Soul' and in the equally hard
cynicism of the Man of Action now reveals itself as inadequate.
Hegel therefore passes on to what he regards as a true compromise
between judging and doing, to a consciousness which achieves
forgiveness (*Verzeihung*), mutual tolerance and indulgence among
persons. In this forgiving consciousness the judge drops all moral
superiority before the man of action: he craves and receives the
indulgence which he likewise extends. In the spirit of mutual
accommodation Hegel for the first time sees *Spirit Absolute* or
God. 'The reconciling *Yea*', he tells us, 'in which both selves
cease to insist on their opposed existence, is the existence of the
self which at once extends itself into duality, while remaining at
one with itself, which in its complete self-externalization and
antithesis enjoys the certainty of itself. This is God showing Himself among these selves who know themselves as consisting in
pure knowledge.'[4] The various forms of moralistic consciousness,
with their insistence on rigid distinctions which it is impossible
to sustain, are therefore superseded for Hegel by the Religious
Consciousness in which such oppositions vanish. It is important

---

[1] *Phen.*, p. 504 (B., p. 666).   [2] *Phen.*, p. 513 (B., p. 676).
[3] *Phen.*, p. 511 (B., p. 674).   [4] *Phen.*, p. 516 (B., p. 679).

to note that this Religious Consciousness has for Hegel a place among the *absolute* forms of Spirit, whereas the Moral Consciousness lies only on their threshold.

V RELIGION IN GENERAL

The long section on *Religion* which follows is one of the most important in the *Phenomenology*. Hegel, as we saw, arrived at the main insights of his system in the course of those long broodings on the meaning of the Christian faith which occurred during his stay at Bern and Frankfurt. His whole system may in fact be regarded as an attempt to see the Christian mysteries in everything whatever, every natural process, every form of human activity, and every logical transition. If this is the case, it is important to know what interpretation Hegel put upon these mysteries, and upon the whole religious frame of mind of which Christianity was for him the highest expression.

Hegel begins his treatment of the Religious Consciousness by noting how often in the previous development we have come on phases that deserved the name 'religious'. There was something religious in the activities of the Scientific Understanding, when it located explanatory forces and laws *beneath* the surface of objective existence. We were studying a mood of Religion when we dealt with the anguish of the Unhappy Consciousness, and its perpetual hopeless yearning for the Unchangeable. In the ethical sphere, likewise, we dealt with a religious phase that was concerned with mysterious family- and blood-ties, with ancestral allegiances and the powers of the 'Nether World'. In the world of the Enlightenment we dealt with a religious phase which placed its object safely and aseptically beyond all Rational Insight: *il y a un Être Suprême* became the whole *Credo* of religion. We also studied the unsatisfactory games played with a Divine Legislator by the Moral Consciousness, a Legislator whose function vanished entirely once Conscience became sure of itself, and of its power and right to make its own moral decisions. But in this Moral Consciousness there was still a distinction, Hegel tells us, between the self-determining moral personality, and the 'world' within which his moral choices were exercised, whether this 'world' were a world of objects in nature or of other persons making *their* moral decisions. The self-conscious spiritual indivi-

dual then rose to the height of its development: in the consciousness of loving forgiveness, which broke down the barriers
between persons, it at length overcame the 'otherness of the
other'. Henceforth, according to Hegel, it has surmounted even
consciousness: it can have no *alien* object before it, but only itself.
In other words, it has achieved the vision of itself as the 'truth',
the *raison-d'être* of everything. The consciousness in which it
first gains possession of this truth is called by Hegel 'Religion',
which is thereby given a content identical with the central theses
of his own philosophy. This Religious Consciousness only differs
from the philosophical in that it retains what Hegel calls 'a form of
representation' (*Vorstellung*): it remains tied up with an imaginative picture or story, and with whatever misleading suggestions of
externality and finitude such a picture or story may suggest.
The religious view will, further, have varying degrees of development according to the development of the 'world', the natural
and social order, of which it represents the explanatory restatement.

In all this Hegel may be held to have given a merely 'persuasive
definition' of 'Religion'. He has (it may be held) defined Religion,
not as it would be defined by those who normally talk of it, but
in a manner to suit himself, his main motive being to secure for
the difficult theses of his philosophy the approval normally
accompanying the words 'Religion' and 'religious'. 'Religion' and
'religious' are terms mainly of praise, not of abuse, and were
certainly more so in Hegel's day than our own: Hegel, it may be
claimed, is simply 'cashing in' on this widespread approval, and
securing its advantages for his own system. He did in fact gain
much approval in his lifetime by being thought to be a defender
of religious and political orthodoxy, neither of which he could
with any depth of truth be held to be. That Hegel's characterization of Religion *is* persuasive, and that it is also largely arbitrary,
can scarcely be gainsaid: Hegel might have stressed its 'form of
representation' rather than its notional content, and might have
emphasized its supersession, rather than its preservation, in
ultimate philosophical truth. But from another point of view
Hegel's account of Religion is by no means indefensible. For the
states of mind called 'religious' *do* show some tendency to develop
from a stage where they seem merely to be talking of facts comparable to the presence of rats in a barn or of cockroaches in the

kitchen, to a stage where they express little beyond a wholly new way of viewing life and experience, and a way which has many of the distinction-overriding features of Hegel's 'Spirit' and 'Idea'. And we may also plead, in extenuation of Hegel's account, that he did not foist philosophical theses, independently arrived at, on the religion he found about him: these theses were the fruits of brooding on that religion, and may even claim to be among that religion's most profound reflective expressions. It was in the course of his wanderings in the neighbourhood of Golgotha and Gethsemane, rather than in his sojourn in Athenian gardens and colonnades, that Hegel first met 'the Idea'.

In the phases of the Religious Consciousness now to be gone through, Hegel tells us that the previous phenomenological relations of Spirit to its 'world' will all be resumed. There will be a sensory, a perceptual, a scientifically-understanding, a customary-ethical, a disintegratedly-enlightened, and a moralistic phase of Religion. These stages will also divide themselves into: (A) Natural Religion, in which the religious consciousness assumes the form of Consciousness Proper, of the awareness of an object, a thing, in which the self-conscious and the spiritual are implicit; (B) The Religion of Art, the product of the Hellenic Spirit, which corresponds to Self-consciousness Proper, and finally (C) Absolute or Revealed Religion, the expression of Christian civilization, in which the actual form of religion is said to be adequate to its 'notion'.

VI PRE-CHRISTIAN RELIGION

The first form of Natural Religion studied by Hegel is the Religion of Light, of which he holds the ancient Zoroastrian religion to have been the historic expression. In this the 'self-conscious essence which is all truth, and which knows all reality as itself' becomes aware of itself in the mode of *Sense-certainty*. It beholds itself, Hegel tells us, in the form of 'being', i.e. of something immediate, 'out there', not, however, as endowed with one or other of the contingent qualities of sense, but as manifesting a certain 'form of formlessness' (*Gestalt der Gestaltlosigkeit*), which will make it into a 'being filled with the notion of Spirit', i.e. into a fit sensuous symbol of self-conscious Spirit. This 'form of formlessness' the religious consciousness finds ready to hand in the 'pure, all-containing, all pervading light of the morning', which may disperse itself over natural shapes, but which remains always the same 'simple, impalpable, splendid essence'.[1]

But just as Sense-certainty finds that it cannot keep its vague object, the immediate 'this', before it, but must proceed to turn it into some more definite object of *Perception*, so too the Religious Consciousness cannot rest content with an object so formless, but must go on to particularize it into a variety of vegetable and animal forms. We leave the pure radiance of the Iranian dayspring, for the pullulating multiplicity of the Indian religious fancy, which, though it may at times show itself in the peaceful innocence of flowers, more often expresses itself in the murderous, guilty forms of warring animal species, each representing some particular national spirit. (Hegel, we may note, held a singularly ill-informed and unsympathetic view of one of the most Hegelian of peoples and religions.)

The warring variety of this type of religious expression is obviously inadequate to the Religious Consciousness: it therefore 'rubs itself away' into the regular expressions characteristic of the *Scientific Understanding*. Spirit becomes an Artificer, revealed to itself in various crystalline, pyramidal and needle-like forms, 'simple combinations of straight lines with flat surfaces and equality of parts, in which the incommensurability of the round is avoided'. These it constructs in an *instinctive* manner like the building habits of bees. We have passed over to the religious expressions of ancient Egypt. In these the creative unrest of consciousness is present mainly in the artificer, and not in his work, but it tends gradually to *invade* his monumental products, showing itself in stylized animal forms faintly touched with humanity, or in hieroglyphs carrying remote and irrelevant meanings. The inadequacy of such instinctive art to self-consciousness then becomes manifest in the form of sphinxes, 'ambiguous beings, a riddle even to themselves, the conscious fighting with the unconscious, the simple interior with the polymorphous exterior, coupling obscurity of thought with clearness of expression'.[2] In the sphinx this stylized, instinctive, constructive religious consciousness may be said to break down: Spirit demands to see itself in a form made self-consciously rather than instinctively, and expressing self-consciousness in a more adequate manner.

[1] *Phen.*, pp. 528–9 (B., pp. 699–700).   [2] *Phen.*, p. 534 (B., p. 707).

We pass from the Nature-religions of the early East to the 'Art religion' of Greece.

The next longish subsection (B) is as much a treatment of Greek art and literature as of Greek religion. In the *Phenomenology* the two modes of spiritual consciousness are not kept apart, as they are in the treatment of 'Absolute Spirit' in the *Encyclopaedia*. Hegel's treatment of Greek religion as a 'Religion of Art' is characteristic of German romanticism. So too is the view that while art may be an expression of the ethical life of the free city-community, with which the individual feels himself at one, the *Religion* of art arises only when the individual's naïve trust in his secure communal ways has been shaken or shattered. Only when Spirit has cause to mourn over the loss of its secure ethical background, will it begin to bring forth an 'absolute art' which is raised high above reality, and whose forms, according to Hegel, shadow forth 'the night in which the Ethical Substance was betrayed, and made into a Subject'.[1] (Again a reminiscence of Gethsemane.) Works of art are said to be the vessels chosen by Spirit to enshrine its sorrow and body forth its pathos. We, living long after the age of Winckelmann, will find in this pathos little beyond a pathetic fallacy.

The artistic religious consciousness has its first typical expression in the *statue* of the God, which combines the externality of nature with an idealized expression of self-consciousness. Here the exact, crystalline forms beloved by the Understanding are discarded: there is a movement towards forms which, though more exact than those of living bodies, still show the essential incommensurability of the rounded forms of life. The human figure is set free from anything natural or brutal, this being left to the Titans or the older generations of Gods. It is Hegel's view that each such marble God stands for the ethical life of a particular people: in worshipping its God, the community is really achieving self-consciousness. Hence the temples of the Gods are for the use of the citizens, their treasure may in time of need be expended by the state, their honour is the honour of 'a high-minded people rich in its art'.

The joyous immobility of religious statuary will, however, afford an inadequate expression of the suffering and effort in the artistic self-consciousness that produced it. This spiritual suffering

[1] *Phen.*, p. 540 (B., p. 714).

and effort demand another medium for their expression, and this Hegel finds in various forms of religious speech, such as the hymn and the oracular utterance: he also finds it in the combination of speech and action which occurs in the religious cult. 'The cult', says Hegel, 'is constituted by a two-sided movement in which a godlike form, moving in the affective element of self-consciousness, and the same form at rest in the element of thinghood, give up their distinct determinations, so that the unity, which is the notion of their essence, comes into existence. In this the self achieves the consciousness of the descent of the Divine Essence from its transcendent beyondness, while what was previously the unreal and merely objective, achieves thereby the genuine reality of self-consciousness.'[1] This two-sided movement occurs elaborately in the religious sacrifice, where the objects sacrificed are said to express both the worshipper's surrender of his own personality, and the descent into actuality and touch with humanity of the God to whom the objects are sacrificed. In other words, the sacrificial ceremony does not merely bring the worshippers to their knees: it also performs the task, at once Voltairean and mystical, of bringing to earth the aloof and self-sufficient Gods. An even more intimate amalgamation of the divine with the human occurs in the various religious mysteries connected with Demeter and Dionysus. These are mysterious and mystical not in the sense of involving hidden secrets, but in the sense that in them 'the self knows itself as one with the Essence, and that the latter is accordingly revealed'. Here the Absolute Being achieves the position of a thing seen, handled, smelt and tasted, it becomes an object of desire and is made one with the self in actual enjoyment.[2] There remains, however, something unself-conscious, something largely natural in this form of religious amalgamation: hence its ready expression in the wild curvets of a swarm of rapt women. 'Its self-conscious life is therefore merely the mystery of the Bread and the Wine, of Ceres and Bacchus, not of the genuine upper Gods, whose individuality includes self-consciousness as an essential element in itself. Spirit has not yet offered itself up to this consciousness as self-conscious Spirit, and the mystery of the Bread and Wine is not as yet the mystery of Flesh and Blood.'[3] In other words, we are as yet only dealing with a

[1] *Phen.*, p. 445 (B., p. 720).
[2] *Phen.*, p. 551 (B., p. 728).   [3] *Phen.*, p. 551 (B., p. 728).

confused anticipation of the Word made Flesh, and its continuance in the life of the religious community.

At this point Hegel might have made a wholly natural and easy transition to his Absolute or Revealed Religion, which was for him historically manifest in Christianity. He prefers, however, to linger longer among the forms of the classical 'Art-religion', though some of these have only minor relevance to the theme on hand. Very characteristically, he treats the activities connected with the major athletic festivals as purely religious activities. Athletes are for Hegel 'animated, living works of art, matching strength with beauty': they represent the 'Essence' in general and also the essence of their people, 'not in the petrifaction of a God, but in the highest bodily expressiveness'.

Neither Olympic athleticism nor Dionysian enthusiasm can, however, be wholly adequate expressions of the union of self-consciousness with the 'essence' of things: in the former there is too spiritless a clearness, in the latter too much confusion and wild stammering. It is in a form of speech more coherent than an oracle's, and less emotional and narrow in its direction than that of a hymn, that such an expression must be found. Hegel therefore passes on to the consideration of the spiritual attitudes lying behind the epic, tragic and comic literature of antiquity, which are for him religious phenomena. We shall not here sum up all the deep and perceptive things he says on these themes. Suffice it to say that he regards the epic as expressing in verbal form the same relations between the human and the divine which are actively expressed in the cult. In the epic, however, the individual self-conscious person is inadequately emphasized, being present merely as the anonymous, background singer. This unemphasized individual person then claims a more adequate expression in the tragic form of literature, where he speaks directly, even if behind a stylized mask, and against the less individualized background comment of the Chorus of Elders. At length, in the comic form of literature, the individual claims his complete and absolute due: he silences the gnomic wisdom of the Chorus, liquidates the abstract forms of the Gods, and reveals himself, under all high masks and appearances, as the everyday, commonplace, vulgar man, at one with actor and audience alike. He performs, in short, in ironical fashion, the same liquidation of the transcendently divine that is more solemnly carried out in the sacrificial cult.

From the resolution of all absolutes in the individualistic comic irony, Hegel now leaps dialectically to the individualized Incarnate Word of Christianity. This extreme leap resembles that from phrenology to the reasonable self in society, or from the death-dealing guillotine to the Categorical Imperative of Kant. The comic consciousness is summed up in the light-hearted proposition: 'I, the Self, am the Absolute Essence' but this light-hearted utterance at once permits conversion to the serious statement: 'The Absolute Essence is I, the self', in which self-consciousness is merely an adjunct, a predicate to something more substantial. The comic consciousness therefore has as its reverse side all the more or less unhappy, abstract forms of self-consciousness which were studied earlier in the *Phenomenology*, and which arose when the secure ethical life of the ancient city-state passed away in the dissolved atomicity and abstract right of the Roman imperial period. We are back once more with the abstract self-sufficiency of Stoicism, the uncommitted freedom of Scepticism, and with the Unhappy Consciousness, which Hegel now sees exemplified, not in the self-abasing, ascetic spirit of the middle ages, but in the intellectual and moral *malaise* of the age of Pater's *Marius*, a *malaise* for which the Incarnate Word could provide the only possible medicine. This Unhappy Consciousness is aware only of its total *loss* of all that previously reassured and filled it: its anguish might find expression in the words of the Lutheran hymn 'God is dead'.

This mortal rupture between the outward and substantial, on the one hand, and the inward and self-conscious, on the other, can be healed (Hegel tells us) only by a twofold movement: by a movement of the Substantial towards the Subjective, and of the Subjective towards the Substantial. In part this need is met by a one-sided spread of undisciplined subjectivity over the whole territory recognized as objective, as in Gnosticism and the Mystery-religions: nature, history and the established faiths become over-run by interpretations and myths, and consciousness wanders crazed in a murky night of its own making. This night passes away only when this one-sided movement of subjectivity towards objectivity is met by a balancing movement from the objective towards the subjective, when self-consciousness finds itself in what is *independently* and *immediately* there. Hegel is here pointing to the essential superiority of the Word made Flesh over the

'Aeons' of Valentinus or the Unconquered Sun of Mithraism. We encounter the former in the concrete particularity of sense, whereas the latter has merely the shadowy, projected being of private fantasy.

'This fact', says Hegel, 'that Absolute Spirit has given itself the form of self-consciousness both *in* itself, and also *for* its own consciousness, now appears inasmuch as it is the belief of the world that the Spirit is there as a self-consciousness, i.e. as an actual human being, that it is there for immediate sense-certainty, that the believing consciousness sees and feels and hears the Godhead. In this manner it is no imagination, but an actuality in the believer. Consciousness therefore does not start from the inner life of thought, and the existence of the God, rather does it start from what is immediately present and recognizes the God in it.'[1]

It will be noted in the above passage that what Hegel thinks important is not the *Incarnatio Filii Dei*, but the *belief* in such an incarnation: if this incarnation is said to be actual and not imaginary, its actuality is one *in* the believer, rather than in the historical person of Jesus. That person was no doubt the vehicle through which 'Absolute Religion', the realization that the divine nature must achieve self-consciousness in man, first became explicit: the realization rather than the vehicle remains the important thing for Hegel. Hegel may therefore fitly be regarded as the father of 'modernism', that ever assailed but unsuppressible, and authentic expression of Christian belief.

VII ABSOLUTE OR REVEALED RELIGION (CHRISTIANITY)

Absolute Religion, to which Hegel now turns, is also what he means by 'Revealed Religion', i.e. a religion in which the Divine Being is known for what it is, a being whose nature it is to be self-conscious, to reveal itself to itself. Hegel remarks: 'There is something secret to consciousness in its object, as long as this appears strange and alien to itself, and is not known *as* itself. This secretness ceases when the Essence becomes objective to Spirit *as* Spirit. . . . Itself is only manifest to itself in its own certainty of self, its object is the self: self, however, is nothing foreign, but inseparable unity with itself, the immediate univer-

[1] *Phen.*, p. 576 (B., pp. 757–8).

sal.'[1] It is this *immediate universality* which is the true content of
a belief in the Incarnation. Hegel uncompromisingly holds that
it is only in speculative knowledge that God can be truly reached:
he holds indeed that God's being *consists* solely in speculative
knowledge. The content of this knowledge is, however, held to
be one with that of Revealed Religion. Philosophy is therefore
alike the saviour and the salvation of men, though this need not
be in every way patent to those whom it saves.

The religious presentation of speculative truth is, as we saw,
an imaginative, pictorial presentation: it has not yet risen to the
pure universality of conceptual thought. The union of universality
with immediacy remains for it their union in the individual self-
consciousness of Jesus, which excludes the believer's own self-
consciousness. The movement towards a fuller universalization
even of such universality-in-particularity, begins when the
Incarnation shifts into the *past*, when its present reality becomes
a matter of memory or tradition. This shift, for Hegel, does not
veil vision, but rather adds to its acuteness. For only if the Absolute
loses the sensuous immediacy of the flesh, can it achieve spiritual
resurrection in the experience of the community. Reference to
the past is, however, only a semi-pictorial form of universality:
though the content of what is thus referred has become universal
—what is past is always a *such* rather than a *this*—it is still pictured
as if present to sense. The Religious Consciousness, according to
Hegel, never wholly rises above the externality of imaginative
presentation. When it seeks for the roots of its spiritual life, it
tends mistakenly to go back to the historical circumstances of its
origin, to the 'soulless recollection of an ideally constructed
individual figure and its existence in the past'.[2] To seek for the
historical Jesus is for Hegel to lose touch with the risen and
ascended Christ.

Hegel now gives a lengthy phenomenological restatement of
the doctrines of the Trinity, Creation, Fall, etc., which throws
considerable light on his own system. Spirit, says Hegel, conceived
abstractiy as a 'Substance' in the element of pure thought, is the
'simple, self-identical, eternal Essence'—the Essence which Hegel
afterwards called 'the Idea', and which religion knows as 'the
Father'. But, says Hegel, this simple, eternal Essence would be
spiritual merely in name, were it conceived *merely* as such an

---

[1] *Phen.*, pp. 577–8 (B., p. 759).   [2] *Phen.*, p. 583 (B., pp. 764–5).

abstract Essence. It must present itself, become objective to something, and in so far as the religious imagination transforms this conceptual entailment into an historical process, the eternal Essence may be said to give birth to something other than itself (God the Son begotten before all worlds). But this procession to otherness is at the same time a return to self, since the conscious Son, and the Father of whom He is conscious, are one and the same spiritual reality. We have therefore the materials for a Trinity consisting of the Essence, of the self-conscious being that knows it, and of the knowledge of the former in the latter. If the self-conscious element represents the Divine word 'which being spoken externalizes and empties the speaker, but which is just as immediately apprehended', it seems that the Spirit is represented by the active identification of the two aspects. 'So that', says Hegel, 'the differences that are made are as immediately dissolved as they are made, and are as immediately made as they are dissolved, and the True and Real is just this movement turned circlewise on itself.'[1] The whole Trinity therefore lives enshrined in the Cartesian *Cogito*. The imagination of the religious community cannot, however, rise to this pitch of abstraction: for it the moments of self-conscious Spirit fall apart in quasi-independence, and in consequent quasi-sequence and interaction.

The same logical entailment which connects the elements of self-consciousness, and which is misleadingly represented as a temporal process, now leads to the existence of a World. The distinction between the pure Essence of Divinity and the self-conscious Word that is conscious of it, is too abstract and categorial to be a *real* distinction: it is, says Hegel (perhaps remembering Augustine's account of the Trinity) a distinction of *love*, in which there is no sufficient opposition of nature. For such a merely categorial distinction to have substance, and to be something that can be genuinely seen through and overcome, it must be exemplified in the immediacy and separateness of sensuous being. The eternal abstract Spirit must therefore create a World, the word 'creation' being merely an imaginative symbol for the entailment holding between the being of an abstract notion and the being of cases in which it may be instantiated. The Spirit which is the sense of the World must itself show an initial aspect of separateness and immediacy: it must at first

[1] *Phen.*, pp. 584-5 (B., pp. 766-7).

appear as a natural individual in this world, and must regard the
world as a system of things foreign to itself. As so individualized,
Spirit may be styled 'innocent', but it cannot as yet be called
'good'. Being Spirit, it must, however, progress from the immediacy of sense-experience to the inwardness of pure thought, and
must in the process lose its innocence: it must become conscious
of what is good, i.e. of its thinking being, on the one hand, and
of what is bad, i.e. its sensuous being, on the other. This epistemological progress from sense-experience to perception and
thought, is turned by the religious imagination into the story of
the temptation and expulsion from paradise. The same imagination translates this progress into the region of pure thought,
into the myth of the fall of Lucifer and his angels.

The world in which the merely natural, self-retreating (*insich-
gehend*) and therefore bad self-consciousness has a place, must
find a place also for the good self-consciousness, i.e. for Spirit
returning to self out of sensuousness. This return the religious
imagination depicts in the form of a free act of 'self-humbling'
on the part of the Absolute Essence, whereby sensuous man is
redeemed. Religion is right, Hegel thinks, in attributing such
redemption to the universal abstract Godhead rather than to the
individual spirit that is conscious of it, precisely because it is
necessary for the abstract Godhead to instantiate itself, in order
to have any real being at all. It is the *abstractness* of God which
forces Him to come down from heaven, and to suffer death by
exemplification. The descent of the abstract universal into sensuous embodiment is also, of course, the elevation of what is
sensuous into what is abstract and notional: the death of God
leads to His Resurrection and Ascension. What is remarkable in
the passage before us is the wholly logical or epistemological
interpretation put upon the Christian mysteries.

From this brief, embarrassed encounter with the Word made
Flesh, Hegel passes on to a stage where Spirit is conscious of itself
in universal form, as the Spirit inspiring a religious community.
The Divine Man who has died is the communal self-consciousness
implicit: the community must make His self-consciousness
explicitly its own. The death and resurrection of the Redeemer
must lose their simple, natural significance as events in the life-
history of a particular individual: they must become phases in the
life of a Spirit which lives and dies daily in the religious com-

munity.[1] The death involved is a death to particularity, which presumably here covers both the particularity of sense and the particularity of interest and impulse, and a resurrection to universality. It is also the death of all imaginative religious presentations, and a resurrection to a more inward, notional form of religious experience. The death of the Mediator must be appropriated by the religious community: His independent, objective self-consciousness must be set aside, and transformed into a universal self-consciousness. With this dissolution of the Mediator in the communal consciousness, will also go the death of the divine Essence, as something abstract and apart: we must learn to sing, not despairingly but exultingly, that God Himself has died. 'This hard saying', says Hegel, 'is the expression of the innermost simple knowledge of self, the return of consciousness into the deep night of I = I, that can no more distinguish or know anything outside of itself.'[2] The ultimate fate of all imaginative religious presentations is therefore to hand over their majesty and authority to self-conscious Spirit, that the latter may be all in all. The religious community does not, of course, realize how revolutionary, how Voltairean a role it is playing. It *feels* its union with the Divine in the form of love, without embracing this in a clear concept.

Though Hegel has veiled his treatment of Religion in much orthodox-sounding language, its outcome is quite clear. Theism in all its forms is an imaginative distortion of final truth. The God outside of us who saves us by His grace, is a misleading pictorial expression for saving forces *intrinsic* to self-conscious Spirit, wherever this may be present. And the religious approach must be transcended (even if after a fashion preserved) in the final illumination. At the same time it would be wrong to regard Hegel as some sort of humanist: he has not dethroned God in order to put Man, whether as an individual or group of individuals, in His place. The self-conscious Spirit which plays the part of God in his system is not the complex, existent person, but the impersonal, reasonable element in him, which, by a necessary process, more and more 'takes over' the individual, and becomes manifest and conscious in him. Hegel's religion, like that of Aristotle, consists in 'straining every nerve to live in accordance with the best thing in us'.

[1] *Phen.*, p. 597 (B., p. 780).   [2] *Phen.*, p. 598 (B., p. 782).

VIII ABSOLUTE OR PHILOSOPHICAL KNOWLEDGE

The last section (*DD*) of the *Phenomenology* is devoted to
Absolute or Philosophical Knowledge, the final reconciliation of
consciousness with self-consciousness. This reconciliation consists in the realization that every object of which we may be conscious is no more than an 'externalization', a presupposition of
our thinking self-consciousness, and a consequent reabsorption
of such externality into our subjective life. At this stage of the
Phenomenology, as in the Homeric book of the dead or the Proustian *Temps Retrouvé*, all the previous forms and attitudes assumed
by consciousness crowd back into life: we realize how seriously
Hegel took the spiral windings of his 'highway of despair', however much they may have seemed arbitrary, and even frivolous to
us. We go once more through the passage from the mere being of
things of sense to the richly determined being they have for the
Perceptual Consciousness, and to the purely universal being they
have for the Scientific Understanding. We recur to the Observing
Consciousness, and to its equation of the conscious I with a mere
thing (as in the ossifying reduction of phrenology), and to the
immediate inversion of this equation, so that any mere thing
becomes equated with the I. This enables Hegel, passing over
many intermediate steps in his treatment, to do a long leap to the
eighteenth-century stress on Utility, the treatment of outer things
as exhausted in their use. From this we move in recollection
through the various stages of the Moral Self-consciousness, and
to its culmination in the act of Forgiveness. We then move to the
reconciliation of consciousness with self-consciousness which
occurs in Religion, a reconciliation treated by Hegel as 'in itself'
or implicit, and contrasted with the philosophical reconciliation,
which is 'for itself' or explicit. Finally the Beautiful Soul makes a
second appearance, somewhat out of its original order. In a sense,
Hegel says, it has approximated more closely to philosophical
self-consciousness than have the imaginative forms of religion,
since it 'knows itself in its pure transparent unity' as a 'pure
knowledge of its pure inwardness as Spirit'. Its steadfast refusal
to realize itself in any objective achievement is the cause of its
dispersal into thin air, and its replacement by a philosophical
insight which is less fastidious as to objectification.

At this point Hegel's exposition defies abbreviation or summarization: so many notes are sounded together that the effect is bewildering and dizzying. What is clear, however, is that we have passed from the imaginative religious view, in which an element of otherness clings to the presented content, to the level of *Wissenschaft*, Systematic Science, at which all content is presented *as* the performance of the thinking self. 'This ultimate form of Spirit,' Hegel remarks, 'the Spirit which gives to its complete, true content the form of self, and thereby realizes its own concept, even as it remains in that concept in so realizing it, is Absolute Knowledge: it is Spirit knowing itself in the form of Spirit or purely notional knowledge (*das begreifende Wissen*). Truth is here not merely implicitly equated with certainty, but has the character of certainty of self. It stands there for the Spirit that knows it in the form of a knowledge of self. The truth is the content which in Religion is not as yet equated with certainty. This equation consists therein, that the content has acquired the form of self. That, therefore, now becomes the element of being, or the form of objectivity for consciousness, which is the Essence itself, namely the Notion. Spirit appearing to consciousness in this element, or (what is the same) brought forth by it in this element, is Systematic Science.'[1]

Hegel's words are dark, but their purport is clear. Since the existence of a 'subject' or 'self' is for him nothing beyond the universalizing activity of thought, a self's consciousness of itself is simply the consciousness of this universalizing activity (which is also an *exercise* of this activity), and in this consciousness of self all particular acts of universalization are in some manner summed up: they will be rethought *as* thoughts, or 'given the form of self'. Spirit in being self-conscious will also be conscious of all it has ever thought, but it will be conscious of them as *its own concepts*, and not as alien objects. Hegel is here saying much what Thomas says when he holds that God *seipsum cognoscendo alia omnia cognoscit*, or what Aristotle means when he refuses to differentiate between thinking of this or that ideal form, and thinking of one's thought in so thinking. Hegel can therefore pass from the pure self-consciousness which is the crowning stage of the *Phenomenology*, to the study of the categories and other abstract determinations of thought and being, which are the content of Systematic Science.

[1] *Phen.*, p. 610 (B., p. 798).

Systematic Science, the understanding of Spirit *qua* Spirit, only arises (Hegel maintains) when Spirit has run through the whole gamut of its preparatory forms. But long before Spirit becomes aware of itself as Spirit, it can be aware of itself in an indirect, concealed manner, by way of categories embedded in various forms of being which appear to have nothing to do with consciousness. What is always there as the inner reality of consciousness is first given conceptually as a series of piecemeal 'moments', which only yield a portrait of self-conscious Spirit when all have been assembled. Hegel here gives a brief, difficult indication of the place of *Time* in his system. 'Time', he says, 'is the Notion itself, as existent out there and presenting itself in the form of an empty intuition to consciousness. For this reason Spirit necessarily makes its appearance in time, and it appears in time only so long as it does not grasp its pure notion, i.e. as long as it does not expunge time. Time is the externally envisaged pure self not as yet apprehended by that self. In so far as the latter apprehends itself, it supersedes the form of time, understands what it envisages, and becomes intuition understanding and understood. Time therefore appears as the doom and the necessity of the Spirit that is not yet perfected in itself.'[1] In this passage Hegel is not teaching any doctrine of the 'unreality' of Time, such as is accepted by McTaggart and Bradley, and is widely thought to be Hegelian. On the contrary he is holding that it is only by achieving self-consciousness *through* a temporal process that self-conscious Spirit can *be* at all. Time, so far from being unreal, is the very form of that creative unrest which represents Spirit as it becomes conscious of itself. Hegel certainly says that, in the final insight of philosophy, Time will be expunged or annulled, but .this 'annulment' stands for no metaphysical or theological timelessness, but for an annulment *in and for philosophy*. It means that, for the philosopher, concepts are universal and principles true, and that the precise moment at which anyone appropriates them is completely unimportant.

Hegel now sketches, in a single long interesting paragraph, the whole previous history of modern philosophy: its main figures appear in dream-like guise, being hinted at rather than referred to.[2] He then indicates, in extremely shadowy fashion, the three sections of his subsequent system: Spirit, he holds, must first

[1] *Phen.*, pp. 612–13 (B., p. 800).   [2] *Phen.*, pp. 614–15 (B., pp. 801–3).

resume, in the new conceptual medium it has entered, the whole passage from the immediacy of sense to articulate self-consciousness, which has been carried out in the *Phenomenology*: this, though Hegel does not explicitly say so, must be the task of the part of Systematic Science called *Logic*. In this logical treatment, however, the concrete *objects* in which alone the categories of thought can be instantiated, will have been lost sight of: they will have been treated merely as limits to thought, not as things important in their own right. Spirit must therefore seek to do justice to this necessary extension of its own being: it must abandon itself to the particularity and the free contingency of existence in Time and Space. Hegel is here forecasting the *Philosophy of Nature*, the second part of his system. Spirit must then, in the third place, resume the contingent modes in which its own subjective life has been displayed in the past: it must run through, in purely conceptual recollection, the historical forms in which its life has been manifested. This task has, to some extent, been carried out in the *Phenomenology* itself, but this has been concerned rather with the typical development of the individual mind than with an historical development through many individuals. In the new philosophical treatment, it is suggested, the historical order will be followed—the *Phenomenology* has merely made leaps across the historical stage—but it will be purged of contingent detail, and lifted, like the rest of the system, into the ether of pure thought. Hegel is here obviously anticipating the third part of his system, the *Philosophy of Spirit*. These final paragraphs of the *Phenomenology* show us how clear was Hegel's plan for his whole system at the time when the *Phenomenology* was written: they also show how clear was his notion of the relation of the *Phenomenology* to that system. Its role was to state, in terms of biographical subjectivity, what was afterwards to be worked out in intersubjective, conceptual terms. That subjective approaches themselves occur in the subsequent system, and that its third part includes a section on Phenomenology, argues no revision of purpose. A continuous mirroring and re-mirroring of everything in everything is of the essence of Hegelianism.

We have now completed our sketch of Hegel's *Phenomenology of Spirit*. Inevitably we have had to follow its windings more closely than is usually necessary in commenting on a philosophical classic. The movement and order of Hegel's thought is unlike any other: it cannot with profit be considerably abridged or rearranged. It must be studied with an absolute *approfondisse-ment* as one must study every note, chord and transition in a great musical work, where form and content are inseparable. The main reward of the study is that there is no notion or principle to be found in the later system which is not sounded in the *Phenomenology*, usually in more penetrating and enlightening fashion. No one can understand the Hegelian Dialectic who has not first seen it at work in the flexible sequence of phenomenological 'shapes' we have been dealing with. And a study of the *Phenomenology* has the further advantage of being so extremely and uniquely difficult as to make everything else in Hegel seem straightforward and plain-sailing by contrast.

CHAPTER SIX

THE LOGIC—I

The Doctrine of Being

I HEGEL'S GENERAL VIEW OF LOGIC

We shall try, in the next three chapters, to give a moderately faithful, moderately critical account of the content of Hegel's *Logic*, the major work which exists in two versions, the long version of the *Science of Logic*, and the shorter version constituting the first part of the *Encyclopaedia of the Philosophical Sciences*. We shall build mainly on the longer version, where there is a large fund of easy, discursive talk to lubricate the difficult dialectical transitions. While the *Encyclopaedia* treatment at times represents a simplification, and while its interstices are crammed with valuable excerpts from Hegel's lectures, its brief, pregnant paragraphs, bristling with new, often barbarous locutions, require a running commentary to play round the knots of their arguments: this Hegel has himself provided in the *Science of Logic*. The style of both *Logics* is, at its hardest, much less exacting than that of the *Phenomenology*. The dry, notional ground that is here cultivated is at once more restricted in range, and less full of the heaped leavings of history and experience, than the over-rich soil of the earlier work. We in our statement will seek to surrender ourselves to the drift of Hegel's treatment, filling in gaps and making modifications in a manner which seems required by that treatment, and not guided by external considerations of 'validity'. The dialectical method as employed by Hegel is unique in the history of thought, and must be judged by standards intrinsic to itself: we must see from his practice what sort of game Hegel is attempting to play, and must then judge in the light of that practice whether he is playing it well or ill. Hegel's dialectical ladder of notions, arranged in their characteristic dimension of intrinsic 'truth', and often linked only by daring and vertiginous leaps, has little in common with a deductive chain of propositions, following from one another according to fixed principles laid down in advance. If it can be said to lead validly to the swaying perch of its last, dizzy conclusion, from which the whole arena of past thought may be systematically surveyed, this validity is not that of a proof or a proven theorem.

The *Logic* may be said, by anticipation, to carry out in the medium of pure thought what the *Phenomenology* carried out in the medium of individual experience. It may be said to show that the *notion*, the *concept* of self-conscious Spirit, has the same explanatory primacy in the realm of concepts and categories that the actual philosophical self-knowledge of Spirit has in the realm of personal experience. In the *Phenomenology* Hegel trod a road which showed progressively, as we looked back along it, how our subjection to the assaults of sense, our probing discovery and explanation of an external world of lifeless and living things, our whole history of violent and co-operative dealings with other persons, could be held merely to be a process of *self*-discovery: how what seemed refractory and alien was there merely to be mastered, and how the order educed from it, or imposed upon it, could properly be said to be *our own*. That it *is* our own is, in fact, for Hegel, a matter of definition, since 'we' means for him the Universal in Action, the factor that imports unity and universality into whatever it touches. Now, in the *Logic*, having reduced all this natural and social material to the 'form of self', i.e. to a set of pure universals or 'thought-determinations', we are to study the same progress from what is most baldly free from distinction and mediation to what is most richly self-differentiating and self-referring, not this time in the material of modes of consciousness, but in the abstract material of concepts or modes of thought. We are to run through a series of extremely general ways of referring to objects, e.g. as merely being there, as being one among others, as being of this or that quality or number, as being in essence this or accidentally that, etc. etc., and are to show how the earlier, more abstract ways of viewing things are unsatisfactory unless made part of more comprehensive, many-sided views, and how ultimately no way of viewing things is satisfactory that does not see them as aspects or conditions in the life of self-conscious Spirit. The sequence of 'views' in the *Logic* will not, however, follow a course precisely parallel to the phases of experience in the *Phenomenology*. Spirit addressing itself in thinking fashion to objects, will develop different emphases, experience different rubs and perplexities, and devise different means for dealing with them, from Spirit embedded in concrete natural and social situations. There are, e.g., many abstract logical and mathematical ideas, generating their own dilemmas and solutions, to which nothing in the field of more concrete experience will be precisely parallel.

It will be plain, from what has been said, that the terms of Hegel's *Logic* are all notions (*Begriffe*), thought-determinations (*Gedankenbestimmungen*), rather than any judgements or propositions into which such thought-determinations enter. The Judgement as such is indeed dealt with at one stage in the Dialectic, but this judgement is rather the form or notion of Judgement in general than any particular judgement or assertion. Hegel does indeed say that his various categories can be looked on as successive definitions of 'the Absolute', as metaphysical definitions of God, but he makes plain that all that is clear in such definitions lies in the notions which form their predicates. Of their subject we have only a wholly inchoate notion which it is the function of the successive predicates to elucidate. It follows that we lose nothing by regarding the dialectical sequence of the *Logic* as purely a sequence of concepts or notions. We should also be doing Hegel no injustice (since he recognizes the closest connection, even an 'identity' between thought and language) in regarding the *Logic* as a sequence of what are now called 'linguistic recommendations'. Hegel recommends for our adoption a given way of talking about the world, then discovers flaws and inadequacies in this mode of speaking, then supersedes it by a further recommendation which also comprehends it, until his last recommendation supersedes and comprehends all others. It is obvious that there can be no question (in the ordinary sense of the words) of either truth or validity in such a series of recommendations. There can only be questions regarding the linguistic or conceptual adequacy or satisfactoriness of its terms.

The fact that Hegel speaks of the terms of his *Logic* as determinations of *thought*, must not, however, lead us to give his treatment too subjective an interpretation. As emphasized in the *Phenomenology*, the mind in Systematic Science has put behind it the whole antithesis between 'certainty' and 'truth', between its own grasp of some objective character or distinction, and the character or distinction which it grasps. The bringing to light of universals, which is 'certainty', and the universals brought to light, which are 'truth', are for Hegel inseparably related sides of the same activity. It follows that Logic as the study of thought-determinations is at the same time a study of things as they really are: it can be given a realistic as well as a conceptualistic interpretation. Hegel remarks in this connection that pure Science 'contains thought in so far as it is just as much the thing in itself, or the thing in itself in so far as it is just as much pure thought. . . . Science is so little formal, so little lacking in the matter for an actual and true knowledge, that its content alone is rather what is absolutely true, or if one still wishes to make use of the term "matter", the true matter. This is a matter whose form is nothing external, since it is rather pure thought, i.e. the absolute form itself. Logic must accordingly be regarded as the system of pure reason, as the kingdom of pure thought. This kingdom is the truth as it is, without covering, in and for itself.'[1]

Hegel indeed goes further in a realistic direction by saying (in the same context) that the content of Logic is 'the presentation of God as He was in His eternal essence, before the creation of Nature and finite Spirit'. The theistic implications of this statement must of course be discounted: as explained in the *Phenomenology*, God's creation of the world is merely that exemplification without which He, as an abstract notional possibility, could have no sort of being. And they are fully discounted in a later passage where Hegel describes the whole system of Logic as 'the kingdom of shadows, the world of simple essences freed from all sensuous concretion'.[2] The realism of the *Logic* means, further, that it includes all the notions connected with Being and Essence which the older metaphysicians dealt with in 'ontology', or the study of Pure Being. The first two parts of the *Logic*, called the 'Objective Logic', are entirely concerned with notions of this kind. Logic, says Hegel, 'coincides with Metaphysics, the science of things set and held in thoughts, and thoughts accredited able to express the essential nature of things'.[3] And even the third part of the *Logic*, the so-called 'Subjective Logic', is subjective only in a Hegelian sense, since the 'Subject' is here the self-realizing Notion or Universal in Action, and since Concept, Judgement and Syllogism are all given an application to objective things and processes. Hegel's logical realism is not, however,

---

[1] *Sc. of Log.*, I, pp. 45–6 (J. & S., I, p. 60; M., p. 49).
[2] *Sc. of Log.*, I, p. 57 (J. & S., I, p. 69; M., p. 58).
[3] *L. Log.*, § 324, p. 83 (W., p. 45).

comparable to that of certain modern thinkers, e.g. Meinong, Russell, and Moore (in the earlier phases of the latter). Hegel draws no distinction between the subjective acts by which logical entities are brought to mind, and the entities which exist independently of such acts. The thought-determinations and categories of Hegel have no subsistence apart from the life of thinking and self-conscious Spirit. (Hegel does indeed show a strong streak of realism in regard to the realm of nature. He thinks its objects exemplify an *unconscious* thought or a *petrified* intelligence, and that they existed before thought brought their generic characters to consciousness. There is no comparable vein of realism in his treatment of the *entia rationis*.)

The *Logic* has the triadic structure characteristic of all parts of the Dialectic. Its three divisions are (*a*) the Doctrine of Being, which is said to be a theory of thought in its immediacy, of the notion implicit or in itself. It studies categories such as those of quality and number, where there is no diremption into distinct levels, and where all is straightforward and on the surface. It then goes on to (*b*) the Doctrine of Essence, which studies thought in its 'reflection' or mediation, where the deeper Being-for-self of the notion is opposed to its surface show. It ends with (*c*) the Doctrine of the Notion, which is said to be a study of thought returning to self, and its developed being-by-self, the Notion in and for itself. These accounts and rubrics obviously mean little till we have seen what Hegel wants them to cover. The Doctrine of Being (the theme of the present chapter) has the following three subdivisions: (i) Determinateness or Quality; (ii) Magnitude or Quantity (which represents Determinateness overcome), and (iii) Quantity qualitatively determined, or Measure.

II BEING, NOTHING AND BECOMING

The notion of Being is chosen by Hegel as the beginning of his logical Dialectic because an acknowledgement of Being— that there is something or other, or that there is this or that— seems to him the simplest and most fundamental of thinking approaches. It is only when there has been such an acknowledgement that we can begin to say of what has been acknowledged that it is so and so determined, so and so related, numbered and so on. *Prima facie*, an acknowledgement of mere Being presupposes nothing whatever, and is in this sense unmediated or immediate, whereas all other thinking approaches presuppose *it*, and are in this sense mediated. In acknowledging Being we are not as yet seeing what we acknowledge *as* anything in particular. As Hegel paradoxically puts it: 'There is nothing to be envisaged in pure Being, if one may speak of vision in this connection, or one has only this pure empty act of vision. In the same way there is as little anything to be thought in it, or it is just this empty act of thinking.'[1] The act of thought or vision which merely sets some object before us *for* determination or characterization obviously cannot determine or characterize that object in any way whatever.

Hegel insists that there is nothing arbitrary in beginning his ladder of thought-determinations with the category of Pure Being. If one began with anything more determinate, it would necessarily be something mediated: anything determinate pre-supposes something *else* as what is really first. 'It lies therefore in the nature of the beginning itself that it should be Being and nothing beyond.' The choice is not therefore comparable to the provisional or problematical choice of a geometrical construction, which proves in the end to be the right one for our purpose. None the less Hegel is conscious of some paradox in making Pure Being his absolute beginning. The system he is about to develop forms a closed, and not an open series, and this would seem to preclude it from having an absolute beginning. It is, moreover, a system in which the later terms represent the ground and completion of the earlier ones, and are in this sense *prior* to them. Being is also itself a dialectical result of the development worked out in the *Phenomenology*. In so far, however, as one abstracts from the rich connections which place a notion in the web of related notions, it is at once reduced to the vestigial notion of Pure Being. The connection of Being with a beginning is in fact tautological: mere Being is what one necessarily has when one *begins* to think. No other notion, Hegel argues, will perform this initial function. The notion of a beginning is itself more complex since it involves an internal opposition: the notion of Being may *be* a beginning, but it is not part of its content to be so. In the same way, such notions as the Ego or the Absolute or God may be what our beginning is 'in itself', or what it will

[1] *Sc. of Log.*, I, p. 88 (J. & S., I, p. 94; M., p. 82).

ultimately turn out to be: a dialectical treatment must, how-ever, ignore any feature not explicitly *posited* in a notion, and discerned in it merely by a privileged oversight or external reflection.

Modern logicians might, however, object to Hegel's choice of Being as his initial conception on grounds quite other than those which Hegel gives. They might hold that Being is anything but a simple, unmediated notion, which other notions presuppose while it does not presuppose them. For modern logicians have been greatly influenced by the view (put forward by Russell in *Principia Mathematica*) that it is quite senseless to affirm or deny existence of something actually before one, in sensory or some other form of acquaintance. One cannot say of a giraffe one meets in the Zoo 'There is that!'; much less can one say of it meaningfully 'There is not that!' The notion of existence, on Russell's widely held doctrine, has application only when one is dealing with a general concept or the meaning of a descriptive phrase: one can say that there are men who have squared the circle, or that there is one man who has done so, meaning that a concept or descriptive phrase applies to something, or that it applies to something and nothing else. On this analysis the notion of Being is to the last degree sophisticated and derivative: it would have its place at a much later stage of the Hegelian dialectic. Hegel's use of the term 'Being' to cover an approach of thought presupposed by all other determinations would seem, however, to have considerable justification. There is such a thing as the mere singling out, or the taking account, or the mere 'hailing' of something, which is presupposed by any act of classification or characterization. This is the sort of singling out that might be expressed by such words as 'Lo and behold this!' or 'Good heavens, that!' or simply by the use of a demonstrative word or phrase. Hegel in fact thinks that such an acknowledgement of mere Being always occurs at the level of simple sense-certainty.[1] And general references to something-or-other, or to everything-whatever, might similarly be held to involve something analogous to such a 'hailing' or singling out: we become, as it were mentally turned towards something, it is after a fashion there before us, and all subsequent classification and characterization merely fills out our original reference. Certainly there is a sense in which a prior acknowledge-

[1] *Phen.*, p. 82 (B., p. 150).

ment of mere Being could be said to be involved in all perception
and all thought.

From the mere acknowledgement of Being, which is the most
elementary of thinking approaches, Hegel now proceeds to work
out his famous triad of Being, Nothing, and Becoming with which
the Logic commences. If an acknowledgement of mere Being is
the first of thinking approaches, it is also the most completely
abstract: by its very nature it can involve no determination in its
references. If, however, we seek to arrest the acknowledgement
of Being at the stage now reached, and to prevent any further
movement towards determination, it will, Hegel thinks, 'pass
over into' or become indistinguishable from another very different
acknowledgment, that of mere Nothing or the absolute absence
of anything. This extremely abstract approach is of course one
not frequently met with in ordinary thought or experience: we
lament the lack of this or that definite determination (e.g. light,
sound, colour, etc.), or the absence of something thus or thus
determined, *not* the absence and lack of anything whatsoever.
And one is inclined to hold that while the mere acknowledgement
of Being might in a sense be said to be presupposed by all determinate references, the notion of the absence of anything would
presuppose the determinate references which it comprehensively
excludes. None the less, just as there are thoughts and experiences
which put *something* before us, without permitting us to determine
it further, so there are thoughts and experiences which rend from
us the whole world of our immediate concern, without putting
anything else in its place, and which may accordingly be said to
be concerned with *Nothing*, or with universal absence. And it is
Hegel's view that, if the two thinking approaches be arrested
at the stage just reached, it is no longer possible to lay one's
hand on any plain difference between them. Between a mere
Being which could be alternatively determined in an infinity of
ways, but which is *not* so determined, and a mere Nothing which
by its nature excludes all further determination, there is, says
Hegel, only a difference of intention (*meinen*): we intend or mean
our two notions to be different, but we are quite unable to say in
what their difference could consist. We are therefore involved in a
conflict. We intend Being and Nothing to be distinct, we feel
they *should* be distinct, and yet we are unable to keep them apart:
as far as their actual content goes, they seem one and the same.

This conflict demands a solution. We must progress to some new notion in which the arrested indeterminacy of mere Being, and the comprehensive negativity of mere Nothing, can in some way be brought together.

Hegel's treatment of Nothing as a possible object of thought will of course raise objection from modern logicians, who are very ready to suspect great thinkers of having fallen into trivial verbal traps. To say that something is true of nothing (it will be argued) is merely to say it is not true of anything: it is a sheer mistake to look on the word 'nothing' as the name of a peculiar entity or object of thought. There are, however, contexts in which the sheer absence of anything seems genuinely contemplated: it seems a perfectly valid notion, and one involved in recognizing the contingency of all that exists. And it would not seem wrong to turn such a universal absence into an *ens rationis* or object of higher order: the absence of all individuals is certainly no individual, but it may very well be treated as a 'thing' of some sort. And it is quite possible to have attitudes to this 'thing': the fear of universal nothingness is quite different from *not* being afraid of anything. In recent times Heidegger has gone further than Hegel in speaking of nothingness both in verbal and substantival terms, and in coupling these two modes of expression together in a sentence which sounds informative while being merely tautological (*das Nichts selbst nichtet*). Hegel has done nothing so misleading, and has moreover only used the idea of Nothing as a stepping-stone to other better-conceived ideas. There is of course *one* profound difference between pure Being and mere Nothing which Hegel has not fully recognized: pure Being is the most abstract and indefinite of notions, while sheer Nothing, which involves the *exclusion* of any and every determination, lies at the opposite pole of definiteness. What Hegel has shown is that indefiniteness artificially arrested becomes indistinguishable from a definiteness that is wholly negative.

Hegel finds a first reconciliation between abstract Being and mere nothing in the notion of Becoming (*Werden*). This notion is held to effect a compromise between Being and Nothing, while at the same time not obliterating their distinction. Where there is Becoming we have a Being on the point of passing into Nothing, or a state of Nothingness into which a state of Being has just passed, or (contrariwise) a state of Nothingness on the point of

turning into one of Being, or a state of Being into which Nothingness has just passed. This notion of Becoming does nothing,
however, to remedy the *emptiness* which is alike characteristic of
pure Being and all-exclusive Nothing: it becomes, perhaps, a
two-edged, vibrant emptiness, but it remains as void of content
as ever. And if this emptiness was a good reason for confounding
pure Being with mere Nothing, it is also a good reason for confounding Becoming with either. Moreover, as Hegel indicates,
the kind of union between Being and Nothing involved in Becoming is inherently uneasy and unstable: it involves a perpetual
borderline hesitation or vacillation between notions, which never
settles down to a harmonious compromise. Hegel is not wrong in
pointing out that our thought hates borderline or transitional
situations, that it is averse to anything that would now be called
a three-valued logic, and that it seeks to break up its subject-
matter into mutually exclusive aspects or phases, so that the
conceptual position of anything is immediately clear.

Hegel now tells us that 'the Being in Becoming which is one
with Nothing, as well as the Nothing which is one with Being are
only vanishing factors' and that the vanishing of these factors
is also the vanishing of Becoming, or the vanishing of vanishing
itself. Becoming, he says, is 'an unsteady unrest which sinks
together into a restful result', it 'falls together through its inner
contradictions into a unity in which both Being and Nothing are
superseded'.[1] This result he calls *Daseyn* or Determinate Being.
The result may seem meagre, and its derivation obscure, but
what Hegel has really shown is that it is only in a *differentiated*
world, with a certain amount of *hard, constant detail* that thought
or language can have purchase or application. A featureless
positivity or negativity, or a featureless flux in which emergence
coincides with disappearance, could afford no foothold for further
conceptual progress (and hence not for spiritual self-consciousness).

Hegel has often been condemned for introducing so empirical,
so temporal a notion as Becoming to heal the breach between two
timeless categories. In a sequence of pure notions, it is contended,
no such empirical borrowings should be admitted. On our view
there can be no substance in such a contention. The Dialectic
must loose its knots in creative fashion, and if it does so by borrow-

[1] *L. Log.*, p. 215 (W., p. 169); *Sc. of Log.*, p. 119 (J. & S., pp. 118–19; M., p. 106).

ing some notion from a richer context, there can be nothing amiss. It is, moreover, not clear that the 'Becoming' here discussed by Hegel, like the 'Development' and 'Process' characteristic of the whole dialectic, is a concept only having application to things in time. Plainly it applies as much to timeless mathematical and qualitative variation, to the point at which a curve reverses its direction, or at which one colour passes over into another. One may, moreover, baulk at the whole suggestion that something so much of the warp and woof of our notions and ways of speaking as are time and tense, can profitably be regarded as being merely empirical or contingent. We may abstract from time and things temporal for certain limited purposes, but our notions are all framed to deal with them, and could have no sense if such abstractions could not once more be undone. This is precisely what Hegel is here trying to show.

III DETERMINATE BEING, THE BAD AND GOOD INFINITES, BEING-FOR-SELF

So far Hegel has shown that the abstract acknowledgement or thought of Being (*Seyn*) can only be sustained if it can be expanded into an acknowledgement or thought of a *Daseyn* or Determinate Being: a Being arrested in mere Being, like the Being of the Eleatics, is self-destroying and absurd. *Daseyn*, says Hegel, is 'determinate being: its determinateness is a determination which has being, i.e. Quality. Through its Quality, something is opposed to others, is mutable and finite, and not merely opposed to an other, but negatively determined in relation to it.'[1] Etymologically, Hegel points out, *Daseyn* means being at some definite place, but this reference to place is here inappropriate. The sort of being involved in *Daseyn* is that of something picked out from an environing background, which is whatever the thing picked out is not, and which performs, in co-operative, complementary fashion, the antithetical role previously performed by mere Nothing, or the exclusion of Being in general.

Hegel now points out, without showing dialectically why this must be so—and tacitly accepting the Identity of Indiscernibles— that the picking out or pinning down of a *Daseyn* is not possible unless what we pin down has some *qualitative colouring*: though

[1] *Sc. of Log.*, I, p. 122 (J. & S., I, p. 121; M., p. 109).

we may not recognize a detachable universal present in a particular instance, yet the thing picked out must in some obscure way assert itself as such and such against an ambient background from which such a qualification is lacking. Hegel likes to envisage even such a purely logical situation in terms of the mystical categories of a Jakob Boehme, by whom having a quality is seen as an activity, a *Qualirung* or *Inqualirung* of the qualified object, which must struggle to maintain itself against a swamping environment. Determinate Being, at one with the quality that it sports, is called by Hegel a Something (*Etwas*). A Something is said to be the first 'Negation of the Negation', i.e. it is what it is by asserting itself against the denying otherness of the environment. It is this Something which the Dialectic will seek to develop into a Someone, and ultimately into a Someone who is also Everyone.

Hegel now proceeds to show that the distinction between a Something qualified in a certain manner, and a background lacking its qualification, must of necessity be variable and shifting. It must be possible to make the background one's centre of reference, and the original Something one's background. In principle it must be possible to select indefinitely many points as one's centre of reference, all else being relegated to the periphery. Language recognizes this principle, Hegel points out, in the varied applicability of the demonstrative pronoun 'this': the symmetry of the situation is even more plainly brought out in the Latin use of *aliud-aliud*, or of *alterum-alterum*, as correlatives. Hegel is saying, what is both arguable and acceptable, that we can only talk significantly of something qualified in one way, in so far as it can be set over against other things otherwise qualified, which themselves permit of precisely the same treatment. How *many* such distinct entities we shall be able to pick out is of course an empirical matter, but in principle there will be indefinitely many such entities. Hegel further maintains that in all such entities there will be two necessarily connected aspects: they will all have a Being-in-self (*Ansichseyn*), and a Being-for-another (*Seyn für Anderes*). It will be by what is most intimately their own that they will be set off against others, and it will be by being set off against others that certain qualities will be most intimately their own. Even coloured patches show something of that life of mutual violence and accommodation which comes to fruition in human society.

Hegel now proceeds to argue (though rather by implication than straightforward statement) that, though we cannot as yet distinguish an object into an inner, underlying nature, and properties which attach to the same—this sort of elaboration will occur later in the Doctrine of Essence—we can none the less distinguish in it definite Determinatenesses (*Bestimmtheiten*), which come out by comparison with other things, and a general inner Determination (*Bestimmung*) which will remain the same in all comparisons. And he suggests further, that a thing picked out by a definite reference is in principle variable in quality: though the picking out which identifies it, and the qualitative colouring which makes possible this picking out, are sides in a single approach, they are none the less sides capable of independent variation. 'In so far as Something changes,' Hegel remarks, 'the change falls in its state (*Beschaffenheit*), which is that in the Something which becomes other. The Something preserves itself in the change, which only affects the unsteady surface of its other-being, not its inner Determination. Determination and State are therefore distinct: Something in its Determination is indifferent to its state.'[1] It therefore makes sense to say of the same Something that it is first thus and now is thus, or that it has it in itself to be qualified in ways in which it is not now qualified. (Some commentators have thought that, because there is no distinction at this level between underlying thing and superficial properties, Hegel could not have thought of his 'Somethings' as having qualitative variability. This is, however, ruled out by the above statements, and is not really incompatible with the *Encyclopaedia* statement that 'in the sphere of Being when Something becomes another, the Something vanishes'.)

Having developed the notion of the Something to this point, Hegel now says that the determinate character of a thing is in a sense a Limit (*Grenze*) to it, that it sets bounds to its more widely ranging *Bestimmung* or Determination. Since the character of each thing is brought out by the other things to which it is opposed, the Limit which gives it its character is indifferently a Limit to these other things as well. In the great web of the world each constituent brings out each other constituent's colour or savour, and a thing may be hindered from filling all its characteristic roles by the fact that other things have taken them up. It is the

[1] *Sc. of Log.*, I, p. 41 (J. & S., I, p. 136; M., p. 124).

nature therefore of a *Daseyn*, a Determinate Being, to be finite, alterable and perishable. It must be hemmed in by things which bring out only some of its inner characters, must be capable of changing to situations where it will be otherwise qualified, and of encountering situations that will remove it altogether. Hegel goes further and characterizes a *Daseyn* in Kantian or Fichtean fashion, as a thing eternally subject both to a Barrier (*Schranke*) and to an Obligation (*Sollen*). As being obliged to be *A*, it is subject to a barrier in being *B*, and it only has a barrier in being *B* because it is obliged to be *A*. It is both true of finite things that they *can* be certain things because they ought to be them, also that they cannot be certain things because they ought to be them (i.e. it is only when they are debarred from being them that they can have an obligation to be them). All this shows how much Hegel conceived of the world on anthropomorphic and personal lines: the most insignificant patch of colour is for him an analogue of self-conscious Spirit. But apart from the merits of such a treatment, Hegel's arguments rest on the solid basis of the inexpugnable relativism, the demand for contrast, characteristic both of perception and thought.

Hegel now shows how the notion of Finite Being just arrived at necessarily pushes on beyond itself into a notion of *Infinite Being*, which first appears in a form which is inadequate, false and bad, and which develops into a form which is adequate, positive and true. The notion of the Infinite necessarily arises as the negation of the Finite: in the notion of a finite thing, as we have indicated, is contained the notion of an indefinite world of other things, otherwise qualified, lying beyond its barriers. One cannot indeed conceive of a barrier as a barrier without in thought passing beyond it. The notion of the Infinite is in fact simply the notion of Indeterminate Being, which has reasserted itself, in intensified form, in contrast to the limitation involved in Determinate Being. It is, says Hegel, 'the nature of the finite itself, to pass beyond itself, to negate its own negation, and to become infinite'.[1]

If, however, we do pass beyond the barriers which limit one finite object, the horizon at once narrows. In rising above one set of limitations, we have merely taken on others. We cannot think of what is other than one definite sort of thing without thinking

[1] *Sc. of Log.*, I, p. 158 (J. & S., I, p. 151; M., p. 138).

of other definite sorts of thing, which are as limited as the first. If we now try to rise above our new barriers the process will be repeated: we shall have what Hegel calls a reciprocal determination (*Wechselbestimmung*) between Finite and Infinite, in which, while there is a perpetual endeavour to pass beyond the Finite, the Finite always manages to reassert itself. Hegel maintains, further, that the very fact that the Infinite is thought of as lying beyond the Finite, and as being exclusive of it, makes the Infinite finite, bounded by what it excludes. The notion of the Infinite here arrived at is called by Hegel the 'Bad Infinite'. Like the notion of Becoming, it involves an inherent, unresolved contradiction, a quest for something that for ever eludes it. 'This Bad Infinity', Hegel remarks, 'is the same in itself as the ever-recurring ought, it is indeed the negation of the finite, but in truth it cannot free itself therefrom. The finite reappears in it as its other, since this Infinite only is infinite in relation to what is finite. The progress into infinity is accordingly only the self-repeating monotony of one and the same tedious alternation of this finite and infinity.'[1] This Bad Infinite must be developed into a True Infinite, which will not engage in this tedious game of abolishing and reinstating barriers.

Modern thought concerning the infinite would accept Hegel's general viewpoint: that the infinite, as something genuinely transcending the finite, cannot be reached along the same serial route as the finite notions of which it represents the negation. There is no *last* member to a series of enlarging finites, and the infinite can accordingly not be reached by pursuing such a series to its *end*. By a subtle switch of thought, which Hegel would certainly have envied and adopted, had it been known in his time, modern thought, inspired by the genius of Cantor, sees the infinite as an attribute or number *of* the whole series of enlarging finites, although it is not in any sense *in* them or among them. (The number, e.g., *of* the natural numbers is infinite, though infinity is not a number *in* the natural number series.) Hegel, however, knowing nothing of Cantor, sought his 'True Infinite' in another direction.

The True or Affirmative Infinite, according to Hegel, cannot represent the mere negation of the Finite, since this would involve a simple contradiction. Being exclusive of, and beyond the

[1] *Sc. of Log.*, I, p. 164 (J. & S., I, p. 155; M., p. 142).

Finite, it would itself be finite. Nor can it be a mere uneasy see-saw or self-cancelling union between finite and infinite, since such a notion would itself be self-cancelling. Rather must it represent a kind of union 'which is not an external bringing together of these aspects, nor an improper connection contrary to their nature, in which opposed, separated, mutually independent entities are incompatibly combined. Rather must each element be in itself the unity, and this only as an overcoming of self, in which neither element has the prerogative over the other, either as regards being-in-itself or determinate positive being. As shown previously, finitude exists only as a passing beyond itself: the infinite, its own other, is therefore contained in itself. And similarly infinity only exists as the going beyond the finite: it therefore contains its other, and so is in itself its own other. The finite is not overcome by the infinite as by an externally existent might, but it is its own infinity whereby it transcends itself.'[1]

The outcome of all this confusing and repetitive talk is tolerably plain: the True Infinite may indifferently be described as an infinity-in-finitude or as a finitude-in-infinity. True Infinity has application, not to a thing as having *no* definite qualitative or other limits, but to a thing as having it 'in it' to pass beyond any and every limit, and also as having the limits it has *in order* to have such an unlimited destination. *True Infinity is, in short, simply finitude essentially associated with free variability.* A mathematical or logical formula is 'infinite' in the Hegelian sense since it admits of an indefinite number of valid substitutions. I, the subject, am likewise truly infinite, since I can, without prejudice to my identity, imagine myself in anyone and everyone's shoes, and conceive myself as having any and every sort of experience. True Infinity, Hegel says in the *Encyclopaedia*, consists not in any progress into infinity, but 'in being by oneself in one's other' or in 'coming to oneself in one's other'. Hegel further says that, in his True Infinite, the element of Infinity will absorb and over-come the Finite, but he might equally well have put it the other way round. What he genuinely believes in is the Beyond brought down to the Here and Now, the Infinite which transfigures the Finite. For an all-inclusive Spinozistic infinite he has absolutely no place.

From True Infinity Hegel passes without a genuine transition to 'Being-for-self' (*Fürsichseyn*), which is also described as

[1] *Sc. of Log.*, I, p. 169 (J. & S., I, p. 159; M., pp. 145–6).

Infinite Being. If Pure Being was wholly indeterminate, and *Daseyn* represented Being as subject to limitation or negation, Being-for-self represents Being which has successfully negated limitation or negation, and which may accordingly be described as the 'negation of the negation'. Hegel somewhat confuses the issue by giving as his example of Being-for-self the advanced case of self-consciousness. 'We know ourselves as existents, as in the first place distinguished from other existents, and related to them. But we further know the breadth of existence as drawn together in a point, as it were, in the simple form of Being-for-self. When we say "I" this word is the expression of an infinite and at the same time negative self-reference.'[1] It is plain, however, that the mathematical unit, to which Hegel immediately passes, is as good an example of Being-for-self. It has on the one hand the finitude of *Daseyn*, Determinate Being, but it has also the indefinite variability, the indifference to qualitative content, which represents a return to Pure Being. When a mathematician deals with a unit, he can at once be said to be dealing with one definite thing, and also with anything and everything.

The remainder of the section on Being-for-self may be regarded as a transition to the mathematical categories of Quantity which occupy the second division of the Doctrine of Being. After some obscure manœuvres, happily omitted in the *Encyclopaedia*, Being-for-self is explicitly identified with the notion of a Unit (*Eins*). Once this has occurred, the otherness which formed the background and foil of qualified being reappears at a higher level as the background to the Pure Unit, which has been wholly emptied of qualifications. This background, like the background of qualified *Daseyn*, soon splits itself into a variety of units, which will all have the same empty Being-for-self as the first unit. In other words, one cannot form the notion of a unit, without thinking of it in contrast to a background of countless other exactly similar possible units. In rising from qualified sensuous objects to the Platonic *Mathematica*, one may rise to what is purged of sensuous content: they will however preserve a vestige of sensuous exclusiveness in that there will be many of them alike.

Hegel unfortunately complicates his treatment at this point by mixing up his consideration of the abstract beginnings of *Mengenlehre* with discussions of ancient atomism, of the Leibnizian

[1] *L. Log.*, p. 227 (W., p. 179).

monadology and of the Kantian conception of the physical world as consisting of centres of attractive and repulsive force. The Pure Unit is said to involve the Void as the non-being which negates it and surrounds it—the Pythagoreans too held that the void kept their mathematical units apart—and this provides an opportunity for transforming the ancient doctrine which made the Void the source of movement into the Hegelian view that the true negativity of the Infinite is the ground of all becoming. In the same way the necessity for the being of a unit, of the other units which form its foil, is transformed into a universal, separating *Repulsion*, which, since it involves the same unitary character in whatever it separates, is straightway transformed into an equally universal *Attraction*. The whole treatment allows Hegel to fit in an interesting discussion of the inadequacies of Kant's *Metaphysical Foundations of Natural Science*, which would be irrelevant in any but a dialectical system.

Being-for-self, from being the notion of a single unit, has therefore developed itself into an indefinitely extensible procedure of positing exactly similar, mutually exclusive units, i.e. into the notions fundamental for Quantity. Hegel writes, with somewhat more than his usual murkiness, that 'the Unit as infinite to itself, i.e. the unit as posited negation of negation referring to self, is the mediation whereby it repels itself from itself as its own absolute, i.e. abstract, other-being (the many). Inasmuch as it relates itself negatively to this its non-being, it overcomes the latter and becomes thereby no more than a relation to itself. . . . This overcoming which is determined merely as a relative overcoming, as a relation to other determinate being, which is itself only indifferent repulsion and attraction, shows itself as passing over into the unending relation of mediation through the negation of external relations from what is immediately there, and as having as result precisely the process just mentioned, which, in the unsteadiness of its moments, is a sinking or coming together into simple immediacy. This being, with the determination just acquired, is Quantity.'[1]

IV   QUANTITY, NUMBER AND QUANTITATIVE INFINITY

The section on Quantity which follows is one of the longest in Hegel's *Science of Logic*, much of it consisting of notes on the

---

[1] *Sc. of Log.*, I, p. 209 (J. & S., I, pp. 190–1; M., p. 177).

mathematics of his time, the differential calculus being treated very fully. The triadic dialectical arrangement has considerable artificiality, and is different from the *Encyclopaedia* treatment. Very often the exposition gains by ignoring it.

Hegel defines pure Quantity, at the outset, as 'Being-for-self overcome'. In it the unit, which by its notion distinguishes itself from other units, and is therefore said to 'repel' them, is also by its notion so *like* the other units which are opposed to it, that it may be said to 'attract' them, to join on to them or coalesce with them. 'The absolute brittleness of the repelling unit', Hegel tells us, 'has melted away into this unity, which, as containing this unit, and determined at the same time by its own inherent repulsion, is, as unity with outside being, also unity with itself.' Being-for-self was 'by its nature the self-overcoming relation to self, a perpetual coming out of self. But what is pushed forth is itself; its repulsion is therefore its own creative forth-flowing. On account of the self-sameness of what is thus repulsed, this discerning is unbroken continuity which, by virtue of its forth-coming, and without being interrupted, is at the same time plurality, which just as immediately remains in equality with self'.[1] The notion of Quantity therefore involves an essential *discreteness* or apartness of units, which is the old 'Repulsion' less animistically renamed: it also involves an essential *continuity* or absence of break in passing from one unit to another, which is the successor of the old 'Attraction'.

Hegel says that the notion of Quantity just reached has many empirical exemplifications. Both space and time are said to be 'extensions, pluralities, which are a going out of self, a streaming', which however only succeeds in perpetual self-reproduction. Pure Quantity is likewise exemplified in matter, which is indeed no more than the 'outer existence' of which pure Quantity is the abstract 'thought-determination'. Hegel quotes with approval Leibniz's dictum *Non omnino improbabile est materiam et quantitatem esse realiter idem.* He also quotes with approval Spinoza's view of real Quantity as *infinita, unica et indivisibilis*, which is to be contrasted with the Quantity of imagination which is *finita, divisibilis et ex partibus conflata*. It is clear, however, that Hegel's picture of Quantity has a dynamic, flowing character quite absent from the idea of Spinoza. Hegelian Quantity is infinite

[1] *Sc. of Log.*, I, pp. 222–3 (J. & S., I, pp. 201–2; M., pp. 187–8).

only in the sense of being indefinitely and freely extensible, not in the sense of being indivisible and complete.

Continuity and discreteness are therefore aspects inseparably united in the Hegelian notion of Quantity. Wherever Quantity applies to anything there are distinguishable units, and there is also a unity in which they are held together. Hegel holds, however, that the notion of Quantity is such as to differentiate itself into two distinct forms, in one of which Continuity is prominent while Discreteness is prominent in the other. The reasoning which leads to the distinguishing of these two species is more than usually lacking in cogency. The two aspects of Quantity (Hegel argues) must be united into a coherent, solid unity and this means that Quantity must be continuous. On the other hand, Continuous Magnitude is Quantity in its first immediate form, and Quantity, that most subtle of notions, is anything but immediate. In so far as it overcomes its immediacy, it therefore returns with an additional stress on the unit of which it is the development, and is accordingly Discrete Quantity.[1] Argumentation apart, Hegel points out how the space in a room, which is usually considered an example of purely Continuous Magnitude, can none the less be broken up into distinct feet and inches, whereas a hundred men, a salient example of purely Discrete Magnitude, are rendered continuous by the humanity which runs through them all. What comes out here is that there is no place in Hegelianism for any of the hard-and-fast independence maintained in certain forms of pluralistic realism. To be separate or independent is, in the Hegelian view of things, merely a pose, a stress, which depends on the background it tries to treat as irrelevant. From this point of view there is no profound difference between the close adjunction which binds feet into a furlong and the ideal affinity which sorts men into a group or collection. Hegel considers in this connection Kant's treatment of his second antinomy, where a one-sided stress on the moment of discreteness leads to the diremption of all extended substances into ultimate simple parts, while an equally one-sided stress on its moment of continuity leads to a denial of real simplicity anywhere. In reality, on Hegel's view, simple unity is to be met with at all levels, but is as ready, on the slightest consideration, to dissolve into an assemblage of mutually external parts.

[1] Sc. of Log., I, p. 239 (J. & S., pp. 213–14; M., pp. 199–200).

From the notion of Quantity in general, Hegel passes to the notion of Quantum, a quantity specified as so-and-so-much-and-no-greater by a particular limit or boundary. Obviously, wherever Quantity has application, some specific quantity will also have application: so much is involved in the very idea of pure Quantity, though Hegel manages to wrap up this logical fact in two paragraphs of the murkiest prose. We therefore proceed to study the development of the notion of Quantity into a system of distinct specific Quanta. At this point Hegel introduces the category of Number, which is for him simply the carrying of Quantity up to a certain point and no further: it makes no difference whether the Quantity so limited be discrete or continuous. Different numbers arise (as in the semi-Pythagorean later teaching of Plato) by the imposition of Limit or Unity on indefinitely expansible (and contractible) Quantity: Quantity carried so far will be fiveness-in-number, so far sixness or six-and-a-halfness, all the indefinitely numerous stopping-places being different ways of arbitrarily limiting the flow of Quantity. Numerical concepts further involve two aspects called by Hegel Unity (*Einheit*) and Amount (*Anzahl*): whatever they cover is a unitary whole, but is also broken up into subordinate units, whose successive recognition is presupposed by the concept in question. Hegel regards the many-dimensional development of geometrical figures as merely a development of numerical concepts: it is not clear whether he is here being advanced or naïve.

Numerical concepts are further said by Hegel to be inert and indifferent: they have therefore to be activated from without, and brought into relation with one another. The modes in which they are so brought into relation are the arithmetical operations of adding, subtracting, multiplying, dividing, raising to powers, and extracting of roots, of which Hegel gives complex but not very interesting accounts. There is interest in his view that it is only *in* such operations that numbers reveal any sense that thought can deal with and seize: apart from such operations they would offer us nothing for contemplation. There is also interest in his view that what issues from such operations does not deserve to be called 'synthetic' in the sense made current by Kant. Kant held that however much we might analyse the notion of the sum of 7 and 5, we should never be able to discover the concept 12 in it: this concept had to be joined *synthetically* to that of 7 + 5 by such procedures as picturing seven fingers and then adding five extra ones to them. As against Kant, Hegel holds that the arithmetical operations reveal nothing beyond what they involve as operations: we merely apply them and that is all. 'The sum of 5 and 7', Hegel says, 'means the unthinking combination of both numbers, and the unthinking continued counting from seven on until five are exhausted can be called a putting together, a synthesis in the literal sense, exactly like counting from one on. But such a "synthesis" is of entirely analytic nature, inasmuch as the connection of the items is quite artificial, and there is nothing in it or added to it, but what lies before one in an entirely external manner. The demand to add 5 to 7 is related to the general demand to count, as the demand to lengthen a straight line is related to the demand to draw it.'[1] Hegel thinks that the necessary truths of geometry are analytic in precisely the same fashion: there is, e.g., no synthesis, no going beyond our notion, in establishing a straight line to be the shortest distance between two points. Straightness in a line entails absolute simplicity, but it also entails spatiality, which is indistinguishable from Quantity in general. The absolutely simple predicated of a Quantum yields the notion of the least, and the least predicated of a line means the shortest.[2]

Hegel thus agrees with much modern thought in holding mathematical, particularly arithmetical, judgements to be analytic of the concepts involved in them, but he does not agree that, in being thus analytic, they are also important and revealing. He indulges in a certain amount of denigration of mathematics, which has reacted on his own reputation: it is said to be opposed to the genuine conceptual grasp of any matter, to represent thought at its last gasp of self-externalization (*aüsserste Entaüsserung*), to move in an atmosphere of unthinkingness, and to exploit connections devoid of any genuine necessity. Since it is the form of thought closest to the mutual outsideness of things of sense, it will appeal most to those childish minds (e.g. the Pythagoreans) who are just beginning to rise from sense to thought. Plato, he says, was right in placing the objects of mathematics *between* those of sense and thought. Mathematical reasoning, is further, so mechanical a matter that it could well be carried on by a

---

[1] *Sc. of Log.*, I, pp. 249–50 (J. & S., I, pp. 222–3; M., pp. 207–8).
[2] *Sc. of Log.*, I, p. 250 (J. & S., I, pp. 223–4; M., pp. 208–9).

machine. Those who try to give mathematics the supreme place in education are aiming at the wholesale mechanization of mind.[1]

Hegel now proceeds to say something about the distinction between *Extensive* and *Intensive* Magnitudes (or Quanta). This is the distinction between a Quantum involving a plurality of parts in itself, and a Quantum involving a mere 'moreness', which is not based on such a plurality. Such an intensive Quantum is what is also called a 'Degree'. The new distinction, Hegel points out, is not the same as the previous distinction between Discrete and Continuous Magnitude. That was a distinction which affected Quantity in general, whereas the new distinction only affects Quanta. There are, moreover, Extensive Quanta which are discrete and others which are continuous. The real novelty lies in the introduction of the notion of Degree. This introduction is effected in a singularly murky manner: Number is said to undergo an 'introversion' in the course of which the mutual externality and indifference of separate units 'vanishes in the unit as a relation of number to itself. The limit of Quantum which, as external, had its existent determinateness in the self-external Amount, passes over into simple determinateness. In this simple determinateness of the limit it is intensive magnitude, and the limit or determination which is identical with Quantum is now also posited as simple: it is Degree.'[2] Hegel, like Plato, would appear to be saying that a numerical concept, *qua* concept, i.e. as 'introverted', is not properly to be thought of as made up of addible units, as are the sets to which it applies, and that its relations to other numerical concepts are intensive and ordinal, not extensive. He maintains, however, that there is not the plain difference between Degree and Extensive Magnitude that we are at first inclined to suppose. If an Extensive Magnitude is determined by its relation to an internal assemblage of parts in the things it applies to, an Intensive Magnitude is determined by its relation to an external assemblage of other Intensive Magnitudes. Hegel points out, further, how many cases of magnitude have an extensive as well as an intensive aspect. The mass of a body has an extensive aspect as being made up of so many pounds, etc., while it has an intensive aspect in respect of the pressure it exerts. Warmth has

[1] *Sc. of Log.*, I, p. 261 (J. & S., I, p. 232; M., pp. 216–17).
[2] *Sc. of Log.*, I, pp. 263–4 (J. & S., p. 233; M., p. 218).

intensive magnitude as a sensation, and extensive magnitude as measured by the rise of mercury. Brightness, a case of intensive magnitude, has extensive magnitude in respect of the distance from which it can be seen, etc. etc. Hegel has been successful in showing that the two sorts of magnitude are 'identical' in the sense of having essential and important relations to each other. It is certainly our fixed policy in regard to Intensive Magnitudes (and in that sense part of their content) to try to tie up what is intensive with what is measurable and extensive. And every magnitude which rests on a multiplicity of parts can also be treated as indivisible and intensive.

Hegel now goes on to develop the notion of *Quantitative Infinity*, a notion parallel to the Qualitative Infinity previously dealt with. The notion has been implicit in Hegel's whole treatment of Quantity, and nothing that has been said in regard to the distinction between Continuous and Discrete Quantity, Intensive and Extensive Magnitude, or the different sorts of arithmetical operation has much relevance to it. The needs of the dialectical method have forced Hegel to traverse a continuous logical path, where a number of divergent tracks would best have covered the conceptual terrain. This appears, too, in the fact that in the *Encyclopaedia* Quantitative Infinity derives from the notion of Degree, whereas, in the *Science of Logic*, it derives equally from Extensive and Intensive Magnitude.

The notion of Quantity readily develops into that of Quantitative Infinity since the limit which marks off one Quantum from what lies beyond it is an arbitrary limit, since the Quanta beyond the limit are quite of a piece with those on *this* side of it, and therefore invite us to push the limit further and further without stop or stay. As Hegel says: 'A Quantum is posited as in absolute continuity with its externality, its other-being. It is not therefore merely *possible* for it to pass beyond every determinate magnitude, not merely *possible* for it to be changed, rather it is posited [i.e. implied in the notion] that it *must* so change. The quantitative determination continues itself in such a manner in its other-being, that it has its being merely in this continuity with what is other; it is not a boundary which exists, but one that becomes. . . . Quantum therefore sends itself beyond itself. . . . The limit which again arises in such going beyond, is simply one which supersedes itself and sends itself on to a further limit and so on into the infinite.'[1] The tendency of Quanta to push beyond their limits operates (as in the parallel doctrines of Plato) in *both* directions: Quanta tend by their nature to indefinite *increase*, but they tend equally to indefinite *diminution*. Hegel's language of dynamic conceptual growth is perhaps confusing and undesirable, as is also his statement that such growth is a matter of necessity, not merely of possibility. But by the endless growth of one notion of definite magnitude into another he means no more than that all such notions are parts of a single, indefinitely extensible system, and by the necessity of such growth he means no more than that membership of such a system is implied by their notional content. These surely are acceptable views.

The Quantitative Progression into Infinity is, however, for Hegel, yet another case of the self-contradictory or 'Bad' Infinite. It represents a conceptual task to which no execution corresponds. What our thought is *endeavouring* to compass is something that will bring to an end the endless slipperiness of our quantitative concepts, that will finish this off in the notion of a Small that permits of no further diminution, or of a Great which permits of no further increase. Both these ideals are, however, inherently self-contradictory: we no longer have Quantity when all possibility of increase or diminution is removed.[2] It can only be by some transformation in our quantitative notions, or by some passage into other notions not purely quantitative, that the demands of our thought can be met. In all this it will be plain that the real contradiction which produces this dialectical unrest lies not in the variable boundaries of our quantitative concepts: to one content with such intrinsic variability there would be nothing self-contradictory to stomach. The real contradiction lies in the conflict between such variability, and the ideal of what is internally rounded off and complete, an ideal which can in the last resort only be realized in the 'Idea', the notion of self-conscious Spirit. Without a persistent sense of Hegel's final goal, we cannot see why he finds inadequacies and contradictions along the path.

Hegel comments characteristically on the notion that there is something sublime and awful in Quantitative Infinity: 'the only really awful thing about it', he remarks, 'is the awful wearisomeness'. The true infinite only becomes present to a man when he

[1] *Sc. of Log.*, I, p. 272 (J. & S., I, pp. 240–1; M., p. 225).
[2] *Sc. of Log.*, I, pp. 275–6 (J. & S., I, pp. 293–4; M., pp. 227–8).

turns his back on such an idle endless progress. Hegel, unassisted by Cantor's work (as remarked before), was not able to conceive of a complete infinite predicable of, without being contained in, the Quantitative Infinite Progression. He was therefore bound to find the True Infinite in a self-understanding, freely variable finite which has simply foresworn the vain advance towards infinity. As remarked before, there is no connection in Hegel's thought between infinity and the all-comprehensiveness of some total system. 'Infinity in a grain of sand and Eternity in an hour' are the only Infinity and Eternity to which Hegelianism can attach any meaning.

The first of Hegel's three long notes on the infinite and infinitesimal, which follows the treatment of quantitative concepts in the *Science of Logic*, abounds in interest and illumination. Here we can only note that the emergence of True Infinity in the quantitative sphere is seen in such fractional ratios as $2/7$ which retain their identity for an indefinite number of possible substitutions, e.g. $4/14$, $6/21$, etc. etc. Infinity is still better represented by a variable fraction like a/b, which admits of an even wider range of substitutions. These passages plainly equate 'True Infinity' with free variability. The contrast between the True and False Infinites is even more plain, according to Hegel, when we equate $2/7$ with its indefinitely extensible decimal expansion $0.285714\ldots$. Ordinary thought sees the Infinite in the decimal expansion, but this is only the False Infinite: the True Infinite is the well-rounded formula $2/7$, which the decimal expansion seeks in vain to equal. Hegel has also much that is interesting to say in regard to the meaning of differential coefficients like dx/dy, expressions important for their influence on his own system, where the notion of a 'vanishing moment' or a 'vanishing distinction' is of such constant occurrence. Hegel is clear that the component expressions in the whole coefficient dx/dy have no meaning in isolation, that they are incomplete symbols, having a sense only as *together* expressing the *principle* of various definite quantitative relationships.[1] The rise from particular quantitative relations to the notion involved in such a differential coefficient resembles the rise from the particularity of empirical existences to the pure concept which is their essence. 'The difference inasmuch as it is no longer the difference of finite magnitude has ceased to be a plurality within

[1] *Sc. of Log.*, I, p. 310 (J. & S., I, p. 269; M., p. 253).

itself: it has sunk together into simple intensity, into the determinateness of one qualitative moment in a relationship to another.'[1]

In all the discussions outlined Hegel has given us nothing like a systematic treatment of the notions and issues central to a philosophy of mathematics. He has rather thrown out a large number of illuminating *aperçus* on all sorts of points, for which the Dialectic furnishes a not always very helpful connecting thread.

V   QUANTITATIVE RATIO AND MEASURE

We shall now deal, in the last section of this chapter, with Hegel's treatment of *Quantitative Ratio*, the last division in the dialectic of Quantity, and with the ensuing treatment of *Measure* (*Maass*), which is notionally continuous with it. The Quantitative Infinite Progression has shown us quantitative concepts expanding and multiplying in an essentially self-frustrating and unprofitable manner, snatching after an exhaustiveness and a finality that cannot be adequately compassed. In the conceptual sphere about to be entered quantitative concepts have only a *relative* application: their function is not to assess quantities absolutely, nor to push on to infinites and infinitesimals, but to illuminate things by the ways in which their various quantitative aspects stand to *one another*, and to the quantitative aspects of other things. Here thought may hope to achieve a poised and stable wholeness which it will never compass in the purely quantitative sphere. 'The Quantitative Infinite Progress', Hegel tells us, 'appears at first to be a continuous extrusion of number beyond itself. But a closer treatment shows Quantity returning to self in this progress, since what is really present in it as regards thought, is the general determination of number by number. And this gives the Quantitative Ratio.'[2] The *futile* reference of one Quantum to another and yet another, which is characteristic of the Progression towards Infinity, is here simply superseded by the *fruitful* reference of one Quantum to a second, which is in turn referred back to the first, each sustaining and giving each other significance, and keeping out the dark night of all other quantitative concepts, into which we may but *need* not enter. In this 'supersession' there is no shade of what would ordinarily be called an argument:

[1] *Sc. of Log.*, I, p. 332 (J. & S., I, pp. 286–7; M., p. 270).
[2] *L. Log.*, p. 251 (W., p. 199).

we have only a general aspiration or direction of thought, and a feeling that one notion satisfies it better than another. Hegel feels that the true function of mathematical conceptions is not to enable us to make senseless statements as to how big things are, how often they occur, etc. etc.—the sort of data accumulated by the universal tourist—but rather to recapture and reconstruct the individuality or quality of things in terms of various quantitative concepts. 'The members of the animal organism have a measure, which as a simple quantum stands in a proportion to the other quanta of the other members: the proportions of the human body are the fixed ratios of such quanta. Natural science has still much to discern concerning the connection of such magnitudes with the organic functions on which they wholly depend.'[1] The notions of mathematics therefore perform their highest service in enabling us to understand and to analyse what to an immediate view seems simply qualitative.

Quantitative Ratio is divided by Hegel into three subsections, which are alleged to represent a dialectical advance: these are Direct Ratio, Inverse Ratio and Ratio of Powers. In a Direct Ratio two magnitudes increase and diminish together in a constant proportion, e.g. 2/7. In an Indirect Ratio the increase of the one is more organically bound up with the decrease of the other so as to yield always a constant product. In a Ratio of Powers the one is a square or some other higher power of the other, its superiority lying in the multiplication of self by self, in which Hegel probably sees an anticipation of self-consciousness. There is not a little of neo-Pythagoreanism in Hegel's treatment of ratios: we are reminded of the identification of the number 4 with 'justice' because in it the doubler is itself doubled. But undoubtedly Hegel's interest in Inverse Ratios and Ratios of Powers was due to their importance in physics.

The treatment of Ratio enables Hegel to pass from Quantity to Measure, a new phase of the Doctrine of Being in which Quantity and Quality are brought together and reconciled. At a previous stage of the Dialectic the variegated scheme of qualitative concepts broke down into the colourless diversity and monotonous extensibility of quantitative notions: the latter have likewise broken down in the Quantitative Infinite Progression. At the level of Measure we recapture the qualities liquidated in the homo-

[1] *Sc. of Log.*, II, p. 411 (J. & S., p. 350; M., pp. 331–2).

geneity of pure Quantity: these become related to various patterns of proportionate variation. Thus the simple qualitative notion of speed becomes based on a ratio between distance and time, heaviness becomes changed into a gravitational formula, the various sense-qualities becomes connected with patterns and rates of vibration, and even higher characters such as the forms of animal species, the expressions of faces and the styles of art and architecture, become connected, though less precisely, with characteristic sets of measures. Hegel does not object to this quantification of the qualitative: he thinks in fact that it has not gone far enough. But he is not enough of a Platonist to believe in the complete reducibility of Forms to Numbers. He holds that a *complete* quantification of the qualitative can be successful only at the mechanical level, where phenomena have the mutual externality which renders them amenable to such treatment. At the higher levels of inorganic, and *a fortiori* of organic nature, measure will be subordinated to other relations, and will not admit of perfect quantification. Hegel, we may observe, draws no distinction between cases where the relation of the qualitative to the quantitative is perspicuous to thought, as where the character of a face is seen to rest on certain ratios, and the quite different sort of case where it is opaque to thought, as where a colour is found to depend on certain rates of vibration. Cases of the second type would have been better dealt with in the two-level manner of the Doctrine of Essence.

Hegel does not, however, conceive that there is a Measure, a Quantified Quality, corresponding to *every* set of quantitative proportions: it corresponds, rather, to a *range* of such proportions. Within such a range there will be variations of Quantity to which no change in Quality corresponds: thus a man may lose hair without being recognized as bald, straws may be thrown down in succession without amounting to a heap, the proportions of a face or an organic body may be varied without altering its type, a note may be sharpened or flattened without reaching a different point on the scale, and a state may increase its territory or population without altering its essential constitution. At a certain point in such quantitative variation a change in quantitative ratio will, however, amount to a change in *Measure*, and the latter to a change in Quality: a new *sort* of thing will confront us in place of the old.

It seems plain that Hegel has here rightly set forth the way in which concepts which may roughly be called 'qualitative' and concepts which may be called 'quantitative' co-operate and interact. Qualitative distinctions are the broad, natural ways of aligning objects which are significant either from the point of view of immediate sensation or appetite, or from more detached intellectual or practical standpoints. Quantitative distinctions, on the other hand, are the distinctions which do not as such matter (whether from an immediate sensuous or detached rational standpoint), which are by their nature colourless and repetitive—'more and more of the same thing', 'the same thing over and over again', etc.—whose indefinite range of sub-variation in any case precludes intellectual or practical mastery. They will be the sort of distinctions which *may* be drawn in order to specify or analyse or explain what is interesting and qualitative, but which are not on their own account worth drawing. It is plain, by the very nature of the distinction just sketched, that qualitative concepts will be broader than quantitative ones, that the latter will multiply in the framework of the former, and that, while the former will vary by the large leaps and bounds necessary to understanding and practice, the latter will involve the indefinite refinement and continuity whose possibility is their essential supplement.

The detailed dialectical treatment of Measure in the *Science of Logic* is one of the most difficult and obscure of Hegel's writings: this is mainly the case because Hegel is trying to incorporate and digest the findings of the sciences of his own time, many of which are irrelevant to his purpose. We shall not attempt to follow all the windings of the treatment, but shall content ourselves with an enumeration and brief explanation of its main headings.

Under the heading of *Rule* Hegel deals with arbitrary metric units such as pound or foot: the arbitrariness of quantitative boundaries is such as to demand in many cases quite arbitrary, conventional standards of measurement. Under the heading of *Specifying Measure* Hegel deals generally with such concepts as Specific Heat, Specific Gravity, etc., concepts which have as their content the degree to which some quality is absorbed or possessed by a particular sort of substance. 'To something in so far as it is a measure in itself, a change in the magnitude of its quality comes from without. The thing does not take over the arithmetical manifoldness in question. Its measure reacts against it, stands over against this manifoldness as something intensive, and adopts it in a peculiar manner. It changes the outwardly posited change, makes out of this quantum something different, and shows itself through this specification as being-for-self in this externality.'[1] In the next section, *Relation of Both Sides as Qualities*, Hegel considers measures of concomitant variation: it is not clear why such a peculiar application of measurement should be regarded as involving peculiar metric concepts. From this Hegel goes on to *Being-for-self in Measure*, where some peculiar magnitude, e.g. gravity or velocity, is entirely analysable in terms of the relations of other concomitantly varying magnitudes. From this there is a passage to *Real Measure* which expresses the quality of various independent *things*. We have here the 'Union of Two Measures' where we study such things as the regular change in volume which occurs whenever two liquids are mixed. Hegel builds a dialectical runway to this doubtful empirical fact by the following verbal arrangement: 'This immanent determining of the quantitative cannot appear in weight (as has been shown), and therefore manifests in the other quality, which is the ideal side of the relationship. Sense-perception may be struck by the fact that after the mixing of two specifically different kinds of matter, a change, generally a diminution of total volume appears: space itself constitutes the being of the mutually external matters. But this being, as against the negativity which the being-for-self has in itself, is the non-subsistent, the changeable. Space is in this manner posited as what it truly is, the ideal element.' In the next section, *Measure as a Series of Measure Relations*, we find the nature of a thing mapped out in the totality of its metric relations to other sorts of things, while the following section on *Elective Affinity* discusses the quantitative side of the peculiar affinities shown in chemical combination. Only gleams of light can readily be gained from the tentative, inchoate sections we have run through, and this is not the place to do deeper research.[2]

The dialectic of Measure returns, however, after all these difficult wanderings, to the themes with which it started. In the section entitled *Nodal Line of Measure Relations* Hegel elaborates the notion of an endless alternation between truly qualitative and

---

[1] *Sc. of Log.*, I, pp. 418–19 (J & S., I, pp. 355–6; M., p. 337).
[2] *Sc. of Log.*, I, p. 436 (J. & S., I, p. 370; M., p. 351).

merely quantitative phases of change, which are involved in the relations of quantity and quality sketched above. Qualities in things rest on a basis of Measures which persist through a long stretch of quantitative variation. Then, of a sudden, variation, from being merely quantitative, becomes momentous and qualitative: we pass a node, there is a transition into another sort of qualitative being. Above the node, progress will again be smoothly quantitative, until another node is reached, and so on, in principle, indefinitely. Hegel stresses that the qualitative change occurring at such nodes is of necessity a leap (*Sprung*). Gradualness, which men appeal to in explaining such changes, has application only when one is dealing with what is merely quantitative. Many famous examples are brought forward to illustrate the categorial relation just outlined: a regular progression through the number-series suddenly introduces one to numbers having new properties and relationships, steady change in musical interval suddenly issues in remarkable harmonies, steady alteration of the amount of the elements present in certain mixtures suddenly leads to a new chemical compound, water after leading a long and tranquil quantitative life as warmer and warmer ice, suddenly jumps a node and becomes liquid water, and after living a long life as warmer and warmer water, suddenly rises to the higher life of steam. Both morals and politics show a similar heaping up of quantitative changes which precipitate changes which are qualitative, a doctrine widely appealed to by Marxist philosophers. Only while, for Hegel, the Nodal Line is practically a tautologial consequence of his notions of Quantity and Quality, for the Marxists it is an important instrument of empirical prediction.

In the Nodal Line we have, Hegel points out, yet another case of the 'Bad Infinite' we encountered in Quantity and Quality. Each measure-relationship, on which a Quality is founded, necessarily passes away, when Quantities change beyond a certain point, into what appears to be sheerly Measureless, the complete negation of all measure. This Measurelessness means, however, the immediate emergence of a new set of Measure-relations, which persist until a new node, and another state of apparent Measurelessness, are reached, and so on indefinitely. Hegel, as before, finds something unsatisfactory and self-contradictory about this progress to infinity, though its contradiction is really with an unspoken ideal of notional well-roundedness. He wishes, once more, to replace it with a 'True Infinite' which will remain the same throughout the whole process. This True Infinite cannot lie in any separate development of the quantitative or the qualitative nor in any oscillation between them. It cannot, in fact, lie in any extension of what may be called surface-thinking. By a leap of thought Hegel affirms that it must be sought in some profounder, non-apparent dimension, in what has traditionally been called a *Substrate*. 'The transition of the qualitative and quantitative into one another, takes place on the ground of their unity, and the sense of this process is merely the existence, the showing or positing that a Substrate underlies it which is such as to be their unity.' The measure-relations just discussed are 'nodes of one and the same Substrate. Thereby the measures themselves, and the independent things posited with them, are reduced to *states*. The change is merely change of state, and that which passes over is posited as remaining the same'.[1]

For a few sections a struggle is made to interpret this Substrate in terms of an 'Absolute Indifference', the notion of something which *rejects* all definite qualitative, quantitative and metric determinations, or of an Indifference which represents the mutual *cancellation* of all opposed determinations, from which they may again be differentiated in inverse ratio of strength: the views of Schelling and Anaximander seem to be momentarily passing under review. But the kind of Substrate that promises hopeful developments is not one in which all definite determinations are rejected or cancelled, but in which they are thought of as springing from some deeper level, as manifesting or expressing an Essence. 'The determinations . . . belong accordingly not to themselves, and do not emerge into independence and externality, but have being as moments. They pertain first of all to a unity which has being-in-self, not released from this, but carried by it as by a Substratum, and entirely filled with it. Secondly, they are the determinations which are immanent in the unity which exists for self, and only have being owing to its extrusion of self from self. . . . Being is thus determined to be Essence, Being which through simple overcoming of Being is simple Being with itself.'[2]

It is not necessary that we should at this point try to analyse or evaluate this new concept of Essence. Suffice it to say that Hegel

[1] *Sc. of Log.*, I, p. 464 (J. & S., I, pp. 392–3; M., p. 373).
[2] *Sc. of Log.*, I, p. 478 (J. & S., I, p. 404; M., p. 385).

has been led to it by inadequacies in the various categories of Quality, Quantity and Measure, and that the passage to it represents a leap of thought which Hegel's dialectical bridging fails to render mechanical and inevitable. We can see how a man weary of the infinite expansion involved in a Nodal Line of Measures should wish to take refuge in the notion of some underlying Essence which embraces this expansion as in a nutshell: we cannot see that he *must* have recourse to this particular way of removing his notional rubs. But there is also no reason why we *should* be able to see this.

SUPPLEMENTARY NOTE

Some of the connections in the Doctrine of Being are much plainer if one carefully studies the *Encyclopaedia*. There it is made clear that, just as Becoming makes explicit the impossibility of keeping apart the two notions of Being and Nothing (which we merely *mean* to be different), so the Qualitative Infinite Progression merely makes explicit the impossibility of separating any determinate Something from the otherwise determined Somethings that serve as its foil or background. 'A Something is implicitly the other of itself and the somewhat sees its limit become objective to it in the other . . . it does not meet the nature of the other as if it had no affinity to it, but being implicitly the other of itself, *thus undergoes alteration*' (§ 92, *Zus.*, our italics). In the same way Being-for-self, the featureless unit, makes explicit the indifference to qualitative content which is implied in the indefinite variability of the Qualitative Infinite Progression, while the categories of Quantity, with their loose extensibility, make explicit the impossibility of drawing a clear line between one such featureless unit and another. The notions of Ratio and Measure put an end to this loose extensibility, since ratios and measures can retain their identity despite infinitely varied application. But they too suffer from a Bad Infinity, which has to be healed by a recourse to deeper *dispositional* concepts (the notions of the sphere of Essence) which express themselves in a clearly *limited* range of surface variation.

CHAPTER SEVEN

THE LOGIC — II

The Doctrine of Essence

I HEGEL'S TREATMENT OF 'POSITEDNESS' AND 'REFLECTION'

In the Doctrine of Essence we deal with an important range of concepts or categories called by Hegel categories of *Reflection*: 'the standpoint of Essence', Hegel informs us, 'is in general the standpoint of Reflection'. He tells us, also, that he has chosen a word from a strange language to express the position of an appearance that has become *estranged* from its own immediacy. He further elucidates his meaning of the word by saying that it has a primary meaning in connection with light 'in so far as in its rectilineal progress it encounters a reflecting surface from which it is thrown back. We have thereby something doubled, in the first place something immediate which has being, and then in the second place the same as something mediated or merely posited (*Gesetztes*).'[1] It seems plain that the origin of the term is to be found in Fichte's account of knowledge, where the activity radiating forth from the Ego encounters various resistances, and is reflected back to its source. Hegel also plays upon the second ordinary meaning of the word as expressing the mental act of reflecting or thinking something over, in which objects are no longer seen as they superficially appear to be, but in various non-obvious contexts and connections. The man who reflects is not content to leave things 'in their immediacy', but seeks to show them as variously mediated or grounded by other things. The connection of 'Reflection' with 'Essence' lies in the fact that the Essence of anything is the antithesis of what it presents to the immediate view: it is something which lies behind or within the immediate surface of appearance, and which is only reached by penetrating beneath it. Such penetration is reflective, and the objects to which it penetrates are postulated or posited, inferred or mediated, rather than given. 'The immediate

[1] *L. Log.*, p. 262 (W., p. 208).

being of things is here imagined as a rind or curtain, behind which the Essence lies hidden.'

The word 'Reflection' is further uniformly connected by Hegel with relativity and relationships. Something is conceived reflectively when it is conceived as in relation to something: it may be seen as in relation to something else, or as in relation to itself. Reflective modes of conception, moreover, occur in pairs: to conceive of *A* under one reflective mode of conception is necessarily to conceive of something, whether something else, or *A* itself, under some correlative mode of conception. When something is conceived as positive, something must also be conceived as negative, when something is conceived as a ground, something must also be conceived as grounded, when something is conceived as substantial or essential, something must also be conceived as unessential or accidental, and so forth. By saying that the concepts of Reflection exhibit this sort of correlative duality, we are not, however, saying that they are concepts in which the necessary connection between correlative aspects is obvious and emphatic: it is in fact characteristic of reflective pairs of concepts that they are kept apart in thought, rather than brought closely together. To conceive reflectively of something as self-identical or causal, is rather to forget that it can only be these things provided that something is also different or caused. When the two correlative concepts are seen as in close and necessary relation, we have, according to Hegel, passed beyond the sphere of Reflection and have reached the higher sphere of the Notion. In the sphere of Reflection we think rather in terms of relational properties and determinations *of* things than in terms of relations *between* things: our standpoint is that of the Aristotelian, not that of the Russellian logic.

What emerges from what we have said is that reflective thinking is a kind of thinking which sees objects as the points of origin or points of convergence of numerous 'rays of relevance', some of which relate the object to other objects, while others are bent round and relate it to itself. It is, moreover, a mode of thinking which sees objects in the *light* of such rays of relevance, rather than concentrating on the rays as such. It is a mode of thinking different from the one pursued in the sphere of Being, where notions occurred singly and not in matched pairs, and where one passed from notion to notion with a shock of surprise, and not with the natural swing to an implied correlative. It is likewise a mode of thinking different from the one we shall follow at the level of the Notion, where antithetical sides will be seen as combined in a single notion, and where there will rather be continuous development than an oscillating swing from one correlative to another. And its connection with the notion of Essence or Substrate is twofold: both inasmuch as the deeper, non-superficial view of things is one that sees things in their bearings on other things, and not in sense-destroying isolation, and also inasmuch as the deeper, essential nature of things is itself one of a pair of correlative notions, being essentially opposed to what is unessential and immediate. Something can only be essential and deeper lying in so far as something is superficial and immediate, and *vice versa*.

Hegel also makes great use in connection with reflective concepts of the notions of *Positing* (*Setzen*) and of *Positedness* (*Gesetzt-seyn*). 'Positing' is what a ray of relevance does when it leads thought to its other end. Thus an object thought of as effect 'posits' something to be its cause, the essential 'posits' the immediate, etc. etc. The term may be variously rendered as 'requiring', 'entailing', 'implying', 'pointing towards', etc. 'Positedness', on the other hand, is the sort of status enjoyed by an object by being at the end of a ray of relevance: an object may have no other status than that of being thus relevant. Thus the status of the thought-objects of physical science is for Hegel merely a *Gesetzt-seyn*: their whole being is summed up in being what underlies and what explains certain perceived appearances. (We shall see shortly how the being of these perceived appearances is itself reduced to a mere Positedness.)

We may note, further, that 'Reflection' has for Hegel an impersonal and objective, as well as a personal and subjective meaning. It is not merely *we* who refer things and thought-determinations to certain correlatives—in so far as this happens we have merely a case of 'External Reflection'—the things and determinations *themselves* point to certain other things and determinations with which their content is connected, and with which they make up a single thought-world. Reflection may to some extent depend on the arbitrary selection of 'angles' or standpoints from which things are regarded, but it depends also on considerations so inescapable as to be properly said to belong to the nature of the things considered. It seems plain that Hegel, in delimiting the sphere of 'Essence' or 'Reflection', has marked off a range of concepts of the utmost interest and importance. Quite plainly there are, in addition to concepts singly significant, other concepts which work only in harness as members of antithetical, mutually entailing pairs. And Hegel seems right in holding these concepts to be the basic concepts of the sciences and metaphysics.

Hegel deals with the points we have been making in the extremely difficult first chapter (entitled *Schein* or 'Mere Appearance') of Section I of the Doctrine of Essence (entitled 'Essence as Reflection into Self') as given in the *Science of Logic*. This chapter condenses to a single paragraph (§ 114) of the *Encyclopaedia*. None the less its matter is extremely important, and we may attempt to give an inkling of what it says.

The results of the Dialectic as the end of the Doctrine of Being was to lead up the notion of Essence or Substrate: we were unable to discover any well-rounded unity in the endless oscillation between definite Measure and sheer Measurelessness, except by postulating some abiding Substrate beneath all this oscillation, something that would hold together in simple unity the vast variety of surface measures. The nature of this underlying reality will be variously determined as the Dialectic proceeds: it will appear as a Thing, a Substance, a Law, a world of non-phenomenal realities, a web of causal connections and so forth. At the present stage the Substrate is merely an ideal: that of something simpler and more constant than the variable surface of what appears. After some unsuccessful attempts to characterize it further, recourse is had to a wholly negative approach: the Substrate is thought of as a wholly blank one-knows-not-what, which nevertheless in the deepest sense *is*, while every determinate form of being becomes a case of mere appearance (*Schein*), and that in the radical sense in which what is merely apparent has no being at all. This, says Hegel, is the view characteristic of certain sorts of scepticism or phenomenalism in which the appearances which are held *not* to be, comprise the whole wealth of the empirical world, while of the Essence which in the profoundest sense *is*, nothing determinate can be said. Hegel has no difficulty in showing up the senselessness of this mode of approach. There can be no meaning in ascribing nullity to appearances unless this nullity means their incapacity for independent being, their necessary dependence on what is essential. In the same way, the negativity of what is essential, its rejection of all mere appearances, is significant only if the Essence is positively connected with such appearances, if it appears in them. We are therefore driven to a position where surface and depth are alike sides of a new conception of Essence, which is thought of as being as much superficial as underlying. This new position is that of 'Reflection' which is here for the first time explicitly introduced.

The notion of 'Reflection' as developed in this section runs through three phases called by Hegel 'Positing Reflection', 'External Reflection' and 'Determining Reflection'. In Positing Reflection everything has a merely posited, i.e. purely relative being, without any absolute foundation to rest on: we have, in consequence, 'a movement from nothing to nothing' and 'a negation which comes into unity with itself'. In Positing Reflection the *whole* function of the apparent, the given, is to afford a starting-point, a presupposition from which there can be a going-back to the essential. As so conceived, the essential may be said to presuppose itself, and the overcoming of this presupposition to be the essential itself. 'Reflection', Hegel finely remarks, '*finds* an immediate before it, beyond which it passes, and from which it represents the return, but this return is itself the prior presupposition of what is thus found before it. The immediate thus found comes into being only in being deserted: its immediacy is an immediacy overcome.' Data, in short, only are data in so far as we go on to interpret them, and may therefore be said to presuppose the interpretations we give of them. Since our interpretations likewise presuppose data, we seem to have before us merely a strange interplay of mutually presupposing transparencies. Such a situation is however unthinkable: there is a call for substance somewhere. We are then led to look for such substance in the direction of what is immediate or given, the movement towards Essence representing an *External* Reflection upon what is thus given, a Reflection generally attributed to the subjective activity of thinking.

In External Reflection a definite starting-point, an immediate datum is presupposed: Reflection 'finds this before itself as the sort of thing from which it begins, and from which it first is a going back into self, the negation of what is negative to itself'. Various determinations then distinguish themselves in the datum thus presupposed and are incorporated into its Essence, but such determining remains *external* to the given: the universals, principles, laws governing the given govern it, as it were, from an outside seat. Such External Reflection has, however, an inadequacy opposite to that of the Positing Reflection previously dealt with: if the latter so strips the given, the immediate, of its initial independence, as to give the rearward interpretative movement nothing firm to start from, the former so stresses the firm starting-point for reflective *approfondissement* as to make the latter intrinsically impossible. For it is only if the datum in which the reflective movement begins is truly revealed in, and in fact identical with the essential account in which it ends, that the latter can deserve to be called 'essential'. We therefore move to a position where we discover that 'the External Reflection is not external, but the immanent reflection of immediacy itself, or that what has its being through Positing Reflection is the Essence which exists in and for self'. In other words, the 'substantial' element we are looking for is as much in the interpretation as in the datum, and we have passed to the standpoint of Determining Reflection.

Determing Reflection is said to be the union of Positing and External Reflection: in it something is granted or posited as the independent starting-point for reflective *approfondissement*, but the fact that it has been so granted once more liquidates the independence thus grudgingly accorded. The given is only given by and for the sense-making activity which starts from it, and which reduces it to the various universal determinations constitutive of its essence. The being of the given is thereby purely a *Gesetztseyn*, a being posited or granted: it exists only through the grace of the sense-making activity into which it is taken back. From Determining Reflection Hegel now hopes to pass on to the detailed study of various reflective determinations, i.e. concepts which involve in themselves an implicit reference to their correlatives.

The above sketch will give some idea of Hegel's account of 'Reflection' in the *Science of Logic*. We have left it with the Hegelian mists clinging to it, without seeking to make it perfectly lucid. We have by no means done full justice to the exuberant richness of the argument, of which it has not always been possible even to keep the thread.

II IDENTITY, DIFFERENCE, LIKENESS, OPPOSITION AND CONTRADICTION

Hegel begins his study of reflective concepts with the notion of Identity, which has the same indefeasible claim to be the beginning in the realm of Essence that Pure Being had in the field covered by the general name of Being. Identity is the undeveloped, the immediate notion of what is essential, just as Pure Being is the immediate form of what develops into Quality and Quantity. Essence is nothing if not what is selfsame and constant in the diversity of appearance: that an essential element runs through a series of appearances entails as a minimum that there is something identical in them all. The notion of Identity that here confronts us is not, however, the abstract sameness we previously met in the sphere of Being: it is the Identity of Locke and Hume, not the Identity of modern mathematical logic. In the sphere of Being an element maintained itself in varying contexts, and even admitted varying determinations in itself, but its self-maintenance was a phenomenon of the surface, something that depended on our power to grip an object and keep it constantly in view. Now, however, Identity has sunk to a deeper level: it is something postulated, inferred, established by criteria. It is an Identity of Reflection, in the Hegelian sense, not one of immediacy.

Being a concept of reflection, Identity is of course inseparably bound up with its correlative concept Difference. Such Difference is, in the first instance, a Difference of the surface, as Identity is an Identity of deeper level. Quite obviously things can only be identical in essence if they can be superficially different, and vice versa. A man is only the same man because he can be continuously identified despite superficial changes: a doctrine or pattern of life is likewise the same in essence only because it can differ in external manifestation. Hegel has here many pointed, famous things to say about the logical laws of Identity and Non-contradiction, which both tell us that the notion of Identity applies to everything. They have a degenerate interpretation appropriate at the level of Being where they are empty and unhelpful tautologies: they have also an interpretation suited to the present level, where they are both significant and synthetic. On the degenerate interpretation the Law of Identity merely bids us identify objects referred to by means of one term or concept with objects referred to by the *same* term or concept. We are condemned to make such Megarian assertions as that a tree is a tree, God is God, etc. At the same level the Law of Non-Contradiction merely forbids us to identify an object referred to by one concept with an object referred to by the *negation* of that concept: of an *A* we cannot say that it is a non-*A*. Whereas, on the deeper interpretation of the present level, an assertion of Identity obliges us to be ready to assert different concepts of what is declared identical, and (presumably) to exclude from it concepts other than those which are merely negative. These additional implications of Identity are, according to Hegel, 'synthetic' and not 'analytic'. At least it is plain that they add to the abstract notion of 'same' formed at the level of Being, even if they only analyse the corresponding notion formed at the level of Essence.

From the reflective concept of Identity Hegel advances dialectically to the reflective concept of Difference (*Unterschied*), which is not, however, the superficial difference just considered, but rather a difference of *Essence*. 'The other of Essence is the other in and for itself, not the other which is other merely in relation to something found outside of it, simple determinateness in itself.' Hegel is here forming the notion of an essential *distinctiveness* which implies relations without being explicitly relational: we use his notion when we think of the things of our acquaintance as being 'different' or 'distinctive' without plainly recognizing (though we no doubt imply) that they are different *from* any particular sort of thing. Difference or distinctiveness so absolutely conceived is for Hegel inseparably connected with Identity and *vice versa*. We cannot pick out anything as distinctive without also picking it out as self-identical in all possible variations, nor can we pick it out as self-identical (or the same in kind) without also recognizing it as distinctive. 'Difference', Hegel paradoxically puts it, 'is the whole and its own moment, just as Identity is likewise the whole and its own moment',[1] i.e. either determination amounts to *both* Difference and Identity.

From Difference Hegel passes on to Diversity (*Verschiedenheit*) where the implication of plurality obscured in sheer Difference becomes obvious and explicit: a single object can be said to be distinctive, different, but only a number of objects can be said

[1] *Sc. of Log.*, I, p. 516 (J. & S., II, p. 43; M., p. 418).

to be various or diverse. Diversity is a reflective concept in which reflection is *external*: the things that are said to be diverse or various are as such *indifferent* to each other's being or properties. They are brought together in an external perspective which is, in general, that of a comparing subject. With such Diversity there necessarily go two additional concepts, that of Likeness or Alikeness (*Gleichheit*), on the one hand, and Unlikeness (*Ungleichheit*), on the other. ('Alikeness' here means *precise* identity in some character rather than mere similarity.) Likeness is an attenuated Identity posited only in an external reflection on things intrinsically indifferent, and Unlikeness is likewise an external Difference, not the same as the essential Difference which is the source of a thing's distinctive being. Hegel points out the deep and obvious dovetailing of the two notions just distinguished, how the positing of Likeness only occurs significantly on a background of Unlikeness and *vice versa*. He also gives an uncompromising assent to the Leibnizian principle of the Identity of Indiscernibles. Two things, he says, are not merely two: numerical plurality is as such absence of variety (*Einerleiheit*) and so things must be diverse by a determination. But the Doctrine of Being has already committed Hegel (without satisfactory argument) to denying an otherness not marked out by quality. What is now rejected is the possibility of *essential* Difference unconnected with Unlikeness, and this, surely, is a trivial rejection.

From mere Diversity Hegel passes on to Polar Opposition (*Gegensatz*), without argument in the *Encyclopaedia*, and with two fairly long arguments in the *Science of Logic*. In the latter Hegel points out how the understanding seeks to turn Likenesses and Unlikenesses into absolute Identities and Diversities: a Likeness, e.g., is held to be an Identity *in a certain respect*, things are said to be the same *in so far* as something is so, etc. etc. As so frozen, Likenesses and Unlikenesses lose their essential mutual relevance, which gives them both colour and meaning: they become a case of Differences which are no Differences, and this, for Hegel, is the essential character of Polar Opposition. (The Negative, e.g., only differs in 'sense' from the Positive, etc. etc.) Alternatively he argues that the presence of Likeness and Unlikeness in the same pairs of things is *itself* a case of Polar Opposition, which we must then explicitly recognize. The giving of two such wholly different derivations seems to show that neither is adequate: Hegel's real motive in passing from mere Diversity to Polar Opposition lies in his dissatisfaction with connections that do not delve deep into the nature of their terms, which depend upon arbitrary, external points of view, which are not, in the last resort, real connections at all. As Hegel remarks: 'In Opposition the thing distinguished has not merely *an* other, but *its* other over against it. The common consciousness treats differents as indifferent to one another. One says: I am a man and round me are air, water, animals and other things in general. Everything there falls apart. Against this the aim of philosophy is to banish indifference, and to recognize the necessity of things, so that the other appears to stand over against *its* other.'[1] It is this aim, here frankly acknowledged, rather than the reasons previously mentioned, which is guiding the Dialectic.

Hegel gives a fair number of instances of Polar Opposition, a category much to the fore in contemporary thought: he points to the Positive and Negative in numbers and magnitudes, in electricity, magnetism and the theory of colour, as well as in the relations of nature to Spirit. He thinks the use of this concept, as opposed to mere random variety, to be a sign of a great advance in science and philosophy. He notes how in Polar Opposition the Negative has barely any character beyond being unlike the Positive—to walk west is just like walking east except that it is in an opposed direction—and how this absence of character in the opposite makes it perfectly natural to make the Negative Positive and *vice versa*. He indicates, too, how the fact that each opposite contains its opposite in its own nature renders them not more dependent upon, but more independent of one another. It is not, e.g., necessary that there should be debts for there to be credits and *vice versa*, though the notion of each 'posits' that of the other. He also gives some amusing if uncompelling reasons why $-a \times +a$ should be $-a^2$ while $+a \times -a$ is not a^2, and also why $-a \times -a$ should be $+a^2$.

By a sharpening of Polar Opposition we then advance to the category of Contradiction (*Widerspruch*), which synthetizes Identity and the various forms of Difference and Opposition in the *Science of Logic*, but which is not separated from Opposition in the *Encyclopaedia*. Contradiction develops out of Polar Opposition when we reflect on the fact that each opposite must in a sense

[1] *L. Log.*, p. 279 (W., p. 222).

contain, and also not contain, its opposite: each opposite, says Hegel, is mediated with self through its other, and so contains that latter, but it is also mediated with self through the *non-being of its other*, and through the exclusion of the latter from itself. Such Contradiction was implicit in mere Difference for there too we had an apparent separateness which was also a form of union. It is (we see) in the attempt to give separateness and independence to opposed determinations that Contradiction arises: Contradiction is therefore the limit towards which all Difference and Opposition necessarily tends.

Hegel goes on to his well-known strictures on the traditional logic for not recognizing Contradiction to be as essential and immanent a determination of things as is Identity: it is, if anything, deeper and more essential, since it is 'the root of all movement and life'. Only in so far as something has Contradictions within itself can it move, or has it drive and activity. It is a mistake, says Hegel, to relegate Contradiction to subjective reflection—if it is out of place in things, it is out of place there—we must recognize, as does ordinary experience, that there are countless contradictory things, institutions, etc. It is plain from Hegel's examples, as from his repeated stress on drive and activity, that he means by Contradiction something as different from the self-nullifying contradiction of formal logic as his Identity differs from its formal identity. Hegelian Contradiction applies to things, whereas formal contradictions do not. Hegel is wrong in saying that formal logicians were prejudiced in their view of Contradiction: it is rather the case that their concept of Contradiction is different from his. Hegel's Contradiction is in fact the Contradiction of much ordinary thought and speech for which it means precisely the presence of opposed tendencies in one and the same thing, tendencies which, in the realm of thought and speech, produce struggling, hesitant, unstable, readily abandoned verbal and thought-combinations, and which, in the realm of things, produce unstable, transitory, readily disrupted conditions and behaviour. Hegel's main innovation is to connect the thought of such conflicting real or thought-tendencies with thoughts and modes of speech which are themselves expressions of such conflicts, and to suggest we should think and speak of the former by means of the latter. He should rather have distinguished between notions, in which conflict is necessarily suspended

(though they may be notions *of* conflict) and transitions *between*
notions which will often be characterized *by* conflict. In the
present phase Hegel is obviously trying to provide us with a
notion of conflict rather than with a conflict of notions.

III GROUNDS, REASONS AND CONDITIONS

Hegel now passes from the reflective determinations just listed,
which are all forms of Identity and Difference to the new category
of Ground. In the *Science of Logic* the transition to Ground is
from the category of Contradiction: in the *Encyclopaedia* Hegel
passes direct to Ground from the categories of Identity and
Difference. Both transitions are assisted by a pun: the dependent-
independence of opposites amounts to a contradiction, and in this
contradiction their opposition falls to the *ground* (*geht zu Grunde*).
What Hegel actually argues is that the notion of Ground effects
a more stable synthesis of the identical and the different than has
been achieved in the reflective concepts so far studied.

Like the other reflective concepts the notion of Ground functions in a logical rule applicable to everything: the Leibnizian
principle that everything has a sufficient ground or reason. This
means, says Hegel, that neither Identity, nor Diversity, nor mere
Positivity or Negativity, is the true essence of anything, but that
it has its being in its other, which as representing its identity
with self is its Essence. In other words, the undecidable quarrel
for primacy between the positive and the negative, and their
attempted synthesis between dependence and independence, has
now led to a one-sided victory: the principle of Ground means
that one thing, the Ground, is independent and essential even
when passing over into something different, i.e. the Grounded,
and that the latter always has its essence in the former, and is
entirely dependent on it. The category of Ground is not, however,
a tranquil union of Identity and Difference, but an explosive
mixture of both: it can, says Hegel, only resolve the contradiction
involved in Essential Difference by pushing forth one of its
essential aspects into something different from itself. 'A Ground
is only a Ground', Hegel tells us, 'in so far as it is the Ground of
something, but that which has gone forth from the Ground is the
Ground itself . . . the Grounded and the Ground are one and the
same content, and the difference between them is the merely

formal difference between a simple relation to self and of mediation and derivation.'

The whole transition to Ground therefore involves a considerable element of arbitrariness. The notions of Ground and Grounded certainly offer a more intimate and interesting union of self-reference and reference to what is other than do mere Diversity or Polar Opposition. In moving to Ground we are likewise nearer to the final solution in the Idea, where one antithetical element certainly triumphs over the other. But it would be vain to argue that the step taken by Hegel is obligatory rather than permissive, and that there are not new, special features introduced in his treatment of Ground which are not an outcome of what has gone before. It seems plain, too, that one reason for introducing the category of Ground at this point is simply that the Principle of Sufficient Ground traditionally goes with the three formal laws of Identity, Contradiction and Excluded Middle, which have been discussed by Hegel in connection with Identity, Difference and Opposition. The use of a joke at this critical point shows, too, that Hegel is much less serious about his Dialectic than are his commentators.

The category of Ground receives a whole chapter with three triply divided subdivisions in the *Science of Logic*: many of its subdivisions, e.g. those of Form and Matter, Form and Content and Conditioning, occur at a later stage in the *Encyclopaedia* treatment. Since the category of Causation is a special case of Ground, Hegel offers many examples that come from the field of Causation. But the notion of Ground is wider than that of Causation: it covers any case in which a *reason* might be offered for applying some concept. And Hegel studies it in relation to many *moral* judgements and decisions, in connection with our reasons for doing something or thinking something right. Much of his treatment is in fact relevant to fairly recent treatments of ethics, e.g. those of Ross, Stevenson and Hare.

The first main division of Hegel's treatment of Ground is entitled 'Absolute Ground', and has the three sub-headings 'Form and Essence', 'Form and Matter' and 'Form and Content'. By the formal aspect of Essence Hegel seems to be conceiving of Essence as active, as grounding or determining whatever flows from it, and as embodying itself and passing away in what it grounds. It is on account of, by virtue of the Ground that the

Grounded must be posited, and as so grounding what follows from it, Essence is considered as active or formative. But grounding or determining involves also a being grounded or a being determined, and this means that the Essence can also be conceived in an inactive undetermined material aspect, as providing a basis or *Grundlage* which is to undergo various grounded determinations. It seems plain that Hegel has pushed the Dialectic in the present direction in order to take in the Aristotelian concepts of Form and Matter. Hardly, however, has the insubstantial distinction been drawn than it collapses by virtue of its very insubstantiality. Hegel has no difficulty in showing that we are dealing with the same essential Ground-relation whether we envisage it as a case of active imposition or passive receptivity. 'Since the Form itself is absolute identity with self, and so contains the Matter in itself, and since the Matter similarly in its pure abstraction and absolute negativity contains the Form in itself, the activity of the Form on the Matter, and the latter's determination by the former, is rather the removal of the *appearance* of their indifference and of their difference. This relation of determination is accordingly the mediation of either with self through its own non-being—but these two mediations constitute one movement and the restoration of their original identity—the re-membering (*Erinnerung*) of their dis-membering (*Entaüsserung*).'[1] (We have tried to translate Hegel's pun.) The above account says little more than that it is indifferent whether we say, e.g., that a certain reason made us act in a certain way, or that we *freely did* something for a particular reason.

We thereby rise to the new notion of Content (*Inhalt*) which can indifferently be taken to represent Materialized Form or Formed Matter; it is the Ground in Action, annulling itself and yet preserving itself in what it grounds. Hegel is eager to distinguish this notion of Content from the common notion which makes Content *indifferent* to the Form in which it is expressed, as where the content of *Romeo and Juliet* is contrasted with its poetic or dramatic form. The Content of a thing in the sense used by Hegel is inseparably one with its Form: *Romeo and Juliet* could not have had the same Content if produced in prose or some non-verbal medium. In the same way its Form is not any and every use of dramatic technique or poetic English:

[1] *Sc. of Log.*, I, p. 562 (J. & S., II, p. 79; M., p. 452).

in actual realization it assumes a wholly particular Form to match the material it organizes. What Hegel seems to be saying is that the ultimate Ground why *Romeo and Juliet* was written as it was written in any respect is that this was necessary in order to produce just the particular work that it is. This notion of Content therefore offers us a Ground which is both determinate and also one with what it grounds: Hegel then passes—with somewhat slight motivation—from the study of Ground Absolute or Ground in general to the more concrete study of Ground Determinate.

Ground Determinate is divided by Hegel into the three sub-divisions of Formal Ground, Real Ground and Complete Ground. In Formal Ground the identity between Ground and Grounded assumes an unhelpful and tautological form: the Ground has to be sufficient to ground what it grounds and this requirement is first met by simply putting into the Ground, with some slight pretence of difference, everything that one puts into what is grounded. Hegel gives as examples of such a merely formal Ground-relation the 'attractive force' which explains the movement of the earth about the sun, and the use of molecules, beams of light, electrical and magnetic 'matters' by physicists to provide Grounds for the phenomena on which such fictions are really themselves grounded. Hegel remarks penetratingly that while such groundings are thought objectionable on account of involving 'occult qualities', the true objection to them is that what they state is only too open and obvious, and that it merely describes familiar phenomena in novel verbal form. The only thing that is really occult about them is the pretended explanation which is not there.[1] The moral realm, too, has cases of such purely formal grounding, as where we hold that a man *should* act in a certain way in certain circumstances, giving as our Ground that it is *right* to act thus in those circumstances.

Formal grounding, however, represents the reduction of Ground to an impossible degree of translucency: for the Ground-relation to obtain at all, there must be some real difference between the form it assumes as Ground and the form it assumes as Grounded. There must, it seems, be additional features in the Ground, features unessential to its grounding function, and merely accompanying it in the same 'Something', which will serve to differentiate it from what it grounds. A Ground so embellished by

[1] *Sc. of Log.*, I, pp. 570–1 (J. & S., II, pp. 86–7; M., p. 459).

unessential additions, whose presence is none the less essential to its being a Ground, is called by Hegel a Real Ground. The weakness of this concept is, however, opposite and complementary to that of a Formal Ground. If the latter allows the Ground-relation to collapse into empty tautology, the former disperses it in externality and arbitrariness. If we do not account for the presence of X by something which is practically only another name for X, we can account for it by practically anything whatsoever. This arbitrariness is particularly marked in the field of moral judgement and decision. 'The hunting up and citation of grounds in which *raisonnement* or argumentation principally consists, is accordingly an endless driving around that includes no final determination. One or more good reasons can be given for anything and everything (as also for its opposite) and a multitude of Grounds may be assembled without leading to a definite result. . . . Grounds are only taken from *essential* determinations of content, relationships and respects of which every matter of fact, like its opposite, has several: in their form of essentiality one is as valid as another. Since they do not embrace the whole extent of the matter, and since other sides demand yet other Grounds, they are one-sided Grounds of which none exhausts the matter, which knits all together and contains them all. None of them is a sufficient Ground, i.e. the Notion.'[1]

From the complementary deficiencies of Formal and Real Ground the Dialectic moves on to Complete Ground, where there is recognized *both* to be a formal element in the Ground, which perpetuates itself tautologically in the Grounded, and also a supplementing real element, by which the Formal element demands completion, if it is to be a Ground at all. In other words, the Formal Ground for anything must be such as to complete itself by one or other out of an indefinite range of additional circumstances or conditions, and the character of what is grounded will depend, likewise, not merely on the formal character of the Ground as such, but on the particular conditions and circumstances which go with it. Thus not only 'attractive force', but a particular collocation of gravitating bodies, is the Complete Ground of some movement, and not merely 'wrongness' or 'wickedness', but a particular wrong done in particular circumstances, is the Complete Ground of punishment, and also determines *what*

[1] *Sc. of Log.*, I, p. 581 (J. & S., II, p. 94; M., p. 466).

degree of punishment should be inflicted. Hegel seems to suggest that while there is arbitrariness and contingency in the completion of the formal element by the real element both in the Ground itself and in what is grounded—we cannot say *a priori* how the ground will be circumstantially completed, not just what outcome it will have if so completed—yet the completion is in *this* sense necessary and essential, that there could be no Ground-relation without it. We pass accordingly to the new concept of a *Condition* as the additional immediate element presupposed by a Formal Ground in order that it may become a Complete Ground.

In the notion of a Condition we have precisely that combination of indifferent immediacy and essential mediation, of independent subsistence and the dependent being of a mere aspect, which the notion of Ground needs for its satisfactory working. A Condition is immediate, merely there, and is as such ungrounded: it is not part of the Ground, and is indifferent to the Ground's existence. None the less it provides the 'material', the necessary foundation for the working of the Ground: it (or some other parallel Condition) is presupposed by the Ground, and (in so far as it is a Condition) may even be said to contain the Ground implicitly or *in itself*.

Hegel now shows how the perfecting of the notion of Ground in the notion of Condition leads us to pass to a wholly new and more adequate mode of conception. We come to regard the whole being of the Condition as consisting merely in the suspension of its independent reality, in its becoming the material or occasion for the operation of the Ground. 'Being (i.e. the immediate being of the Condition) is in general merely the becoming of Essence: it is its essential nature to turn itself into something merely derivative and into the identity which achieves immediacy through the negation of itself.'[1] The Conditions which occasion a Ground's operation are accordingly there merely to elicit what is implicit in the Ground, to try it out, to put it through its paces, much as everything in nature and history will be shown to be there merely to elicit the self-consciousness of Spirit. The independence of the Condition is therefore merely an appearance: it is there as a complement and stimulus to the Ground, which accordingly becomes *self-dependent* or *absolutely unconditioned*. If it be objected that Conditions always have further Conditions *in infinitum*,

[1] *Sc. of Log.*, I, pp. 588–9 (J. & S., II, p. 100; M., p. 472).

Hegel deals with this recrudescence of the Bad Infinite by holding that *all* the Conditions of an operative Ground, however remote, can be regarded as being there to elicit its operation: the Ground accordingly becomes the True Infinite which resumes all its 'others'.

The Ground considered in the complete context of its Conditions becomes for Hegel a new category, that of the *Sache* or Matter of Fact. 'The Absolutely Unconditioned', he writes, 'is the Absolute Ground which is identical with its Condition, the immediate Matter of Fact as what is truly essential. As Ground it relates itself negatively to itself, turns itself into a merely posited being, but a posited being whose notion has shown itself as the complete reflection into its aspects and as the Form-relation which is identical in them all. This posited being is accordingly, in the first place, the suspended Ground, the Matter of Fact as the immediate without reflection, the side of the Conditions. This is the totality of the determinations of the Matter of Fact, the Matter of Fact itself, but cast forth into the externality of Being. . . . The other side of this appearance of the Unconditioned is the Ground-relation as such, determined as Form over against the immediacy of the Conditions and the Content. . . . The movement of the Matter of Fact, to be posited by its Conditions, on the one hand, and by its Ground, on the other, is merely *the vanishing of the appearance of mediation*. The positing of the Matter of Fact is accordingly an emergence, a simple entry into existence, a pure movement of the Matter of Fact to itself. When all Conditions of a Matter of Fact are present, it enters into existence.'[1]

What Hegel is here saying is that we only regard a Matter of Fact truly or adequately when we see every external Condition as leading up to it, or as presupposed by it, and as in that sense a part of it. The whole universe of fact and possibility is involved in my present act of writing, which can from this point of view be regarded as absolutely unconditioned, as *causa sui*. We must here note the vast difference between Hegel's conception of the relation of the individual Matter of Fact to the complete Universe of conditioning Matters of Fact, and the conception held by modern British idealists. While the latter hold that an individual Matter of Fact can be truly seen only in its full context in the total system of facts, Hegel rather believes that this total system

---

[1] *Sc. of Log.*, I, pp. 592–4 (J. & S., II, pp. 103–5; M., pp. 474–7).

of facts is truly seen only as bearing on, and as involved in, the individual Matter of Fact. For the British idealists the Finitude of the individual thing or occasion is parasitic on the Infinity of the Universe: for Hegel the Infinity of the Universe (which is as such 'Bad') is parasitic on the True Infinity of the individual thing or occasion.

Hegel now moves from the various categories of Ground to the categories of Existence or Phenomenal Being, the kind of being characteristic of a Matter of Fact which emerges out of a multitude of Conditions. In what follows he rather loses sight of the ethical illustrations which have made his treatment of Ground so interesting. We shall be exclusively concerned with the conceptual anatomy of Phenomenal Being.

IV PHENOMENAL THINGS, MATTERS, PROPERTIES AND LAWS: WHOLES AND PARTS, FORCES AND MANIFESTATIONS, INSIDES AND OUTSIDES

Phenomenal Being (*Erscheinung*) is opposed to the Mere Appearance (*Schein*) which we previously dealt with. Phenomenal Being is the sort of being that has come *out* of the Ground, and which may accordingly be said to *ex*ist. Punning apart, it is the sort of being characteristic of an object set in an orderly and connected world, where everything has other things as the conditions of its being. Phenomenal Being is studied by Hegel in three dialectical subdivisions: 'Existence', which deals mainly with the notions connected with a Thing, 'Phenomenal Being Proper' which reverts to a two-world treatment of the essential and superficial, and 'Essential Relationship' which deals with relations (Whole and Part, Force and its Manifestation, Inward and Outward) in which this two-world treatment is more and more fully overcome. The arrangement here differs considerably in the *Encyclopaedia* and the *Science of Logic*: we in our treatment shall follow the *Science of Logic*. The material of the present section is largely a restatement of themes developed at the beginning of the *Phenomenology* in connection with Sense-perception and Scientific Understanding.

The Thing (*Ding*) is introduced by Hegel as the result of the absorption of mediation into the existent, so that one is now confronted by something self-mediated rather than mediated by external circumstances. This Thing is obviously only a slightly more settled version of the Matter of Fact (*Sache*) of the previous section. In the concept of the Thing Hegel distinguishes two sides. It will have an aspect of surface-immediacy and reflectedness-into-what-is-other which will correspond to the Condition-aspect of the Matter of Fact, and also an aspect of reflectedness into-self, of reference to its own being, which will correspond to the Ground-aspect previously dealt with. The Thing will have an intrinsic being in respect of which it will be a Thing-in-itself, indifferent to the colours, smells, etc., which are due (Hegel assumes without question) to its interactions with other Things. Hegel now makes an apparently circular though not self-cancelling series of moves. He passes first of all from the notion of the relation of the Thing-in-itself to its surface-determinations to its relations to other Things-in-themselves. It is (as we said) part of our notion of a Thing-in-itself that it gains its surface-determinations by coming into relation with other Things-in-themselves. But it is likewise part of our notion of a Thing-in-itself that these relations to other Things-in-themselves merely serve to bring out the nature of the original Thing-in-itself, that it is in them only related to itself. (In Lockean terms, secondary qualities are in a sense not part of the 'real essences' of substances, but in a sense they do 'flow' from them.) By this move towards other Things-in-themselves and the subsequent return to the first Thing-in-itself, Hegel now reaches the new notion of a *Property*, of a determination *proper* and peculiar to a Thing-in-itself, which none the less stems from its relationship to other Things-in-themselves.

At this point Hegel stresses the absurdity of the Kantian doctrine of the Thing-in-itself, which attributes to consciousness all the properties of the Thing, while leaving to the Thing only an abstract, indeterminate form of reflectedness-into-self. The Properties of a Thing are as essential to it as are its mere inwardness and unity, and it is more reasonable to treat the 'I' of self-consciousness as a self-reflected unity indifferent to what it cognizes, than to do so in the case of the Thing and its Properties. Hegel emphasizes further that it is through their Properties that Things come into relation with one another, and even that Things only achieve distinctness from each other through the Properties that mark them off. Apart from some definite criterion involving

Properties, we cannot say whether we are dealing with one Thing (e.g. a book), or very many things (e.g. leaves). The dialectical line here being pursued readily leads to a complete alteration in the status of the underlying, essential Thing: it ceases to seem essential, and becomes merely a 'powerless bond', a 'mere also', a blank 'this', by which Properties are held together. As so conceived, the Properties of Things pass away into 'Matters', a notion current in Hegel's time according to which material substances contained 'luminous matter' 'olfactory matter', 'thermal matter', 'electrical matter', etc., to account for their various Properties. Such Matters owe no allegiance to one particular Thing above another: they float from one combination to the next, and their interweavings make up the very being of Things. At the same time, Hegel maintains, there is a deep and irremoveable contradiction in their relation to one another: they must be thought of as coexisting and interpenetrating in the same spatial region, but this interpenetration also liquidates their independence. Faced by this difficulty, Hegel maintains, both ancient and modern thought have had recourse to the naïve hypothesis of pores, e.g. Matter for Warmth is located in the interspaces of Matter for Magnetism, the latter in the interspaces of Matter for Warmth, and so on. As Hegel remarks: 'Where the difference-in-self, the contradiction and the negation enters, where recourse must be had to concepts, picture-thought submits to the sway of an external, quantitative difference. In the face of generation and destruction, it takes refuge in gradualness, and in the face of being, in smallness, wherein a vanishing moment is reduced to one that is unnoticeable, and the true relationship is played over into an indefinite picture whose murkiness saves the notion that is in process of breaking down.'[1]

The true outcome of the difficulties which have emerged is said by Hegel to be the dissolution of the Thing. The world can no longer be conceived as a plurality of self-subsistent Things, each giving the others Properties through its interrelations with them. It becomes demoted to a system where all is phenomenal, 'a posited being not opposed to an essential Ground, nor an appearance attached to what is self-subsistent'. We have passed into the sphere of *Erscheinung*, Phenomenal Being Proper. Despite appearances, Hegel emphasizes that we are not here returning to

[1] *Sc. of Log.*, I, pp. 619–20 (J. & S., II, p. 126; M., p. 497).

the category of Mere Appearance, which we considered previously. Phenomenal Being is a richer category than either Being
or Existence, since it involves in itself a deeper essential dimension,
even if this lies rather in the interrelation of phenomena than in
any entity postulated beneath the surface.

When the Thing vanishes as the nucleus holding various
Properties together, its place, says Hegel, is at once taken by the
Law of the Phenomenon, a new category expressing the way in
which various phenomenal features hang together or vary together.
Such a Law expresses, in the form of abstract universal consequence, what in the field of appearance will often be a relation of
conflict or succession: it may therefore be said to provide us with
an *abiding, tranquil* model of the existent or phenomenal world.
It will likewise reduce to a *simple* correlation what in the phenomenal world appears as a rich variety of changing factors. And it is
called a Law, a *Gesetz*, because it is something merely posited
(*gesetzt*), derivative in opposition to the immediate data of appearance, and also because it expresses merely *hypothetical* relations
between determinations in which they may be said to posit one
another. Hegel further stresses that the Laws of Phenomena do
not lie beyond phenomena but are present in them. So much is
this so that they preserve something of the contingent immediacy
of the features connected in experience, and in no sense involve
a necessary passage.

Hegel now argues that these Laws of Phenomena must, by
their nature, be ever more and more extended so as to cover every
detail and winding of phenomenal fact. They must be perfected
into a system, a realm of legal principles, with special rules flowing
from more general ones, so as to cover every possible combination
of circumstances and conditions. In the end the realm of Laws
must cover, in tranquil, merely hypothetical form, the whole
content of whatever exists or might have existed in the whole
universe: there will, e.g., be a purely legal formula expressing
exactly what *would* happen if a man exactly like Caesar *were* to
cross a stream exactly like the Rubicon in circumstances exactly
like those existing in the late Roman Republic. As so developed,
the realm of Laws will acquire every feature of contingency and
inessentiality previously attributed to the world of phenomena:
it will include, *sub specie legalitatis*, whatever is real and concrete
in the empirical world. And the world of phenomena, by exempli-

fying the completed realm of Laws, will also acquire the close connections of content characteristic of the latter. When this point is reached, Hegel maintains, it will no longer be possible to differentiate the two worlds from one another. They will become mirror-duplicates of each other, identical both in form and content, in which case it will no longer be possible to regard one as the original and the other as its reflection. If they differ at all, Hegel suggests, it will only be in respect of some wholly senseless inversion, the North Pole in the realm of phenomena becoming the South Pole in the realm of Laws, positive electricity being transformed into negative, and evil and unhappiness into happiness and good. (Hegel is here faithfully reviving the strange fable of a topsy-turvy non-phenomenal world which we found so puzzling in the *Phenomenology*. But it is not clear what light it can throw on the deep contrast between hypothetical legality and categorical existence, which would seem to remain however much the content of the two worlds were assimilated. That Caesar *crossed* the Rubicon because, etc. etc., cannot by any dialectical legerdemain be made to mean the same as that Caesar *would* have crossed the Rubicon *if*, etc. etc.)

Hegel is, however, on firmer ground when he holds that the truth of Phenomenal Being lies in what he calls the 'Essential Relationship', the next set of categories to which he passes. Quite obviously the whole meaning of hypothetical statements of Law is to mirror in ideality and universality what appears as a merely factual, phenomenal connection, and obviously it is the ideal destiny of every factual phenomenon to have its content completely covered by hypothetical statements of Law. An Essential Relationship is one which maintains the distinction between the immediate, self-subsistent surface of reality and its reflection into a deeper legal dimension, but which also sees both sides of the distinction as essentially connected. Hegel then studies what he calls an immediate form of the Essential Relationship, the Relationship of Whole and Parts, in which both sides are equally self-subsistent, a more developed form, the relationship of a Force to its Manifestations, in which one member, the Force, is alone regarded as self-subsistent, and finally the consummating Relationship of Inner to Outer, in which the whole distinction between immediacy and reflectedness goes to the ground, and the Essential Relationship develops into the new category of Actuality.

In the Relationship of Whole and Parts the role of immediacy, of surface, is taken by the Parts, while the Whole represents reflectedness into a deeper dimension. Either side, however, can be regarded as the side which is self-subsistent, in which case the other side will enjoy a derivative, merely posited being. But it is impossible to give self-subsistence to one member of our antithetical pair, to make it include the whole relationship under consideration, without finding that self-subsistence at once shift to the other member. In this lies the contradiction and inadequacy of the Whole-Part category. Thus we cannot conceive of a Whole as a self-subsistent totality without conceiving that, since it is a Whole, it consists of its Parts, and we cannot treat the Parts as a self-subsistent totality without realizing that, if they ceased to form a Whole, they could not even be many at all, but would even coincide in the abstraction of their isolated being. The Whole and the Parts are likewise from one point of view indivisibly identical, while from another point of view it is only the Parts *together*, i.e. as assembled into a Whole, which amount to the Whole, and it only the Whole divided, i.e. broken into Parts, which amounts to the Parts. (Hegel is here dealing with the puzzles which agitated both Plato and Russell, as to what things can properly be said to be many: it seems that neither things without relation, nor things related to form a Whole, can fitly claim the title.) A situation in which two correlated categories thus repeatedly defer to each other's precedence, like two courtiers endlessly bowing before some doorway, is a case of opposition sharpened to self-contradiction, which demands supersession by some less inhibiting form of thought. This Hegel finds in the notion of a Force and its Manifestation.

In the notion of a Force and its Manifestation there is the same oscillation in priority between the two correlated determinations: at one moment the Force passes over into its Manifestation, at another time the Manifestation is withdrawn back into the Force. But the Force does not merely yield place to the Manifestation which expresses it, as the Whole divides into its Parts, and is lost in them, but is in some sense still present and active in it: it can be overt and manifest as well as covert and unmanifest. And even when a Force is unmanifest, it is still thought of as attaching to something which enjoys manifest existence. Hegel maintains, further, as in the *Phenomenology*, that it is part of what we understand by a Force that it should be *solicited* or provoked by something external to itself, and that what solicits it should itself be a Force and not merely a Thing. The dialectic now takes a familiar turn: since it is of the essence of a Force that it should be solicited by another Force, the soliciting Force is not really alien, but is merely posited as such. The outside influence provoking a power into exercise is merely the power's own 'presupposing activity' which assumes the form of another power. This presupposition is, moreover, mutual, and the soliciting power can also be regarded as presupposing the activity of the soliciting power, without which it could not exercise its soliciting vocation. The outcome of all this Dialectic, as in all previous cases of limitation or conditioning, is that the various dynamic factors which seem to interact in producing a given result are one and the same, and that Force or power must be thought of, not as finite and externally provoked, but as infinite and self-provoking. 'The impulse whereby it is solicited into activity is its own solicitation: the outwardness which approaches it is nothing immediate but mediated by itself, just as its own essential self-identity is not immediate but mediated by its negation. In other words, power makes *this* manifest or outward: that its outwardness is identical with this inwardness.'[1] With this Hegel passes to the last form of Essential Relationship, that of Inner to Outer, or Interior to Exterior.

In the Inner-Outer Relationship we have a single self-identical Matter of Fact (*Sache*) which is conceived under two forms, a form of essentiality or reflectedness-into-self, and a form of immediacy or reflectedness-into-another. The former is its interior, the latter its exterior aspect. The two forms are really a vestige of dialectical history: a Matter of Fact conceived as Exterior is conceived as consisting of Parts, conceived as Interior it is conceived as a Whole, conceived as Exterior it is manifest and expressed, as Interior it is dynamic and dispositional. Now, however, there is complete coincidence between the two sides of the notion, and it is only past history that enables us to differentiate them. Hegel's distinction of Inner and Outer is not therefore like the distinction between the inner life of thought and the outer life of overt behaviour, where many inner changes are not outwardly expressed and there are outer changes without an

[1] *Sc. of Log.*, I, p. 655 (J. & S., II, p. 154; M., p. 523).

inner backing. It is much more like the Aristotelian distinction between convex and concave, where every convexity is from an opposite point of view a concavity, and *vice versa*. Hegel, however, allows us to say that a certain Essence is *merely* inward, but only by coupling it with the paradox that such a merely inward Essence is also merely outward. Thus the rationality which appears in a merely inward form in the child, also appears in a merely outward form in its parents and instructors, and the will to violence that appears merely inwardly in some criminal appears merely outwardly in the violence which punishes him. The merely inward and merely outward are, in Hegel's language, an 'untrue' expression of the categorial relationship in question, which is 'truly' expressed only when the two sides coincide in the same reality. Hegel has much that is profound and edifying to say about the hollowness of claiming to have a noble inner nature, remarkable talents, etc., to which outer circumstances have denied an adequate expression. Nothing, he holds, can significantly be said to be *in* a man's nature which is not effectively brought out of it.

Hegel is now able to pass, with little more than the shade of a transition, from the Essential Relationship of Inner and Outer to the new notional field of Actuality (*Wirklichkeit*). In the Relationship of Inner and Outer there is still a distinction of aspect in regard to a content which is through and through identical. In the category of Actuality this distinction will be altogether dropped. The sustained brilliance of Hegel's treatment of the three forms of Essential Relationship will be evident: they provide one of the happiest and most successful instances of the Dialectic.

V THE ACTUAL, THE POSSIBLE, THE CONTINGENT AND THE NECESSARY

The treatment of Actuality occupies the third main division of the Doctrine of Essence: the notion is obviously of the first importance in Hegel's philosophy. By what is actual Hegel means what is actualized, fully realized and operative: it entails, at least in principle, individuality, definiteness, sensuous concreteness, being here and now, and a complete context of conditions. Hegel's philosophy has absolutely no final place for realities that are non-individual, beyond human apprehension, merely posited or prescribed, infinite in the bad sense, supersensuous and without a firm lodgement in the Here and the Now. He emphasizes repeatedly that his Absolute Idea is nothing elusive and far-off, but both actual and present, that it is in fact what is absolutely active and actual. The entailment between Actuality and immediate sensuous concreteness is not, however, reciprocal: not everything that is palpable and accessible is thereby elevated to Actuality. There are many things immediately present which, in the Hegelian sense, fall short of Actuality, which are 'low and untrue existences', by no means actually what they have it in them to be. There is an implicit reference to the long view and the full view in the Hegelian conception of Actuality: what is said to be Actual certainly *will* achieve full presence in chosen moments of human experience, but the whole Dialectic would be put out of action were it *always* so achieved. It is in this sense, and with these qualifications, that we must understand Hegel's attribution of Actuality to his Absolute Idea, as well as his hard saying that the 'Rational is the Actual, and the Actual the Rational'.

Hegel begins his treatment of Actuality in the *Science of Logic* by a first section on 'the Absolute', which deals with the main concepts of Spinozism: this is omitted in the *Encyclopaedia*. It is subsidiary to the development of the Dialectic, but is of some interest owing to the Spinozistic inspiration of much Anglo-Saxon interpretation of Hegel. The Absolute is here sketched by Hegel as the self-identical *Ground* in which all previous categorial determinations—Essence, Existence, Whole, Parts, Force, etc.— have gone to ground and suffered shipwreck. The Absolute is thus negatively related to the categories previously considered: it is the abyss (*Abgrund*) in which they all have vanished. But it is also positively related to them all, since they can only have an apparent application if the Absolute appears *in* them. This positive relation is, however, of the nature of an external reflectedness: as in Bradley, the setting forth of the appearances of the Absolute falls outside of the treatment of the Absolute as it is in itself. Hegel holds this whole position to be dialectically self-destroying: the Absolute cannot be absolute unless it takes into its identity all the distinctions of Being and Essence, and unless it *itself* carries out the exposition of the appearances which was credited to external reflection. It must be shown to be of the nature of the Absolute to express itself, not only in all-embracing Attributes, but also in Modes corresponding to the forms and phases of finite existence. These Modes, says Hegel, must be the Absolute's *own* reflective movement: it is only in them that the Absolute can be what it is, 'an identity with self as negativity which refers self to self, an appearance which is set down as an appearance'.[1] Hegel holds that Spinoza, among other most serious faults, failed altogether to establish a necessary transition from his Absolute Substance to its inessential Modes, to show that it could not be an Absolute Substance except as so differentiating itself. The Spinozistic procession of Modes is really an oriental doctrine of emanation in which the production of finite beings remains an inexplicable fact, involving an ever-increasing loss of lustre as the emanation proceeds further. Leibniz, Hegel maintains, remedied these defects of Spinozism by bringing in the principle of monadic individuality, by concentrating the world's content in self-conscious, self-determining individuals. The comparative favour shown to Leibniz is extremely revealing: it shows how the Hegelian Absolute has no other seat or vehicle, no other location for its infinity or its absoluteness, beyond the experiences and decisions of particular conscious persons.

From this interesting digression Hegel returns to the treatment of Actuality, which the concept of the Absolute has developed in an unsatisfactory manner. From the Modes of the Spinozistic Substance he proceeds to study the Logical Modalities, between which he claims to see a more than merely verbal connection. Since 'the Absolute' is expunged without loss in the *Encyclopaedia*, we may ignore this transition from its Modes to the Modalities. In his treatment of these Modalities Hegel is hampered by his passion for triadicity. He distinguishes three stages, one of Contingency or merely Formal Actuality, Possibility and Necessity— one of Relative Necessity or Real Actuality, Possibility and Necessity—leading up to a final third stage of Absolute Necessity.

Actuality, it will be remembered, is the Whole which has reached identity with its Parts, the Force fully expressed in its Manifestations, and the Interior that has become the completely Exterior. As so conceived, Actuality has an immediate being corresponding to the immediate side of the above categories, and another aspect which corresponds, in vestigial form, to their inward, essential side. This latter aspect will be the modal aspect

---

[1] *Sc. of Log.*, I, p. 670 (J. & S., II, p. 166; M., p. 535).

of Possibility, which must necessarily be thought of as present in Actuality, since whatever is actual, is also possible. The most elementary form of Actuality is one that abstracts from a necessitating context, which is thought of as immediate and not as mediate. As so conceived, it is merely a *pro forma* or Formal Actuality, and the Possibility which corresponds to it is likewise a merely formal, abstract Possibility, one that is sufficiently established by the mere *absence of contradiction*.

Hegel stresses the extreme emptiness and nugatoriness of *this* sort of Possibility, the fact that everything, if sufficiently detached from the Conditions required by its nature, can be held to be possible in this sense: it is possible, e.g. that the moon may fall to the earth, that the Sultan may become Pope, etc. etc. It is rather the first abstract blue-print of the notion of Possibility than the complete working notion. It involves, in fact, an immediate and obvious contradiction, for by calling something possible we imply that it is something *less* than actual, and we imply also that it must remain so as long as it is merely possible. What will in no circumstances be actual is, however, the *Impossible* rather than the Possible: every possibility is therefore, *qua* merely possible, also impossible. Hegel points out further how the merely Possible *excludes* itself from actualization since it is a two-sided, ambivalent Possibility, as much the Possibility of not-A as it is of A. Until and unless one of these sides can be held back from realization, the Possible will remain the Impossible. The self-contradictory notion of a Possible which is less than the Actual must therefore be replaced by the notion of a Possible incorporated in the Actual, which will accordingly make of that Actual something merely *contingent*, since the possibility incorporated will as much be the possibility of *something else* as of the state of affairs realized. (There are obvious fallacies in the above arguments, which we need not waste time in pointing out in detail.)

Hegel emphasizes that the notion of Contingency, of a merely chance being, is a legitimate phase of the Idea, and has also a genuine application on the surface of nature and mind. There are many more or less superficial matters of fact which are also matters of mere fact, for which no scientific or philosophical reason can be given why they should be thus and not otherwise. The 'chequered play of the particular sorts of plants and animals', 'the complex changes in the formation and grouping of clouds', as well as the casual fancies and caprices entertained by the individual mind, are all given as examples of superficial Contingency, for which it would be wrong to seek a necessitating explanation.[1] The fact, however, that Contingency enjoys free play on the surface of nature does not mean that, *qua* category, it is not imperfect and self-destroying, and it is this self-destruction that Hegel next proceeds to help on.

Quite obviously we mean by what is Contingent what is without sufficient Ground, that whose contrary is as possible as the thing itself. But this Possibility of an unrealized contrary is the merely Formal possibility which has already been ruled out as senseless: there must therefore be some Ground from which it follows that an unrealized alternative *is* unrealized and that a realized one has been realized. 'The Contingent', Hegel says, 'has for that reason no Ground in that is it Contingent, but just as well it has a Ground in that it is Contingent.'[2] In the notion of the Contingent the two aspects of the Actual and the Possible are unsatisfactorily and restlessly combined: we therefore pass to the notion of the Necessary where their combination is stable and satisfactory. The Necessary is on the one hand Actual, and *qua* Actual in no need of a Ground, but it also includes in itself a Possibility which has been made into an Actuality through the elimination of the contrary Possibility by some sufficient Ground. The only *genuine* Possibility is in fact the *only* Possibility, a Possibility which has been raised to Necessity, and which coincides with the Actual.

Hegel now passes from the purely abstract, Formal Possibility, Actuality and Necessity so far considered to such as are *Real*. Obviously the abstract categories just studied demand a content with which they may be connected, and without which they could have no significance: this content must be borrowed from the Things with their many Properties which act and interact in the existent world. The Real Possibility of such things and their states is plainly not the mere absence of contradiction in which Formal Possibility consisted: it is rather the actual manifold of circumstances, of Conditions, which are relevant to such Things and their states. It is in *other* Things that such things have their Real Possibilities, just as they have their Formal Possibilities in

[1] *L. Log.*, p. 327 (W., p. 264).
[2] *Sc. of Log.*, I, p. 684 (J. & S., II, p. 177; M., p. 545).

themselves. These Real Possibilities are, however, in Hegel's sense self-contradictory: their Formal Actuality is at odds with their Real Possibility. Hence when the conditions of a thing are all assembled, they inevitably pass away into the Actualities of which they are the Real Possibilities. These Actualities are, however, Real Necessities in the sense that, the Conditions and circumstances being what they are, no other outcome is possible. Real Possibility is therefore, in Hegel's use of the terms, inseparable from Real Necessity.

Hegel now points out that the Real Necessity thus reached is, from another point of view, really Contingent, since it has Contingency at its point of origin. Given the totality of the Conditions, the outcome *must* follow, but its Necessity rests on Conditions that are severally Contingent, and whose coming together proceeds by stages, and is likewise Contingent. Real Necessity, having a Contingent foundation, is therefore not really Necessary at all. But this unsatisfactory, inwardly discrepant notion 'swings over' at once, into one that is satisfactory and harmonious. It becomes plain that it is *of the nature* of the Necessary to have something Contingent to serve as its antecedent Condition, and in this understanding the Contingency of the Contingent is in a certain sense overcome. *Being a Necessary Condition of the Necessary it is also after a fashion Necessary.* 'It is accordingly Necessity which is as much the overcoming of what it posits as the positing of immediacy and undeveloped being, as of the determination of this overcoming as having a merely posited being. It is therefore Necessity itself which determines itself as Contingency, in its very being repulses itself from itself, and in this repulse has only returned to self, and in this return has likewise, as from its very being, repulsed self from self.'[1] Through the rich redundancy of his phraseology Hegel's meaning is plain: Contingency is only overcome in Necessity in the sense that it is the necessary Condition of all necessary connection, in which 'overcoming' it is of course eternally preserved. Hence Contingency does not merely sport on the surface of Nature, but lives enshrined at its heart: there are and always must be things which merely *are so*, in which Necessities have their origin. Science or *mediate* understanding can exist only by taking up into itself an element that is *immediate*, and which can at best become self-mediated. And empiricism,

[1] *Sc. of Log.*, I, p. 693 (J. & S., II, p. 184; M., p. 551).

which recognizes the starting-point of all knowledge in the immediate and Contingent, is a permanent facet of ultimate truth.

'Absolute Necessity', Hegel maintains, 'is the truth in which Actuality and Possibility in general, as well as Formal and Real Necessity, go back. . . . It is therefore as much simple immediacy or Pure Being, as it is simple reflectedness-into-self or Pure Essence; it is the fact that these two are one and the same. The Absolutely Necessary only is, because it *is*. It has otherwise no Condition and no Ground. It is just as much Pure Essence, its being is simple reflectedness-into-self, it is *because* it is. As reflectedness it has Ground and Condition, but it has only itself as Ground and Condition. It is Being-implicit, but its implicitness is its immediacy, its Possibility is its Actuality. *It is accordingly because it is*: as the *coming together* of Being with itself it is Essence, but because this simplicity is an immediate simplicity, it is Being.'[1]

Hegel is here saying what Bosanquet says when he holds all necessity to have a 'categorical basis'. Only while for Bosanquet this categorical basis lies in the all-inclusive system of the Universe, Hegel's categorical basis lies in the infinitely numerous individual realities, the nature of which involves responsive conditioning by all others. This basis explains why Necessity is said to be *blind*, and also why it is said to *shun the light*. The various individual elements of the world carry no mark on their faces of their relationships to each other. From the point of view of their surface being these relationships appear as external, as coming to them accidentally from without. Such relations belong to the depth, to the Essence of objects, and only 'break out' and reveal themselves in their contacts with other objects.[2] It is only in the exhaustive testing of things by other things that it becomes clear what they essentially are. It seems plain that there is nothing in Hegel's doctrine of Necessity which could affront the most austere empiricist. It is quite free from the doctrine that we can deduce the plan of the universe, or any segment of it, merely by scrutinizing one of its parts.

[1] *Sc. of Log.*, I, pp. 693–4 (J. & S., II, pp. 184–5; M., p. 552).
[2] *Sc. of Log.*, I, p. 695 (J. & S., II, pp. 185–6; M., p. 553).

VI SUBSTANCE, CAUSE AND RECIPROCAL INTERACTION

Hegel now winds up his treatment of Essence by considering three categories which are held by him to exemplify Necessity with ever-increasing adequacy. These are the categories of Substance and Accident, of Cause and Effect and of Reciprocal Interaction (*Wechselwirkung*), which have so important a place in Kant's *Critique of Pure Reason*. In these notions the Absolute Essence is said to set forth and expound *itself*, in contrast to the external exposition it received in Spinozistic philosophies.

Substance is set forth by Hegel as the being which is because it is, the unity of posited reflectedness and apparent or surface being, which involves a continual 'swing over' from the possible to the actual, and *vice versa*, while retaining its deep Essence in all such changes; its tranquilly proceeding 'actuosity' is revealed in the movement of its Accidents, and its provocation *ab extra* is merely a vanishing appearance. Its simple identity of being is inseparably one with the ceaseless change of its Accidents, in relation to which it appears as the Absolute Power, always creative and destructive at once: its Accidents have in themselves no power, and certainly no power over each other. It is Substance in the form of Accident *A* which solicits the development of Accident *B* or which does away with Accident *C*, and which is accordingly *self*-solicited and *self*-directed. Hegel thinks, however, that Substance, so conceived, is *too* emphatically self-identical, its Accidents *too* shadowy and evanescent, to rise to its full notion. Having none but a shadow-other to box with, Substance itself is nerveless and shadowy, a mere formal 'inner' to its outward Accidents. The Accidents, which are all thought of as being Substance *au fond*, must therefore *show* their substantiality in their being and working: they must each *be* Substance in one of its phases, if the identity which resumes them is to be genuine, embracing real differences and oppositions in itself. The full working out of Substantiality therefore leads Hegel on to the category of Causality.

In the *Encyclopaedia* Hegel connects this treatment of Substance with the philosophy of Spinoza, which is, in the *Science of Logic*, dealt with in his earlier discussion of 'the Absolute'. This might lead one to think that Substance as here treated involves singleness in its notion, that there can be but *one* Substance of which all things are the Accidents. To draw this inference would, however, be wrong. Hegel's treatment of Substance is quite neutral as regards the opposition between monism and pluralism. And the subsequent movement of the Dialectic is towards a world of interacting substantial units rather than to a Spinozistic unity. Hegel's use of the word 'substance' in other contexts has moreover no all-comprehensive Spinozistic suggestions: he speaks of 'substance' in connection with the half-conscious ethical life of primitive society, which is certainly *not* thought of as all-inclusive.

In the treatment of Causality which follows, Hegel rather perversely emphasizes the *identity of content* between the Active Causality exhibited by one Accident, and the merely Passive Consequence shown by another. An Effect, he holds, can by its notion contain *nothing* that is not contained in its Cause, and *vice versa*. In so far as Cause and Effect *differ*, they do so only in respect of supplementary features which are wholly contingent and external. By virtue of this identity of content, statements of causal connection become for Hegel basically tautological. Hegel gives several pregnant illustrations of this famous doctrine, whose inspiration is very probably Aristotelian. Thus rain is the Cause of moistening in the things it wets, but it can be so only because of the moistness or wateriness which it *has* as much as it imparts. In the same way a pigment colours an object only by being of the very colour it gives it, a body moves another body by imparting an unaltered quantum of movement, and the style manifest in a painter's other products and way of life merely shows itself in the pictures he paints. Hegel admits that there are important exceptions to this principle of Cause-Effect identity. It has no application where the inorganic acts on the organic or the spiritual, since in such cases Causality itself only has partial application. The living and the spiritual are such as to break with causal chains, to transmute them in characteristic, discontinuous ways. Thus the damp which occasions a fever does not continue in the fever it sets up, nor is the Ionic climate continued into the Homeric poems for which it provided the needful setting. But even with these qualifications, Hegel's doctrine of Cause-Effect identity may be regarded as unfortunate and uncharacteristic. It is doubtless the case that we *do look* for a continuing content among states held to be causally connected, and are much happier when we have found one: we like, e.g., to see causal connection as a communication of motion, or energy, or quality, or of a pattern of life and ideas. But even where such a continuing content can be pinned down, we still want to hold that Cause and Effect reveal this content in a different *manner* or *form*. Energy manifest in motion is and is not the same thing as energy manifest in heat: the Buddhist way of life as developed in ancient India is and is not the same thing as the Buddhist way of life as developed in Ceylon and China. Hegel might here have stressed the necessary union of significant identity with difference which was so emphasized at an earlier stage of the work.

The further development of the Dialectic does not, however, depend on this doctrine of Cause-Effect identity: it rests on the inevitable development of Causality into a 'Bad' Infinite Progression. Obviously a content which can be shifted without let or hindrance from Cause to Effect, can be shifted with equal ease and smoothness from an Effect to yet another Effect, or from a Cause to yet another Cause, and so on *in infinitum*. The Cause may be dominant or essential as against the dependent, accidental Effect, but, being limited by that Effect, it is itself finite and dependent, and in need of another determining Cause. In the same way the Cause passes over into, loses its causal virtue in the Effect, which thereby carries that causal virtue implicit in itself, and accordingly becomes a new Cause. We thereby reach a situation in which Causality perpetually extinguishes itself in Consequence, and emerges like a phoenix refreshed from its ashes, while Consequence equally passes away into Causality, to re-emerge from the outcome.

Hegel now explains how the Bad Infinity involved in the logical situation just outlined necessarily resolves itself in a manner parallel to the way in which previous Bad Infinities have also been resolved: by being 'bent round' into a circle, so that the Effect no longer exerts its causality *away* from the Cause, but rather reacts *back* on this same Cause. The argumentation by which this result is reached assumes that the phase of being in which Causality is located must be thought of as different from the phase of being in which the corresponding Consequence has its seat: if a Substance can be said to act on itself, it must, in Aristotelian phrase, act on itself *qua* other. We must therefore, in our thought of causal transactions, oppose a *Passive* Substance on which causality is exerted, to an *Active* Substance which exerts it (even if in special cases these should be one and the same). Not only is this so, but the Passive Substance must be the right sort of Substance for the Active Substance to act on, and it must be thought of as inevitable, as of the essence of the Passive Substance, that it should be thus acted upon. The Passive Substance must accordingly be thought of as *Active* in the causal transaction, and not only as Active, but as acting *on* the Active Substance which also acts on it. Only in so far as the Passive Substance is there to suffer violence, can the Active Substance exert violence on it, and the Passive Substance also *strips* the active Substance of its causality by permitting itself to be acted on. We are in a position similar to the one previously studied in the case of Forces and their mutual solicitings. What emerges from the whole discussion is that the Cause-Effect transaction is in itself reciprocal and complete: the Cause meets its precise match in the Effect, and the Effect likewise is exactly matched in the Cause. If there is a further spill-over of Causes into remoter Causes, and of Effects into more distant Effects, all this is logically a redundancy and an irrelevancy: we may extend a causal chain as far as we like, but we need not extend it beyond the smallest link. Just as a single sample of a wall-paper may embody in itself the whole of an indefinitely repeated pattern, so does the whole content of the causal relation appear perfectly in a single transaction. We have here yet another instance of Hegel's individualistic absolutism: for him the single causal transaction concentrates within its narrow bounds all the well-rounded completeness and explanatory unity that the widest system could embrace. This conclusion explains and justifies Hegel's puzzling indifference to the temporal aspect of Causality, an aspect generally thought to be of its essence. Within the limits of the single causal transaction the Cause is to all intents and purposes contemporaneous with the Effect.

From the notion of Causality Hegel now passes to the notion of Reciprocal Interaction (*Wechselwirkung*), the third member of Kant's famous trio of the categories of 'Relation'. We are no longer to think in terms of a single Substance of whose nature changing states are the inevitable outflow, nor in terms of Substances acting unilaterally on themselves and other Substances, and exerting on each other an endless interchange of influence:

we are to think rather of Substances as *conspiring* together to move in a common direction and to contribute to a joint result. This notion, with its total symmetry, brings out what is only implicitly present in the seemingly asymmetrical notion of Cause and Effect. (Whether this is what *Kant* understood by *Wechselwirkung* may, however, be gravely questioned.) 'At this point', Hegel maintains, 'Reciprocity presents itself as a reciprocal causality of presupposed and self-conditioning Substances. Each is in the relation to the other of being at once an Active and a Passive Substance. Both being thus as much Passive as Active, every distinction between them is already transcended: it is a perfectly transparent show. They are Substances only inasmuch as they are the identity of Active and Passive.'[1]

It is now easy for Hegel to pass out of the whole field of substantial and causal notions, and of the reflective determinations that preceded these. A Necessity in which there is no mutual interference among Substances, but only perfect harmony and conjoint action, is obviously indistinguishable from Freedom. When a Substance merely uses its varied intercourse with other Substances to bring out its own nature, and can never be Passive without in the same relation being Active as well, it can no longer be a victim of an alien Causality, but has become free, self-developing, inwardly complete. Hegel is here bringing into his Dialectic a vision undoubtedly borrowed from Spinoza, but he is bringing it in with a difference. While Spinoza sees Freedom merely in the realization of one's union with the necessity and infinity of the Universe, Hegel rather sees it in the extension of one's nature so as to take in all the influences and relationships that impinge on it from without. We are free for Spinoza by losing ourselves in the Universe: we are free for Hegel since the only Universe that there can be is in us. This Freedom is, however, only implicit at the present level. It must be worked out in the various categories of the Notion that will concern us in the next chapter.

We have now finished our account of the Doctrine of Essence, of Hegel's study of the categories of 'Reflection'. That he has dealt with a definite and important province of notions—those involving mutually determining pairs of correlatives, rather than single concepts—cannot be doubted. Nor can one doubt that he

[1] *Sc. of Log.*, I, p. 718 (J. & S., II, p. 203; M., p. 569).

has said many highly illuminating things about Identity and Difference, Ground and Consequent, Force and its Manifestation, Possibility and Necessity, Substance and Causality. Whether the successive treatments make up a genuine progress, rather than an interesting oscillation, is not so clear. The great difficulty of certain sections, those e.g. dealing with Ground and Cause, would seem to be due to the dispersed treatment of topics that really belong together. Everywhere the treatment is hampered by the determination to take everything in, and to do so along a single line of advance: no 'grand tour' of Europe was ever more crowded or more pressed. It is not worth the pains to try to amend Hegel's treatment at every point, nor even to enquire into the precise meaning of all its finer windings. As a method, the Dialectic is plainly one for rearward gazing admiration, and not for contemporary use. Through the grandiose sweep of its failure it, however, makes plain the profound affinity of notions too often and too lightly thought to be unrelated, and their constant connection with certain central ideals of intelligibility which are rightly held to spring from man's spiritual nature.

SUPPLEMENTARY NOTE

It will simplify the approach to the concepts of the sphere of Essence if one stresses that they are concepts of *disposition*. What enjoys *Gesetztseyn* in something else is what is *virtually*, *dispositionally* present in it. While the concepts of the sphere of Being deal only with what *manifestly* is, the concepts of the sphere of Essence deal also with what is *latent*, with what *would* or *could* be in certain circumstances. They are therefore a class of concepts much to the fore in contemporary discussion, e.g. in analyses of physical objects and mental states.

I also feel that the transition from Polar Opposition to Ground has perhaps stronger motivation than my remarks in the text might suggest. In Polar Opposition one deals with superficially antagonistic, independent features, which none the less depend upon and entail each other. In Ground this mutual dependence simply becomes explicit, since the Ground *plainly* involves the dispositional presence of what it grounds.

CHAPTER EIGHT

THE LOGIC — III

The Doctrine of the Notion

I THE NOTION AND ITS 'MOMENTS'; UNIVERSALITY,
SPECIFICITY AND INDIVIDUALITY

In the Doctrine of the Notion or Concept (*Begriff*), which forms the third main part of Hegel's Logic, the treatment of abstract categories or thought-determinations enters on a radically new stage. The notions hitherto dealt with, those, e.g. of Number, Measure, Difference, Appearance, Substance, Cause, were all *objectively* oriented: it was their function to grasp and organize things and materials which were not as such thoughts, nor posited as in any way essentially related to thoughts. Now, however, the notions we deal with will be *subjectively* as well as objectively oriented: they will be notions *of* notions, explicitly relating what they deal with to the central, co-ordinating life of thought. Hitherto, we may say, we have been employing notions, but not thinking of them as notions. Our notion of Causality, e.g., was the notion of two distinct but correlated determinations in two distinct natural objects: it included no awareness of the overarching unity which made it one notion rather than two, a notion of correlation rather than a correlation of notions. We have also, in the past, been more concerned with particular thought-determinations than with the universal that ran through them all: we have operated with thoughts rather than considered what it was to be a thought. Now the movement of the Dialectic, according to Hegel, has forced thought to become *self*-conscious: whatever it deals with will be henceforth seen as an expression of thought. With this change there will go an accompanying change. Our thought will no longer pass from one set phase to another quite different one as it did in the sphere of Being, nor will it be reflected to and fro among correlated determinations as it was in the sphere of Essence: it will instead tranquilly *develop*. By a change in internal emphasis it may specially light up one or other of its aspects or 'moments', but it will not permit others to pass wholly into shadow, nor to enjoy a fancied severance. In the sphere of the Notion one picture is always before us: we only become more clearly aware of its parts and their interrelations.

We should be able to see what Hegel means by 'the Notion' by seeing how its concept develops out of the three concepts of Substance, Causality and Reciprocal Interaction. Necessity there 'swung over' into Freedom, and the concept of Substance was replaced by the concept of the Notion. 'The Notion', Hegel tells us, 'is not the abyss of formless Substance, nor the Necessity which is the *inner* identity of mutually distinct, self-limiting things or states, but, as Absolute Negativity, it is the formative and creative element. Since its determination is no limit, but is absolutely overcome and reduced to a Positedness, so its appearance is an appearing of what is identical. The Universal is therefore Free Might: it is itself, and overreaches its other, not as it were by violence, but by being tranquilly with itself in it. Just as it is called Free Might, it might also be called Free Love and Unlimited Blessedness, since it stands to what is different only as it stands to itself, since in this other it has returned to self.'[1] What is implied in all this is that the melting of the walls between interacting Substances can, if it occurs at all, only be a *conscious melting*: it is only thought, with its concentration of multitude into unity, which can bridge the gulf between distinct Substances, and can transform foreign violence into unfettered self-expression. A Substance will, after a fashion, be expressing its own nature, even if it is buffeted and pushed about by other Substances, but it cannot, so long as it remains a mere Substance, be all this *for itself*: it remains, *qua* Substance, subject to Necessity, and its behaviour can be raised to Freedom only in so far as it begins consciously to understand and enjoy it, since it is only in such conscious enjoyment that things alien, dispersed and disparate can be made part of a thing's being. The emergence of conscious categories at this stage of the Dialectic is therefore intelligible and quite in order: interacting objects can at best exhibit an undeveloped analogue of Freedom, which can only be fully explicit in the unique reduction of the manifoldness of existence into single pulses of mind.

If doubt should exist as to the subjective implications of Hegel's term *Begriff*, one has but to look at his identification of the Notion with the Self or Ego. 'The Notion', Hegel tells us, 'in so far as it

---

[1] *Sc. of Log.*, II, pp. 39–40 (J. & S., II, p. 237; M., p. 603).

has risen to an existence which is itself free, is none other than the I or pure self-consciousness. I certainly *have* notions, i.e. determinate concepts, but my I is the pure Notion itself, which as concept has come into existence. When one reminds oneself of the basic determinations which constitute the nature of the I, it may be supposed that one is referring to something well known, familiar to picture-thinking. But I is first of all the pure unity which refers self to self, and this not immediately, but in so far as it abstracts from all determinateness and content, and retires into its illimitable sameness with self. To this extent it is *universality*, i.e. unity which only is unity with self through that negative attitude which appears as abstraction, and which thereby holds all determinations dissolved in itself. But secondly I is just as immediately negativity which refers self to self, individuality which opposes itself to what is other and excludes it, i.e. *individual personality*.'[1] The Notion is accordingly one with a man's thinking being, the same universal thinking nature in all, but individualized in this or that thinking person.

But lest passages like the above should seem to give too subjective an interpretation to the Hegelian Notion, one must remember that Hegel, like Kant, identifies the self with the unifying and universalizing agency of thought, with the emergence of unity and universality out of the confused mass of sense-experience. Such agency is not subjective in the sense of being arbitrary: the unity of consciousness for Hegel alone constitutes the relation of thoughts to objects, and thereby their objective validity. The self so conceived is simply objects revealing themselves as they truly are, as instances of a kind, terms in a relational unity, and so forth: it is not a special content set over against other contents, and counting as 'subjective' while they count as 'objective'. 'The conceptual grasp (*Begreifen*) of an object', Hegel tells us, 'consists, in fact, in nothing else but in that the self makes this object its *own*, penetrates it, and brings it into its own form, i.e. the form of a universality which is immediately determinateness and a determinateness which is immediately universality. The object in direct envisagement (*Anschauung*) or picture-thinking remains something external, foreign. Through the conceptual grasp (of the mind) the being-in-and-for-self that the object enjoys in direct envisagement and picture-thinking is transformed into a merely posited being: the I penetrates the object thinkingly. But as the object is in thought, so is it for the first time in and for itself. As it is in intuitive and picture thought it is an appearance.'[1] The self in short is the Universal in Action, and an object comprehended by the self is simply an object brought under the universals which make up its Essence.

The Hegelian Notion is, in fact, an entity straddling several spheres, that can be approached from several directions. It is an element in the individual's experience, and can as such be approached by way of feeling, sense-awareness and imagery as Hegel will do in the *Philosophy of Spirit*. It can be approached in terms of an ideal spiritual education as was done in the *Phenomenology*. But its logical aspects are concerned solely with the self-revelation of objects, in terms of various universals, without regard to the pictorial ways in which such a revelation may be brought home to the individual, and in this direction the Notion has its ancestry in the abstract concepts of Being and Essence, of whose notional character it represents the explicit statement. But the Notion also has a footing in the realm of Nature in which, says Hegel, it appears as a 'blind, unspiritual Notion, one that neither apprehends nor thinks itself'; such a Notion is only a Notion implicitly or by courtesy. Hegel's Notions have, in fact, much the same variety of role as the Forms of things have in Aristotle: they have a being in nature, whose variety and changes they produce and explain, they also have an immaterial being in the mind in which role they are led up to by various psychic states and accompaniments. But *the* Notion as such resembles Aristotle's Intelligence in Act or the self-thinking thought of God, which in thinking itself also thinks every determinate notion.

If the Notion thus lives finely poised between subjectivity and objectivity, it also, on Hegel's view, extends itself in three different logical directions, which are none the less interdependent and incapable of separation. These are the directions of Universality, of Specificity (or Particularity) and of Individuality (or Singularity). To have a Notion is to think universally of things, to range them under common characters in which their specific differences and crude individual immediacy will be submerged. But it is just as definitely to be ready to pass to more precise specifications of character within this universal framework, or to treat one's Notion

[1] *Sc. of Log.*, II, p. 16 (J. & S., II, p. 219; M., pp. 584-5).

as specifying others which are more general: only along a ladder of generality and specificity can either direction have meaning or importance. To have a Notion is, lastly, to refer, even if in remote and sidelong fashion, to the possible individuals to whom such a Notion might be applied. To have the Notion of man is not merely to think of certain generic or specific properties, but also to think of *something* that might have them. Hegel says: 'The Universal is the self-identical expressly so taken that in it the Specific and the Singular are contained. The Specific moreover is the distinct or determinate, but so taken as to be Universal in itself and also Individual. Just so the Individual has the meaning of being a subject, a basis which contains the Genus and Species in itself and is itself substantial. This is the posited inseparability of the moments in their difference, the clearness of the Notion which no distinction interrupts or perturbs, but which always remains equally transparent.'[1]

Hegel points out further how the attempt to separate the three 'moments' in question only leads to each developing the marks of the others. Thus a Universal cut off from Individuals or from further specification becomes itself a mere Individual, plainly the *gravamen* of the Aristotelian criticism of Plato's Forms. An Individual, likewise, cut off from the Genera and Species which pin down its nature, becomes emptily universal, a mere One or This. The most Specific Determination is further purely Universal if not seen in relation to universals of higher order, and the widest Genus would lose its Generality were there nothing Specific to be ranged under it.

The Universality which thus involves Specificity and Individuality is said by Hegel to be a *Concrete* Universality, and is opposed to the Abstract Universality in which conceptual thought is generally held to consist. 'The Universal of the Notion', Hegel tells us, 'is not merely a *common feature* which has its self-subsistence over what is specific, but it is much rather something self-specifying and self-particularizing, which remains unperturbedly by itself in its other. It is of the greatest importance, both for knowledge and practice, that the merely *common* should not be confused with what is truly Universal.'[2] Hegel's doctrine of Concrete Universality must not, however, be interpreted in too

[1] *L. Log.*, pp. 361–2 (W., pp. 294–5).
[2] *L. Log.*, § 163, p. 359 (W., p. 292).

mystifying or too mystical a fashion. It is not the doctrine that a Generic Notion *includes* all its specifications as part of its intension, nor is it the doctrine that such a Notion somehow leads to a precise deduction of the Species or Individuals falling under it. What it does involve is that a Generic Concept is only a Generic Concept is so far as its use implies a reference to *possible* Specifications and to possible Individual Applications, that these do not come to it surprisingly from without, but represent the fulfilment of what it is. Hence the Universal is not merely common to the Species and Individuals it informs: it is *differently* realized in each of them. And there is, and should be, no problem in seeing how a Universal like 'being greater than ten' can specify itself in different numbers, or how a Universal like 'man' can specify itself in the various sorts and conditions of men, nor how either concept can apply to the Individuals or sets of Individuals that exemplify it. The thought of Logic, in particular, while in a sense purely formal, without the rich content which will accrue to it from the study of nature and mind, has, none the less, Hegel holds, a content, a material, a 'reality' peculiar to itself.[1] If it does not (we may say) include the kind of references which are expressed by individual and predicate *constants*, it at least contains the kind of references which are expressed by individual and predicate *variables*. It is in this sense and no other that Hegel holds Universal Concepts to be 'concrete' and 'self-specifying'. There is no trace in his practice, despite some use of generative metaphors, of any attempt to beget what is Specific or Individual out of the mere Universality of the Notion.

Hegel's doctrine of the interdependence of the three moments of Universality, Specificity and Individuality in the Notion is crucial for the understanding of his system. The Idea, we must remember, is merely a more experienced self-conscious form of the Notion, in which the moment of Objectivity, implicit in Individuality, has been allowed to develop itself more fully. Absolute Spirit likewise, in which the Dialectic of Nature and Spirit culminates, is merely the Idea brought down from formal ideality to full embodiment in human experience: Spirit, too, is therefore a fuller expression of the Notion. But the Notion is essentially something Universal whose nature it is to specify itself in various definite ways, and be expressed in a multitude of

[1] *Sc. of Log.*, II, p. 27 (J. & S., II, p. 227; M., pp. 592–3).

mutually exclusive individuals. It follows that the Absolute Spirit and Idea of Hegel are to be understood as something Universal, something common to all self-conscious beings, but also such as to specify itself in varying ways in countless mutually exclusive individual minds. We shall get Hegel's meaning awry if we lay undue stress either on the natural Individuality and human Specificity of his Absolute, or on its overarching, pervasive Universality and Unity.

We may note, further, that *Abstract* as well as Concrete Universality plays a part in Hegel's Notion. Though its three moments are in Hegel's view inseparable, and may each be regarded as the *whole* Notion, of which the others are only aspects, yet the Notion does, in some fashion, set its aspects against one another, so that the merely Universal and merely Specific confront each other as two species of what is Concretely Universal. Hegel strangely suggests that this self-diremption of Concrete Universality into Abstract Universality, on the one hand, and Abstract Specificity on the other, is the model and pattern for all good logical divisions, which should accordingly be dichotomic. Nature, indeed, often offers us Genera with more than two Species, but this, says Hegel, is only Nature's impotence, its inability to rise to the rigour of the Notion, and its consequent lapse into a blind notionless multiplication of kinds which awakens wonder only in the irrational.[1] Whatever one may think of this astonishing opinion, Hegel certainly holds that the Notion can in some sense be doubled, dislocated from itself, divided into moments whose inner identity is implicit and not posited in the moments themselves. As so dislocated each moment is Abstractly Universal, is the Notion 'reduced to notionlessness' and not posited as a Notion. Such Abstract Universality is, however, *essential* to the life of the Notion: by giving hardness to its various notional determinations, it calls into action its own dialectical power, which will reduce them to mere moments in its unity. Abstract Universality is accordingly part of the being of the Notion, since it is only through its nullification that the Notion can achieve concreteness.

From the general treatment of the Notion and its moments Hegel passes on to a treatment of the various forms of Judgement and Syllogism, which will show us the Notion concretely at work, at once distinguishing and reuniting its moments. This part of

---

[1] *Sc. of Log.*, II, p. 46 (J. & S., II, pp. 241–2; M., pp. 607–8).

Hegel's Logic is the only part that answers to the traditional concept of Logic. It is of considerable interest itself, but is also important as having inspired the *Logics* of Bradley and Bosanquet, both works in which Hegelians may be held to have followed and improved upon Hegel. If a work like Bradley's *Appearance and Reality* now seems little more than an undistinguished pastiche of Hegelianism, eked out with Spinozistic memories, his *Logic*, and the twin *Logic* of Bosanquet, remain worthy attempts to turn the undeveloping classifications of the traditional formal logic into an ascending, Hegelian ladder of judgemental and inferential forms.

II   THE JUDGEMENT AND ITS VARIETIES

In his treatment of the Judgement Hegel stresses the line it draws between the three notional moments of Individuality, Specificity and Universality rather than the union or connection it effects among them. The Judgement, he says, is rightly called the *Ur-theil*, the primeval partition between Subject and Predicate, or between the Individual, on the one hand, and a Sort or Kind, on the other. We tend, says Hegel, to picture the Subject of a Judgement as an object, an individual, existing 'out there' in the world, while the Predicate (a Sort or Kind) is an 'idea in my head': these two are bound together in the Judgement, but in a manner so external that each would be exactly what it is even if no such bond existed.[1] The Judgement itself, Hegel holds, justifies this mode of picture-thinking since it emphasizes the independence, the self-subsistence of the various moments it combines rather than their interdependence and logical interpenetration. None the less, the Judgement contains in itself a perpetual reminder of the inseparability of the elements it holds apart: this reminder lies in the Copula, the verb 'to be', which is always assuring us that, despite appearances, the Individual *is* the Universal, the Individual *is* the Species, the Species *is* the Universal and so forth. Hegel assumes that the Copula expresses the *identity* of the terms it unites : he does not draw the modern distinction between the Copula as sign of Characterization and the Copula as sign of Identity. Nor is this so very reprehensible when one considers Hegel's fluid notion of identity, so much more like the identity of

[1] *Sc. of Log.*, II, pp. 68-9 (J. & S., II, p. 260; M., pp. 625-6).

ordinary speech than the rigid concept of logicians. To make a Judgement, Hegel is insisting, is not to put together things which have nothing to do with each other: it is to distinguish pieces which belong together and which dovetail deeply into each other's being.

Hegel holds, none the less, that the 'identity' of Universal, Species and Individual (variously placed as Subject or Predicate in a Judgement) is not so much clearly posited in the Copula, as *present* (*vorhanden*) in it. It is not merely implicit (*an sich*) as it is in the mere Notion, but it is not explicitly posited (*gesetzt*). The Judgement (we may put it) that this rose is red, does not affirm this Individual to be that Universal, it rather *shows* this by employing the Copula. This showing is, however, fraught with an inner tension or 'contradiction': the two sides of the Judgement may not be so perfectly matched as to live up to the identity 'present' in the Copula. Obviously the *whole* being of this rose is not exhausted in its redness, nor of redness in this rose. Hegel holds, therefore, that Judgements will arrange themselves in a scale or series in which there will be an ever more perfect identification or overlap of the elements distinguished in them. From the almost peripheral contact of the rose and its redness, we shall rise to the close and intimate union between this man and his goodness, where the goodness represents something precisely adjusted to the specificity and individuality of the man. As we move along this series we shall, according to Hegel, pass to forms which more and more deserve the name of 'Judgements'. There is little that deserves to be called 'Judgement' behind such asseverations as 'This wall is green' or 'This stove is hot'; judgement emerges where there is a reasonable amount of doubt regarding some matter, and is most emphatically present in questions concerning aesthetic and moral worth. The deeper the Predicate digs into the Subject, and perfects its overlap or identity with it, the more Judgement will there be in the whole performance. In all this Hegel is surely mirroring ordinary usage, as opposed to the levelling tendencies of logicians. This is perhaps also evinced in his curious treatment of 'propositions', which he holds to be a class wider than Judgements: to say, e.g. that Aristotle died in the fourth year of the 115th Olympiad is in most cases to state a proposition, and not to make a Judgement. It is only if one were in doubt regarding the date of Aristotle's death, and were hazarding some more or less grounded surmise about it, that one would have reason to speak of a 'Judgement'.

Hegel is rather less in harmony with ordinary speech in holding that, as one passes along his scale of Judgements, one also passes along a spectrum of increasing 'truth', that there is little 'truth' in affirming this rose to be red or Cicero to have been a great orator, while there is much 'truth' in affirming the rose to be plant, or a man to be a good specimen of his kind. A Judgement is 'true' in proportion as the moments distinguished in it concide in their content, in proportion as they represent the conformity of a thing to its Notion. In proportion as they fall short of such coincidence, Judgements will be more and more untrue, though Hegel does not question that that may be right (*richtig*), that they may agree with their objects and set forth their state correctly. Ordinary usage would here speak of 'profundity' or 'importance' where Hegel speaks of 'truth', and would equate *its* 'truth' with his 'correctness'. We may here note how little Hegel connects his 'truth' with the notions of system and coherence, which are so prominent in the teachings of many Hegelians.

Hegel's Judgement has, further, the somewhat puzzling dual status that we saw attributed to his Notion: if in some passages —e.g. that which stresses its relation to doubt and grounded surmise—he would seem to make of it something subjective, there are other passages in which he stresses its objectivity, its capacity for a thought-independent, even merely natural being. Thus the growth of a plant is said by Hegel to be its 'Judgement': it is, we may gather, a sort of setting forth of the Notion of a plant, which occurs in a somewhat different fashion in a conscious assertion. Here, as in the similar case of 'Contradiction', Hegel seems to be widening the use of a logical term in a manner more likely to confuse than to illuminate. But he would seem to be on firmer ground in making the Judgement as much declaratory of the nature of things as of the mind that makes it, since this is undoubtedly part of what we mean by a 'Judgement'.

In contrast with what has been said, Hegel's account of Judgement involves no clear account of the differing functions of Subject and Predicate. They are not pronounced in his treatment, as they are in the *Logics* of the British idealists. Hegel has no teaching as to the ultimate subject of all Judgements, nor any equation of the latter with the total system of reality. Hegel says that it is impossible to explain the distinction of Subject and Predicate in advance: our idea of it must develop with our idea of the Judgement. We can at best characterize the Subject, in preliminary fashion, as the Individual against the Generic, or the Individual against the Specific, or the more determinate over against the more general, and the Predicate conversely.[1] We tend likewise to start by regarding the Subject as what exists for self, whereas the Predicate merely inheres in it or illuminates it, but Hegel holds that these characterizations are all capable of a reversal, and that it is as possible to regard the Predicate as the focal point of the Judgement, and the Subject as what merely illustrates or embodies it. He makes plain, in fact—what modern philosophers have done to a much greater extent[2]—that the Subject-Predicate distinction is a more multifarious and Protean thing than its uniform grammatical form would suggest. The *point* of a Subject-Predicate utterance may be wholly different, while its grammatical form remains the same. If there is any one view of the distinction more especially stressed by Hegel, it is that which sees the centre of gravity of a Judgement in its Predicate. The Subject of a Judgement, Hegel holds, is for the most part a mere name or a thing indicated by a mere name: *what* this thing is, is for the first time made clear by the Predicate. Hence most disputes about God, Spirit, Nature, etc., are merely verbal, since what such things are becomes for the first time plain in what we say of them. If the Notion is alike represented by the Individual, the Species and the Genus, there can be no doubt which is the first person in this Hegelian Trinity. Specificity and Individuality exist merely to give the Universal concreteness, and the Subject of Judgement, which is for the most part individual or specific, exists only to be taken up into the Predicate. Like most sweeping statements about Hegel this last statement must be made with some reserve.

Hegel's treatment of Judgement runs through the traditional fourfold division according to Quality, Quantity, Relation and Modality, in each of which Hegel discovers the three subdivisions previously found in them by Kant. There are (A) Judgements of Existence or Inherence (covering the traditional distinctions of

---

[1] *Sc. of Log.*, II, p. 66 (J. & S., II, p. 259; M., p. 624).
[2] See, e.g., J. L. Austin, 'How to Talk: Some Simple Ways', in *Aristotelian Society Proceedings*, 1952–3.

Quality). Here we have (Aa) Simple Positive Judgements, e.g. 'This rose is red'; (Ab) Simple Negative Judgements, e.g. 'This rose is not red'; (Ac) Infinite Judgements, e.g. 'This rose is non-red', in which the Subject is put in the *infinite* remainder of a given class. We have also (B) Judgements of Reflection (the traditional distinctions of Quantity). These are (Ba) Singular Judgements, e.g. 'This is a man'; (Bb) Particular Judgements, e.g. 'Some men are happy'; (Bc) Universal Judgements, e.g. 'All men are rational'. We have also (C) Judgements of Necessity (the traditional distinctions under 'Relation'). Here we have (Ca) Categorical Judgements, e.g. 'The rose is a plant'; (Cb) Hypothetical Judgements, e.g. 'If wax is warmed, it melts'; (Cc) Disjunctive Judgements, e.g. 'A colour is either violet, indigo, blue, green, yellow, orange or red'. Finally we have (D) Judgements of the Notion (corresponding to the traditional distinctions of Modality). Here we have (Da) Assertoric Judgements, e.g. 'This act is right'; (Db) Problematic Judgements, e.g. 'This act may be right', and (Dc) Apodeictic Judgements, e.g. 'This act (being one of pure benevolence) must be right'.

Though Hegel has superficially followed the traditional and Kantian classification of Judgements, he has profoundly modified its significance. The traditional classes are four alternative modes of classifying Judgements which may overlap in the particular case, e.g. the same Judgement 'Some men are not learned' which is negative as regards Quality, is particular as regards Quantity, categorical in respect of Relation, and assertoric as regards Modality. In Hegel's treatment, by contrast, the four Judgement-classes do not overlap at all. In the traditional treatment, likewise, the classes are merely co-ordinated: none of them represents a higher and more adequate form of judging than another. In Hegel's classification, on the other hand, the Judgements dealt with form an ascending series: there is development within each main class of Judgements and also development in passing from one main class to the next. These differences necessarily go together with differences in the content of the various levels of Judgement. Thus at the stage of Quality Hegel deals only with Judgements of contingent particular fact, at the level of Quantity only with Judgements whose predicates are relational, e.g. mortal, useful, at the level of Relation only with Judgements stating necessary connections, and at the level of Modality only with

Judgements of Value. The names of the various classes are altered to suit these modifications. Obviously Hegel is pouring the new wine of his theory of Judgement into the old bottles of the traditional and Kantian classification.

Under Judgements of 'Inherence' or 'Existence' Hegel first deals with simple positive qualitative assertions such as 'Caius is learned' or 'This rose is red'. These Judgements, in Hegel's manner of speaking, affirm an identity between an Individual and a Universal. Hegel makes various strange moves at this point, holding that while it is proper to regard the Subject as Individual and the Predicate as Universal, it is also possible to reverse the relation and to regard the Subject as Universal and the Predicate as Individual. We can, e.g., treat 'red' as signifying some individual datum before us, while 'rose' signifies a universal something running through this and similar data. Whatever may be thought of these subtleties, and of others to which they give rise, Hegel's reason for finding the Positive Individual Judgement defective lies in the inadequacy of the overlap between its Subject and Predicate. The Judgement is trying to find a Predicate which shall altogether exhaust and illuminate its Subject, but in actual fact it does nothing of the sort. The Predicate applies to countless other things besides the Subject, and the Subject, likewise, rejoices in a Bad Infinity of properties besides the Predicate. Being thus beset by an inner tension between what it is and what it means to be, the simple, positive Judgement of Inherence is, in the Hegelian sense, self-contradictory. It therefore leads on to a form in which the disparity between Individual and Universal becomes explicit, and this Hegel finds in the Negative Judgement, which asserts in principle the impossibility of a true overlap, a Hegelian identification, between an Individual and one of its accidental qualifications.

Hegel says that the force of the Judgement that an Individual is *not* a Universal tends to the effect that it *is* something Specific and Particular. (He jestingly remarks that for the Individual *not* to be Universal is for it to be non-Universal and therefore Specific.) Significant negation, Hegel then argues, on lines similar to those of the British idealists, always occurs on a positive Ground. To deny the rose to be red is to affirm implicitly that it is coloured and that it has some specific colour. But even as so developed the Predicate of our Judgement remains inadequate to its Subject, and this inadequacy is best expressed in the complete nugatoriness of the Infinite Judgement, where the Predicate ceases to say anything of the Subject, and the whole form of Judgement becomes a hollow sham. To say that the rose is no elephant, or the understanding no table, may be to say something formally correct: it is not to say anything illuminating, or in the Hegelian sense 'true'. We pass, therefore, in quest of such truth, to Judgements which do not qualify objects with accidental qualifications. We must leave Judgements of Inherence and Existence for Judgements of Reflection.

In Judgements of Reflection the Predicates are said to be the 'essentialities' (*Wesenheiten*) which relate objects in a profound manner to other objects: Hegel gives such examples as 'perishable', 'harmful', 'elastic', 'happy'. He holds further that in such Judgements there will be development on the part of the *Subject* and not of the Predicate. Previously the Predicate was modified so as to become less and less obviously inadequate to the Subject. Now, however, the Subject will be continuously adjusted so as to become more and more nearly adequate to the essential Predicate. At the present stage this will be done by varying the *Quantity* of the Subject. Thus if I say '*This* hellebore is poisonous', there is an obvious inadequacy of the singular Subject to the essential Predicate. If I try to remedy this inadequacy by saying '*Some* hellebore is poisonous', the inadequacy is less glaring but is not yet removed. Plainly the best to be achieved along this line of development is the Universal Judgement '*All* hellebore is poisonous'. This Judgement involves, however, a merely *enumerative* universality: it applies a Predicate to an assemblage which is an instance of the 'Bad Infinite' since it can never be comprehended or exhausted. It expresses a task that can never be completed, and what it says is valid only subject to the proviso that contrary instances shall not be forthcoming. Hegel contrasts this false infinity and universality with the true universality and infinity of a mathematical *rule*, and holds that we cannot cure its inadequacy except by passing on from Judgements whose Subject is enumerative and collective to Judgements whose Subject is generic and essential. Instead of talking about *all* hellebore or about *all* perfect squares, we must make Judgements about Hellebore-*as-such* or about *the* Perfect Square in general. We rise, accordingly, with a 'logic' quite intelligible even if it is not formal, to Hegel's next class of Judgements of Necessity.

Judgements of Necessity are, in the first place, Categorical Judgements, by which Hegel understands Judgements connecting some specific concept, e.g. hellebore as such, with a generic concept which is part of its content, e.g. being a plant. It is, says Hegel, absurd to follow the common Logic in ranging a Judgement like 'Hellebore is in flower' in the same class as a Judgement like 'Hellebore is a plant', and referring to both as 'categorical'. But this common mistake is due to the fact that the Categorical Judgement *veils* the necessity which it inwardly implies, and therefore seems to be saying something merely external and contingent. What is merely implicit in the Categorical Judgement accordingly becomes explicit in the Hypothetical Judgement, e.g. 'If that is hellebore it will kill you'. This tells us that if anything is of a certain sort, it must also be of some other general sort. The Ground of such a Judgement will, according to Hegel, always be some specific nature, carrying with it what is generic, or some generic nature necessarily carrying its features into every possible specification. But this connecting Ground may not be fully explicit: there are (to use Bosanquet's term) many 'broken-backed' hypotheticals, in which the connection between antecedent and consequent does not seem necessary, because not resting on an explicit identity. This defect is remedied in the Disjunctive Judgement where the same genus appears both .as Subject and Predicate, at one time in its pervasive Universality, at another time in the totality of its Specifications. If we say that an *A* must by its nature be either *B* or *C*, we achieve the identity, the accurate overlap between Subject and Predicate, at which all previous judgement has been obscurely aiming.

Hegel emphasizes that the Disjunction which here rounds off the edifice of Judgement must be necessary and not merely empirical. To this obscure requirement he adds one that is barely intelligible: that a genuine Universal disjoined in a Disjunctive Judgement should include *itself* (or some pure form of self) among its own members, and that its other member should embrace the totality of its specifications. To say that colour is either violet or indigo or blue or green or orange or red is to disjoin in a barbaric, quasi-empirical fashion: the true form of such a disjunction is that colour is either pure colour, on the one hand, or the unity of light and dark, on the other. We shall not comment on this queer piece of logical doctrine, which seems part of Hegel's general polemic against Newton and in favour of Goethe. It will be plain that Hegel's account of the Generic, Hypothetical and Disjunctive Judgements has inspired some of the best treatments in Bradley and Bosanquet.

In the Disjunctive Judgement, on Hegel's view, the Judgement has achieved identity between the Universal, on the one hand, and its many Specifications, on the other. This identity is, however, defective in so far as it does not as yet extend downwards to the *Individual* objects in which the Universal is manifested.[1] The accomplished unity of all *three* moments of the Notion is found only in the *Judgement of the Notion*, which for Hegel at once exhibits modal distinctions and is also a Value Judgement. It is the latter, because in saying that an individual man is good, or that an individual picture is beautiful, we are expressing the complete conformity of an Individual both to its Specific and its Universal Notion. The Notion which a good man satisfies is precisely what *he*, as an individual, has it in him to be: it is his peculiar personal vocation, not shared by mankind as a whole, nor by any subsection of mankind. In the same way the Notion expressed by a fine picture is a Notion peculiar to itself, and not capable of being stated in terms of a general canon. In the Judgement that something is good or beautiful we accordingly achieve that complete sublimation of the Individual into the Specific and Universal, and that perfect incarnation of the Specific and Universal in the Individual, of which all Judgement has been in quest. Hegel thinks, further, that the modal distinctions of the traditional Logic are here in place. The Judgement of Value will be merely *assertoric* in so far as it merely predicates goodness or beauty of a particular object. Such an assertion can however readily be met with a counter-assertion of badness or deformity, and will accordingly pass over into a Judgement that is merely *problematic*. The problematic character of such a Judgement will lead to a search for a reason or Ground, and will become *apodeictic* when this reason is found. Hegel implies that the object will ultimately justify its claim to have satisfied its notion precisely by being the individual object that it is. Socrates was a good man simply because he was . . . Socrates, *The Tempest* is a fine play simply because it is . . . *The Tempest*. If this is not a *theory* of value, it is perhaps better than any such theory.

[1] *Sc. of Log.*, II, p. 112 (J. & S., II, p. 295; M., pp. 658-9).

It would take us too far afield to comment critically on Hegel's doctrine of Value Judgements which has plainly been introduced in somewhat hole-and-corner fashion. Something was required in the ascending Judgement-series to take the place of the modal classification which occupied the fourth place in the traditional scheme of Judgements. Hegel had already dealt with the modal distinctions in the Doctrine of Essence. Hence the origin of this inadequately argued, brilliant fragment. The recognition of a sense of probability attaching to Value Judgements is also interesting. Hegel is at one with the great Jesuit moralists in admitting this species of probability.

From the Judgement Hegel now passes on to the Syllogism, the next topic in order in the traditional exposition of Logic. The Apodeictic Judgement we have been studying gives a *reason* for what it asserts, and is therefore a Syllogism in germ. It will become a full Syllogism when this reason is allowed to become a Middle Term, whose connection with the two extremes of the Judgement justifies their connection with one another.

III   THE SYLLOGISM AND ITS VARIETIES

In his treatment of Syllogism Hegel practises the same pouring of new wine into old bottles that we have just seen in the case of Judgement. Superficially his treatment is on traditional lines. He deals at first, under the new heading of 'Syllogism of Existence' or 'Syllogism of Understanding', with the three Aristotelian Figures of Syllogism, the First Figure in which the Middle Term is Subject in the Major Premiss and Predicate in the Minor Premiss (*All men are mortal, Caius is a man, so Caius is mortal*), the Second Figure in which the Middle Term is Subject in both Premisses (*All men are mortal, some men study eternal truths, therefore some who study eternal truths are mortal*), and the Third Figure in which the Middle Term is Subject in both Premisses (*All men are mortal, Gabriel is not mortal, therefore Gabriel is no man*). We may note, however, that Hegel, for his own purposes, has altered the *numbering* of the traditional figures. The Hegelian Second Figure is the *Third* Figure of tradition, and the Hegelian Third Figure the *Second* Figure of tradition. This change is extremely confusing unless constantly kept in mind. Hegel feels bound, further, to introduce a Fourth Syllogistic Figure to match the one later added to the Figures of Aristotle: it is as redundant as the latter, though otherwise quite different. Hegel then goes on to discuss Syllogisms which are inductive rather than deductive, Syllogisms which argue enumeratively from particular cases to general rules, and Syllogisms which argue analogically from particular cases to other similar particular cases. Finally he deals with three types of Syllogism of Necessity, distinguished according as they have Categorical, Hypothetical or Disjunctive Premisses.

But though Hegel's framework may be traditional, he means by a Syllogism something quite different from what it was traditionally thought to be. The Syllogism is for Hegel the clearly posited unity (in their distinctness) of the three notional moments of Individuality, Specificity and Universality: what was in bud in the Notion, and 'present' but not 'put' in the Judgement, is both present and put in the Syllogism. The Syllogism shows us Individuality ascending to Universality by way of Specificity, or Specificity and Universality connected by way of Individuality, or Individuality and Specificity linked by Universality: it shows us, in short, the interdependence of the three notional moments, as something realized in their actual working, and not posited by external reflection. The traditional arrangement of Syllogism is, moreover, for Hegel a developing series: connections which are casual and external in earlier types of Syllogism, come to be necessary and intrinsic as we advance to the later. The Syllogism is further no mere empty form in which the most various subject-matter can be cast: it is not for Hegel merely the expression of 'reason' in the sense of ratiocination, but of 'reason' in any form in which we recognize and value it. Hegel, like Kant, identifies the Reason which soars to the transcendent ideals of God, Freedom and the Moral Law with the Reason which is the humble faculty of Syllogisms. The latter *shows* the necessary unity of Individual, Species and Genus, which the former tries to express.[1] Hegel further sees his whole system as a gigantic triad of Syllogisms, in which Nature and Spirit are mediated by the Logical Idea, the Logical Idea and Nature mediated through Spirit, and Spirit and the Logical Idea mediated through Nature.[2] The same basic Syllogisms are at work in the relations of the divine Persons of

---

[1] *Sc of Log.*, II, pp. 119–20 (J. & S., II, pp. 301–2; M., pp. 658–9).
[2] *L. Log.*, pp. 391–2 (W., p. 322).

the Trinity, in the Incarnation and Passion, in the redemption of the individual, and in the life of the Spirit in the religious community.[1] Hegel does not hesitate, in fact, to make any and every object syllogistic: any object whatever represents a Universal made Specific, and descending into Individuality. And there are certain natural objects whose make-up is in a special degree 'syllogistic': thus a magnet exhibits syllogistic unity in the connection of its polar extremes through a mediating point of indifference.[2] The exuberance of these analogies should not be allowed to blind us to what is illuminating in them.

The first type of Syllogism considered by Hegel is the simple Syllogism of Existence, in which Individuals, Species and Universals are connected in an apparently casual and external fashion. It appears in these to make no difference to the Individual whether or not it has certain generic or specific features, and so *mutatis mutandis* in the case of the other notional determinations. In Syllogisms of the First Figure an Individual is connected with a Universal by way of a certain Specific Attribute: Caius, an Individual, e.g., is inferred to be long-nosed (Universal) by virtue of being Roman (Specific Feature—all Romans being assumed to be long-nosed). The form of such a Syllogism is expressed by Hegel in the symbolic pattern $I-S-U$ (or $I-P-U-$ if 'Besondere' is translated by 'Particular'). Hegel points out the inherent inadequacy of this form of syllogistic deduction. Since its Middle Term is only contingently connected with its two Extremes, it can yield only a contingent, externally cemented conclusion: a contrary conclusion could as readily have been reached by employing some different, just as loosely connected Middle Term. Hegel here gives several confusing, apparently fallacious examples. He holds, e.g., that it is right to infer that a wall will be yellow because it has been painted yellow, and also right to infer that it will be blue because is has been painted blue. None the less, despite *both* these valid syllogisms, the wall in question will be neither blue nor yellow, but green. He holds similarly that it is both right to infer that the earth, being heavy, must fall into the sun, and that, being centrifugal, it will not so fall: its actual movement in a circle combines and negates both these valid conclusions.[3] What Hegel is probably suggesting is that Premisses which fail

[1] *Phil. of Sp.*, pp. 456–8 (W., pp. 300–2).   [2] *L. Log.*, p. 88 (W., p. 50).
[3] *Sc of Log.*, II, pp. 127–8 (J. & S., II, p. 308; M., p. 671).

to state essential connections are as likely to lead to false as to true conclusions. He is perhaps also suggesting that Syllogisms resting on such Premisses only *pretend* to certainty and confidence, that we are ready to retract the Premisses if the conclusions are unacceptable, and that the whole Syllogism consequently implies alternative Syllogisms with conflicting conclusions. Apart from this weakness, Syllogisms stating non-essential connections readily lead to the 'Bad Infinite': we have to provide Prosyllogisms to prove each of our Premisses, *their* Premisses likewise require other Prosyllogisms, and so on indefinitely.

Hegel seeks to evade this infinite regress, as in previous cases, by twisting it round into a circle. This will necessitate passing from the First Figure Syllogism just given to another Syllogism in the Second, and to yet another Syllogism in the Third Figure, each of the three Syllogisms then being justified by the other two. The Syllogism I–S–U joins I with U by way of S as Middle Term: it involves the unjustified connections of S with U and of I with S, and we can justify the former by the Syllogism S–I–U, and the latter by the Syllogism I–U–S. S–I–U is a Syllogism which connects the Specific with the Universal by way of the Individual: it is represented by the argument 'Caius, Marcus, etc., are Romans, Caius, Marcus, etc., are long-nosed, therefore all Romans are long-nosed'—valid if the enumeration is exhaustive—and would ordinarily be said to be in the Third Figure, though in Hegel's nomenclature it is in the *Second* Figure. In the same way the Syllogism I–U–S connects the Individual with a Specific Property by way of a Generic Property: it is exemplified by the argument 'All non-Romans are flat-nosed, Caius is not flat-nosed, therefore Caius is a Roman (i.e. not a non-Roman)', and would ordinarily be said to be in the Second Figure, though Hegel classes it as in the Third Figure. The point of these movements from Figure to Figure is to show that it does not matter which of the moments we use as a Middle to justify us in connecting the remaining two. Since each moment can justify the connection of the other two, and this connection with either of the remaining connections can justify the last one, each moment in a sense justifies its own connection with either of the other two moments, and the whole system of connections is self-justifying. We are in fact dealing with one Matter of Fact which can be differently broken up into Data and Conclusions.

At this point the Dialectic digresses into dealing with the Mathematical Syllogism, a pattern of inference where the connections are those of the mathematical equation, where all distinctions between Extremes and Middle terms, and consequently all Figures, vanish. The form of such Syllogisms is simply U–U–U, the Universal connected with the Universal by way of the Universal: it does not matter, in such reasonings, which terms we regard as Extremes and which as Middle. If I equate A with B by way of C, I can use my conclusion to help justify either of my previous Premisses. Hegel rightly sees nothing shameful in the potential circularity of all mathematical demonstration. He thinks, however, that the Mathematical Syllogism represents a degeneration from the Syllogisms previously mentioned: its extreme self-evidence stems from the 'notionless' suppression of the distinctions there present. It is not by way of this dead-end, but in a new notional direction, that the Dialectic must take us. (Hegel has here many pertinent things to say about the early formalization of Logic attempted by Leibniz and certain other symbolists.)[1]

The inadequacy of the Syllogism of Existence lay in the contingency, the externality of the connection of its terms. This is to some extent lifted when they are seen as merely playing into each other's hands, as essentially 'reflected' into one another. But a full lifting demands that there should be a better approach to coincidence among the Individuals, the Species and the Genera which enter into our reasoning: this is found when the Individuals concerned are grouped into a *class*, and the inference concerns the whole of this class. The Syllogisms now dealt with are called by Hegel 'Syllogisms of Reflection' since in them there is this attempted equation between intension and extension, each being the counterpart or reflection of the other. The first Syllogism to be dealt with at this stage is the Syllogism of All-ness or Complete Enumeration: we reason that Caius is mortal, since Caius is a man and all men are mortal. This Syllogism differs from the corresponding Syllogism of Existence in that being a man is not a contingent property that Caius may or may not have: Caius with all his properties is contained in the class of men, and the connection of humanity with mortality is taken to be established for the *whole* of this class. Hegel then raises the now familiar criticism of the Syllogism of mere Allness that it

[1] *Sc. of Log.*, II, pp. 142–8 (J. & S., II, pp. 319–24; M., pp. 681–6).

involves a *petitio principii*: it is only *if* Caius is mortal that the Major Premiss can be allowed to be true, and the mortality of Caius consequently does not rest on the Syllogism in question.

The Syllogism of Allness is accordingly a mere sham of a Syllogism; the Individual Caius appears to be connected with mortality by way of humanity, but in truth humanity only comes to be connected with mortality through the countless Individuals like Caius who are both human and mortal. The scheme *I–S–U* therefore alters to the scheme *U–I–S*: instead of the Deductive Syllogism given above we have the Inductive Syllogism

Caius

Human — Marcus — Mortal

Balbus

etc.

which represents its 'truth'. This new Syllogism in its turn is no more than the appearance of an inference, since the enumeration of the individuals concerned is only a *task* involving a progress into the Bad Infinite, and leaving its conclusion always *problematic*. The 'truth' of the Inductive Syllogism is accordingly the Syllogism of Analogy, which reasons from Particulars to Particulars, from certain Universal features common to a set of Individuals to certain Specific features only known to be present in some of them. The pattern of this Reasoning is *I–U–S*. Hegel gives the now well-worn examples of the moon's probable habitation on account of its somewhat superficial analogy to the inhabited earth.[1] What is interesting in this part of Hegel's treatment is the accuracy and brevity with which he both anticipates and resolves the difficulties afterwards hit upon and puzzled over by Mill.

The inferential defects of the Syllogism of Reflection can only be cured in the Syllogism of Necessity, where the Middle Term is no longer a class or collection, incapable of being exhausted, and therefore incapable of functioning as a true Middle, and becomes the Essence, the Specific or Generic nature of the Individuals concerned. For Hegel as for Aristotle the knowledge-producing Syllogism is one mediated by 'essential nature'. Here

---

[1] *Sc. of Log.*, II, p. 155 (J. & S., II, p. 330; M., p. 692).

Hegel deals with the Categorical Syllogism, again the familiar 'Caius is a man, a man is mortal, etc.', only now understood as mediated by the Essence of Caius, and so avoiding the defects connected with Induction and Analogy. This Categorical Syllogism is defective in its selection of an *arbitrary* Individual Minor Term, and in the fact that its two extremes have many aspects irrelevant to the Middle. In the Hypothetical Syllogism which next emerges (If A then B, but A, therefore B), we have a Middle Term A which is also an immediate existent: we see necessity at work, both positing and overcoming certain initial conditions. (Hegel's treatment of this type of Syllogism is extremely obscure.) Finally the Syllogism finds a completely adequate embodiment in a Disjunctive pattern of reasoning: A is either B or C or D; but A is not B and not C; therefore A is D (or: but A is B; therefore A is not C and not D). Here the Middle is the 'fulfilled Universal', the Genus completely developed into its Species, and the Individual A is united with a Species D by way of it. Hegel's exaltation of the Disjunctive Syllogism and Judgement is the source of the similar exaltation in the *Logics* of Bosanquet and Bradley.

Hegel now makes a somewhat 'hard' transition from the Disjunctive Syllogism to the notion of an Object: the latter is needed to provide the element of 'otherness' at the level of the Notion. The Disjunctive Syllogism exhibits the complete interdependence of the Universal, the Species and the Individual: the extremes in this Syllogism, says Hegel, have a merely 'posited being', and the distinction between mediation and mediated has fallen away. The Notion is now fully realized, he informs us, and has achieved the kind of status which is called Objectivity. An Object, in short, is a real Individual being which is thought of as penetrated through and through with Generic and Specific meanings, a higher stage of being than that of mere Existence or mere Substantiality. It is a being on which syllogistic processes have, as it were, left a crystalline deposit, in which everything that a thing is, it is by virtue of its indwelling Concept or Notion. The Object is what Syllogisms illuminate, and it is that in which they terminate and are absorbed. This transition is no more fundamentally obscure and arbitrary than many previously met with in the Dialectic.

IV   CATEGORIES OF OBJECTIVITY: MECHANISM,
CHEMISM AND TELEOLOGY

Objectivity, in the sense Hegel now proposes to give it, is not what is *opposed* to Subjectivity: it is not to be equated with the resistance put up by the phenomenal order to the caprices and preferences of the subject. It rather represents what thought *must* think if it is to be true to its universalizing self, if it is to see the individual realities before it as individualizing and specifying Universals. 'At the present standpoint of our treatment', Hegel declares, 'Objectivity has in the first place the meaning of the in-and-for-selfness of the Notion, the Notion that has transformed the mediation posited in its self-determination to an *immediate* relation to itself. This immediacy is accordingly itself immediate and completely suffused with the Notion, just as its totality is immediately identical with its being.'[1] The in-and-for-selfness just sketched is, however, something that Objectivity must achieve by stages. It will at first appear, Hegel tells us, as the Objectivity of Objects seemingly independent, whose notional union has a merely implicit, external form: we shall be concerned with Objects *mechanically* interrelated. From this we shall rise to a stage where notional connection assumes a more intimate, deep-cutting character: we shall be dealing with Objects *chemically* connected. Finally we shall rise to a stage where notional connection wholly suppresses the independence of distinct Objects: we shall be dealing with Objects *teleologically* bound together. Objectivity, duly softened by all this notional penetration, will then be ripe to pass over into 'the Idea'.

Hegel's treatment of Mechanism starts with a sketch of the Mechanical Object as Such: this is defined as 'Universality which permeates Specificity and is immediate Individuality in it'. Owing to the collapse of the syllogistic moments into each other, the Mechanical Object is without distinct Individual or Specific features: difference at this stage resolves itself into 'indeterminate determinateness' (*unbestimmte Bestimmtheit*), i.e. into mere numerical diversity. Each Mechanical Object is therefore one among other precisely similar Objects, and must itself be an aggregate of such Objects: the realm of Mechanism must extend

[1] *Sc. of Log.*, II, p. 179 (J. & S., II, p. 348; M., p. 710).

to the embracing Universe on the one hand, and to endless parts within parts on the other. Atoms, being thought of as indivisible entities, will be defective instances of Mechanical Objects: Leibnizian monads, with their 'true unity', will be likewise defective. Truly Mechanical Objects, Hegel suggests, will be as much 'heaps', mere aggregates, as the wholes they compose, and must therefore be divisible *without end*. They can exhibit no character but such as is analysable, on reflection, into the mode of arrangement of indifferent, independent parts, nor any behaviour which is self-determined, but only such as is due to the behaviour of other like Objects within them or outside of them, whose behaviour is likewise determined.[1] Hegel is here sketching an ideal of Pure Mechanism to which mechanical systems only imperfectly approximate. It will have the closest approach to application in the phenomena of impact and inertia: it will become less and less applicable as we advance to such phenomena as those of Light, Heat, Magnetism and Electricity, and will be quite inapplicable to the *characteristic* performances of Life and Mind. None the less, Hegel insists, Mechanism has the status of a general logical category, and will have *some* application at all levels of discourse, including the spiritual. There are, e.g., associative connections, phenomena of rote learning, cases of custom and social uniformity, which in every way admit of a mechanistic explanation. Since Mechanism represents the *first* pattern of notional interpretation, the naïve mind will always apply it with peculiar confidence: it will be regrettably tempted to stick to it in regions where it no longer applies.

The contradictions in the mechanical ideal sketched above will have been obvious. In seeking to preserve the apartness and distinctness of Objects, it has rendered them indistinguishable: in seeking to make them wholly *indifferent* to each other, it has made them wholly *determined* by one another. As an explanatory category, it has likewise failed by involving the Bad Infinite: everything is ascribed to the putting together or interference of *something else*, while nothing is *self*-organizing or *self*-determining. In the Mechanical Process, the next stage in the Dialectic, we see this contradiction explicitly posited: the Objects show themselves to be not really indifferent to one another, by communicating influences, and by interfering with and doing violence to

[1] *Sc. of Log.*, II, pp. 181–4 (J. & S., II, pp. 350–3; M., pp. 711–14).

one another. Hegel here deals (under the heading of 'Formal Mechanical Process') with the transmission of Motion, Electricity, Magnetism, etc., from one body to another, and notes how far they are from conforming to the indifference of Pure Mechanism. He also deals (under the heading of 'Real Mechanical Process') with the more pointed conflict shown when a Mechanical Object resists some influence communicated by another Object, and this resistance is finally overcome. Finally Hegel suggests that Mechanism, which in its abstract form knows no privileged or central Objects, tends none the less to produce just such Objects, and to lead to Laws which bind all Objects to just such central Individuals. Such dialectical tendencies show themselves in the production of solar systems, but are also shown in the creation of vast central aggregations of power and wealth in society. The Mechanical, Hegel argues, shows itself to be *not* merely mechanical by its inherent capacity for self-organization: the soul may be sunk in its mechanical body, but it none the less gives undeniable signs of its presence. We pass therefore to a stage where there will be no longer that hollow pretence of self-sufficient independence characteristic of Mechanism, but where Objects will *admittedly* have a *penchant* or bias towards one another, i.e. we pass on from Mechanism to Chemism. Hegel's treatment of Mechanism in the *Science of Logic* is rendered difficult by its close entanglement with his Physics. One grasps without confidence at the wraiths of discarded doctrines through the double fog of scientific misunderstanding and philosophical obfuscation.

The Chemical Object, to which we now rise, distinguishes itself from the Mechanical Object in that it is not posited as by its nature indifferent to other Objects, but as with *specific leanings* to some of them. Implicitly it may be said to exemplify the same *Notion* as its opposite number (or other half) even if, outwardly and existentially, it may subsist apart from it. This specific leaning, and unifying Notion, shows itself in the need to 'annul' such outward apartness: Chemical Objects must as such strive to be as one in their outward being as they are one in their Notion. Hegel emphasizes that the names 'Chemism' and 'Chemical Object' do not limit his category to the chemical sphere. It is as much exemplified in sexual relations at the organic level, and in love and friendship at the spiritual.

Hegel uses the language of *Syllogism* to cover the facts of chemical union: in a chemical union we have two Extremes, a Major and a Minor, brought together by a Middle Term, the result being a Neutral Product, in which the properties of both extremes are for the time being cancelled. The Middle Term which effects this strange sort of physical inference is, on the one hand, the inner nature of the two chemical substances, their common concept revealed in their mutual affinity. But it is also often manifest in a material or psychic *Medium*, in which the two extremes will be brought into direct communication. (This Medium exists in Nature, since Nature, being an externalization of thought, loves to present as a separate existent what is really a mere phase of the Notion.) In the chemical sphere the Medium will generally be water, though air sometimes performs the same functions. In the spiritual sphere, Hegel tells us, this role of a Medium will be performed by symbols and by language. (Since Love is a case of 'chemical' interaction, what happens, one wonders, in cases of *verschwiegene Liebe?*) The Syllogism that leads to the neutral union of two Chemical Objects by way of a Medium is, further, capable of reversal. Just as the underlying unity of two Chemical Objects may look for an opportunity to cancel out their differences in neutrality, so, when neutrality is attained, their suppressed differences may look for a suitable excuse to pass back to the state of separated, mutually unconcerned existence, where the disused Medium alone represents their previous union. (The rustless iron is free from water, the lovers no longer on speaking terms.)

Hegel now points to a radical defect in the two 'Syllogisms' just sketched. Though they are but two sides of the same Chemical Notion, operative now in the form of union, and now in the form of diremption and separation, their identity is to some extent masked and obscured. The elements chemically united will not *of themselves* proceed to separate themselves, nor will the elements chemically isolated *of themselves* proceed to unite. In both cases external conditions and provocations are needed to reverse the process. (If the results of a chemical reaction could of themselves start a new, reversed reaction we should have, not chemistry, but life: life is, in short, no more than a chemical process made perennial.) The inadequate, external chemical mode of conceiving the relation of Objects points therefore to a more intimate, internal mode of conception where the provocative, conditioning

element will be part of the notion of the Objects involved. This
new view of things Hegel finds in the Teleological or Purposive
mode of viewing Objects, which makes explicit the deep unity
and mutual dependence which is largely masked both in Mechanism and Chemism. 'The Notion', Hegel remarks, 'which has
hereby absorbed all moments of its objective being as externalities
and has put them into its simple unity, is thereby completely
freed from objective externality, towards which it directs itself
as to an inessential reality. This objective and free Notion is the
End.'[1]

With the passage to Teleology we move to a sphere where
Hegel is more lucid, and where what he says has a genuine
philosophical importance, and is not merely a reflection and
interpretation of the science of his time. Teleology, Hegel maintains, is the 'truth' of the Mechanical and the Chemical: he
reprobates the traditional forms of thought that treat the three
categories as *co-ordinate* forms of interpretation and explanation,
and that merely ask under *which* of them phenomena must be
brought. Such a merely co-ordinate view of Teleology was
assisted, Hegel believes, in the forms of thought in question, by
the merely piecemeal, finite nature of the Teleology postulated.
The Mechanical Order was not subjected throughout to sweeping
purposive explanation: it was eroded and interfered with by
niggling purposive intrusions, the offspring of a purblind piety.
Before Kant wrote his *Critique of Teleological Judgement*—Hegel
seems strangely forgetful of Aristotle—purpose was always thought
of as external, not as indwelling and internal. Such being the
case, it is not remarkable that Mechanism, with all its radical
contingency and externality, should have been thought of as a
more genuinely 'immanent' mode of explanation than Teleology.
Hegel does not, however, start with the wholly immanent purposiveness which represents the category at its highest. He starts
with a purposiveness which *subordinates* the Mechanical and
Chemical order to itself, while leaving the latter intact in seeming
independence. The End imposed on a world which would otherwise be purposeless, and which operates by way of teleologically
indifferent means, must be allowed to enjoy its brief dialectical
hour before being absorbed in the all-dissolving unity of Absolute
Purpose.

[1] *Sc. of Log.*, II, p. 208 (J. & S., II, p. 373; M., p. 733).

The End first studied by Hegel is the Subjective End, by which he means, not necessarily an End entertained in conscious intention, but a slant or direction, whether conscious or unconscious, which is superimposed on a Mechanical or Chemical basis, and which guides its performance to one definite result. (It might be as much shown in the reflex movements which sustain balance, as in the conscious fulfilments of animal wants and appetites.) An End so conceived is not, Hegel tells us, to be confused with a Force that expresses itself, nor with a Substance or Cause made manifest in its Accidents or Effects. The latter concepts involve an element of unfreedom and externality: Forces require external circumstances to solicit them, and Substances and Causes only have full reality in their Accidents or Effects. An End, on the other hand, may be thought of as a Power which solicits *itself* to expression, or as a Cause which merely carries out and perpetuates *itself*. The notion of End is in fact 'the truth' which these former concepts reached in their final development. Hegel, we may note, might very well have passed directly from Substance, Cause and Reciprocal Interaction to this category of Purpose. The long detour through Concept, Judgement and Syllogism, and through the categories of Mechanism and Chemism, is only necessitated by the unilinear demands of the Dialectic. An End is further described as self-specifying: it must expand itself into a series of detailed contents, in the full unfolding of which it will be executed or realized. This content will, however, in the first instance, be arbitrary and finite, since only thus can the End have definite content. The End will therefore at first relate itself to a merely presented environment, on which and through which it will exert its purposive activity. The world must, in the first instance, provide us with something to do, as well as with the wherewithal to do it. Only thus can we rise to a plane where purpose will become internal, and will have no materials or setting that it does not itself demand or create.

From the notion of End thus sketched, Hegel passes, without much show of a transition, to the related category of Means. The Subjective End, as a mere design or plan, relates itself to some Means present in the outer environment, and through this Means passes over to full realization. The Means of such purposive action again functions as the Middle Term of a Syllogism: the

German terms *Mittel* and *Mitte* here suggest a closeness of connection not suggested by the corresponding English words. This
Teleological Syllogism, Hegel tells us, resembles the Syllogism
of Existence, in that its Middle Term stands in a merely contingent
relation to its two Extremes: Socrates may be connected with
philosophy by being mentioned in Diogenes Laertius, and just
so a purpose may be carried out by whichever out of a wide range
of alternatives comes readiest to hand. Being thus contingently
related to the End and the realization, the Means appears as a
merely Mechanical Object, with an independent existence and
way of working. None the less, Hegel insists, the Means only
mediates because it implicitly involves the whole of the Notion:
its secret destiny is to enable the End to realize itself, and it
must therefore prove unresistant towards this End, however
much it may withstand other Mechanical Objects.

Hegel expresses this subservience of the mechanical order of
Means to the overriding order of Ends in the famous metaphor
of the Cunning of Reason. 'That the End relates itself directly
to an Object, and makes the latter a Means, as also that it determines another Object thereby, can be regarded as violence, in
so far as the End appears to be of an entirely different nature
from the Object, and both Objects are likewise independent
totalities over against each other. But that the End puts itself into
mediate relation with the Object, and fits in another Object
between itself and the latter, can be regarded as the Cunning of
Reason. The finitude of reasonableness has, as observed, this
aspect, that the End relates itself to an external, presupposed
Object. Were it directly related to the latter it would, however,
itself be involved in Mechanism or Chemism, and would therefore be exposed to contingency and to the destruction of its
notional integrity. For this reason it puts forth an Object as
Means, lets the latter work itself out externally instead of itself,
surrenders it to attrition and preserves itself behind it against
mechanical violence.'[1] Teleology, we are to understand from this
passage, does not violate Mechanism or Chemism: it merely
makes use of them. Mechanical and chemical connections foster
deep-set Ends to which, *qua* mechanical or chemical, they are
entirely indifferent.

Hegel now points to a radical defect in teleological mediation:

[1] *Sc. of Log.*, II, pp. 225–6 (J. & S., II, p. 387; M., p. 746).

it entails the same endless intercalation of Middle Terms that we saw in the case of the Syllogism of Existence. The End passes into execution only by way of the Means, but this implies that the Means must itself be 'worked up to' by further Means, and so on *ad infinitum*: a Purpose, it might seem, cannot get under way at all, since every step in its fulfilment requires another step to be first made. (This is not intended to be a practical dilemma, but a puzzle arising out of the complete dovetailing of Mechanism with Teleology.) In the same way, Hegel holds the series of terms between a Means and its executed End is of necessity transfinite and 'compact'. Whatever we achieve, being only contingently related to the End, can embody it only in a one-sided, inadequate and temporary manner: it is itself merely a Means which will require further Means to be added to it, if the End is to be persistently pursued. Thus the performance of a symphony to which all efforts of conductor and performers have been devoted proves to be a mere Means towards the unending aim of keeping the symphony alive and before consciousness: it achieves this aim only if it leads to other similar and perhaps better performances. In the same way a house, as the End of the efforts and tools of the builder, is really a mere Means to the continuous provision of protection and shelter: it is in being rubbed away in use that it comes closest to fulfilling this function. In a sense all fulfilments fall short of, and may therefore be said to frustrate, their underlying aims. Strictly speaking, we have no finite Ends, but only 'the End'. This End, says Hegel, never finds a true Means, since it will always require a prior execution in order that this Means may bring it into being.[1]

The category of external, finite Teleology now hastens to its dissolution: its 'truth' must be found in a Cunning yet more devouring. The independence and externality of the Object worked upon, as opposed to the design that works on it, must reveal itself as a mere show: the activity of the End must consist solely in the staging and dissolution of this show. We are, in other words, facing the central message of Hegelianism: that 'otherness' in all its forms exists only to call forth the energies, and to intensify the self-awareness of Spirit. The Objective World, with its glittering prizes and its multitudinous hazards, must be seen as no more than the row of ninepins that self-conscious Spirit must

---

[1] *Sc. of Log.*, II, p. 231 (J. & S., II, p. 391; M., pp. 749–50).

bowl over in order to *be* self-conscious Spirit. In the Realized End, the last category of objectivity, there is no longer an inner world of subjective design set over a mechanical world of merely instrumental reality: subjective design will be such as to require and therefore to include in itself the instrumental mechanical order, which thereby loses all independence. In the Realized End there is no Means, however trivial, which is not taken up into the End: the *whole* End is likewise present in the most trivial of its Means.

'The finitude of the End', Hegel tells us, in a justly famous passage, 'consists therein that in its realization the material used as Means is merely externally subsumed under it, and rendered conformable to it. But now, in fact, the Object is implicitly the Notion; if the latter as End is accordingly realized in it, this is no more than the manifestation of its own inner nature. Objectivity is as it were a mere veil under which the Notion lies hidden. In the finite we cannot rise to the vision or the experience that the End has been truly reached. The carrying out of the infinite End consists therefore merely in overcoming the illusion which makes it seem as yet unaccomplished. . . . This illusion it is in which we live, and yet it alone is the activating factor on which all interest in the world reposes. The Idea in its process makes itself that illusion, and opposes an other to itself; its activity consists in overcoming this illusion.'[1] In other words the imperfection of Teleology consists in the fact that it appears as a journey in which starting-point and end-point are the things of importance, while the journey itself derives its importance from them. When both starting-point and end-point are seen as mere terms to the journey, in which alone anything of importance is included, the true goal has been reached. With this step Hegel reaches 'the Idea', the last group of categories in his Logic.

V THE IDEA IN ITS IMMEDIACY

The Idea, the final stage of the Logic, embodies for Hegel a perfect unity and balance between the 'Subjectivity' he studied in the Universality, Specificity and Individuality of the Pure Notion, and the Objectivity treated under the three headings of Mechanism, Chemism and Teleology. It represents, on the one

[1] *L. Log.*, p. 422 (W., pp. 351–2).

hand, a pure concept which can only be the ideal and universal thing it is, in so far as it subdues, penetrates and explains the concrete detail of the individuals which stand over against it, and are objective to it. On the other hand, it represents an Object no longer subject to external mechanical connections or chemical bias, but moulded through and through by a Teleology which not only uses it as a Means, but also explains its total make-up and mode of operation. The origin of the Idea in the notion of Teleology throws immense light on Hegel's philosophy. The Idea does not explain things by being their cause, or their underlying Substance, or the Whole of which they are the parts: it explains them by being the End towards which they must be thought of as tending. It is not, however, an external End imposed on the world by a pre-existent intelligence, but one which the things in that world by their nature pursue. And it is an End, moreover, which it is impossible to divorce from the Means which bring it about or the process through which it is realized.

Hegel tells us that his use of the term 'Idea' is derived from Kant, for whom the transcendental Ideas of God, the Soul and the World were the last products of Reason, the syllogistic faculty, intent always on explaining the facts of experience by subjecting them to higher and more embracing principles. (Since Kant's use of the term 'Idea' is derived from Plato, the Hegelian Idea has its roots in the Platonic Idea, and in the principle of Unity or Good in which the Ideas have their source.) Hegel agrees with Kant in connecting his Idea closely with Reason, yet not in such a way as to oppose Reason to Understanding: any Understanding which goes deep and far, and is not merely an application of narrow categories to present materials—as when one 'understands' someone's explanation of the way through a wood—must be in terms of the Idea. But while he agrees with Kant that the Idea has no full expression in sense-experience, he refuses to treat it as a merely regulative conception, something which it is profitable to aim at, but not possible to reach. The Idea, he emphasizes, is nothing far off and elusive: it is rather that which is most absolutely present. It is in fact what all things *truly* are, and to the extent that sensible things fall short of it, it is they, not the Idea, which are defective in 'truth' and reality. This last statement shows that there is more of the regulative in Hegel's conception than his words recognize. This comes out further in his statement that the Idea is no abstraction, no empty logical form, but that it is present in things as an active *Trieb* or Urge, an Urge to heal the division between 'the simple notion existing in and for itself' and the 'empty subsistence' which is opposed to it. The thought which 'lifts reality into the light of the Idea', Hegel maintains, 'must not conceive of the truth of reality as dead repose, as a mere picture, dull, without urge or movement, a genius, a number or an abstract thought. In the Idea the Notion achieves freedom, and for the sake of this freedom must include the toughest opposition in itself. Its peace consists in the security and certainty with which it eternally creates the opposition and surmounts it, and so closes with itself.'[1] One would perhaps do justice to Hegel's thought on the Idea by saying that, since it is its *whole* business to organize and inspire the drift of things in a certain direction, it is, in so inspiring this drift, manifest and actual in the only sense in which actuality can be predicated of it, and in a sense *more* genuine than applies to the transient things of sense. A finite End can be said to be realized if exhaustively carried out in some particular concrete arrangement, unrealized if this is not yet the case. But since the Idea is by nature inspirational and regulative, the fact that it is such cannot be set down as showing it to be imperfectly realized. It can only fall short of actuality to the extent that it is inadequately conceived in various mythical or metaphysical terms.

Hegel now deals with the Idea under three successive headings: in the immediate, relatively inexplicit form of Life, in the more deeply sundered and therefore more profoundly unified forms of Cognition and Volition, and lastly in the form of the Absolute Idea, where Cognition and Volition merge in a difficult union, whose content is paradoxically identified with the whole course and method of the previous system.

Hegel first endeavours, not very clearly or convincingly, to differentiate the treatment of Life as a logical category from its treatment as a phase of Nature or a presupposition of Spirit. Certainly there is vastly more geographical, botanical and zoological detail in the treatment of Life in the *Philosophy of Nature*, and much more physiological detail in the treatment in the *Philosophy of Spirit*. But the logical treatment also involves much

[1] *Sc. of Log.*, II, p. 242 (J. & S., II, pp. 399-400; M., p. 759).

detail which seems ill-placed in a general treatment of organismic categories.

For Hegel the distinguishing mark of an organism is its all-pervasive unity: whatever part of function can be distinguished in it has the 'whole notion' in itself. Hegel also agrees with Kant in seeing a thoroughgoing *immanent* Teleology as characteristic of an organism. The organism is a manifold not of parts but of *members*, which, though they may be mutually external, and to that extent mechanically or chemically related, are also swayed by a unifying Urge, which makes them reciprocally End and Means, each member sustaining and being sustained by the others. The organism is not only the instrument of its indwelling purpose, but also the complete execution of that purpose. Homoeostasis, self-production and self-maintenance among ever-varied conditions, is its task and being. Hegel remarks that this self-directedness and pervasive unity of the organism only seems self-contradictory to the diremptive understanding. The living is, in fact, the type of all that is comprehensible and intelligible, and our incapacity to understand it reflects only on the finitude and nullity of our thinking approaches.

Hegel develops his treatment of the category of Life in three subsections: the Living Individual, the Process of Life and the Genus or Kind. In the first he deals with little beyond the generalities we have mentioned, though space is found for a reference to the three biological functions of Sensibility, Irritability and Reproduction so much discussed in the science of the time. Sensibility is said to represent the Universality of the organism, its capacity to take outward particulars into itself and resume them in simple 'self-feeling'. Irritability is said to represent Specificity, while Reproduction is connected with Individuality. Under the heading of 'The Life-Process' Hegel then goes on to discuss the way in which the organism takes practical steps to ensure the 'nullity' of the indifferent environment, of which nullity it is 'inwardly certain'. The external world may be good in essence, may exist only to forward Spirit and Idea, but its immediate role is to foil and 'contradict' the organism, the sense of which 'contradiction' Hegel says is embodied in the actual experience of pain. 'When one says that a contradiction is not thinkable, it is rather the case that, in the pain of a living organism. it is an actual existence.' Such pain, however, arouses urges to abolish the tension between organism and environment: the environment becomes conformable to the organism, which in a sense reproduces itself in it, penetrates it with its own pattern. This provides a transition to the yet more pregnant self-perpetuation shown in the life of the Genus or Kind, where the Universality of the Notion is said to be revealed in sexual intercourse, and in the living germs passed from one individual organism to another. It also shows itself in the form of the Bad Infinite Progression of the living generations. 'In generation the immediacy of the living Individuality perishes: the death of this life is the emergence of the Spirit.'

It is now not hard for Hegel to claim that the *immediate* union of subjective notion and objective reality found in the living organism, must point the way to the much more adequate expression of the same union which is to be found in the Idea of Knowledge. Knowledge of the objective world plainly represents a more thorough subjugation of its objectivity, and its more thorough penetration with unity and universality, than can be achieved at the level of life. 'The Idea which as Genus is *in itself*, becomes *for itself* in so far as it has overcome its particularity, which the living generations constitute, and has thereby given itself a reality, which is its simple Universality. Thus it is the Idea which is related to itself as Idea, the Universal which has Universality as its determination and being—the Idea of Knowledge.'[1]

VI THE IDEA AS KNOWLEDGE

Hegel begins his treatment of Knowledge by discussing the idea of Soul or Spirit: he discusses this notion as it occurs in the bad metaphysic of philosophers like Mendelssohn, and in the good metaphysic of philosophers like Aristotle. He also says how the treatment of Soul and Spirit in *The Phenomenology of Spirit* or in ordinary empirical psychology, differs from the present *logical* treatment. Here we are dealing with Spirit as a form, a category, disentangled from all the less-developed categories which attend it in experience and existence. The whole discussion makes plain—if indeed it needed to be made plain—that the Hegelian Idea is no more than the categorial form of self-con-

---

[1] *Sc. of Log.*, II, p. 262 (J. & S., II, p. 415; M., p. 774).

sciousness, which will show itself to be the last 'truth' of everything.

Hegel conceives of Knowledge as an undertaking, a process of enquiry, rather than as a product or result of such enquiry. It is always the resolution of a 'contradiction', the contradiction between the absolute self-certainty of the thinking self, which feels all reality to lie within its explanatory grasp, and its humbling confrontation with what is merely given, with what seems to come from without, for whose precise form and occasion of irruption no reason can be given. All experience thwarts the unbounded ego-centricity and self-sovereignty of the thinker, and the thinker can accordingly not rest till he has subdued and mastered the alien and intrusive element. 'The Knowing Subject', Hegel remarks, 'relates itself through the very nature of its notion, its abstract being-for-self, to an external world, but it does so in the absolute certainty of itself, in order to raise the reality it has in itself, this formal truth, to *real* truth. It has it in its notion to be the complete essence of the objective world. Its process is to posit the concrete content of the latter as identical with the notion, and contrariwise the notion as identical with objectivity. . . . The Notion is the absolute certainty of itself, but its being-for-self is opposed by its presupposition of a world which exists in itself, but whose indifferent other-being means something inessential for its self-certainty. It is therefore the urge to resolve the other-being and to behold an identity between itself and the object.'[1]

This urge which is Knowledge, is also the urge towards *truth*. Just as objective truth is the conformity of objects to their notion, of which the highest expression is the Judgement of Value, so the goal of Knowledge is precisely to secure this conformity, to *see* objects as being what they are because this is what they have it in them to be. Knowledge cannot, however, while it remains Knowledge, entirely achieve this result. The object remains something *given* to thought for assimilation and explanation, and while thought can progressively reduce and dissolve it, there is always something of the old hardness left. Only at a stage beyond Knowledge and Practice (the stage of the Absolute Idea) will this hardness finally melt into softness, leaving no problem concerning the 'external world' or 'empirical fact'.

[1] *Sc. of Log.*, II, pp. 274–5 (J. & S., II, pp. 424–5; M., pp. 783–4).

In his treatment of Knowledge Hegel first considers **Analytic Knowledge**, in which, he tells us, 'the Notion remains in pure identity with self, but in which this its immediate reflection-into-self has just as much the determination of objective immediacy. What is for it its *own* determination, is just as much a being, since it is the first negation of the presupposition. The determination therefore counts as a presupposition merely discovered, as the apprehension of something given.'[1] Hegel here seems to be stressing what many modern philosophers have disregarded, that an analytic truth may be as much discovered in quasi-empirical fashion as one that is substantial and synthetic. That $7 + 5 = 12$ may be true by the very content of my notions, but I may discover its truth, in the particular case at least, by making use of those notions on empirically given particulars. Knowledge, however analytic, remains Knowledge of objective reality: the manner in which things are conceived by us may be *read off* from the actual things.

Hegel's brief treatment of Analytic Knowledge contains much that is penetrating and important. He maintains that it is as wrong to regard analysis as the mere *putting* of distinctions into a notion, as to look on it as the *discovery* of distinctions which are independently there. It is in the diremptive crucible of thought that analytic distinctions first come to light, but we may say that what comes to light represents what the object always was 'in itself'. Thought produces the character of its object much as the dramatic producer produces that of his caste: his efforts bring out what is latent, but what would not be latent were such as he not there to bring it out.[2] Arithmetic and all sciences of discrete magnitude are, according to Hegel, completely analytic. For this reason, he maintains, we have no genuine *theorems* in such sciences, only particular problems. It is worth while carrying out a special counting process in order to discover $7 + 5$ to be 12, but it is not right to regard such an application of arithmetical procedures as a contribution to arithmetic. When the problem is to add several numbers, the only solution is to add them: for a proof to show such a solution to be correct, could only be to show that it *is* a sum in addition. Analytic Knowledge remains, however, in the sphere of abstract identity, but this is merely a

[1] *Sc. of Log.*, II, p. 278 (J. & S., II, pp. 427–8; M., p. 786).
[2] *Sc. of Log.*, II, p. 280 (J. & S., II, p. 429; M., p. 788).

limiting or degenerate case of a genuine identity of distincts, of which the Knowledge must be *Synthetic*. To such Synthetic Knowledge the Dialectic accordingly turns.

The treatment of Synthetic Knowledge which follows is divided into (*a*) Definition, (*b*) Division and (*c*) the Theorem. In the treatment which follows Hegel seems rather to be amending and developing traditional philosophical accounts of Knowledge (those e.g. in Aristotle's *Posterior Analytics*) than dealing with the actual enquiries of common life and science. He manages, however, to breathe life into the traditional approaches, and to make them more empirical and concrete than his headings would lead one to expect.

Definition is conceived by Hegel as real rather than nominal: its aim is to circumscribe *Individuals*, to reduce the manifold richness of their empirical being to a few simple notional determinations. That the Individual continues to elude the ever narrowing definitory net, and remains given, *vorgefunden*, merely there, is no more than the fundamental flaw and inadequacy in Knowledge: it is in no sense part of its *aim*. Hegel points out the extreme difficulty of arriving at even an inadequate and approximate real definition of objects. Except in the case of artefacts, whose nature as artefacts is determined by *us*, or in the parallel case of geometrical figures, which merely are what *we* mean them to be, the task of defining objects involves an ineliminable aspect of arbitrariness and contingency. The things of nature and Spirit manifest an endless richness of properties, and there is no simple rule for deciding which are to be chosen as definitory and which as accidental. (To try to make this choice by rule of thumb might result in defining Man as the animal possessed of ear-lobes, a property as distinctive of human beings as it is inessential.) Hegel thinks, however, that a genuine definition of natural kinds is possible, but that it must spring, not from some rule, but from 'an obscure feeling, an indefinite but deeper sense, a divination of what is essential' (*ein dunkles Gefühl, ein unbestimmter aber tieferer Sinn, eine Ahnung des Wesentlichen*). It must likewise recognize that, in the external realm, Essence will dissolve into features external to one another, that there will not be *one* feature of a genus of objects which will be essential to them and definitory of them all. It will, moreover, be impossible to find a definition of a Genus from which certain poor specimens do not, at certain points, depart. In a bad plant, or a degenerate man or state, says Hegel, there will be certain aspects quite obscured which would otherwise seem the most characteristic marks of their kind. In all this Hegel would seem to be wholly alive to the actual procedures by which scientific concepts are built up, and to what we should now call their essentially 'open texture'.

Definition, however, must necessarily pass over into Division, the single notion find its place in the classificatory scheme. Hegel here points to the pragmatic and shifting character of scientific classification: principles of division must continuously be reshaped to fit new cases and transitional forms, and principles that seemed to hit off essence, will, with a slight widening or shift of field, become totally useless. In all this physical nature is herself at fault: a contingency which extends to sixty-seven distinct varieties of parrot will obviously extend to anything. Only an obscure 'instinct of reason' can guide us through this wilderness of contingency. It is this, e.g. which leads us to classify animals by their teeth and claws, the organs by which they actually maintain themselves against 'otherness', and plants by the form of their reproductive organs, the highest function of which they are capable.

From Definition and Division, Hegel passes on to Theorems (*Lehrsätze*), the proven propositions of science. These are said, somewhat strangely, to represent the *individualization* of Knowledge: in proofs Knowledge comes as close as it ever can come to applying principles to individual cases. Hegel also holds, equally strangely, that proof alone brings an element of genuine synthesis and necessity into Knowledge: while Definition and Division merely *monstrate* the given, the proven Theorem *demonstrates* it. Hegel is clear, however, that there is no sharp line to be drawn between Theorems and Definitions. We may very well put into a Definition something we afterwards demonstrate from more fundamental Definitions. Hegel maintains, further, that *all* principles in science must be capable of proof. The so-called axioms of one science must be demonstrated in another: only pure tautologies can be accepted without proof. Hegel does not make plain at this point how he imagines such universal proof to be possible. If his treatment of similar issues is any indication, he is probably approving of a *circulus in probando*: the theorems of a scientific system will all 'prove' one another inasmuch as *some* of them can be selected as premisses from which the rest can be demonstrated. Hegel points out, further, how proof really merges into and completes Definition. We start by defining a triangle as a plane figure enclosed by three straight lines, but we have not advanced far in Euclid before reaching a logically more fecund definition of triangle as a single angle enclosed by two lines of given length. The Pythagorean theorem, Hegel maintains, is the best definition of a right-angled triangle, and also indirectly (as covering deviations from its conditions) of all triangles whatever.[1]

Hegel has so far used Euclidean geometry as the paradigm of all Knowledge. It is, in fact, the paradigm of *scientific* as opposed to philosophical Knowledge, but it is none the less unable to complete its programme, to lubricate with proof every rough surface and connection in the given. Not only does it not descend to Individuality, but even in its own sphere, that of abstract externality, it meets with paradoxical facts of incommensurability, which Hegel does not think are amenable to its principles. This is much more obviously the case in sciences such as Physics, where the attempt to press fact into abstract deductive form, merely means that our first principles rest precariously on empirical facts, which are in their turn triumphantly 'deduced' from such principles. Explanation in such sciences, according to Hegel, is in part mere tautology, in part a 'cooking' of the data of experience to fit the requirements of theory, in part a blind granting of principles whose full force is clear only in application.[2] It is plain, in fact, that Synthetic Knowledge is most perfectly systematic only where it abstracts most severely from concrete Individuality: where it attempts seriously to deal with the latter it must sacrifice its systematic perfection. Its object never becomes adapted (*angemessen*) to itself. In its tight fabric of Definitions and Theorems, there always remain holes through which we look through to what is crudely external.

Here as previously, however, Necessity is the matrix of Freedom: the unsuccessful attempt to dissolve empirical givenness into the meshes of theory gives way to the attempt to produce it freely, in one blow, as it were, by an Act of Will. The theoretical Idea of the True therefore passes over into the practical Idea of the Good.

[1] *Sc. of Log.*, II, p. 309 (J. & S., II, p. 452; M., p. 810).
[2] *Sc. of Log.*, II, p. 315 (J. & S., II, pp. 457–8; M., pp. 815–16).

VII   THE IDEA AS PRACTICAL ACTIVITY

In the Practical Idea, which Hegel now sketches, the Notion no longer appears as a pattern of intelligibility which must derive its data, its content from without: it is thought of rather as an active urge which imposes an intelligible order on what is given. Instead of trying to discover what the world independently is like, this urge rather seeks, with Marxist imperiousness, to make it what it ought to be. This Practical Idea also descends to the Individual in a manner impossible to the Idea of Knowledge: a Theorem may be a *Specific* application of a Universal principle, but a genuine descent to what is Individual can be achieved only in *practice*. Hegel further seeks to point out both the analogy and difference between the Practical Idea now reached, and the notion of End which went before. The Practical Idea *gives* itself this or that definite content, and thereby retains its essential freedom and infinity, whereas an End is essentially bound up with some content or other, and therefore leads to an endless supersession of one realized purpose by another. In the Practical Idea execution or fulfilment is as such indifferent: it is its own endeavour, the free play of its self-determining vitality, that is alone important, the world about it being merely a 'kingdom of darkness', a stimulus and foil to practical activity.

Hegel now points out how this Practical Idea involves that curious self-deception and double-dealing which he has already treated in the *Phenomenology*. The Practical Idea is at once seriously and unseriously concerned to impose itself on the world. It is seriously concerned to do so, since only so can it *be* the Practical Idea, the Notion that nullifies and masters the Object. It is again *not* seriously concerned to do so, since with the total conformity of the Object to itself, it would extinguish its *raison d'être*, and consequently its activity. If the defect of the Cognitive Idea lay in its irremediable dependence on what is outside, merely there, the defect of the Practical Idea lies in its lofty indifference to execution and actuality, its inability to make anything objective the true fulfilment of itself. What the Practical Idea lacks is the clear consciousness of *success* which it can only have by associative with the Cognitive Idea. By its insistence on its *own* endeavours as the sole source of value, and by its repudiating, negative attitude to the Object, it stands, as it were, in its own path, and can never fully translate itself into objectivity.

Hegel now points out how the Practical Idea remedies its own deficiencies and so leads to the notion of the complete union of Theory and Practice. This is achieved simply by rendering it clear that there is not that opposition between the use of the Object as a Means to the life of Active Endeavour (which will push back the barrier of objectivity indefinitely), and that Active Life itself. The Object is there to be mishandled, to be pushed back, and this pushing back is integral, rather than merely instrumental, to the life of Practical Endeavour. The two Premisses of the Practical Syllogism (which Hegel here introduces), in the former of which the Will seizes on some immediate thing (called by Hegel the 'Middle Term' of the Syllogism), and in the latter of which it seeks through this immediate thing to achieve its general aim, are said to fall together in the conclusion, in which the Will only realizes *itself*. 'The execution of the Good', Hegel remarks, 'in the teeth of an opposed and alien reality, is the mediation which is essential for the immediate relation and realization of the Good. For this (mediation) is merely the first negation and other-being of the Notion, an objectivity which would submerge the Notion in externality. The second is the overcoming of this other-being whereby the immediate execution of the End first becomes the actuality of the Good as the Notion which has being-for-self, inasmuch as therein it becomes identical with itself, not with something alien, and is thereby posited as alone free.'[1]

Hegel makes plain that the final overcoming of the otherness of the other, the passage from the Idea of Will to the Idea Absolute, lies ultimately in the *view* (*Ansicht*) that is involved in either. Active Endeavour will continue to strive against an ever re-emerging alien barrier until it comes to see this barrier as merely its shadow, as merely the reflex of its own activity. The Absolute Idea when it emerges out of the Practical Idea does not therefore people the world with new distinctions: it merely reverses its perspective. As Hegel remarks in an unforgettable passage in the *Encyclopaedia*: 'The Will knows the End to be its own, and the Intelligence sees the World as the Notion Actual. This is the true attitude of rational cognition. Nullity and transience are merely the surface, not the true Essence of the World. The true Essence is the Notion

---

[1] *Sc. of Log.*, II, p. 325 (J. & S., II, p. 414; M., p. 822).

in and for itself, and the World is thus itself the Idea. Unsatisfied endeavour vanishes when we realize that the purpose of the World is just as much accomplished as it is for ever accomplishing itself. This is in general the attitude of the mature man, whereas youth believes that the World is given over wholly to evil, and must be remade into something quite different. The religious consciousness, on the contrary, treats the World as ruled by Divine Providence, and as accordingly agreeing with what it ought to be.' And, lest this should seem too total a concession to a blind conservatism, Hegel adds: 'This agreement of what is, and what should be, is none the less not rigid and stationary, since the Good, the Purpose of the World, only exists in so far as it perpetually engenders itself. Between the spiritual and natural worlds there is still this distinction, that while the latter only returns continuously to itself, in the former there also must be progress.'[1]

VIII   THE ABSOLUTE IDEA

We have now reached the final stage of Hegel's ladder of categories: we are face to face with the Absolute Idea, which is variously described as the unity of the Subjective and the Objective, the unity of Life and Theory, or the Unity of Theory and Practice. It is also explicitly identified with the Aristotelian νόησις νοήσεως, the pure thinking which can have no object outside of itself. While the Theoretical and the Practical Idea each involve an ever unfulfilled endeavour—whether to explain the given exhaustively, or to transform it practically—the Absolute Idea surmounts both by the simple expedient of bringing them together, so that the provocation and compliance which the world yields to our practical endeavours, becomes also the last theoretical truth about it. In this consciousness endeavour in a sense collapses: the problems of theory and practice become solved by being dissolved. This collapse of endeavour involves something like a return to the tranquil immediacy and balanced poise of Life. The Absolute Idea, however, according to Hegel, retains in itself an element of the intensest opposition (*den höchsten Gegensatz*), which is characteristic alike of Intelligence and Practical Action. 'The Notion at the level of the Idea', Hegel tells us, 'is not merely Soul, but the free Subjective Concept, which exists for self and

[1] *L. Log.*, p. 445 (W., p. 373).

therefore has *Personality*—the practical, objective Notion determined in and for itself, which as Person is impenetrable, atomic subjectivity—but which is just as much not exclusive Individuality, but is for itself Universality and Knowledge, and which has its *own* objectivity as Object in its other. All else is error, murk, opinion, endeavour, caprice and perishability: the Absolute Idea alone is Being, imperishable Life, Truth that knows itself and the whole of Truth.'[1] Hegel may be forgiven the extreme gorgeousness of this passage: its import is perfectly clear. To conceive things with adequacy and truth is to see them as having no other meaning or function but to call forth the intellectual and practical efforts of conscious persons, beings who are and must remain atomically separate in their self-enclosed personality, but who also share an endless open horizon of rational enterprises, for which the rest of the world provides no more than the stepping-off place or the stimulus. There is no reference here to any absolute, timeless or supra-individual experience: the Absolute Idea is merely the categorial form of self-conscious Spirit, something we all exemplify when we admire art, practise religion or cultivate philosophy.

It might have been expected that Hegel would at this point have continued and expanded his praise of the Absolute, that he would have shown in detail how it sums up all previous categories in its final lucidity. He does nothing of the sort. The summing-up in question has, in his view, been effectively performed at earlier stages of the treatment. If the vision of the Absolute arose by a simple reversal of perspective, so that the endeavours which seemed to lead up to it were suddenly seen as having achieved it, so now, by a reversed reversal of the same perspective, Hegel comes to regard the Absolute as 'having no other content than the whole system of which we have so far been studying the development'.[2] It is, he says, like the old man who utters 'the same creed as the child, but for whom it is pregnant with the whole meaning of a lifetime'. The only new thing that can still be brought out at this stage is the *method* that has led up to the Absolute Idea. With the achievement of the Idea we can become fully conscious of the method we have hitherto followed without being explicitly conscious of it. That a discussion of method should absorb Hegel's

---

[1] *Sc. of Log.*, II, pp. 327–8 (J. & S., II, p. 466; M., p. 824).
[2] *L. Log.*, p. 447 (W., p. 375).

final utterances in the *Logic*, shows that for him, as for many mystics and religious persons, the ultimate truth is best thought of as a 'way'.

We shall not here attempt to summarize Hegel's brilliant, difficult characterization of the dialectical method, nor the train of reasoning which leads him to regard Dialectic as the inmost nature of personality, and to see in the latter the highest, most sharply pointed climax of Dialectic.[1] Obviously a person is not unlike a passionate argument, as in arguing we are most deeply conscious of what we as persons are. We shall also leave aside Hegel's account of Systematic Science as a circle of circles in which each member's return to self becomes the point of origin for a new member.[2] This last statement leads Hegel on to the much discussed transition from the *Logic* to the *Philosophy of Nature*, which we shall consider in our next chapter.

[1] *Sc. of Log.*, II, p. 349 (J. & S., II, p. 483; M., pp. 840–1).
[2] *Sc. of Log.*, II, p. 351 (J. & S., II, p. 485; M., p. 842).

CHAPTER NINE

THE PHILOSOPHY OF NATURE

I THE NOTION OF A 'NATURPHILOSOPHIE'

We shall be concerned in the present chapter with Hegel's *Philosophy of Nature*, his study of the Idea in a 'self-estranged' state, its diremption into existents external to one another in Time and Space, out of which it must raise itself to complete self-consciousness. This part of the system is one that many Hegelians have thought fit to ignore entirely, mainly on account of the outmoded character of the science on which it reposes. Nothing can, however, be more unfit than this ignoring, and, in view of Hegel's undoubted greatness, more impertinent. The *Philosophy of Nature* is an integral part of Hegel's system, and one can no more understand that system without taking account of it, than one can understand Aristotelianism while ignoring the *Physics* or the *History of Animals*, or Cartesianism while ignoring the physical portions of the *Principles of Philosophy*. In Hegel's theory of Nature, as in the parallel theories of Aristotle and Descartes, one sees the philosopher's principles at work, casting their slant upon our talk and thought about the world around us. The complete misunderstanding of Hegel's idealism by British philosophers, and its reduction to a refined form of subjectivism, are probably due to their ignoring of the *Naturphilosophie*.

That the natural science appealed to by Hegel is outmoded is, moreover, irrelevant. The scientific views of Hegel's day are as deserving of respect as the transitory opinions of our own. They are in some respects superior, in that the *élan* of scientific thought had not yet lost itself in a wilderness of detail, nor been paralysed by difficulties beyond its effective mastery. It was a time when a world-mind like Goethe could write easily and deeply on plant-morphology and the theory of colour in a manner impossible to the poets of our own day. Hegel's grasp of contemporary science was, moreover, informed and accurate: the reading of the *Naturphilosophie* is made easy by its wealth of experimental illustration, and by its long citations from contemporary treatises. Hegel *gives* one the science of his own day, together with the interpretation he puts upon it. Moreover, since the concepts of the *Naturphilosophie* are not meant to fit the empirical facts closely, but only to follow them generally, and in another medium and manner, there is much that he says that could be used to illuminate *our* science, or that could, with a whirl of the distaff, lighten the science of the future. Hegel's peculiar teleological way of viewing things may not appeal to us greatly: it remains as worthy of study, and of detailed scholarly comment, as are the views of Aristotle, or (in recent times) of Whitehead. The present exposition must of necessity be summary: we shall have done our task if we have made plain the role of the *Naturphilosophie* in Hegel's system, as well as the fact that it deserves a closer treatment.

The passage from the *Logic* to the *Naturphilosophie* has occasioned much difficulty, mainly on account of Hegel's riddling, anthropomorphic choice of expression. While 'the Idea' sketched at the end of the *Logic* has been liberated from further transitions, while its pure transparency is no longer sullied by a breath of otherness, it is still, Hegel suggests, capable of further development: we must think of the Idea as 'freely letting itself go' (*dass die Idee sich selbst frei entlässt*), while remaining 'certain of itself and tranquil within itself'. This complete freedom of self-determination leads to a result as completely free: the mutual 'outsideness' of Space and Time, 'existing absolutely to itself without subjectivity'.[1] The *Encyclopaedia* endorses and echoes this puzzling talk of 'free decision'. 'The absolute freedom of the Idea', Hegel tells us, 'is that it does not merely pass over into Life, nor as finite Knowledge allow the latter to show itself within itself, but that rather, in its own absolute truth, it decides to release from itself, as its own mirror-image, the moment of its own Specificity, and of the first determination or other-being, the Idea Immediate, i.e. Nature. Now once more we have the Idea as Being: but the Idea which has Being is Nature.'[2]

These passages suggest doctrines of Neoplatonic emanation or Thomistic creation quite foreign to Hegel: other passages, however, make plain what is involved in all this talk about the Idea's free decision to let itself go. It is often asked, Hegel remarks,

---

[1] *Sc. of Log.*, II, p. 353 (J. & S., II, p. 486; M., p. 843).
[2] *L. Log.*, § 244, pp. 451–2 (W., p. 379).

how the Universal determines itself, or how the Infinite makes itself finite, or, what is the same, how God comes to create a world. The answer simply is that God, the pure-self-active Idea, would be a mere abstraction without a Universe to unify and interpret, and a wholly abstract God or Idea is a contradiction in terms. 'God', says Hegel, passing from the formal to the theological mode of speech, 'has two revelations, as Nature and as Spirit. Both these divine formations are temples of God that He fills by His presence. God as an abstraction is not the true God: only as the living process of positing His other, the World (which conceived in divine terms is His Son), and first, in the union with His other, as Spirit, can He be subject.'[1] In other words, the *Logic* merely provides us with the *Idea*, the abstract *Form* of Spirit vanquishing its other and seeing itself in the latter: this abstract form is nothing except as realized in an actual struggle, in which otherness and externality are elaborately posited as Nature, and just as elaborately done away with in Spirit. The philosophical statement of the struggle will, of course, be in some degree abstract, but it will not touch the severity of abstraction aimed at in the *Logic*. The Idea, therefore, only 'decides' to release its moment of Specificity in the wealth of Nature, inasmuch as Specificity without Species would be sense-less and contradictory. And its decision is 'free' only inasmuch as there is an irremediable arbitrariness, an indeducibility from principle, in Nature's specific detail: the Idea presupposes and demands such detail, but it does not *qua* Idea, logically entail it. In spite, therefore, of much quasi-theological mystification, there is nothing but the utmost intellectual sobriety in Hegel's transition from the Idea to Nature.

Hegel opens his *Philosophy of Nature* by acknowledging, and richly apologizing for, the bad repute of his subject: an external formalism of concepts, arbitrarily applied to natural phenomena, has rightly estranged sober students of Nature from the 'con-structions' of philosophers. None the less, he holds, there is still a place for a rational, philosophical treatment of Nature, one that will lay violent hands on the physical Proteus—which both attracts thought by its promise of what is akin, and also shocks it by its barbaric inconsequence and diversity—to make it stop changing its forms, and to declare itself in more intelligible and

[1] *Phil. of Nat.*, pp. 47–8.

simpler fashion. Hegel gives no wholly clear account of the precise relation between his rational physics and the flourishing empirical sciences on which it obviously depends. At times he holds that we must take the concepts hammered out in the empirical sciences, a .d transform them in the 'quietude of thought':[1] more commonly he holds that we must first frame notions of the abstract 'other' of the Idea, and *then* look for empirical cases which more or less illustrate them. Thus the abstract notion of an *Aussersichseyn*, of *partes extra partes*, finds its empirical illustration in our intuition of space,[2] just as the equally abstract notion of an identity pervading differents finds an empirical illustration in the magnet.[3] If we turn, however, to Hegel's practice, it seems plain that his notions have all been framed and moulded so as to cover empirical phenomena, that he has been trying to find ways to talk in Hegelian fashion about phenomenal features such as cohesion, light, magnetism, colour, digestion, procreation, etc., rather than to *find* phenomenal features which correspond to ideas independently arrived at. There is nothing discreditable in this fact, since it is not Hegelian to attempt to deduce the content of the world. What Hegel achieves, therefore, is a new and often illuminating characterization of natural phenomena in terms of their relation to an ideal standard. The wisdom of Hegel's practice exceeds the wisdom of the accounts he gives of it.

In his general characterization of Nature, Hegel says that it is the Idea in the form of *other-being*. In Nature the pure categories and unities of thought have a sort of immediate reflection, which appears *other* than those categories and unities, just as it also appears *other* than the conscious intelligences that rise to contemplate it. Being fundamentally characterized by such otherness, Nature will likewise exhibit otherness in each phase of its manifestation. All its varied manifestations will seem mutually external, and even phases that belong together logically, that are in fact sides of a single phenomenon (e.g. the poles and indifference-point of a magnet, two chemically responsive substances, the individuals of a single species) will put on a brave show of independence and outward indifference. In Nature, says Hegel, in theological language, we have the Divine Idea momentarily excluded from the Divine Love: everywhere it shows anticipations

---

[1] *Phil. of Nat.*, pp. 39, 44.
[2] *Phil. of Nat.*, pp. 70-1.   [3] *Phil. of Nat.*, pp. 274-6.

and vestiges of intelligence, but in a frozen, petrified form, in which God may be said to be dead.[1] Nature, in short, is the raw material of self-conscious Spirit, and, being raw, it is, in its immediate form, the exact antithesis of anything spiritual.

As regards the relation of Nature to Time, Hegel says that it would be as wrong to say that the natural world had a beginning in Time as that it had no such beginning. It is not eternal, since for Hegel, as for many philosophers, eternity is connected only with things to which pastness and futurity, priority and posteriority, are without application. It is infinite as regards past and future time only in the sense of the Bad Infinite, that which we cannot complete, which always points beyond itself to farther terms of the same sort: in *ordinary* terms, then, Hegel grants that the natural world has always existed, and that it always will exist. Hegel certainly thinks that Nature existed for long periods in the past without living or conscious components, that there were long geological ages in which the 'Earth Spirit' (which is only the *possibility*, not the actuality of conscious life) had not yet risen to the opposition involved in awareness. Its history, he writes poetically, was 'the movement and dreams of one that sleeps, until it awakes and achieves its consciousness in Man, and stands over against itself as a tranquil structure.'[2] It is in this unconscious, inorganic setting, when its cataclysmic period is over, that Life suddenly emerges, fully armed and equipped, like Minerva from the brow of Jove.[3] What is plain from these passages is the complete *realism* of Hegel's treatment of Nature. Hegel is an idealist in the sense of acknowledging a necessary movement in Nature from death and unintelligence to their opposites, but not in the sense of holding Nature to be the construct of a mind. 'Nature', says Hegel, 'comes first in time, but the Absolute Prius is the Idea; this Absolute Prius is the Last Thing, the true Beginning, the Alpha is the Omega.'[4] In other words, Spirit in the form of Idea is logically prior to Nature, since it is to produce Spirit that Nature exists at all. Spirit, however, as an actual reality comes *after* the rest of Nature in time.[5]

Nature, the immediate, self-dirempted reflection of the Idea, is necessarily conceived by Hegel as having a need to get rid of its diremption and immediacy, to pass out of death and achieve

---

[1] *Phil. of Nat.*, p. 50.   [2] *Phil. of Nat.*, p. 463.   [3] *Phil. of Nat.*, p. 463.
[4] *Phil. of Nat.*, p. 58.   [5] *Phil. of Nat.*, §§ 247–8.

Life and Spirit. This being so, Nature will necessarily manifest itself in a series of grades or levels, each of which arises out of what has gone before. Hegel is, however, keen to stress that the necessity which leads Nature on from level to level, is a logical and dialectical, rather than a *natural* necessity. Because Cohesion represents a higher natural level than Inertia or Gravitation, this does not mean that matter was at first merely inert and gravitating and *then* acquired cohesion, or that the former features causally led to the latter. In the same way, because living forms grade themselves as better and better approximations to the Idea and its fluid unity, this does not mean that living forms have given rise to each other in this order, that plants have evolved into animals, invertebrates into vertebrates, etc. There are large leaps and gaps in the natural series: the order and connection lies on the reverse side of the fabric, in notions and ideas, not in immediate phenomena. Hegel therefore repudiates any doctrine of the actual historical evolution of living forms in time. Conscious Spirit inevitably reveals itself in history, and inorganic Nature had a cataclysmic pre-history before the emergence of Life, but there is no history of the varying patterns of Life. Hegel maintains this doctrine even in the face of the geological record, which was fairly well established in his time. He holds that the organic forms found in early geological strata never really lived: they are merely paintings or sculptures of the living, imitations and anticipations of organic forms, but produced by forces that were inorganic.[1] It seems plain that Hegel is here holding a doctrine as much at variance with his own principles as it is out of harmony with the facts. Possibly it is his cautious, genuinely empirical spirit which made him hesitate to launch forth in far-reaching evolutionary speculations, like those of some of his contemporaries. Had the Darwinian and later data been available, he would almost certainly have acknowledged the historical trends in Nature that he admits in the realm of Spirit: if any philosopher is a philosopher of evolution, that philosopher is Hegel. As it is, he sees in the notion of evolution merely a convenient conceptual schema. It may, he holds, be supplemented by the equally convenient schema of emanation, in which the scale of Nature is read downwards from higher to lower, and the lower forms are held to have degenerated from the higher.

[1] *Phil. of Nat.*, p. 480.

Hegel makes plain, further, that there is only a loose relation of fitting between the ideal determinations ot *Naturphilosophie*, and the empirical phenomena that correspond to them. 'Contingency and determination *ab extra*', says Hegel, 'come [in Nature] to their right.' Nature is, in fact, *impotent* to follow out these notional determinations in their purity, and it is also impotent to prevent their indefinite distortion and perversion by external influences. This does not mean, however, that *traces* of conceptual connection may not be found even in the most haphazard individual contingencies. *Naturphilosophie* does not, therefore, provide us with a set of laws and notions from which the detail of Nature can be foreseen: it is not, in modern terms, a set of *scientific* notions and hypotheses. But equally it is not an arbitrary, merely external way of looking at things, to which natural detail is irrelevant. Natural arrangements are either such as positively to fall in with, or not to square readily, with the requirements of our thought-determinations. And Hegel is not unwilling to refute a particular hypothesis like Newton's colour-theory by pointing to one crucial empirical fact he thinks at variance with it (i.e. that coloured lights appear darker than white light, as they should not on the Newtonian view that white light combines all coloured lights). It seems plain, therefore, that the descriptions and characterizations of *Naturphilosophie* occupy a position intermediate between those that are strictly scientific, and those that are, in a modern sense, 'metaphysical'. Not everything in the observed realm of Nature makes a difference to Hegel's philosophical theorizing, but some things certainly do so.

In the body of the treatise which follows Hegel deals first with Mechanics, the study of inert Matter or Matter impelled into action by outside influences, then with Physics proper, the study of Matter secretly biassed towards other Matter, and involved in various kinds of necessary *liaison* with the latter. Finally he deals with Organics, in which Nature strives valiantly to rise above its original *Aussereinander* or *Aussersichseyn*, and to make each feature and manifestation manifest one *total* reality. The unity thus achieved will then be ready to pass over into the more abiding, immaterial unity of conscious thought. As in Aristotle, the various levels of Nature are each contained and resumed in the levels that lie above them. Hegel follows Schelling in comparing this to the way in which the lower powers of a number are factors in its higher powers.

II PHILOSOPHICAL MECHANICS; SPACE, TIME, MATTER, MOTION, GRAVITY

We shall now range with seven-leagued boots over the vast terrain of Hegel's Dialectic of Nature. We shall at times come down to treat more fully what seems memorable and salient, but we shall in general skim over matters whose full treatment would require much background. This will involve ignoring many curious, often deep-cutting transitions: the reader will, however, have had enough experience of Hegel to guess what these were like.

In Mechanics, the study of inert Matter, we have Nature at its most natural: we deal with it first in the form of an abstract *partes extra partes*, of which the empirical exemplifications are the two orders of Space and Time. 'The first or immediate determination of Nature', says Hegel, 'is the abstract universality of its externality, its immediate indifference, i.e. Space. Space is the wholly ideal side-by-sideness (*Nebeneinander*) because it is externality, and it is absolutely continuous, because this mutual outsideness is as yet entirely abstract, and involves no definite difference within itself.'[1] In Pure Space, Hegel tells us, we have that uneasy, struggling unity between Discreteness, on the one hand, and Continuity, on the other, which is characteristic of all quantitative conceptions. Space essentially breaks up into points which are, however, nothing apart from their position in Space, which therefore remains unbroken in the process. Such pure Space is nothing real and substantial. It is, says Hegel, 'a non-sensuous sensibility and a sensuous supersensibility' (*eine unsinnliche Sinnlichkeit und eine sinnliche Unsinnlichkeit*). The things in Nature are in Space, merely because Space is the form of their universal externality and otherness. As regards the three spatial dimensions, Hegel sees in them a reflection of the three notional determinations of Universality, Specificity and Individuality. But since Space is a form of mere Quantity, the difference between these moments becomes a *mere* difference, which is,

[1] *Phil. of Nat.*, pp. 70–1.

in a sense, *no* difference. Obviously it makes no difference whether we call a distance one of length, breadth or depth.

Time, as opposed to Space, is held by Hegel to be the genuinely *punctual* element in the mutual outsideness of Nature. Space can, in fact, only be broken into points by the diremptive action of Time, which is associated successively with different points of Space. Hegel is clear that Time and Space are inseparable: in Time we have in fact the 'truth', the necessary complement of Space. It is not *we* who pass subjectively from the one to the other: Space itself necessarily completes itself in Time. A position in Space means nothing unless coupled with a moment of Time: a Here is inseparable from a Now.[1] Hegel is therefore thoroughly conversant with the modern notion of Space-Time. He further repudiates any spatialized view of Time: it is wrong to think of Time as extended, as having the Past, Present and Future as its dimensions. Time is nothing if not the form of Becoming intuited: it is 'the being which, inasmuch as it is, is not, or which, inasmuch as it is not, is'. In the Time of Nature, he holds, only the present moment is real: only in the Time of Spirit can the Past be spread out in memory, or the Future projected in expectation or hope. 'In the positive sense of Time,' Hegel sums up, 'one can therefore say that only the Present is, while what is before and after is not. The concrete Present is, however, the result of the Past, and is pregnant with the Future. The true Present is therefore identical with eternity.'[2] We shall not develop the implications of these brief but interesting utterances, which obviously anticipate much fairly recent thought.

How Space and Time lead on to Motion and Matter may be incomprehensible to the Understanding: to Hegel the transition presents no difficulty. Obviously Space and Time are the aspects of Motion: Motion is in fact the passing away and the self-reinstatement of Space in Time. But the unending, self-contra-dictory restlessness of such Motion is, from another point of view, abiding continuity and self-identity: Motion, in short, is insepar-able from Matter, from what is movable. 'People', says Hegel, 'have often started with Matter and then looked on Space and Time as its forms. What is right in this is that Matter is what is real in Space and Time. But these latter, on account of their abstraction, must be treated by us first, and then Matter must

[1] *Phil. of Nat.*, pp. 78, 87.   [2] *Phil. of Nat.*, p. 86.

appear as their truth. Just as there is no Motion without Matter, so also there is no Matter without Motion.'[1] The dialectical method here plainly appears as the simple undoing of initial abstractions.

In the complicated Dynamics which follows Hegel holds Matter to be necessarily the seat of two balancing forces, a repulsive force which holds Matter apart, and which maintains a difference which would otherwise be *no* difference, and an attractive force which expresses the complete sameness of what is thus held apart. Gravity, says Hegel, is as it were a perpetual acknowledgement of the real nullity of the mutual outsideness of Matter.[2] Hegel is therefore unwilling, in seemingly modern fashion, to separate Gravitation from Inertia: it is nonsense, he holds, to ask what a body *would* do were it immune from gravitational attraction, or were it not slowed down by friction (which for him depends on pressure, as pressure depends on gravity). It is for Hegel essential to what is material to have movement towards a centre external to itself, just as it is accidental to it to impart, to receive or to maintain motions through impacts with other bodies. Both the motion and existence of material bodies depend on a balance between the diremptive, centrifugal tendencies credited to Inertia, on the one hand, and its unifying, centripetal gravitational tendencies, on the other.

It follows that for Hegel there is nothing accidental in the development of such a gravitating assemblage as the Solar System. Matter necessarily organizes itself about a main central body (the Universal Centre), which is as such immobile. It also necessarily organizes itself round many subordinate centres (the Specific Centres) which move, since it is not in them to have one fixed position, and which move in circles or in near-circles, since the Universal Centre would be no centre unless other centres moved about it. Hegel is insistent that the centrifugal force of the planets is not due to some external impetus: it is not owing to a past accident that they fail to fall in the sun. He tells us, in Aristotelian or Platonic phrase, that the heavenly bodies are not pulled hither and thither by competing forces, but that they go on their ways in freedom, like blessed gods.[3] Hegel then engages in a long, embittered defence of the organically unified astronomy and cosmology of Kepler as opposed to the dualistic, mechanistic,

[1] *Phil. of Nat.*, p. 95.   [2] *Phil. of Nat.*, p. 95.   [3] *Phil. of Nat.*, p. 123.

chapter-of-accidents hypotheses of Newton. Kepler, he says, did not make Newton's mistake of separating the centripetal force of Gravitation from the centrifugal force due to some external, rectilineal blow. Kepler also recognized the propriety and naturalness of the elliptical course of the planets, which is, says Hegel, superior to the circular, since there is an abstract arbitrariness in the precise equality of radii. Hegel sketches the position in the Solar System of its Universal Centre, the Sun, its Specific Centres, the planets, and its looser Individual elements, the satellites and comets. The last represent the 'lunatic fringe' of the Solar System: Hegel reluctantly finds a place for them in his theory (and makes much subsequent use of them) since 'what is actually present must of necessity be contained in the Notion' (*was vorhanden ist muss nothwendig im Begriffe gehalten seyn*).[1] It may be noted here, in view of a widespread legend, that Hegel does *not* teach that there can only be seven planets— he knows of the existence of the asteroids Vesta, Juno, Ceres and Pallas and also of Uranus—and that he specifically warns against the attempt to deduce too much philosophically, or to seek too exact an illustration in Nature of the notions our thought finds firm and clear.[2] If Hegel's Mechanics is too 'organic' for our modern taste, it is none the less far from absurd. Possibly, too, there may ultimately prove to be more of Keplerian organism in an assemblage like the Solar System than our science has unthinkingly denied.

III PHILOSOPHICAL PHYSICS: THE ELEMENTS, COHESION, SOUND, HEAT, ELECTRICITY, MAGNETISM, CHEMICAL ACTION, ETC.

From Mechanics Hegel passes on to Physics proper, the study of Matter in its 'reflectedness', its essential relativity. The transition, being obscure, may be quoted at some length. 'The substance of Matter, Gravity', Hegel says, 'developed to the totality of form has no longer got the externality of Matter outside of itself. The form appears at first, as regards its differences, in the ideal determinations of Space, Time and Motion, and as regards its being-for-self as a Centre fixed outside of the self-external Matter. In the developed totality, however, this mutual outside-

---

[1] *Phil. of Nat.*, p. 123.   [2] *Phil. of Nat.*, p. 150.

ness is posited as something wholly determined by Matter itself, and Matter is nothing outside of its mutual outsideness. The form is in this manner materialized. But conversely Matter, in this denial of its externality in the totality, has obtained in itself the Centre that it formerly merely sought, its self, the formal determinateness. Its dull, abstract, being-in-self, the heavy in general, has been determined to form. It is qualified Matter—Physics.'[1] In other words, the complicated extended pattern of organization seen in the solar system is now seen as inherent in *every* piece of Matter, which therefore ceases to seem lumpish and homogeneous, with an organization coming from without. We rise to the notion of Matter as being as rich in intrinsic differences as it is in extrinsic organization. Just as the mechanical process of adding unit to unit leads to the bizarre intricacies of incommensurables, infinitesimals, etc., and is thereby shown to be a mere abstraction from what is by no means straightforward, so do our first lumpish pictures of Matter reveal themselves as abstractions from what is indefinitely subtle and internally complex. We therefore pass on to Physics, in which this subtle complexity will be made overt.

The long section on *Physics* which follows first deals (under the heading of 'Physics of Universal Individuality') with the various 'elements' out of which the natural world is composed: these include the traditional elements of Fire, Air, Earth and Water, and also Light. It then goes on to deal with the 'Physics of Specific Individuality', in which Hegel discusses the four material properties of Specific Gravity, Cohesion, Sound and Warmth. Finally it moves on to discuss the 'Physics of Total Individuality', which covers the phenomena of Magnetism, Crystallization, Refraction, Colour, Taste and Smell Differences, Static Electricity, and finally Chemical Process. We shall not plague ourselves with the fragile links leading from each of these topics to the next, but shall merely sketch their contents in general outline.

Hegel conceives of Light, perhaps under the inspiration of Kant's Third Analogy of Experience, as the Medium or Agent which holds the material world together, which makes of it *one* world. It is, he says the 'pure existent power of spatial occupancy, its being the absolute velocity, the present pure materiality, the

_____
[1] *Phil. of Nat.*, p. 150.

actual existence which is in itself, or Actuality as a transparent Possibility' (i.e. Light will show things up if they are there to be shown up). 'Space is merely an abstract subsistence or being-in-self, but Light, as actual being-in-self, or as Existence which is in itself, and is therefore pure, is the power of Universal Actuality to be outside of itself, as the Possibility which coalesces with all, the community with all which remains in itself, and whereby the existent surrenders none of its independence. . . . Light brings us into universal connection. Everything, because it is in the Light, stands for that reason in theoretical, unresisting manner before us.'[1] He goes on to say that Light represents the ideality of Matter, as Gravity represents its reality: he also declares it to be a lower form of the all-pervasive self-sameness of the Ego. If Gravitation represents a somewhat crude denial of the mere outsideness of Matter to Matter, which takes effect in the slow act of falling, Light represents a more subtle denial of this mere outsideness, for it brings everything to everything else without locomotion, merely by making it manifest. For those interested in such anticipations there is undoubtedly a flavour of relativity-physics in some of the things Hegel says about Light.

From Light Hegel passes on to the four canonical elements Air, Fire, Earth and Water. He defends their elementary status against that of such substances as Carbon, Oxygen, etc., on the ground that the latter are merely 'sides' of genuine elements, artificially forced into isolation. Air is said to be the element of negative Universality which, unlike Light, is heavy: through it, as through Light, everything is revealed to everything, but in the slowly diffused, quasi-material form of fragrance. Fire, as opposed to Air, is a negative Universality which is consuming and destructive: it steadfastly eats up what is other, resembling in this respect the tooth of Time and the self-assertive Universality of the Ego. Water, in its turn, is said to be the element of passive Neutrality. In it fiery processes quench themselves: in itself it is without cohesion, smell, taste, form or opacity. But it is also a universal solvent, and adheres to all things and wets them. Earth, finally, is said to be the element of Individual Determinateness and Developed Difference: it represents the hard, definite aspect of Nature. The elements thus sketched are then made to engage in an elaborate meteorological ballet. Hegel thinks in Aristotelian

[1] *Phil. of Nat.*, p. 157.

terms and denies that Water remains Water when it passes into vapour, and becomes patent as Water when it again falls as rain: rain, he points out, appealing to experience, sometimes falls from a wholly dry sky. He is a remorseless foe of all forms of latency. 'What is not subject to observation, does not exist in the physical field, since existence is merely being-for-something-else, the making of oneself noticeable.'[1]

In the Physics of Specific Individuality which follows, Hegel deals with an ascending series of determinations in which Matter becomes increasingly self-centred (*selbstisch*), in which it stamps a unifying and distinctive individuality on all its parts. In Specific Gravity, Matter is said to rise to self-centred individual distinctiveness by its refusal to fill Space uniformly: Hegel spurns mechanistic theories which account for varying Specific Gravities by differing amounts of void. In Cohesion, Matter goes further in individual distinctiveness by *clinging* together: it is not satisfied to *compare* itself with other bodies, as in Specific Gravity. In Sound a body even dares momentarily to negate the whole mutual outsideness of parts characteristic of its material being, though it returns to normal materiality an instant after. Sound is in fact the regular periodic abandonment of spatial materiality and its periodic replacement by temporal ideality. The Shiver or Quiver (*Erzittern*) involved in this periodic intermission of materiality is for Hegel distinct from the material Vibration (*Schwingung*) it produces. Sound, says Hegel, is either the complaint of the ideal against alien violence, or its cry of triumph in maintaining itself against the latter. Heat, in its turn, is Sound transformed into something *real*: we observe, says Hegel, that not only the musician but also his *instrument* becomes hot. Through Heat Matter loses its rigidity and rises to abstract homogeneity and shapelessness: the most diverse substances then tend to mingle and coalesce. In all these physical forms Matter is trying, with increasing success, to negate its clear-cut separateness of properties and individual being: we pass, therefore, to the Physics of Total Individuality, where the properties of bodies are inseparably bound up with their relation to other bodies. Hegel confesses that the task of matching thought-determinations to empirical moments has, in the phenomena just treated, been particularly taxing: totality has been present only as an impulse, and the

[1] *Phil. of Nat.*, p. 203.

determinations studied have accordingly seemed isolated. Our summary has made Hegel's treatment sound more of a fairy tale than it actually is, since in him elements of interpretation are subtly mixed up with the detail of science.

In the Physics of Total Individuality the most interesting treatments are of Magnetism, Crystallization, Colour, Electricity and Chemical Process. We shall content ourselves by quoting a few vivid definitions and sayings. Of Magnetism Hegel says: 'The activity of the form is none other than that of the Notion in general, to posit the identical as differing, and the differing as identical, here, therefore, in the sphere of material spatiality. But to posit the identical as different in the case of a spatial thing is to remove, repel it from itself, just as to posit differents as identical is to bring them closer, and into contact with each other, i.e. to attract them together. This activity, since it exists in a material thing, and is as yet abstract (and only as such is it Magnetism) only ensouls something linear. In such an object the two determinations of the form can only appear separately in its differences, i.e. in the two ends, and their active magnetic difference consists solely in this: that one end (the one pole) posits as identical with itself the same third thing which the other end or pole removes from itself.'[1] Hegel refuses to look on Magnetism as mysterious: it involves none of the invisible currents beloved of the Understanding. It is a mere assertion of the unity of the Notion over the surface separateness of Matter. That the two magnetic poles should be so peculiarly distinct is described by Hegel as a 'naïveté of Nature'. The forms of crystals, according to Hegel, represent the magnet's restless activity reduced to tranquillity, while the 'abstract linearity of its place-determining power' is now spread over a body's whole surface. The Notion in crystals no longer generates approach or withdrawal, but is manifest statically.

Hegel sees in Colour a joint product of the Luminous or Transparent, which is homogeneously neutral in existence, and the Dark, which is said to be individualized to being-for-self, and to be connected with metallic forms of Matter. Metals are for Hegel the universal Colour-stuff. All colours are combinations of simple Light, the principle of homogeneous connectivity, and metallic Darkness, through which bodily Individuality is manifest. Hegel's

[1] *Phil. of Nat.*, pp. 288–9.

definition of Colour prejudges the question of its nature in favour of Goethe's Colour-theory, of which Hegel gives a passionate defence against Newtonian views. According to this strange theory, as set forth by Hegel, we have yellow whenever a brighter ground shows through a duller medium, blue when the medium is brighter and the ground darker. Green is the simple, neutral mixture of yellow and blue, while red arises when yellow is shaded or blue illuminated. Red, according to Hegel, is the kingly colour, the light that has overcome darkness, and penetrated it through and through. Elaborate connections are then found between the primary colours and the four elements, and between them and specific attitudes of mind.

In the Electrical Relationship Hegel sees a direct expression of the *selfhood* of a body in relation to other bodies. It is not an expression of a single body, like Sound, nor of so profound a relationship between bodies as chemical coalescence. An object's corporeity, Hegel tells us, does not enter into the Electrical Relationship, which accordingly reveals itself in a cold flash without physical effect, and in the evanescent shock which accompanies this. Hegel emphasizes that there is nothing mysterious in electricity: it is not a universal fluid or agent, nor need it be explained in terms of particles or currents. Electrical behaviour is simply the 'self' of a body responding angrily to the friction or pressure of surrounding bodies. Hegel writes: 'We, however, conceive electrical tension as the proper selfhood of the body that is physical totality, and that maintains itself in contact with another body. It is a body's own anger, its proper ebullition. No one else is present beside itself, least of all a foreign material. Its youthful spirit strikes out, it raises itself on its hind legs: its physical nature gathers itself together against the relationship to something else, and does so as the abstract ideality of Light. It is not merely *we* who compare bodies, but they compare themselves, and maintain themselves physically in doing so.'[1] This comparison of electrical tension to the snarling of hostile dogs is a vivid piece of picture-thinking.

In the Chemical Process, the last phase of the Physics of Total Individuality, we have at once the most complete distinctness of material individuals, and also their most complete fusion and union. Both are but sides of the same Notion, which manifests

[1] *Phil. of Nat.*, p. 375.

itself in two opposing Processes, at one time gathering the separate chemical substances into the compound which neutralizes them, at another time dissolving this close-knit unity and restoring the separate individualities. This Chemical Process is, in a sense, the same thing that has appeared previously as Magnetism and Electricity, though Hegel rejects the widely accepted doctrine of their mere identity. In the Chemical Process we start with more separateness than we have in the case of a Magnet, and we end with more fusion than we have in the brief flash and shock of electrical recognition. Hegel attacks in an expected manner Dalton's atomic picture of chemical union: there is, he holds, no occult survival of elements in a chemical compound. The root-defects of the Chemical Process are however the facts (a) that it merely represents an uneasy swing from one kind of one-sidedness to another, and (b) that it depends on external conditions to set it off, and never becomes self-renewing and cyclical. The components will not unite unless externally brought together, nor will the compound dissolve without an external stimulus. All this, however, represents a lameness in the expression of the underlying Notion, which can only be remedied in the Vital Process, where, precisely, we see a concrete unity assembling itself out of distinct bodies, and again specifying itself into distinct parts and functions. Hegel is therefore able to pass from Physics to Organics, the study of the Living Organism. This Organism has secretly been the guiding star in the whole previous course of dialectical navigation. With this transition, Hegel tells us, we are able to leave the prose for the poetry of Nature.[1]

IV ORGANICS: PHILOSOPHICAL GEOLOGY, BOTANY AND ZOOLOGY

Hegel begins his section on Organics with the following passage: 'The real totality of body, as the infinite Process, that Individuality determines itself to Specificity and finitude, and also negates the same and returns into self, is accordingly a rise into the first ideality of Nature, so that it has become a satisfied, and essentially self-centred and subjective unity, inasmuch as it is one that refers self to self. The Idea has therefore come to existence, and first to an existence that is immediate, to Life.'[2] In Life there is a

[1] *Phil. of Nat.*, p. 445.   [2] *Phil. of Nat.*, p. 449.

constant self-differentiation of Matter into separate organs and functions, but also a constant use of such dirempted aspects in the interests of a single economy. Hegel finds his necessary triad in Organics by including in it the 'Geological Organism', the Earth treated as the basis and background of Life, and described in quaint zoological metaphors. This is followed by a treatment of the Vegetable and Animal Organisms, the last being the crown of Nature and the matrix of self-conscious Spirit.

Of Hegel's views on Geology and Geography little deserves comment. He holds that the Earth has been the scene of a large number of cataclysmic shapings, involving flood and fire, which now lie entirely in the past, that it has settled down completely and sustained the lightning-stroke of Life, after which it has remained the quiescent background of living forms. These, as we said before, came forth unheralded like Minerva from Jove's front. Hypotheses as to the pre-organic state of the earth have for Hegel no rational interest: factually well attested they may be, but not philosophically 'true'. They merely translate the senseless side-by-sideness of things in Space into the equally senseless before-and-after of states in Time. From a philosophical standpoint the Natural World is timeless and ahistorical, since its long aeons of past development contribute nothing to our understanding of it. As mentioned before, Hegel thinks that the living forms found in geological strata never really lived: they are the dead products of an 'organic-plastic' impulse resident in the earthly elements, which works like an artist producing creditable likenesses of the living. On the other hand, Hegel does believe that the Geological Organism is at present the seat of an indefinite amount of spontaneously generated, momentary life. The atmosphere gives birth to such living things as miasmata and honey-dew. The sea is always ready to break out into infusoria or phosphorescence: its surface is an 'immeasurable, unsurveyable sea of light, which consists solely of living points, which organize themselves no further.'[1] The land equivocally generates lichen, mushrooms and vegetable mould. There are no germs or seeds for such products, since seed only exists where subjectivity is explicit. Such transitory forms of life provide, however, a good dialectical transition to the Vegetable Organism. Here life ceases to be diffuse, and becomes gathered into individual points of life,

[1] *Phil. of Nat.*, p. 486.

which sustain themselves for a time and produce other similar individuals, maintaining thereby a continuity of kind. In this the Notion, always obscurely counteracting the externality of Nature, is more obviously explicit.

In the Vegetable Organism subjectivity is said by Hegel to develop itself into an 'Objective Organism', a bodily form articulated into distinct members. The unity of the one Organism, and the distinctness of its members, are as yet somewhat rudimentary. The different parts of a plant, e.g. a bud or a branch, are separate individuals, each in a sense is the whole plant, and the whole plant is their unifying ground rather than the one individual of which they are the members. The differing functions of the various plant-organs are accordingly superfluous: vary the circumstances and each organ assumes the other's functions. The whole plant can be entirely regenerated from its most inconsiderable fragment. There is also in the plant no clear distinction between individual growth and the generation of new individuals: since being-for-self is implicit, the individual merges in the kind. Plants exhibit most of the paraphernalia of sex and go through complex rituals of fructification and the production of seeds. All this, however, is a mere *analogon* of true sexual reproduction, which can be enjoyed only at the animal level. The sexual commerce of plants is a game, a luxury, altogether superfluous for reproduction: the latter proceeds as readily by budding, grafting or similar processes. A plant, moreover, lives submerged in the mutual outsideness of material being and cannot bring this latter to a unitary focus. It cannot, therefore, determine its place by locomotion, nor can it enjoy sensation, since it lacks a 'centre of negativity' towards which the thrillings in its members can be referred back. Sensitive plants, despite appearances, are not truly sensitive. Being thus imperfectly unified, the plant has its true centre of unity, its 'self', outside itself. The 'self' of a plant is the light towards which it constantly turns: were it conscious, this light would be its God.[1] Understanding, as opposed to Reason, is dominant in plant morphology: they affect straight lines and fixed numbers. Here as elsewhere Hegel makes use of the strange intuitions of Goethe. Obviously the plant is a mere half-way house between a geological and a true Organism. We therefore pass on to an Organism whose form agrees with its notion, which

[1] *Phil. of Nat.*, p. 500.

has parts which are truly members, and a 'subjectivity' which exists as the pervasive unity of the whole. The Vegetable Organism passes into the Animal Organism.

Hegel characterizes the Animal Organism in the following terms: 'Organic Individuality exists as subjectivity in so far as the proper externality of its form is idealized to members, while the Organism invariably preserves its selflike unity (or selflike Sun) in its going forth towards the outside. This is the Animal Nature, which in the actuality and externality of immediate individuality, is by contrast just as much the self-reflected self of Individuality, subjective Universality which exists in self.'[1] Hegel somewhat fantastically compares the Animal Organism to a solar system in which the Sun has absorbed all the other bodies. He goes on to stress the Aristotelian platitude that a member cut from an animal body is a member only in name: this was not true at the vegetable level. The Animal Organism is further said to reveal an 'ideality' which renders it independent of a precise position in space: it is a 'free Time', endowed with arbitrary locomotion, through which it fixes its place. It is endowed with a 'self-feeling' in which the most varied organic affections can be brought back to a 'centre of negativity'. It has a Voice in which its inmost quivers can, at its own impulse, be given objective being: inorganic objects only sound when struck, whereas animals sound spontaneously and voice themselves in such sounding. Each animal has a peculiar voice used only in the throes of violent death, in which it expresses its own overcoming or nullification. It expresses itself also in the phenomenon of animal warmth, as sustained and constant as chemical warmth is transitory.

From this general characterization, Hegel goes on to a detailed treatment of the ever recurring, supremely tedious organic functions of Sensibility, Irritability and Reproduction. These are here related to the Nervous System, to the Muscular and Vascular Systems, and to the Digestive and Glandular Systems respectively. Hegel deals at length with the physiology and functions of the sense-organs, and with various elementary animal instincts and needs. Like Aristotle he devotes much space to the processes of digestion and nutrition: a philosopher who looks for the 'truth' of things in the swallowing up and assimilation of what is alien, must obviously have strong nutritive interests. He says much that is

[1] *Phil. of Nat.*, p. 576.

interesting but not memorable about sexual relations and reproduction, and then goes on to a long treatment of the relation of
an animal Genus to the Species and Individuals which fall under
it. This last leads him to consider Disease and Death, in which we
see the inadequacy of the Individual Organism to its Generic
Notion, an inadequacy which is the original disease of all Individual
Organisms, of which they all sooner or later and on varying
pretexts die. In old age the Universal becomes 'bogged down'
and 'physicalized' in the routines that it has built up. Having no
longer an 'other' to work upon, or a task to perform, it must of
necessity depart or withdraw.

The topic of death smoothes the dialectical passage from
Nature to Spirit. The Universality which can only realize itself
in a series of perishing Individuals, must of necessity pass to the
more adequately realized Universality which exists only in the
enjoyments of conscious Thought. 'The subjectivity in the Idea
of Life', Hegel tells us, 'is the Notion, it is therefore implicitly
the absolute being-in-self of Actuality and concrete Universality.
Through the indicated annulment of the *immediacy* of its reality,
it has gone together with itself. The last outsideness-of-self of
Nature is overcome, and the Notion which merely exists *in itself*
in Nature has thereby become *for itself*.'[1] 'The aim of Nature',
Hegel continues, 'is to compass its own death, to break through
the rind of the immediate and sensory, to burn itself like a phoenix,
and to appear out of this externality rejuvenated as Spirit.'[2] Those
who understand the basic acceptances involved in Hegelianism
will find nothing untoward in this last transition. Hegel ends by
apologizing for the imperfection of his *Naturphilosophie*. These
arise mainly from the refractory resistance of material realities
to the unity of the concept, and to the accumulated detail with which
they clog and vex the mind. Reason must maintain its faith in
itself despite these difficulties: it must let the Notion speak to the
Notion behind all the externality and unending variety of natural
forms.

[1] *Phil. of Nat.*, p. 719.   [2] *Phil. of Nat.*, p. 721.

CHAPTER TEN

THE PHILOSOPHY OF SUBJECTIVE SPIRIT
(*Hegel's Psychology*)

I DEFINITION AND EMERGENCE OF SUBJECTIVE SPIRIT

The *Philosophy of Spirit*, the third section of Hegel's *Encyclopaedia*, deals with *Geist*, Spirit, as 'the self-knowing actual Idea, raised to the concept of the living Spirit which in necessary wise draws distinctions in itself, and returns to unity with itself out of its distinctions'.[1] This actual Spirit, Hegel tells us, has both Nature and the Logical Idea as its presuppositions, while in a sense it remains prior to either. It must be prior to the Logical Idea, since this represents merely the possibility, not as yet the actuality of self-conscious Spirit. The 'knowing' involved in the Logical Idea is (Hegel declares) only 'the notion of Knowledge that is thought by us, not the Knowledge that is there for itself, not actual Spirit, but only its possibility'.[2] Since the actual is prior in notion to the merely possible, it is in Spirit that we see the fully carried out meaning of the Idea. In the same manner Spirit is in a sense prior to Nature, since the whole of Nature represents a half-thwarted striving to lay aside its externality to self (*Aussersichseyn*), and it is this tendency which achieves its unthwarted realization in Spirit. 'All activities of Spirit', Hegel tells us, 'are no more than diverse ways of reducing the external to the inwardness which Spirit itself is, and only through this reduction, this idealization or assimiliation of the external, can it become and be Spirit.'[3]

The emergence of Spirit from Nature (as also from the Logical Idea) must accordingly not be regarded as the coming forth into being of something epiphenomenal, derivative or resultant. Spirit, Hegel tells us, is in a sense its own result: 'it itself brings itself forth out of the presuppositions it makes for itself—out of the Logical Idea and external Nature—and is the truth as much of the one as of the other'. In its 'sovereign ingratitude' Spirit sets aside the thing on which it seems to be consequent, and

---

[1] *Phil. of Sp.*, p. 15.   [2] *Phil. of Sp.*, p. 20.   [3] *Phil. of Sp.*, p. 24.

makes of the latter its own consequence, thereby achieving absolute self-sufficiency.[1] This setting aside of the Natural World in Spirit must not, however, be thought to involve some Kantian doctrine of the covert manufacture of phenomenal Nature by the 'productive imagination' or by some similarly conceived faculty. We do not half-consciously build up a phenomenal order in Space and Time, in order afterwards to discover the marks of our own workmanship upon it. Such a subjective interpretation Hegel explicitly repudiates, and it is quite foreign to his thought. He remarks clearly that the fact that what is sensed by the intuiting Spirit has a spatial and temporal form does not imply that Space and Time are subjective. 'The things themselves', he tells us, 'are in reality spatial and temporal: that double form of mutual outsideness is not merely put on them one-sidedly by our intuition, but is provided for them from the very beginning by the infinite Spirit which is in itself, by the creative eternal Idea.'[2] The last phrases mean no more than that the spatial and temporal orders are a presupposition of spiritual self-consciousness, and that this, in the last resort, answers the question *why* they are there. There is no suggestion that they were consciously or unconsciously fabricated by some actual Spirit, since the Idea which is said to have made them is no more than the *possibility* of self-consciousness.

The passages we have quoted, and many more like them, will have borne out the account of Spirit given in our third chapter, and the central position of this notion in Hegel's philosophy. It will not therefore be necessary for us to follow the course of Hegel's dialectical treatment of Spirit in very close detail. We may also claim exemption from a very detailed exposition inasmuch as the *Philosophy of Spirit* is largely a restatement, in the systematic mould of the *Encyclopaedia*, of the living tangle of notions and experiences that has already been sketched in *The Phenomenology of Spirit*. Compared with the tortured, palpitating vitality of that work, the *Philosophy of Spirit* certainly seems flat and obvious. This flatness and obviousness descend into the uninspired obscurantism of the long restatement of the treatment of 'Objective Spirit' which is to be found in the fourth and last of Hegel's written works, the fruit of his Berlin elevation, *The Philosophy of Right*. As this work has been twice translated, and has also been much commented on in English, and has been

---

[1] *Phil. of Sp.*, p. 29.   [2] *Phil. of Sp.*, p. 323.

regarded both as more wonderfully inspiring and more wickedly corrupting than it can with any reason be held to be, we shall sketch in its outlines lightly.

The *Philosophy of Spirit* has, of course, the usual triadic structure, subdivided triadically to a number of stages. In its first section it deals with Subjective Spirit, Spirit as yet unconscious of all it is, Spirit which is only Spirit for *us*, the philosophical commentators or observers, and not for *itself*. In this section there is an Anthropological, a Phenomenological and a Psychological chapter. Spirit in this section stands opposed to a natural world in which it does not as yet see anything akin to itself. Being so opposed, it is also largely in bondage to what it opposes and is accordingly at first a nature-bound Spirit. The dialectic then passes to Objective Spirit, where Spirit develops itself into a complete 'world' held together by a 'necessity' of which 'freedom' is the central pin. Objective Spirit passes through the three sections of Abstract Right (or Law), Morality, and Social Ethics, the last of which terminates in the famous Hegelian treatment of the State and History. The content of this section is given in condensed form in the *Encyclopaedia*, more discursively in the *Philosophy of Right*. We then pass to the third crowning division of Absolute Spirit, where Spirit becomes conscious of itself as the informing principle of its 'world', as well as being the 'truth' of all that leads up to it. Here we have three chapters on Art, Religion and Philosophy, each developed into a complete history of human development in these spheres. Our present chapter will be confined to the treatment of Subjective Spirit.

II 'SOUL', OR SPIRIT SUNK IN NATURE (ANTHROPOLOGY)

Spirit emergent from Nature is, in the first instance, manifest as Soul (*Seele*). Such Soul, Hegel tells us, is simply the latent ideality or immateriality of Matter: in it the *Aussersichseyn*, the outsideness-of-self, which is the basic determination of Matter, is 'volatilized' (*verflüchtigt*) into Universality, into the subjective ideality of the Notion. Hegel also says that Soul is the *truth* of Matter, the truth that Matter has no truth. Soul is, however, only as yet the *sleep* of Spirit, the passive Mind of Aristotle, which involves in itself the possibility of all forms of conscious awareness, without bringing such possibilities to active fulfilment. (What these descriptions suggest is the obscure massive life of bodily feeling, in which there are certainly contributions from distinct environmental regions and bodily parts, but in which these contributions are also lost in a profound unity, and not as yet discriminatively appropriated by 'consciousness'.) The question as to *how* the body is related to this Soul Hegel regards as a product of confusion. People imagine that the body as spread out in Nature is one particular thing, and that the same body with its environment *as felt internally* is another particular thing: it is not then clear how something so disjoined as the Body, and something so conjoined as the Soul can have commerce with one another. In truth, however, Hegel tells us, the immaterial is not to be opposed to the material as one particular to another: it must rather be thought of as 'overreaching, genuine Universal', against which the material has neither strength nor truth. The whole 'sense' of the material, extended body is to be the 'other' of a Soul that can feel itself at one in it, and that can lead back its multiplicity of parts and processes to the simple unity of 'self-feeling'. Matter with its mutual externality of parts has been striving towards this completion in the long course of its mechanical, physical and organic development. There is, therefore, nothing that particularly requires explanation when the keystone finally falls into place in the arch.

Hegel begins his treatment of Soul with a difficult section on Natural Soul, by which he means a sort of psychic life diffused throughout wide segments of Nature, and not yet parcelled off into separate individual Souls. It is *not*, he says, a Soul of the World of the sort Plato believed in, but rather a 'substance' out of which individual Souls may be carved. This Natural Soul is said to bestir itself within itself (*sich in sich regen*), and to condense the environing natural world in itself, and reduce it to something qualitative. The Natural Soul will have qualitative differences corresponding to various climates, seasons and times of day which will permeate through to the individual Souls that arise in it: animals will be wholly swayed by such qualities of psychic atmosphere, and men too will feel them, though they will be able to counter them with their wills. (The winter mood of the Natural Soul, for instance, drives men towards inner self-collection and the life of the family hearth, whereas its summer mood impels them towards journeys, to pilgrimages and to life in the open.[1]) The Natural Soul will further be differentiated according to the climate and other features of the geographical environment, and will impose special qualities on those living in its sphere of influence. There will be an Arab Soul as unchangeable as the desert, a Greek Soul geographically divided into Spartan, Theban and Athenian sub-varieties, as well as special Souls allotted to the various modern Western European nations. (The English Soul is credited by Hegel with a special power of 'intellectual intuition', which enables its particulars to see rationality in the individual rather than in the general case, and to excel in poetry and not in philosophy.) Hegel gives no clear elucidation of his notion of an unindividualized Soul-stuff, nor does he give instances of its working beyond such as bear upon the psychic life of individuals. All that he says about his 'Natural Souls' might well have been said without them: he could simply have held that our individual psychic life is profoundly at one with the geographical environment in which it arises. It seems strange, too, that Hegel should have laid so much stress on geographical influences rather than on those which stem from culture and history.

From studying the Natural Soul in its Universality and its Specificity, Hegel passes on to study it when 'broken up like light into countless *individual* stars' (an image first used in the *Phenomenology*). The Natural Soul here shows itself in various innate differences of individual capacity, of temperament and of character. (Hegel so uses the term 'character' that the foundations of character, e.g. a tendency to self-will, can be said to be innate.) It also shows itself in certain typical lines of individual development, among which Hegel lists the variations characteristic of youth, maturity and age, of the two sexes, and finally of the alternating states of Sleeping and Waking. Sleeping and Waking provide Hegel with a jumping-off place for one of his more arbitrary transitions: he passes from them to Sensation (*Empfindung*), which in Hegel covers all states of obscure awareness. 'Sleeping and Waking', he writes, 'are at first not merely changes, but alternating states (progress towards infinity). In this their formal negative relation there is, however, as much the affirmative relation present. In the being-for-self of the awakened Soul,

[1] *Phil. of Nat.*, p. 67.

being is present as an ideal moment. It therefore *finds* the content determinations of its sleeping nature, which are implicit in the latter as in their substance, in itself, and indeed for itself. As a determination this specific content is distinct from the identity of the being-for-self with itself, but also simply contained in its simplicity—Sensation.'[1] (The German text contains an untranslatable verbal play on the words *finden* and *Empfindung*.) In other words, Sensation is simply the bringing to conscious clearness of the obscure mental modifications of the slumbering Soul. Hegel gives to the word *Empfindung* a connotation of 'noticing' absent from most philosophical uses of the English word 'Sensation', for which it would be the slumbering, rather than the waking Soul that lead a life of pure Sensation. 'Sensation' includes for Hegel a certain amount of looking and investigating, and also the use of one's obscure mental modifications to mediate the awareness of external objects and of one's own subjective life. Thus touch (*Berührung*) is the link through which the Soul senses an object outside itself, and also affirms its own conscious being. But though there is thus *some* subject-object structure in Sensation, Hegel regards it as altogether too rudimentary to amount to the *consciousness* of an external object or oneself. It is, he says, a 'dark weaving of the Spirit in its unaware, uncomprehending individuality' in which determinateness is as yet 'immediate' and 'part of its most particular, natural ownness'.[2] There would seem to be inconsistent emphases in this account of Sensation.

In the account of the life of Sensation which follows Hegel not only deals with the five recognized types of sense-experience, which represent for him the psychic internalization (*Erinnerung*) of the Soul's corporeity (*Leiblichkeit*): he also deals with various sensory externalizations of the soul's inner states, which involve a certain natural quasi-symbolism. Thus our experiences of colour are not merely pleasant or unpleasant: they are also sober, gay, fervent, cold, melancholy or tender, and these qualities are for Hegel qualities of Sensation. In the same way he stresses that various passions and emotions have their sensational (and thereby also their bodily) side: grief is felt as obdurately visceral, rage lives in the breast and muscles, and even thinking is marked by

---

[1] *Phil. of Sp.*, pp. 119–20 (W., pp. 175–6).
[2] *Phil. of Sp.*, pp. 122, 123.

obscure sensations in the head. The whole life of the heart, including morality and religion, and even the intellectual passions, therefore enters into the Hegelian account of Sensation, though it is not in these, but in other non-sensational experiences, that the true content of these states of mind can be adequately set forth.

From Sensation Hegel passes on to Feeling, which differs from Sensation only in being inclusive and comprehensive. Sensations are evanescent and particular, whereas Feelings represent the condensed psychic outcome of vast masses of Sensations: they also represent the obscure psychic resultant of innumerable relationships to things and happenings, to the whole of a man's personal universe or world. 'We are in ourselves', says Hegel, 'a world of concrete content and infinite periphery' containing an unnumbered multitude of relations and connections, which are always in us, even when they do not enter into our Sensations and ideas, so that 'the human Soul on account of the unending richness of its content may be called the Soul of a World, or an individually determined World-Soul.'[1] It is not wholly clear what Hegel is covering in this notion of 'Feeling'. In part he may be covering the vague states called *Bewusstseinslagen* or moods of consciousness, in which the whole of some region recently traversed in experience collapses into a 'nutshell' or remains as an 'atmosphere'. In part he would seem to be dealing with the merely *dispositional* riches of a much-experienced Soul, which can bring to light whatever bears on the particular matter on hand. This last would seem to be the dominant meaning, since Hegel talks of the 'indeterminate pit' in which endless sensations, ideas, knowledge, and thoughts are 'stored up, without existing', and speaks of people who in abnormal states recover knowledge that had long passed into forgetfulness. The dialectical linkage is at this point vestigial: the topics treated have neither a dialectical, nor any other clearly discoverable expository order.

It is characteristic of the Soul in the state of mere Feeling that it can have its 'self', its conscious directive individuality, in another person, who in this case is called the feeling Soul's *Genius*. A child in the womb has its mother's Soul as its Genius, and there are married couples, members of one family, or 'nervesick' male or female friends who thus at times play Genius to one

[1] *Phil. of Sp.*, p. 152.

another. In somnambulistic states the Soul, temporarily reduced to a state of mere Feeling, has its own waking self as its Genius, in some cases the waking self of the 'magnetizer' who has induced the somnambulistic state. Hegel here pours out a vast amount of lore concerning clairvoyance and telepathy, which does not differ materially from what would be cited in our own day. He describes the methods and experience of dowsers, the peculiar clairvoyant aptitudes of the pit of the stomach, the veridical hallucinations which concern sick friends in distant countries, the telepathic sharing of emotions and pains by close friends and relatives, also the remarkable frequency of 'second sight' in the Scottish Highlands, which Hegel ascribes to the extraordinary absorption of the people in individual contingencies (i.e. gossip), so that even *future* contingencies manage to seep through to them. Hegel's ready credence for these reported phenomena is due to their conformity with the principles of his own philosophy. That Spirit is, as he says, the truth that Matter has no truth, is confirmed by each case in which the normal outsideness of bodies is set aside, and in which profound long-range unities become operative. Only the unemancipated Understanding, not Hegelian Reason, finds something mysterious in these breakdowns of mechanical materiality,[1] which has in any case done nothing *but* break down even at the physical level. At the same time Hegel is unwilling to see signs of a deeper wisdom in the obscure deliverances of the feeling Soul. Whatever may be revealed in its visions and divinings will be more reliably and coherently revealed in the clear thoughts of waking consciousness.

Hegel now passes, by a barely noticeable transition, to talk interestingly on insanity and other mental disorders. Insanity, he says, consists in the one-sided domination of some particularity of 'self-feeling', which is not fitted into the systematically ordered 'world' which likewise has its correlate in self-feeling. Such a quasi-mechanical disorder is possible only in the Soul, which retains traces of Matter's mutual externality of parts: fully self-conscious Spirit is of necessity immune from madness. In madness the duplex condition characteristic of the somnambulistic state becomes actual in one individual person. In him the coherent world of waking thought lodges with dream-content which cannot possibly be reconciled with it. Such madness is not, however,

[1] *Phil. of Sp.*, § 406, p. 169 (W., pp. 183–4).

merely a disorder: it may be seen as the stigma of our spiritual greatness. For a man's Soul, being implicitly Spirit, is by its nature detachable from all finite content, *capable* of association with *any* form of being. I, who am an impoverished bank-clerk, might very well have been a king, a dog, or a being possessed of wings: if I become mad, I think I am these things. The one defect in being mad is that I turn a true and noble possibility, inseparable from the negativity of self-consciousness, into an ignoble and often absurd actuality.[1]

The freedom of a man's Soul from the particularity of circumstance is shown in yet another way in the phenomena of Habit. Here, Hegel tells us, 'the Soul possesses the contents of Feeling in such a manner, and contains them so in itself, that in such determinations it is not sensitive, that it does not distinguish itself from them, or stand in any relation to them, and is not absorbed in them, but rather has them by itself without Sensation and consciousness, and moves itself in them. It is to this extent free from them, that it is uninterested in, unconcerned with them. Inasmuch as it exists in these forms as its possession, it is at once open to further activity and concern—for Sensation and for the consciousness of Spirit in general.'[2] Hegel here stresses the importance of unconscious Habit in the life of a conscious being, how things done heedfully become more and more unheedingly done, until at last they proceed without consciousness, thereby liberating the mind for more difficult activities. Hegel recognizes to the full that consciousness has its place in the challenging, the critical situation, that it can delegate its direction to well-disciplined, even responsible mechanisms: he is free from the mythology of constant conscious supervision. The mastery of particular ideas which the madman fails to achieve, is fully achieved by the Man of Habit: in him detached systems of ideas are driven from consciousness, so as to become its humble executives rather than its dissident disturbers.

Hegel now winds up the Anthropological section of his treatment of Soul, by a brief section on 'Actual Soul'. This is a Soul perfectly accommodated in a body trained to express its every nuance and mood. Such a Soul is called 'Actual' as being the 'identity of inward with outward', the latter being wholly subordinated to the former. It has, says Hegel, 'in its corporeality

---

[1] *Phil. of Sp.*, p. 214.   [2] *Phil. of Sp.*, pp. 235–6 (W., p. 191).

its free form, in which it feels itself and makes itself felt, which, as the Soul's work of art, has human, pathognomic and physiognomic expression'. Gait, tone of voice, facial expression become at this stage as much psychic as bodily: the inertia of mere Matter is wholly overcome. Through this total domination of its body, the Soul is able to rise above its merely natural, matter-sunk being, to regard this as objective and alien to itself. 'The Soul', Hegel tells us, 'that opposes its being to itself, that has liquidated it and determined it as its own, has lost the meaning of Soul, of the immediacy of Spirit. The Actual Soul, having become accustomed to Sensation and to its concrete self-feeling, is in itself the ideality-for-self of its determinations, turned inwards in its outwardness, and become infinite relation to self. This being-for-self of the free Universality is the higher awakening of the Soul to the I—the abstract Universality in so far as it is *for* the abstract Universality—which accordingly is Thought and Subject-for-itself, and definitely the Subject of the Judgement in which the I excludes (and relates itself to) the natural totality of its determinations as an Object, a World outside of itself, so that it is immediately reflected back into itself in the same—Consciousness.'[1] By this wordy passport Hegel is able to cross the frontier from Anthropology to Phenomenology, the study of the forms of Consciousness. Consciousness of the subject-object type has been implicit in the states of Feeling hitherto studied: with the relegation of the problems of immediate bodily control to Habit, it has become explicit.

The contents of the Anthropological section just studied present no great difficulties for interpretation. They are interesting for the extremely rich fund of empirical material on which Hegel draws, and which he shows to be in harmony with his Idealism. The claims of that Idealism are for Hegel definitely strengthened by the supernormal phenomena of clairvoyance, telepathy, somnambulism, etc., which many of his interpreters would regard with contempt. To Hegel no phenomenon is contemptible that shows the might of Mind over Matter. Hegel's treatment of insanity and mental defect, as well as much detail of psychological physiology, is likewise as much empirical as philosophical: much of it reads like a slightly old-fashioned American textbook of moderately behaviouristic tendency. The defects of the section

[1] *Phil. of Sp.*, p. 252 (W., p. 195).

lie in the loose links of connection that string its headings together:
the Dialectic, in particular, is merely a pretence, artificially
imposing triadicity on material with other natural articulations.
The only logic lying behind the series of phases run through
is the need for Mind to assert its mastery over body and environment so as to come closer to seeing itself as the *raison d'être* of
both.

III PHENOMENOLOGY: THE STUDY OF CONSCIOUSNESS

From the naturalistic Anthropological treatment of Spirit,
Hegel goes on to treat it Phenomenologically and Psychologically.
The Phenomenological Section recapitulates, in brief outline, the
main course of the Dialectic in *The Phenomenology of Spirit*, and
has subdivisions devoted to Consciousness, Self-Consciousness
and Reason. The Psychological Section develops many of the
later themes of the *Phenomenology*, though it follows their pattern
less closely. We shall not devote much space to the recapitulated
Phenomenology, nor consider its divergences from the original.
Nor shall we again raise the question as to whether Hegel meant
the new treatment to supersede the old, or whether (as seems
probable) he thought that the same material which occurs at
one place in the idealized history of experience, will occur also
at another place in the systematic study of the forms of thought
and being.

The phase of subjectivity studied by Phenomenology is said
by Hegel to be that in which the 'I', as the 'absolute negativity'
or 'infinite self-relation of Spirit', has come to distinguish itself
from the natural life in which, as Soul, it was previously embedded,
and to look on the latter as an independent or external *Object*.
The 'I', in so far as it has risen to this stage, is implicitly the
identity underlying this show of opposition: it is, says Hegel,
both *one* side of the conscious relationship, and also the whole
relationship, the Light that reveals itself and other things besides.
But though the existence of other things *for* Consciousness may
be the ultimate truth about them, which we, the philosophical
commentators, understand and appraise, it is not at first manifest
to Consciousness itself, to whom the content of Nature seems to
spring from a dark source beyond itself. For Consciousness so
circumstanced, the stages of its own growing self-acquaintance

will appear as a gradual change in the Object before it: this will seem ever differently determined, though each new determination will be the shadow of a new phase in Consciousness. This development of Consciousness will reach a limit when Spirit recognizes *itself*, its own rational unfolding, in the changing show before it, when it raises its original self-assurance to truth. Consciousness is from the beginning *sure* that it grasps its object correctly, an assurance that may, however, prove ill-founded or absurd: it is only when the object is thoroughly understood, explained by categories that are the subject's own, that 'truth' (which for Hegel entails inerrancy) is attained. The above summarizes the content of §§ 413-416: it must be borne in mind that the self-recognition involved is merely the discovery in the object of that unity and universality which is, for Hegel, inseparable from the pure 'I'.

Hegel now traces the development of Consciousness through the three phases previously studied in *The Phenomenology of Spirit*. He begins again with Sense-awareness, in which the object *seems* to display an unparalleled wealth of content, but in which, in fact, nothing whatever can be said about it, except that it is something, or that it is there. Only in so far as object and thought rub together, and the former is allowed to yield many abstract offprints of itself, can this wealth of content be more than an empty claim. For the object to change in this manner is, however, for Consciousness to pass over from Sensation to Perception. Perception in its turn passes over into Understanding, when it is found impossible to *think* the object's undisciplined diversity of appearances without bringing them under principles which delimit their variations, and which so trasnform the ever-shifting surface of things into a 'tranquil kingdom of Laws'. Hegel then passes from Consciousness to Self-consciousness by a manœuvre like the one previously employed in the *Phenomenology*. In the notion of Law, he argues, we have a difference which is no difference, the same general principle, e.g. gravitation, appearing under the most widely different phenomenal guises. But a difference which is no difference then also obtains between Consciousness and its Object, since in subordinating this Object to Laws, Consciousness sees in it nothing but itself. Granted the peculiar Hegelian view of the Self there will be nothing so strange in this transition.

The phases of Self-consciousness are now traversed in a manner similar to that followed in the *Phenomenology*, though the concrete and exciting sections on Stoicism, Scepticism and the Unhappy Consciousness are left out, probably as being irrelevant to the study of *subjective* mind. The first stage distinguished is that of the Desiderative Self-consciousness. This is said to arise on account of a conflict or contradiction between Self-consciousness, on the one hand, and Consciousness, on the other, between our general sense of ownership of the world and of its consequent intelligibility, and the actual opacity and alien character of its contents, which do not lightly yield up their secrets. In the Desiderative Self-consciousness, according to Hegel, we have an Urge (*Trieb*) to overcome the conflict just mentioned, and to show up the object's nullity by straightforwardly consuming or remoulding it, so as to abrogate its pretensions to independence. In this process the object seems to submit to an alien violence, but this submission is a show: the immediate object must by its nature be liquidated, since its Individuality falls short of the Universality of its notion. The Desiderative Self-consciousness is, however, by its nature unappeasable. Having consumed or remoulded one object, it must forthwith experience the sting of the old contradiction, the stirring of its original hunger. Once more its claim to be all-in-all will have to struggle with its sense of narrow objective restrictions, and will lead to new consumptions and new remouldings. This contradiction is resolved, as in the *Phenomenology*, in the Recognitive, or Social Self-consciousness, where the object is brought into closer harmony with the Self by being made into another 'I', a second Self-consciousness. Hegel does not, of course, mean that the mind solves its inner conflicts by constructing a fantastic world of other persons. What he means is that a multitude of mutually recognizing persons is a presupposition of Self-consciousness in any, and that this ultimately is the reason *why* the plurality of persons exists.

The recognition of other persons involves, however, for Hegel an enormous contradiction, the contradiction between the essential community of those who thus recognize one another, and their mutual impenetrability and rigidly cut-off apartness.[1] For Hegel the problem concerning other minds is not how we know that

[1] *Phil. of Sp.*, p. 282.

they *are*, but how, being known to be, they can still genuinely be *other*. This contradiction leads, as in the *Phenomenology*, to the Life-and-Death Struggle between persons, to the relationship between Lord and Bondsman, and finally to the Universal Self-consciousness which is 'the affirmative knowledge of oneself in the other self, in which either has the absolute independence of free individuality'. Only in an environment of other persons, who freely acknowledge us as we acknowledge them, can we be finally freed, not merely from outside pressures, but also from the restrictions of our particular personality. It is this acknowledgment, however dim and confused, which is for Hegel the foundation of Reason, Reason being a subjectivity which is *inter*subjective and therefore objective. Quite obviously the realms of meaning, of scientific verity, of well-conceived planning and execution, are all realms which have a public as well as a private status, which are inseparable from that use of language to which Hegel is to give so important a place. Phenomenology therefore passes over into Psychology, the study of the individual functioning in a way which presupposes a *social* setting and experience.

IV PSYCHOLOGY: THE STUDY OF THEORETICAL, PRACTICAL AND FREE MIND

The Psychological section of Subjective Spirit has the three subdivisions of Theoretical Spirit, Practical Spirit and Free Spirit. In Theoretical Spirit we deal with the activities through which the seemingly strange object loses its character of the merely given and gets taken up into the rational life of the subject. It is said to differ from the Understanding of the Phenomenological section, in that Understanding thinks it is exploring something independent, whereas Reason is sure that the object will conform to itself. In Practical Spirit we study Spirit imposing its designs on objective reality: it is said to differ from the Desiderative Self-consciousness of the last section, in that Spirit is sure that the object will yield to it. Finally we come in Free Spirit to the unity of these two one-sided phases, just as, on the level of pure categories, the ideas of Cognition and Volition were blended in the Absolute Idea. It must be confessed that Hegel's Psychological section does not really build on the Phenomenological section that preceded it: it is an independent treatment which might have followed on straight from the Anthropological section. The Phenomenological section was probably put in to obtain a threefold scheme, or perhaps simply because Hegel could not bear to leave out the brilliant treatment of his youth.

Theoretical Spirit is articulated in the three phases of Direct Intuitive Acquaintance (*Anschauung*), Imaginative Reproduction (*Vorstellung*) and Pure Thinking. In the first of these we have a variety of direct, unanalysed awareness like the 'Sensation' dealt with in the Anthropological section, or the Sense-awareness discussed in the Phenomenological section. Here, however, the sensation or feeling involved is capable of containing in a nut-shell a highly intellectual content. 'All our ideas, thoughts, and concepts of external Nature, of Law, Morality and the content of Religion, develop out of our sensitive intelligence, and after they have had their complete exposition, are concentrated once more in the simple form of Sensation.'[1] This Intuitive Acquaintance is, on the one hand, the same as the Kantian *Anschauung* which reads into the data of sense-experience complicated spatial and temporal measures and relationships which they do not simply exhibit. (Hegel is careful to remark that Space and Time are not merely subjective forms imposed by *us* on the material of sense-experience: they are out there in the objects, and are imposed on them by the eternal action of 'the Idea'.) But Intuitive Acquaintance extends also to the data of the inner life: these too can be looked at and contemplated, not merely *had*. Hegel holds in fact that all mastery over the emotions, such as occurs, e.g. in art, involves an ability to look on them in a more or less detached manner. It becomes plain, as Hegel proceeds, that Intuition is inseparable from the activity of *attending*, by which he means, not merely passive, but voluntary attention. In such attending the mind voluntarily surrenders itself to some matter on hand, in order that this may appear with more clearness: without such voluntary and controlled surrender there can be no adequate apprehension of what is before us. Hegel emphasizes further that Intuitive Acquaintance involves a grasp of the *whole* character of some object or situation, not merely a puzzled groping among its details. 'Intuition', he says, 'is a consciousness filled with the certitude of reason, whose object has the character of being reasonable, not accordingly an individual torn apart into distinct

[1] *Phil. of Sp.*, p. 317.

sides, but a totality, a coherent fulness of determinations. . . . A talented historian, e.g. has the *whole* of the states and events to be depicted by him in lively intuition before him, while the man without talent in historical exposition remains stuck in details, and overlooks what is substantial.'[1] The Hegelian notion of *Anschauung* is therefore a notion belonging more to popular usage than to the analyses of philosophers, but it is not less interesting on that account.

From Intuition the Dialectic passes on to Imaginative Reproduction (*Vorstellung*): here the ownership by the thinking mind, implicit in the case of Intuition, simply becomes explicit. What is before me is now wholly mine, something I can carry about with me and can shape to suit myself, whereas in the case of Intuitions all these implications were covert. (This new ownership and mastery over my data is expressed, according to Hegel, by the auxiliary verb 'have' in such statements as 'I have seen this'.) This imaginative possession runs through the three forms of Recollection (*Erinnerung*), Imagination (*Einbildungskraft*) and Memory proper (*Gedächtniss*). In Recollection there is an intuitive picture which is the subject's possession in the sense of being cut adrift from the universal, continuous framework of Time and Space, and fixed in the mind's *private* Space and Time. It is also the subject's possession in that it lapses, after its momentary emergence, into the 'dark pit' of his unconscious, merely virtual 'being-in-self', which he carries about with him at all times (though not, Hegel insists, in the form of actual traces on nerve-fibres). In Imagination the mind's implicit mastery over its detached pictures becomes explicit. It can summon them up, can associate them as it wishes, and can also use them as signs or symbols carrying a more than merely individual meaning. Hegel is emphatic that such universal meanings are no mere by-product of mental picturing, the resultant of mutual attrition or mental chemistry. They are rather the actively ensouling forces which govern our associative transitions, and which are misrepresented in the so-called laws of association.

At this point in the treatment occurs an extremely interesting digression on Language (§ 459), in which, according to Hegel, we see the Imagination extending backwards into the field of Intuition, and overcoming the hard immediacy of sight and hearing

[1] *Phil. of Sp.*, p. 425.

by making these the vehicles of imagined contents different from themselves. In this connection Hegel prefers the *pure* sign to the sign that is pictorial or hieroglyphic, as affording a greater mental liberation. He also prefers the short-lived spirituality of the spoken, to the long-lived fixity of the written, word. A further step in mastery occurs when the word is itself 'internalized' and becomes a private image: with this we have passed from Imagination to the case of Memory Proper. (It is not clear why Hegel uses the word so eccentrically.) Here the mind can at last discourse with itself in signs that have the clear fixity and lastingness of what is outward, while they also have the ready manipulability of what is subjective and inward. Hegel holds that such subjectively manipulated words are essential to thought. 'We only then know of our thoughts, only then have actual, definite thoughts, when we give these the form of objectivity, of a distinctness from our inwardness, i.e. the form of outwardness, and indeed of such an outwardness as also bears the impress of the highest inwardness. The only inward-outward of this sort is the articulated tone, the word. To seek to think without words—as Mesmer once tried to do—seems therefore to be a piece of unreason, which drove this man, according to his own account, almost to madness.'[1] Hegel counts it a further step in intellectual mastery when the mind, having enshrined and fixed its thought in verbal signs, can repeat these signs *mechanically* without troubling itself with their sense. Having liberated itself from the bondage to concrete objects, and even from their signs and images, by employing only unspoken, private words, it now frees itself even from the bondage to these, by making their use merely outward and mechanical. The mind in a sense rises *above* words by putting itself entirely *into* words, by making them wholly adequate vehicles of its meaning, in which there is no longer any effort to say the right thing. When words are used with this intelligent automatism they no longer *have* a sense: according to Hegel, they simply *are* their sense. Since the sense, the Universal, cannot really be separate from the thing which instantiates it, Word, Sense and Thing now become for Hegel identical; we reach an extraordinary fusion between nominalism, conceptualism and realism. The activities of Intuition, Imagination and Memory therefore pass over into Thought, the most absolutely 'inward' of psychic

[1] *Phil. of Sp.*, p. 355.

states which is also, on the above showing, the most wholly 'outward'.

Since the transitions just traversed are among the most astounding in Hegel, a few quotations may be added. Hegel says: 'Just as the true Thought is the Thing, so also is the Word when it is employed by the true Thought. Inasmuch, therefore, as the intelligence fills itself with the Word, it takes up the nature of the Thing into itself.'[1] 'The existent as Name needs something else, the meaning of the representing intelligence, in order to be the Thing, the true objectivity. The intelligence as mechanical memory is this external objectivity and the meaning in one. . . . Memory is in this manner the transition to the activity of Thinking, an activity that ceases to *have* meaning, i.e. the subjective element in it is no longer distinct from its objectivity, just as this inwardness is now in itself existent.'[2] 'The intelligence is recognitive: it knows an intuition in so far as this latter is already its own, and in the Name it recognizes the Thing. But now its universal element is there *for* the intelligence in the double meaning of the universal as such, and of the same as immediate or existent. It is, in short, the true universal, which is the over-reaching unity of itself and of its other, being.'[3]

Theoretical Spirit therefore starts by being something private and personal to which the real world stands opposed: its strategy is to transform that private personal life into an impersonal system of symbols in which the essence of the world will be fully captured and perspicuous. This capture is complete when our Thought takes the form of using precisely the right words to express the real facts, without any 'thinking' in the sense of fumbling about for the right expression. The pregnant phrase, that sums up the situation effortlessly, represents the fusion of Word, Thing and Notion that we have now reached. Hegel next goes on to consider the distinctions of Concept, Judgement and Syllogism, which have been expounded in the Logic, but which are now reconsidered from a psychological point of view. We need not cover this territory anew. Theoretical Intelligence, however, must move on unhaltingly towards that complete ownership of its contents in which they will no longer present it with a problem, but will be fully and freely determined by the Intelligence itself.

---

[1] *Phil. of Sp.*, p. 355.   [2] *Phil. of Sp.*, pp. 357–8 (W., p. 228).
[3] *Phil. of Sp.*, p. 359 (W., p. 229).

But this, the ideal and goal of Theory, is something that can be actually achieved only by the Practical Intelligence, the Intelligence that *makes* things to fit the subject's requirements. To this Practical Intelligence the Dialectic accordingly turns.

In the study of Practical Spirit which follows we move among some of the familiar concepts of Butler's *Sermons*, obscured by Hegel's haste and by the exigencies of dialectical exposition. Practical Spirit, seeking to subdue the world to itself, must make various demands on that world, each of which will express itself in an Ought (a *Sollen*), a requirement that what exists should fulfil certain conditions. The demands of Practical Spirit are first experienced in the form of Practical *Feelings*, from which they afterwards pass over into action. These Practical Feelings are of varying type: the most elementary are those of simple Agreeableness and Disagreeableness, more complex are the affections of Joy, Sorrow, Hope, Fear, Anxiety, Contentment and Gaiety, yet more complex are the various moral and religious Feelings, of which Hegel gives Remorse and Shame as examples. The Practical Feelings, confronted with a world that fails to agree with them necessarily pass over into Impulses (*Triebe*). Hegel seems to regard his Practical Feelings as the *springs* of action: he does not realize the Butlerian point that they must themselves depend on prior impulses, and cannot be the source of the latter. The Impulses or *Triebe* are said to differ from the Desires of the Phenomenological Section in that they are to some extent rationalized: despite their unsuitable name, they represent long-term, co-ordinated policies of action rather than unco-ordinated, short-term urges. But though rationalized, they retain the contingency due to their source in a particular subject, a contingency which Hegel thinks cannot and should not be eliminated. The Rational Will would be an empty and formal thing could it not adopt into itself the concrete impulses of invididuals, living in them as its *Interests* and Passions, without which Hegel rightly thinks that nothing worth while can be accomplished.

The complementary side of Practical Spirit lies, however, in the Universality of Reason, which must of necessity practise reflection, be reflected-into-self, and distinguish itself from particular Interests and Passions. This universal element is manifest *subjectively* in the form of *Willkühr* or Free Choice, an orientation indifferent to the particularity of Feeling and

Impulse, that can as readily 'side' with one of them, make this its own, as with another. It is also manifest *objectively* in the notion of Happiness or Self-interest, the notion of what will satisfy any and all of our Interests and Passions, rather than some special one among them. From the notion of Happiness Hegel passes on to the notion of the Really Free Will by the following remarkable transition: 'Happiness is the merely imagined abstract universality of content which merely should be. The truth, however, of the *Specific* determination (of Impulse), which is as much real as it is also abolished, and of the abstract Individuality of Choice, which as much gives itself, as it does not give itself, an end in Happiness, is the *Universal* determination of the Will-in-itself, i.e. its very self-determination or Freedom. Choice is in this way Will as the pure subjectivity which is at once both pure and concrete, inasmuch as it only has that infinite determination, Freedom itself, as its content and end. In the truth of its self-determination, in which action and object are identical, the Will is the Really Free Will.'[1] The notion that lives enswathed in these verbal casings is one that has met us repeatedly in the Dialectic: it is that of the contingent and arbitrary which is, in a sense, divested of arbitrariness and contingency by being shown to be a necessary condition of what is universal and rational. The rational, universal Will *requires* a body of contingent material purposes which it can organize and unify, and without which it simply could not be rational at all. These contingent purposes are, by this necessity (and without loss of their contingency) taken up, or done away with, in the overriding rationality of which they furnish the presupposition. The ultimate reason *why* we have Passions and Interests is that we may have something to control and harmonize: in realizing this, the last wildness and wilfulness of passion sinks subdued. The supreme cunning of Reason consists, therefore, in making it seem that we have unreasonable passions, though these are merely the condition of reasonableness, and are, in the Really Free Will, made to seem and feel so.

Hegel now leaves the field of Subjective Spirit, the study of Mind detaching itself from Nature and building up its own rich cogitative and practical life. His treatment has often been brilliant and suggestive, but it has also been incoherent and hasty.

[1] *Phil. of Sp.*, pp. 378-9 (W., p. 237).

He now passes on to the study of Objective Spirit, i.e. Spirit externalizing itself in an ordered world of institutions, usages and prescriptions. The transition consists simply in restressing the intersubjective, social origins of rationality which were brought out at the end of the Phenomenological Section, but which have temporarily been forgotten. The rational freedom which shows itself in ordering an individual's impulses, and in recognizing it to be their function to be so ordered, remains imperfect and formal: it can be concrete and real only in a world of rational agents, among whom Freedom will take the form of an ordering Necessity which compels each to acknowledge the claims of all. There may be such a thing as a rational Robinson Crusoe, but he can be so only because his life in society has made him look on himself and his passing interests from the outside. Self-interest, on this view, has its roots in the respect for others. We pass, accordingly, from Hegel's Psychology to his treatment of Morals, Politics and History.

CHAPTER ELEVEN

THE PHILOSOPHY OF OBJECTIVE SPIRIT
(*Hegel's Theory of Law, Morals, the State and History*)

I FORMAL RIGHT: THE PHILOSOPHICAL BASES OF LAW

In the present chapter we shall deal with Hegel's doctrine of 'Objective Spirit', the complete world of ethical institutions and laws in which Spirit 'utters' itself, and in which the necessary connections among persons are held to reflect their fundamental spiritual freedom. This doctrine is triadically articulated into a section on Abstract or Formal Right, a section on Subjective Morality, and a third last section on Social Ethics (*Sittlichkeit*), which includes Hegel's doctrine of the State and History. These topics are briefly treated in the *Encyclopaedia*, and with much greater fulness in the *Philosophy of Right*, Hegel's last published work. We ourselves shall adhere to the later treatment.

By 'Law' or 'Right'—both unsatisfactory translations of the German word *Recht*—Hegel means an intersubjective order which is the necessary expansion of the Free, the Reasonable Will, the Will which uses the contingencies of impulse as the material for its own organizing activities, and which must, by virtue of its detached and universal character, be as respectful of the organizing activities of others as it is of its own. 'The absolute urge of the free Spirit, that its own Freedom should be its Object —objective both in the sense that it is its own self rationally systematized, and in the sense of being an immediate actuality— in order to be *for* itself as Idea, what the Will is *in* itself—the abstract conception of the Idea of the Will is, in general terms, *the Free Will* that wills the Free Will. . . . This, that there should be an existence which is the existence of the Free Will, is Right (or Law).'[1] Hegel's starting-point in this part of his system is obviously Kantian: some of the details which follow are also reminiscent of Kant's treatment of Law and the State. Hegel's deep immersion in the concrete actuality of social arrangements, and his repudiation of a subjective, abstract morality, represent, however, his own emphasis.

[1] *Phil. of Rt.*, §§ 27, 29, pp. 78–9.

In the section on Formal Right Hegel deals with those fundamental legal relations between persons which were studied in the
classical jurisprudence, and which formed the great contribution
to human thought and life of the decaying 'atomistic' Roman
imperial world. Though these rules are backed by the authority
of the State, Hegel suggests that, apart from this, they have a
foundation in the 'absolute negativity' or free universality of
Spirit. (In a sense, therefore, Hegel believes in 'natural rights',
but since the State, too, is for him a necessary outgrowth of
Reason, this acceptance is somewhat unimportant.) Free, self-
determining Spirit must appear, in the first instance, in an
'immediate' form, and this it does in the Will of an individual
person, a Will affected by a large number of personal interests
and passions, and blankly exclusive of the Wills and interests
of other persons, as also of the common, neutral world in which
they all *find* themselves. At this level, Hegel tells us, the injunction
of Abstract Right is simply to be a Person, and to respect others
as Persons. The precise content of the personal Will is from this
point of view indifferent, and the Rule of Right insists merely
that individuals should be *allowed* to do what they choose to
(within certain limits) and that others should be forbidden to
interfere with this formal exercise of their freedom.[1]

Hegel now studies the development of Formal Right through
the three stages of the Ownership of Property, the Making of
Contracts, and the commission of Torts and Crimes. He bases
the right of Ownership, not on the need of a person to use outer
objects to satisfy his desires, but on the sheer fitness that the
Free Person should have infinite dominion over the unfree,
impersonal Thing. The Free Person should be permitted to
'put his Will' into any and every external object, and to make it
his own. In so doing, he merely acts as an 'Idealist' (in the Hegelian sense), effectively doing away with the seeming independence
and self-sufficiency of the thing. Even animals (Hegel recurs
to this point) are 'Idealists' in this sense: they show their contempt
for the claim to reality of external objects by incontinently devouring them. Possession in this sense can, however, be exercised
only on rightless, natural objects. It cannot be exercised on
Persons, whether infant or adult, and pre-Christian legal systems,
Hegel insists, deviated from Abstract Right in permitting such

[1] *Phil. of Rt.*, §§ 34–38.

things as Slavery or an unlimited *patria potestas*. (These unequi-vocal statements should be remembered when Hegel is accused of being an instigator of the National Socialist Slave-State.) Property does, however, extend to our organic bodies, since it is open to us to use them or not to use them, and a person can also freely destroy his body, as a beast cannot. Being what it is, Property must be acquired by an Act of Seizure (*Besitzergreifung*), of which use is merely the expression. It is not because someone uses an object that it is his own, nor does it cease to be his merely because he refrains from using it. To use and train one's body must be recognized as an Act of Seizure, one so sacred that offences against the body count as offences against the Person. But the Act of Seizure which makes an object a man's own must occur in a *public* setting. The object seized must previously have been masterless, and the Act of Seizure must be duly *recognized* by others. (Hegel does not discuss the rights of cases where such recognition is not general: presumably these are deviations from the ideal 'truth' of Property.) Being due to the free putting of a man's Will into an Object, Possession can only be liquidated by an equally free act of Alienation. (Lack of use, therefore, only liquidates possession because it is presumed that a man is no longer putting his Will in an object.) Such alienation can, how-ever, only be exercised on things genuinely separable from my personal existence, though I can within limits alienate the *use* of my spiritual capacities. Life itself is inalienable, since the Person cannot dispose of what is essential for its existence as a Person, can have no right over itself. Only a higher realization of Reason than the finite Person can rightfully demand the sacrifice of life: this higher realization is the State. Hegel holds, further, that Property is by its nature personal and individual; communism of Property represents a deviation from its rational Idea. The State may, however, make exceptions to this principle, but only *it* may do so, and that sparingly. In general, it may be held that Hegel sufficiently recognizes 'basic' individual rights, and nothing he says in later parts of his work must be allowed to obscure this fact.

From Property Hegel passes on to Contract, a possibility necessarily rooted in the possession of Property. It lies in the sovereign disposal of the Free Person to take his will out of the property into which he has put it, and it lies likewise in the disposal of another Person to put his Will into the property thus alienated. It is also possible for one Person to come to his decision just in so far as, and because, another comes to his. The agreement of Wills that thus arises is an arbitrary agreement concerning a single external object. Though it may give rise to rights and duties, based on the general command to respect other Persons, it is not of itself a matter of obligation. Hegel then gives a classification of possible contracts mainly borrowed from Kant's *Metaphysical Foundations of Law*. We have Contracts of Gift, in which one party dispenses Property and another party takes it up, Contracts of Exchange in which both parties dispense and receive Property, and finally Contracts completed by the giving of Securities or Guarantees (*Verpfändung*). (These last are probably introduced for dialectical reasons.) Obviously, however, since Contract depends on a contingent agreement of Wills, it is by its nature capable of a breach. The respect for Persons which alone could maintain it may be overcome by diverging personal interests. We pass therefore to Wrongs and their Correction.

In his treatment of Wrongs, Hegel first deals with Civil Wrongs, which involve no questioning of the general injunction to respect Persons, but merely dispute what this Rule of Right entails in a particular case, and adduce *grounds*, based on different facts of Property or Contract, to sustain one interpretation rather than another. From Civil Wrongs he passes on to Fraud, where there is a pretended respect for Persons, and for their rights of Property or Contract, but in which this pretence corresponds to no reality. Finally he passes on to Violence and Crime, where we have neither the reality nor the pretence of a respect for Persons or for their contractual or property-rights. Such Crime Hegel compares to the Infinite Judgement (S is non-P) in that it not merely removes itself from a particular category of person-respecting conduct (as in the case of Civil Wrongs) but from all person-respecting conduct whatsoever.

The treatment of Wrong-doing leads on to the complementary topic of Desert or Requital. Since Civil Wrongs are merely would-be right actions done under a mistaken or specious label, they are liquidated by a mere restitution or compensation. Fraud and Crime, however, demand Punishment. Hegel then puts forward his celebrated account of Punishment as the mere cancelling out of a wrong act or the demonstration of its nullity.

This view he admits to be hard for the Understanding to grasp, since it can make no sense of merely adding the evil of present pain to the evil of past wrong-doing, and must introduce all sorts of *raisonnements* concerning deterrence or moral reform. On Hegel's view, a criminal, like another rational being, necessarily wills his own freedom and everyone else's, and is accordingly concerned to cancel out his own act of disregard for the freedom and rights of Persons. He demands this annulment as a right, and does not merely submit to it at the hands of alien authorities. 'The injury that is meted out to the criminal is not merely right in itself', Hegel tells us, 'as right it is at once his implicit Will, a creature of his freedom, *his* right: but it is also a right in the criminal himself, i.e. posited in his *existing* Will and in his act. For it lies in his action, as being that of a reasonable being, that it is something universal, that through it a law is set up, that he himself acknowledged it in the act, under which he also may be subsumèd, as under *his* right.'[1] Despite much eloquence Hegel does not explain how a pain or personal evil suffered now, manages to blot out an irrational act done in the past. He does not, e.g., suggest that Punishment is some sort of natural symbolism through which the demands of Reason are given a penetrating and reforming hold on the merely finite and personal Will, unreason being pregnantly symbolized and brought home by unease. As it stands, the theory is an impressive arch from which the keystone is missing.

Punishment, however, cannot adequately annul Wrong as long as the punishing authority remains external to the person punished: as so external, Punishment remains tainted with revenge, and with the Bad Infinity of retaliation to which revenge must lead. To avoid this, the punishing authority must pass inward into the man's own self-consciousness. It must be the man himself who lays down the Law of Right, and who also liquidates his own transgression of it. This internalization of the Law is really the reference of it to its true source and locus, but to the wrong-doer it represents an advance. We learn our morality by being painfully forced by others to respect *their* rights, but morality is truly learnt only when the rights and the force have alike become our own. With this, according to Hegel, the Will ceases to be the Free Will merely *in itself*, one that stands opposed to a

[1] *Phil. of Rt.*, § 100, p. 155.

seemingly immediate outer Rule of Right, and becomes the Free Will *for itself*. 'Its personality, which is all that the Will is in Abstract Right, has now become the Will's object, and the infinite subjectivity of Freedom which is for self therefore constitutes the principle of the Moral Standpoint.'[1]

II   PERSONAL MORALITY AND ITS PERPLEXITIES

The Moral Standpoint, to which Hegel next passes, is said to be that of a Will which is not merely infinite, i.e. unrestrictedly universal, *in itself*, but also *for itself*. The principle of Formal Right, which represented this boundless self-reference implicitly, under the form of respecting *other* persons and their interests, is now explicitly posited as self-referring. It is I, the subject, who must prescribe this general principle, and it is I also who must decide how it shall be applied. No principle can in fact have relevance to my conduct but such as I myself acknowledge and approve. In the standpoint of Formal Right, Hegel suggests, it was important that persons and their Wills should be respected, but we were not concerned with the content, and in particular not with the remoter principles and motives of those Wills. In the Moral Standpoint, the Morality of the Will itself concerns us: it is for their disinterested person-respectingness that persons themselves deserve respect. The agreement of Wills at the Moral level must therefore be a necessary agreement: it is not like the contingent coincidence underlying a contractual relation. Hegel also stresses that, while the attitude to the interests of others is, at the level of Formal Right, merely permissive and negative— each being allowed to do as he likes as long as he remains in his 'sphere of freedom'—at the Moral level it is both positive and obliging. Morality is concerned with the 'Good' and with the Welfare of other persons. The Moral Standpoint involves further a division in the Will of the Moral person: what he wills as a universal, person-respecting being may not agree with what he wills as a particular finite person, and will appear, therefore, in the form of a Requirement (*Forderung*), or of an Obligation (*Sollen*). Lastly, Hegel points out that the infinite, self-determining character of Morality is as such void of content: it is, he says, 'the pure restlessness and activity that cannot as yet come down

[1] *Phil. of Rt.*, § 104, p. 162.

to anything that is'.[1] The whole of Hegel's criticism of pure Morality is that it remains empty and abstract, open to a filling that is merely capricious or even evil, until it finds its completion in the customary ethics of an established social system.

The above summarizes the somewhat wordy treatment of §§ 105–113. Hegel then divides his subject-matter triadically. His first section, entitled 'Design and Blame' (Der Vorsatz und die Schuld), will deal with the formal, subjective conditions of morally relevant Willing, the next, entitled 'Intention and Welfare' (Die Absicht und das Wohl), will deal with the necessary content of such Willing, and the last, 'The Good and Conscience' (Das Gute und das Gewissen), will attempt to integrate the two former, but is in fact unable to do more than frame an ideal for which organized social ethics must provide the concrete fulfilment.

In 'Design and Blame' Hegel runs through some of the features definitory of morally relevant actions or decisions, of actions for which I can be held morally accountable. Plainly I can be brought to book only for what I specifically intended, or for acting in circumstances to the extent that I knew of them, or for bringing about consequences to the extent that I foresaw them, or had grounds for thinking them likely. These conditions obviously enter into the form of those actions which can be legitimate objects of moral concern. Hegel doubtless assumes, without specifically mentioning it, that the Rule of Right, the general principle of respect for persons, must be obscurely recognized in the background of my actions, whether I choose to flout it or fulfil it: without some such background my action would plainly not qualify as an object of moral concern. But the fact that he says nothing on this point makes his treatment somewhat confusing.

In the section on 'Intention and Welfare' Hegel stresses that the Willing relevant to Morality must have a content as well as a form: it must be directed to ends which afford satisfaction to the needs, desires, passions, etc., of the agent, and which provide him with reasons for his Willing. All such ends can be ranged under the general heading of Welfare (das Wohl), and Hegel rightly holds that the issues which affect Morality are all issues where Welfare is in question. To recognize this is merely to recur to the notion of 'interest', which was part of the concept of Formal Right. The subject with its 'absolute negativity' and its tendency

[1] Phil. of Rt., § 108; Zus., p. 167.

to infinity must now necessarily extend the pursuit of such Welfare to others as well as himself, and to all such others. Its utilitarianism must necessarily take on a universalistic flavour, even if this quarrels with another merely egoistic direction. Hegel emphasizes further that, for an Act of Will to be morally satisfactory, it must not merely regard the Welfare it pursues as a means to its own morality. Like Scheler in his treatment of Pharisaism, Hegel recognizes the pursuit of Morality for Morality's sake as a dangerous moral temptation.[1] It is, further, not morally sufficient that great results should have been intended, but also that they should have been achieved. 'The laurels of Mere Willing', Hegel remarks, 'are dry leaves that have never been green.'[2] The necessity of bringing Welfare into our notion of Morality is shown further by the facts of the *Notrecht*, the suspension of the canons of Abstract Right in cases where personal survival is at stake. (On the other hand, it is *only* in such cases that these canons may be dispensed with: one many not, like St. Crispin, steal leather to make the poor shoes.) Obviously, Hegel sensibly concludes, some sort of compromise between Formal Right and the pursuit of Welfare is essential to Morality.

This compromise Hegel seeks to provide in his third section, entitled 'The Good and Conscience'. The Good is the somewhat vague concept of a 'unity between the notion of the Will and the particular Will—in which the Abstract Right, like Welfare and the subjectivity of knowledge, and the contingency of external existence, are alike set aside as self-sufficient in themselves, but are none the less contained and preserved in it—Freedom Realized, the Absolute Purpose of the World. . . . It is not something Abstractly Right, but possessed of content, which content constitutes the Right as much as the Good.'[3] In this Good there is said to be no Welfare apart from the Rule of Right, and this Right is not the Good in abstraction from Welfare. (*Fiat justitia* may not therefore have *pereat mundus* as a consequence.) The notion thus arrived at by Hegel is, however, merely abstract or formal: if we ask *what* it prescribes, we can get no answer but 'Do what is right and consider your own welfare and the general welfare', or the equally vague scriptural command to love God supremely and our neighbour as ourselves. The only way to

---

[1] *Phil. of Rt.*, § 124.   [2] *Phil. of Rt.*, § 124, p. 184.
[3] *Phil. of Rt.*, § 129, pp. 187–8.

provide content for the Moral Good is to drag in Conscience, the faculty of particular moral decisions, a move previously explored in the *Phenomenology*. This Conscience 'expresses the absolute justification of the subjective self-consciousness, to know in itself and from itself what is Right and Duty, and to acknowledge nothing except what it thus knows as the Good, together with the assertion that what it thus knows and wills is in reality Right and Duty.'[1]

This particular move does not, however, free us from our predicament. A faculty of moral decisions may solve moral problems, but it does so only by cutting through them. It does not live up to its claim to be rational, since it applies no regular, intrinsically valid procedure (*die Regel einer vernünftigen, an und für sich gültigen allgemeinen Handlungsweise*). Such a Conscience, Hegel insists, is as likely to deliver itself in a perverse as a sublime and noble manner: it is, in fact, a product of moral and social decay, as may be seen in the case of the age which produced Socrates or the Stoic sages. Hegel goes further, and holds there to be an intrinsic connection between Abstract Conscientiousness and Wickedness: both rest on the unbounded, capricious self-assurance of personal judgement. 'Self-consciousness in the vanity of all otherwise valid determinations, and in the pure inwardness of the Will, has just as much the possibility to take what is in and for itself Universal for its principle, as the choice to elevate its own Particularity above the Universal, and to realize this through its acts—i.e. to be wicked. Conscience as formal subjectivity is just this, to be on the very point of turning over into what is wicked.'[2] Such Wickedness can hypocritically hide behind a semblance of Morality, and find plausible grounds for its decisions. The probabilistic techniques of the Jesuits are for Hegel a typical instrument of moral evasion, but they are also an ill to which pure Moralism naturally leads. The true giving of content to Morality cannot occur at the level of conscientious inwardness: it demands, says Hegel, a surrender to *Sittlichkeit*, the concrete ways of a well-organized society. Oddly enough, Hegel compares the moral despair which leads conscientious persons to take refuge in *Sittlichkeit*, with the despair which leads Protestants to become converts to Rome. In the latter case people are prepared to accept unthinking subordination to

---

[1] *Phil. of Rt.*, § 137, pp. 196–7.   [2] *Phil. of Rt.*, § 139, p. 200.

authority rather than endure any longer the disease of inner emptiness and negativity. Hegel suggests that a recurrence to *Sittlichkeit* is a more rational act than this, but he does not make plain *why* it should be reasonable to seek the filling for one's ideals in the customs of a society rather than in the prescriptions of an historic Church.

The whole section on Morality we have been examining is one of the least satisfactory in Hegel. The writing shows signs of haste, as if Hegel were profoundly sick of conscientious 'inwardness', and of the subversive work that it can do. The transition from Conscientiousness to Wickedness is quite scandalous, since the problem of Conscience is surely one of *applying* the Rule of Right, or of giving *content* to the vague notion of Welfare, whereas the principle of Wickedness is that of rejecting these notions root and branch. Hegel would have done better to make his Wickedness the colossal Wickedness of the Nazis, whose principles certainly represent a *sort* of Morality, a systematic inversion of the Rule of Right as interpreted by all Western European Culture. These would have provided him with a better instance of perverters of Morality than the poor Jesuits whom he cites. But how the emptiness of mere Conscientiousness and the Rule of Right can be cured by appealing to largely unreflective moral and political arrangements, rather than to the collective conscience of all deeply reflective, mutually responsive persons— which would have corresponded so much better with the notion of Spirit—Hegel does not explain.

III   CUSTOMARY MORALITY: THE FAMILY
AND CIVIL SOCIETY

From Conscientious Morality we accordingly pass to Customary Morality (*Sittlichkeit*), the Morality of the 'Concrete Ethical Substance' of which individuals are said to be the Accidents. This Ethical Substance, like the Substance of Spinoza, posits various fundamental differences in itself, and these Hegel identifies with its Laws and Institutions; these enjoy a subsistence raised high above the subjective beliefs and preferences of its individual members. The Ethical Substance is manifest in the universal, customary modes of behaviour of its members; it is their 'second nature' superimposed on their original, merely natural Will, and is 'the pervasive Soul, meaning and actuality of their being'. Hegel insists that the rules of this Ethical Substance are not alien to the individual subject, but are felt to belong to his essence, are incorporated into his 'self-feeling'. The individual believes and trusts in the ethical system to which he belongs, and rises through it to 'substantial freedom'. In performing the duties it enjoins, he is freed from dependence on the urges of nature, from oppressive reflections on what is obligatory or permissible, and from the unbounded subjectivity which cannot come down to what is existent and determinate.[1] Though the individual's life in the Ethical Substance is, in the main, unconscious— Hegel here again quotes Antigone's statement that no one knows whence the eternal laws are—yet the Ethical Substance *has* a self-consciousness, and can be made an object of knowledge: it can come to realize its own absolute might and authority, much more firmly founded than anything in nature. Hegel does not say in whom or where this self-consciousness of the Ethical Substance comes to fruition: presumably it is in members of the 'thinking estate', in philosophers like himself. And lest anyone should identify the Ethical Substance with what is cosmopolitan, Hegel assures us that it is the actual Spirit of a Family and a Nation. The development of this Substance is now to be studied in the three phases of the Family, Civil Society and the State.

The above summarizes the content of §§ 142–157 of the *Philosophy of Right*. It will be observed that Hegel has moved far from the position of the *Phenomenology*. There he discussed the same Ethical Substance, but he discussed it *before* he dealt with Legal Right, and long before he dealt with Conscientious Morality. And there the dialectical breakdown of Conscientious Morality did not lead back to customary *Sittlichkeit*, but on to the emancipating experiences of Religion and Philosophy. In the *Phenomenology* the custom-sunk ethical life was something immediately harmonious, with the remote, childlike beauty of the ancient city-state, but it was also something essentially self-eliminating, which must lead to a more reflective, critical mode of adjusting human interests. Here, in the *Philosophy of Right*, Hegel shows himself to be literally a reactionary. His dialectic, contrary to its principles, simply harks back to the immediacy in which it had its origin. That Hegel could have come to write as he does, certainly

[1] *Phil. of Rt.*, § 149, p. 230.

points to a deep loss of integrity both in his character and his thinking.

The study of the Family which succeeds is more elaborate, but less charming, than that of the *Phenomenology*. This Family has 'as the immediate substantiality of the Spirit, its self-sensitive unity, Love as its determination, so that its prevailing mood is to have the self-consciousness of one's individuality in this unity as what is essential in and for self, so as not to be in it as a person on one's own account, but as a member.'[1] With this ultra-substantial view of Family Life, it is not remarkable that Hegel should hold that husband and wife are not merely one flesh, but one person, and that he should prefer marriages to be arranged by parents rather than based on individual inclination. It is also not remarkable that he believes that children should be disciplined and not reasoned with, since their elders represent for them the 'universal and essential'. A toleration of divorce, with a proviso that it should be made extremely difficult, is the only liberal note in the whole treatment.

When the Family Substance yields to the might of death, its members become independent legal persons. We pass from the unitary and substantial Family, to the atomistic Need-State or State of the Understanding, in which universal self-seeking begets a system of intricate interdependence, and a profound interweaving and interlocking of the welfare and rights of all. Hegel sees a deep confirmation of his own philosophy in the economic principles of Adam Smith and Ricardo, which connect the selfish pursuit of individual good with the realization of the collective good of all. It is better, in fact, that Reason should work underground in this manner than that it should carry out its designs in the light of day. A planned economy (such as Hegel thinks Plato intended) could do no better, since Particular and Universal only exist through each other, and automatically 'swing over' into one another. An apparent economic anarchy has therefore its part to play in Hegel's organic society, and the freedom which he denies to conscientious persons must be allowed to unprincipled money-makers.

Civil Society, the atomistic Need-State, is sketched in the three divisions of the System of Wants, the Administration of Justice, and Police and Corporation. In the System of Wants Hegel shows

[1] *Phil. of Rt.*, § 158, p. 237.

how the rise above animality leads to an indefinite multiplication and refinement of needs, of which he fundamentally approves, though he speaks scornfully of the progress towards infinity involved in the English pursuit of 'comfort'.[1] The multiplication of needs leads naturally to an extensive Division of Labour, and ultimately to the formation of fixed Social Classes or Estates (*Stände*). Of these Hegel distinguishes three: the Substantial, rooted in the soil and embracing agricultural labour and the landed aristocracy, the Acquisitive, embracing manual and factory labour, and all who live by trade, and the Universal Estate, the salaried bureaucracy who pursue the business of society. Each of these Classes has its own peculiar code of 'righteousness' and its peculiar Class-honour: it is, in fact, in connection with such stations and their duties that Morality has its richest development. A young man may find it repugnant to be tied down to a particular Social Class, but as he grows in maturity he will see that a class-less private individual necessarily lacks genuine universality, that a man only can be *something*, or achieve 'substantiality', by associating himself with a Class and its interests.

The distribution of Property essential to Civil Society must be protected and precisely determined by legal processes: Hegel therefore turns to study the Administration of Justice. His treatment is in no way remarkable, apart from its unequivocal stress on the equality of persons before the law. A human being must be treated as such whether he be Jew, Catholic, Protestant, German, Italian, etc., and this principle, says Hegel, is of *infinite* importance. He also stresses the need of a conscious, codified law, as opposed to one that relies on custom and judicial precedent. English practice in this respect he thinks deplorable. Hegel further demands that legal proceedings should be public, and that judgements should be intelligible to the laity, both as regard the facts, and the application of the law to those facts.

The Police (Public Authorities) and Corporations (Trade Guilds) now make a somewhat comic entrance on the dialectical stage, as the detailed administrators of law and order, and of their application to the contingent individual case. Hegel is sufficiently remote from the Police-State to lament the tendency of these public authorities to pedantic or inquisitorial interference, though he also says that we cannot draw an exact line as to where they

[1] *Phil. of Rt.*, § 191; *Zus.*, p. 273.

should or should not interfere. The extension of governmental care to the poor, as practised in England, is held to be destructive of shame and honour. Hegel holds, further, that the Corporations and Guilds peculiar to the Acquisitive Class serve a valuable purpose in giving a public aspect to individual life, which the irresponsible, uninstructed individual cannot, without damage to society, find in affairs of state. Such Corporations, with their strong guild-honour, he thinks second only to the Family in importance as the bases of State-life.

IV THEORY OF THE STATE AND STATES

The dialectic substructure of the State has now been laid: Hegel defines the latter as 'the actuality of the Ethical Idea—the Ethical Spirit, as the Substantial Will, revealed, lucid to itself, which thinks and knows itself, and which carries out what it knows in so far as it knows it. In Custom it has its immediate existence, as it has its mediate existence in the self-consciousness of the individual, his knowledge and his activity. The latter, through his sentiment, has his substantial freedom in it, as his essence, end, and the product of his activity. . . . The State, as the actuality of the substantial Will, which it has in the particular self-consciousness raised to its universality, is that which is rational in and for itself. This substantial unity is the absolute, unmoved End-in-itself, in which Freedom comes to its highest right, just as the final End has the highest right over the individuals, whose supreme duty it is to be members of the State.'[1] The State so described is of course the Idea of the State: actual States may conform to it very inadequately. But they will still have vestiges of its essence in them, just as malformed, diseased and criminal men retain vestiges of humanity.

The totalitarian suggestions of the above account must not be given undue weight. Hegel insists that the Modern State, as opposed to Asiatic despotisms, and the undeveloped States of antiquity, must allow 'freedom to its particularity', and must consider the well-being of individuals, and protect their private rights. The State cannot achieve its universal status without the understanding co-operation of groups and individuals, whose subjectivity and 'inwardness' must be allowed to develop in the

[1] *Phil. of Rt.*, §§ 257–8, pp. 328–9.

fullest and most lively manner. There must be no legal barriers between Social Classes, nor restrictions which limit individuals in their choice of occupation. Religion, in particular, which represents in the 'form of totality' what the State represents in 'mutual outsideness', must enjoy the widest range of freedom, except where it interferes fanatically in the detail of state-management. Even religions which oppose the State in certain directions, e.g. Quakers, Anabaptists, must be tolerated in a strong and secure State. Hegel strongly recommends that complete political rights should be accorded to Jews. It must constantly be kept in mind that the Hegelian State reposes on the respect for persons which is the basis of Abstract Right, and that, whatever may be added to this principle, it at least never overthrows it. Hegel proposes to study the State under the three headings of Internal State Right, External State Right and Universal History.

Hegel holds that the traditional divisions of States into monarchies, aristocracies and democracies is inapplicable to the 'developed Modern State', where there is necessarily a Monarch, a plurality of government functionaries and a large number of legislators. Only in undeveloped States does the State-power reside in a unique individual or set of individuals, concerning whom we may well ask whether they (or it) are one, or a few, or many. In the undeveloped State such a question is important since it is possible for the ruling individual (or group or mass) to act without laws, and without a definite constitution, whereas the developed State, being a 'hieroglyph of Reason', necessarily involves both. In the developed State the whole State may be said to be in a sense self-conscious and personal, and it operates as a single Person whether through its Monarch, its ministries and bureaucracy, or its legislative assembly. Presumably the State operates in this manner when the citizens are patriotic and loyal, and do whatever they do *for* the State. Hegel certainly does not believe in any mystical, supra-individual State-Person, however much some of his unguarded language might lead one to think so. It is, in fact, because the State is not as such a Person among Persons, that Hegel thinks it fit that it should operate, at least in the last instance of decision, through a genuine Person among Persons, i.e. an individual Monarch.

Hegel's belief in constitutional monarchy is perhaps the central doctrine in his political theory. The immanent development of philosophical science, Hegel tells us, 'has this peculiarity, that one and the same notion, here that of the Will, which at the beginning (since it is the beginning) is abstract, preserves itself, and condenses its determinations purely through itself, and in this way achieves a concrete content. So it is the basic feature of the abstract personality which is at first present in immediate Right, which has developed itself through varied forms of subjectivity, and which is here, in absolute Right, in the State, in the complete concrete objectivity of the Will, the Personality of the State, its certainty of itself—that ultimate thing, which cancels all specifications in its simple self, interrupts the weighing of grounds and counter-grounds, among which there is always a vacillation from side to side, finishes them off with an "I will", and initiates all action and actuality. Personality and subjectivity can further, as infinitely self-related, only have absolute truth, and have their nearest immediate truth, as a Person, a subject that is for self, and what is thus for itself must be absolutely *one*. The Personality of the State is only actual as a Person, the Monarch.'[1] Any attempt to substitute for this actual Monarch a moral Person such as a republican assembly, is declared by Hegel to mark an undeveloped political State, in which Personality is merely an abstract moment. It is likewise impossible to substitute the People in general for the Monarch, since the People without its Monarch, and his dependent organization, is merely a formless mass, and cannot exercise any state-functions.

The functions of the Monarch in the State is simply *to take the last decisions*. Even in undeveloped States, the need for a Monarch is shown in times of stress, and where there is no Monarch to make last decisions, recourse is had to such deciding factors as oracles, omens, etc. The monarchical majesty resides, further, in the complete *groundlessness* of these last decisions: when all counsel and countercounsel has been offered, the last move is the simple *fiat* of personal decision. The same monarchical majesty resides in the fact that *who* shall be Monarch is decided groundlessly by nature, and not by a process of choice. A hereditary monarchy is the only one that can be raised high above factions, and that can give real unity to the Estates. Hegel in fact compares the transition from abstract State Personality to the naturally born Monarch to the speculative transition from the Idea to

[1] *Phil. of Rt.*, § 279, pp. 381–2.

Nature. He admits that his dialectical arguments for Monarchy must give great anguish to the Understanding (as they certainly do).

Despite Hegel's strange belief in hereditary Monarchy as the crowning truth of the State Idea, his view of the Monarch's functions are far from feudal, and are, in fact, in accord with modern British constitutional practice. The Monarch is merely the necessary apex of the State-structure, and as such he is merely someone who dots the *i*'s, and whose individual character is not of great importance. Though he may have the Individual Moment of making last decisions, he also has the Specific Moment represented by his advisers, and the Universal Moment represented by the Constitution and Laws, which it is not in his power to alter. The more positive functions of the Monarch lie in his choice of ministers, for whose actions he is not, however, responsible, and in the extension of mercy to condemned criminals, an essentially groundless and therefore properly monarchical act.

Hegel's account of the remaining State-authorities and legislature is less interesting. He holds that, while the heads of Corporations may be elected, and small ambitions and passions thereby find an appropriate jousting-place, all official posts must remain in the gift of the Crown. Like Aristotle, he stresses the importance of a strong middle class, the pillar of righteousness and intelligence, without which no State (witness Russia in his time) can be highly developed. In the Legislature he holds that the Monarch, the State-authorities and the Estates of the Land must all be represented. While the People as such scarcely knows what it wills, and would be best guided by the higher State officials, its representation has value as expressing the needs and interests of various Classes, and as providing a public opinion, the fear of whose censure is good for those involved in State business. It is through the Estates, and the speeches of their representatives, that the State and its acts enter into the popular consciousness. Hegel believes in a bicameral Legislature, one chamber representing the landed aristocracy, the other the commerical part of Civil Society. The landed aristocracy is peculiarly fitted for State functions. As a 'substantial' Estate, founded upon the 'nature principle', it has, through its great sacrifices for political ends, achieved a vocation for, and a right to State-functions, and this by birth, and without the contingencies of choice. Again

Hegel seems to endorse the traditional arrangements of England. Public opinion should be both respected (*geachtet*) and despised (*verachtet*). It represents the eternal, substantial principles of justice, but mixed up with false beliefs and prejudices. While a people cannot be deceived as to its substantial basis, it can deceive itself indefinitely in regard to all detailed matters of fact. The truly great man will therefore scorn immediate public opinion, knowing that he will ultimately have it with him. Hegel's attitude to the freedom of the Press is sensible but unfanatical. In a strong state, it should be almost indefinite, except where writing is libellous, seditious, incites to violence, and so forth.

Hegel's view of the State's internal structure is now completed by an account of its external relations. Spirit, he tells us, 'in the freedom of its infinite negative relation to self, is just as essentially being-for-self that has taken the subsistent difference up into itself, and is for that reason exclusive. The State in this determination has Individuality, which essentially exists as an individual, and exists in the Sovereign as an actual immediate individual. Individuality as exclusive being-for-self appears as a relationship to other States, of which each is independent over against the others. Inasmuch as the being-for-self of actual Spirit has its being in this independence, it is the first freedom and the highest honour of a people.'[1] It follows from this, that Hegel rejects the notion of a supra-national State which will regulate the relations of particular States to each other, and will ensure perpetual peace. States are, and should be, in a state of nature over against one another. The welfare of the State is essentially a *particular* welfare, and the government that concerns itself with it must essentially be a particular wisdom, not a universal providence —strange statements from a philosopher whose principles are the 'absolute negativity' and the active universality of the Notion. It follows, further, that Hegel sees an ethical element in war, and that he quotes with approval his own statement in the *Phenomenology* about war preserving the ethical health of peoples and saving them from the stagnation due to a long peace. The State, he says, is individual, and to individuality negation is essential. As soon, therefore, as States assemble themselves into alliances, such associations must automatically create enemies to which they can be opposed. Through external conflict, nations

[1] *Phil. of Rt.*, §§ 321, 322, p. 132.

gain internal peace, and arise refreshed from the hazards due to 'hussars with shining sabres'.

We need not go further into Hegel's account of the State. It is an unedifying piece of writing, largely lacking in thought and argument, and without any deep coherence with his own principles. It describes with faithful accuracy the political arrangements of the monarchy in which Hegel spent his later years. And it presents these arrangements as the final fruits of the historic development of Spirit. Hegel, it would seem from this work, was not really gifted with deep political and social understanding. He was profound in his appreciation of speculative puzzles, of aesthetic and religious experiences—of what constitutes the higher solitude of man—but he was not profound in his grasp of the political and the social. This limitation he shared with Plato and other noble thinkers. His narrowness of view is shown, above all, in his carping strictures on the political arrangements of France and England, the two great creative nations of his own time. On the other hand, there is absolutely nothing *vile* in his political philosophy. At its worst it is small-minded and provincial, at its best it achieves the level of inspiration of an average British back-bench conservatism. The atmosphere of Hegel's State is the enclosed atmosphere of the small, stuffy waiting-rooms of Prussian officials, in which Professor Hegel himself probably often waited, when intent upon minor academic intrigues. It has absolutely no affinity or connection with the colossal wickedness of Dachau or Auschwitz.

Hegel's best excuse for the unsatisfactory character of his political theorizing lies perhaps in a revealing passage from the *Vorrede* to the *Philosophy of Right*. There Hegel says that a philosophical study of the State must be far from attempting to construct a State as it ideally should be. The task of philosophy is to understand *that which is*, since that which is is the reasonable. 'As far as concerns the individual,' he remarks, 'each is undoubtedly a son of his time, philosophy is the same, it is its own time comprehended in thought. It is just as silly to suppose that any philosophy goes beyond its contemporary world, as that an individual can jump beyond his time, can leap over Rhodes. [A reference to the proverb *Hic Rhodus, hic saltus*, which is addressed to those who boast of feats done in foreign lands.] If his theory really goes beyond his time, if he builds himself a world as it should be, it indeed exists, but only in his opinion, a soft element in which anything one likes can be imagined. With a little modification our proverb reads: Here is the Rose, here dance.'[1] (Hegel here plays on the ambiguity of *Rhodus* and *saltus*.) This passage comes as near as anything in Hegel to a modest acknowledgement that his philosophy can do no more than represent the philosophical consciousness of the German romantic epoch, and that it is open to others (as it is not open to Hegel himself) to criticize it from the higher vantage-points that the World-Spirit and the Idea *will* attain.

V THE PHILOSOPHY OF HISTORY

The *Philosophy of Right* ends with a section on World History, which Hegel expanded into a famous series of popular lectures on the Philosophy of History. In this part of the system Hegel passes from the study of the developed State, the supreme self-objectification of Spirit, to a study of the less developed States that lead up to it. This Philosophy of History is no independent part of the system, which can be studied in isolation. It is part and parcel of the teleological movement of the system as a whole, as of the particular teleology of the political theory.

According to Hegel, the recognition of an unbounded right to respect to be accorded to each person by each person, with the rules of Property, Contract and Requital of Wrong-doing which this entails, together with the inward spirit of Conscience that makes these principles its own, and the institutions and persons which embody these principles in the State—all these are things that cannot *be*, except in so far as they are *made* to be. They require a series of stages in which the merely natural in Man is more and more brought under the universality of the Will, in which the rights of Persons become more definite and more widely conceded, and in which these things are increasingly safeguarded by better institutions and dispositions of power. These stages will, in so far as they exist in the natural world in Space and Time, share in its *Aussereinander*, or mutual outsideness of parts. Though the half-developed forms of State are correctly seen as one-sided abstractions from the fully developed State, yet they will exist apart from it in Space and Time. They will not, however,

[1] *Phil. of Rt.*, p. 35.

like the forms of natural being, merely exist side by side in Space, and have an order of approximation to their Idea which *we*, the outside observers, ascertain and pin down. Each more developed State will arise *historically* out of less developed ones, until the fully developed State is achieved. The reason for this historical development of States lies, of course, in the fact that it is only in States, the 'Second Nature', that Spirit can achieve full self-consciousness, that it is only by detaching itself from finite individuality through the rules of an established State-order, that it can be aware of itself as universal and 'infinite'. And this detachment must, in a conscious being, necessarily take place in Time. Time is, in fact, as Hegel showed in the *Phenomenology*), merely the intuitive form in which Spirit carries out its own self-elucidation.

Each State will therefore only be able to reach its characteristic consciousness of Right, in so far as it has sprung historically out of States less lucid and less equitable, and in so far as the memory of those less lucid, less equitable States has become part of its present self-consciousness. Thus the modern world of Christian States can only have its universal, absolute sense of human dignity in so far as it both remembers, and in remembering transcends, the much less universal, less absolute Graeco-Roman sense of human dignity, and the still less universal, less absolute sense of human dignity found among the peoples of the ancient East. History therefore enters, not merely into the origin, but into the present being of States. Each State only has the degree of development it has by consciously remembering its origins. It follows that, for Hegel, where there are no historical records, there can also be no real political development. Historians do not therefore merely record political development: they also render it possible.

What Hegel attempts in his Philosophy of History is therefore a philosophical restatement of that continuous memory of the past which is already part of the self-consciousness of those living in a particular political State: it merely deepens that self-consciousness by connecting it with a philosophical outlook. The Hegelian Philosophy of History therefore builds on the original histories which constitute the source-material for the past, and also on the more reflective histories which subject this source-material to various critical tests, or which use it to answer certain special questions. It only differs from both because its aim is in part evaluative: to discover in past States different stages in the developing consciousness of Right, to discover a *line* of development running through all such stages, and to show, further, how events which seem unconnected with this development have none the less contributed to it. The Philosopher of History is, for Hegel, a theodicist, one who not only believes in a quasi-providence, a deep-set drift leading to more developed political arrangements, but who also thinks that the workings of this quasi-providence can be laid bare, that one can come to see what new state of political consciousness events are producing, and just how they are producing it.

In developing this theodicy Hegel holds that the Philosopher of History must follow the principle (previously mentioned) of the Cunning of Reason. This principle means that persons whose aim is not the production of a new stage in political self-consciousness, who are perhaps only vaguely conscious of this possibility, and who are motivated by personal interests and passions, none the less help to bring the new stage about, in co-operation with others with like but independent motives, and do so frequently to the frustration of their own ends. The Cunning of Reason 'lets passions forth, whereby that which is put into existence through these, pays the penalty and suffers loss'. This Cunning of Reason is shown at its highest in the careers of certain World-historical Individuals, men like Alexander, Caesar or Napoleon, who in aggrandizing themselves, or in defending themselves against rivals, make the transition to completely new levels in self-consciousness, generally destroying themselves in the process. Despite the mystical tone of Hegel's popular lectures, and his frequent appeals to the agency of the World Spirit, it seems plain that he does not think that these World-historical Individuals are quite ignorant of what they are bringing about. 'Such Individuals', he says, 'did not in their purposes have the consciousness of the Idea in general, rather they were practical, political men. But at the same time they were thinking men, who had insight into what was needful, and for what it was time. This was the truth of their time and of their world, so to say the next kind of thing which was already present inwardly. Their business was to know this universal, the necessary next step of the world, to make this their end, and to place their energy in it.

The World-historical Individuals, the heroes of a period, must therefore be acknowledged as the men of vision. Their actions and their speeches are the best of their time. . . . The further developed Spirit is the inmost soul of all individuals, but also the unconscious inwardness which the great men bring to consciousness. Therefore the others follow these leaders of souls, since they feel the irresistible force of their own inner Spirit that encounters them.'[1] Reason, in short, operates on men in general, and particularly on World-historical individuals, by being obscurely or implicitly recognized in the background of what they do or say, so that it affects the course of their actions and utterances. At a later stage what is thus obscurely recognized becomes manifest in a new historical state of society.

Hegel then puts forward as a principle for the Philosophy of History that there is but one *single* historical line of States representing the unfolding of the State-Idea. Only *one* State at a time plays a significant role in this development, the rest serving as mere satellites or onlookers, or as States that have been or will be politically important. When a State has passed out of this phase of historical significance, its vicissitudes may be important for the annalist, but they have lost all significance for the Philosopher of History. 'The Nation', says Hegel, 'is moral, virtuous, vigorous, inasmuch as it brings forth what it desires, and defends its work against outward violence in this labour of its objectification. The discord between what it is subjectively in itself, its inner aim and essence, and what it actually is, is lifted: it is with itself, it has itself objectively before it. But even so this activity of the Spirit is no more needed: what it wants, it has. The Nation can still achieve much in war and peace, internally and externally, but its living, substantial soul has as it were become inactive. The essential, supreme interest is accordingly gone from its life, since interest is only present where there is opposition. The Nation lives like the individual passing from manhood to old age, in the enjoyment of itself, and in being what it wanted to be and could attain.'[2]

Hegel then sketches a philosophical restatement of the past which distinguishes four historical 'Kingdoms'. There is an Oriental Kingdom characterized by 'substantiality', where the individual is dumbly, rightlessly submerged in the mass, where

---

[1] *Phil. of Hist.*, pp. 60–1.   [2] *Phil. of Hist.*, p. 114.

Religion, Morality, Law and Custom are undifferentiated, where social life is hardened into castes, and where only one individual, the despot, is free. There is a Greek Kingdom, where substantiality yields to an individualized spirituality 'born in the daylight of knowledge', and 'moderated and transfigured into free and joyous ethical life'. Here there are several distinct National Spirits, supreme decision is left to oracles and not to a personal sovereign —few thinkers have so stressed the importance of the oracular in Greek history—and the incomplete consciousness of Freedom permits the existence of a class of slaves. We then have a third Roman Kingdom, characterized by the complete diremption of ethical life into private personalities, on the one hand, and into the abstract universality of State authority, on the other. It develops out of a clash between the 'substantial insight' of the patricians, and the 'free personality' of the plebs, into a struggle between ruthless, self-seeking power and a corrupt rabble, and ends in the complete destruction of ethical life. Finally we have the Romantic Modern German Kingdom (in which all Western Europe is included) which has learnt from Christianity the essential unity of the human and divine natures, and which, beginning with an opposition between *this* world and the eternal world *beyond*, ends by bringing both worlds together in the rich spiritual and cultural life of modern Europe. The actual application of this scheme to the detail of history is by no means arbitrary and *a priori*. Hegel builds on contemporary sources, shows a lively historical sense, and certainly casts interesting lights on the subject-matters he treats.

This is not the place to evaluate so complex an undertaking as a Philosophy of History, nor to consider what sociologists, Marxists and others may have made of it. Suffice to say that Hegel's own construction is part of his higher-order philosophical way of looking at the facts of experience, and that it makes absolutely no attempt to supplement or replace accepted historical facts, nor to establish them in some novel manner. It takes these facts as established by ordinary historical methods, and merely seeks to rethink them, or 're-see' them, in its own peculiar frame of reference. It is, above all, no attempt to deal with ordinary historical facts in some 'scientific' manner: it makes not the smallest attempt to extrapolate or predict, nor does it even take as its province *all* historical truths. Many such truths it, in fact, discounts as having no philosophical significance. It is doubtful whether it is 'historicistic' in the sense condemned by some modern philosophers. It proceeds on the vague assumption of a progressive series of consciousnesses of Right, discoverable in the States that have swayed history, and finds an abundance of historical facts that fit in with, and in a general way confirm this assumption. It does not consider the possibility that more than one such ordering assumption might be found to work, and also pays insufficient regard to the existence of factors which are disruptive and dysteleological, and to the sad possibility of their long-term reign or their final victory. It seems a pity that it recognizes no coexistence of independently significant historical cultures. The Incas or Mayas are condemned to non-significance merely because they were contemporaries of our Western European culture. But the obvious provincialism of Hegel's philosophical reconstruction of history will not entail that *any* such reconstruction must be valueless.

CHAPTER TWELVE

ABSOLUTE SPIRIT AND RETROSPECT

(*Hegel's Aesthetics, Philosophy of Religion and History of Philosophy*)

I   TRANSITION TO ABSOLUTE SPIRIT

Hegel has so far shown us Spirit separating its subjective life from the objectivity of external Nature, and then proceeding to construct a 'Second Nature', an objective world of its own, *in* the latter. This Second Nature has culminated in the State, that 'hieroglyph of Reason' and that 'actual God upon earth'. This Second Nature, like the first, is, however, the jumping-off place for a renewed flight into subjectivity, this time no longer hieroglyphic, into the final, all-absorbing subjectivity called by Hegel 'Absolute Spirit'. Spirit must now not merely shape the world to its will: it must also see the world as having no other function but to be so shaped, it must see itself, in short, as the 'truth' of everything. This vision it can obviously only have in the security and convenience of a well-ordered State, where the cruder problems of subsistence and adjustment have been met. And it will enjoy this vision immediately and sensuously in Art, emotionally and representatively in Religion, and thinkingly in Philosophy, the three forms of Absolute Spirit. These are briefly sketched by Hegel in the *Encyclopaedia*, but are also worked over with incomparable richness in his three courses of lectures on *Aesthetics*, on the *Philosophy of Religion* and on the *History of Philosophy*. Here Hegel's empirical spirit seems to range in barefoot delight over the broad fields of beauty, worship and speculation, quite freed from the pinch and creak of the dialectical boots. We shall in the present chapter merely suggest the wealth and colour of those fields, and shall then look back, in general retrospect, over the whole landscape we have traversed.

The transition from the State to Absolute Spirit is simply managed. The Ethical Substance of the State may be infinite *in itself*, but is also limited and particular, infected with contingency, and with a relation to what is immediate in Space and Time. 'But', says Hegel, 'it is the Spirit which *thinks* in this ethical life, which transcends in itself the finitude which it has as the Spirit of a Nation in its State, and its temporal interests, its system of laws and customs, and raises itself to the knowledge of what it essentially is (a knowledge which, however, has itself the immanent limitations of the National Spirit). But the thinking Spirit of World History, in so far as it strips off these limitations of the particular National Spirits and its own worldliness, grasps its own concrete universality, and raises itself to the knowledge of Absolute Spirit, as the eternal truth, in which cognitive reason is free for itself, while necessity, nature and history merely minister to its revelation and are vessels of its honour.'[1]

There is as much or as little rigour in the above transition as in any previously met with in the Dialectic. Self-conscious Spirit always *was* the explanatory essence of everything, and now that the State has given it the organized, spiritualized setting in which this truth can be adequately appreciated, it simply proceeds to do so. Hegel must not, however, be interpreted as saying that Spirit's vision of itself ever quite rises above the limitations of a national culture, of which Art, Religion and Philosophy are an integral part. The perspective of World History will rob these last of a great deal of provincialism and one-sidedness, but there must be a remaining one-sidedness and provincialism which it cannot hope to remove. This Hegel, as we saw in the last chapter, admits fully, and against which he makes no vain protestations: it is the unavoidable predicament of a particular phase of experience which can only be overcome, and profitably discussed, from the vantage-point of another, later phase. But though the highest Art, Religion and Philosophy of a particular culture may be, from a later point of view, limited and superseded, they remain, from another point of view, dateless and absolute. For Hegel does not believe in the endless vain chase of a higher vision lying beyond the horizon, but regards absolute truth as being always in essence *contemporary*, as representing the best, most impartial vision possible at a given time. It is this vision of the German Romantic age which Hegel now proceeds to give us, and which we, living in a much more visionless, confused age, will do well to take account of in framing our own.

[1] *Phil. of Sp.*, § 552, p. 433.

II THE IMMEDIATE FORM OF ABSOLUTE
SPIRIT: ART

Art, the first of the forms of Absolute Spirit, is held by Hegel to express the Idea in an 'immediate' manner, in connection with material given to the senses. This sensuous material is seen as completely penetrated or dominated by some indwelling notion or meaning, and this penetration *itself* signifies, in an obscure, symbolic manner, the absorption and overreaching of the 'other' by self-conscious Spirit. A Work of Art does not *say* that self-conscious Spirit is the truth of everything, nor need it have any speculative content whatsoever, but it triumphantly *shows* how what is non-spiritual, even painfully and aggressively so, can be taken up and overcome in Spirit. It therefore provides us with an evangelic preparation for the higher illuminations of Religion and Philosophy. 'Works of Art,' says Hegel, 'although they are not thoughts and notions, but a development of the Notion out of itself, an alienation towards the sensuous, none the less have the power of thinking Spirit in them, a power not merely of apprehending itself in its peculiar guise of thought, but just as much of recognizing itself in its externalization to sense and the sensuous, of grasping itself in its other, inasmuch as it transforms the alienated to thought, and so leads it back to itself. . . . In this way the Work of Art also, in which thought has externalized itself, belongs to the realm of understanding, thought and Spirit, in so far as it subjects it to scientific treatment [i.e. in aesthetic criticism or theory] merely satisfies the need of its inmost nature. Since thought is Spirit's essence and notion, it is only finally satisfied when it penetrates all products of its activity with thought, and so makes them truly its own. Art, however, as we shall see more definitely, far from being the highest form of Spirit, attains in Science its first genuine validation.'[1]

Hegel stresses the curious *fusion* of notional meanings with sensuous material which is characteristic of Works of Art. The maker or enjoyer of a Work of Art does not merely see it as an instance of a number of general features or relationships which he runs through in thought. He sees all this wealth of significance *in* the object itself, as somehow one with its sensuous immediacy.

[1] *Aesth.*, I, pp. 34–5.

'The agreement of the Notion and the Appearance must', says Hegel, 'be complete penetration (*Dúrchdringung*). For that reason the external form and shape does not appear as separated from an external material, or mechanically impressed on it for an alien purpose, but rather as the Form dwelling and shaping itself in the reality in question.'[1] Hegel does not further analyse this notion of fusion and penetration, but plainly it lies in the power of certain appearances to *suggest* a given notion, to bring it home, with peculiar vividness and impressiveness, to the conscious person. One instance of certain qualities may have this suggestive power, while another quite lacks it.

The construction of forms richly soaked in notional meanings is said to be the task of a special power of Imagination (*Phantasie*), which operates unconsciously or instinctively, and not by applying rules or recipes. One man naturally builds up structures of sound or visual patterns fitted to clothe certain notional meanings, while another man wholly lacks the 'genius' or 'talent' to do so. Hegel does not suggest that genius or talent obeys *no* general principles merely because it fails to formulate them. The principles it follows are in fact those which Hegel is setting forth in his *Lectures on Aesthetics*, though the imaginative artist need not and should not have regard to them. Nor is Hegel inclined to underestimate the hard labour, the extensive background of experience, that are needed for artistic creation, and the absurdity of the current romantic theories of 'inspiration'.

Since the aim of Art is to create sensuous forms suggestively soaked in significance, it will be indifferent to the *reality* of what it thus suggests, or to any other unsuggested features of reality. The task of Art is to make notions sensuously or imaginatively *apparent*, not to produce actual things which *are* what thus appears. Hegel of course stresses that this preoccupation with show or appearance involves no real fraud or deception. What is thus shown in notion-soaked appearance may be more important, more 'true' than much that really exists. Since the aim of Art is thus quasi-theoretical, it will use for its shows the material of the theoretical, the distant senses. Art, according to Hegel, works entirely through sight and hearing, which alone permit us to enjoy objects as showing forth notions, without passing on to consume them or remake them or to use them in the urgency of

[1] *Aesth.*, I, pp. 165–6.

animal desire. It will be plain throughout his treatment how much Hegel owes to Kant's analyses in the *Critique of Aesthetic Judgement*.

Hegel further lays great stress on the transforming, the *idealizing* tendency of artistic creation. What is represented in Art may be taken from Nature, but it is not presented *as* Nature presents it. In Art one or other universal meaning must be brought out, made sensuously apparent, and whatever is not relevant, favourable to such bringing out must be dropped from the picture, replaced by what is relevant and favourable. The resultant work will not be abstractly schematic: it will be ripely and richly individual. But it will have an individuality in which *all* features are such as to bring out one dominant notion. In Art everything must be purified, concentrated, pregnant. Hegel says of the representations of the Greek gods that 'the liveliness of the ideal consists in this, that this determinate spiritual basic meaning, which must be brought to representation, is completely worked out through all particular sides of their external appearance, carriage, position, movement, features, form and shape of members, etc., so that nothing empty or meaningless remains, but rather everything shows itself as penetrated by that meaning'.[1] In the Venus of Art everything must be profoundly Cyprian, etc. etc. Hegel also compares the way in which Art makes natural objects poignant to the way in which the *eye* carries the whole sense and soul of the living body. The aim of the artist is to make his works 'all eye', to turn his shapes 'into a thousand-eyed Argus so that the inner soul and spirituality may at all points be seen in the appearance.'[2] He quotes with approval Schiller's reference to the 'still shadow-land of beauty', and says that Art must by its nature deal with shadows which are 'dead to immediate being, cut off from the defects of natural existence, freed from the bonds of dependence on outside influences, and from all perversions and distortions attendant on phenomenal being'. The underlying tone of aesthetic absorption must be throughout one of glad peace (*heitere Ruhe*), even when its object is tumultuous and full of struggle. Hegel prefers this characterization of the emotional tone of Art to the somewhat morbid emphasis on 'irony' favoured by his contemporary von Schlegel.

Hegel's stress on ideality means that for him some contents or

---

[1] *Aesth.*, I, p. 238.   [2] *Aesth.*, I, p. 213.

meanings are more intrinsically presentable in Art than others. The conscious Spirit, particularly in an assured pose of mastery over what is natural or immediate, is the most supremely presentable of contents, just as the human form is its most adequate vehicle of expression. The Greek God, with his transfigured human individuality and accomplished sculptured naturalness, remains for Hegel the aesthetic paradigm, whether as regards 'notion' or external embodiment. But the more tortured, struggling phases of spiritual life also merit artistic presentation. Romantic Art can put as much triumphant soul into its martyrs as Classic Art puts into its serene Gods. Even the *particularity* of human spirituality may be, after a fashion, universalized and idealized, as it regularly is in the portrait. Hegel here mentions the manner in which certain old German and Flemish altarpieces—one has but to think of the Donne triptych—combine the expression of a pure universality with that of a universalized particularity. The former appears in the Virgin and Saints, in whom each feature of bodily structure centres in one glorious expression, while the latter comes out in the kneeling donors, whose faces may shine with the single emotion of piety, but which also betray a long knightly, civic or household past, as well as 'powerful passions and solid vital virtues'.

But though the conscious Spirit and the human form are the supreme channels of aesthetic effort, the life of mere Nature affords a possible, if less fruitful field. The geometric symmetries of crystals, the flowing individuality of living forms, the complex, characteristic patterns of landscape, all deserve artistic disentanglement from whatever obscures them, so as to afford a vehicle for spiritual self-envisagement. Even in their natural existence such forms have aesthetic significance, though their entanglement with irrelevances, with the mere prose of concrete existence, renders disengagement more difficult. Natural objects may, further, be imaginatively 'humanized' (Hegel's equivalent for *Einfühlung*), and may have various passions and spiritual attitudes read into them, which give them aesthetic significance. Such a general 'humanization' may be further spread to the appurtenances and appearances characteristic of ordinary life in a given civilization, as in the masterpieces of Dutch painting, where, says Hegel, 'velvet, the glitter of metal, light, horses, servants, old women, peasants blowing smoke from their pipe-ends, the gleam of wine in transparent glasses, fellows in dirty jackets playing with old cards' all become expressive of a single spiritual content, which Hegel ultimately declares to be simply the gay, secure, historically tried, energetically triumphant national consciousness of the Netherlands.[1] This spiritual content is what comes out alike in Dutch still-lifes, in their landscapes or seascapes, and in their dignified or convivial genre-pictures.

From his general treatment of the Ideal, or Aesthetic Idea, Hegel passes on to a philosophy of Art-history, as well as to a philosophy of the various Art-forms. Art-history is studied under the three headings of Symbolic, Classic and Romantic Art. Symbolic Art covers for Hegel the exuberant, bizarre, but for him formless and tasteless Art of India, Persia, Egypt, etc. It is an Art which rather strains after the ideal of spiritual self-envisagement than actually attains it, which brings out the negative relation of inadequacy between sensuous representation and Idea, rather than makes the one adequate to the other. Symbolic Art is, in short, *sublime* Art, in the precise Kantian sense of the word: it in effect expresses the Idea through its sheer inability to express it. The inadequacy of such a technique of success-in-failure leads on, however, to the complete adequacy and success of Classic Art, where the self-consciousness of Spirit finds an entirely satisfactory sensuous house in the glorified, idealized human body. In Classic Art we have the highest of which Art, as Art, is capable. In Romantic Art, which comes after it, we see Art struggling to what is in fact a higher form of spiritual life. There must always be an inadequacy, from the point of view of spiritual self-envisagement, in that union of ideal meaning and sensuous content which is the aim of all Art. In Romantic Art this inadequacy itself receives artistic expression. Romantic Art, in fact, returns to the lack of definition and measure characteristic of Symbolic Art. It only differs from the latter in its clear sense of what it fails to express.

Hegel also deals in turn with the three visual Arts of Architecture, Sculpture and Painting, and with the two auditory Arts of Music and Poetry. Architecture, operating on Matter in the form of 'mechanical heavy mass', and moulding it into symmetrical forms agreeable to the Understanding, belongs really to the Symbolic phase of Art: it does not create an expression of self-

[1] *Aesth.*, I, pp. 224, 234.

conscious Spirit but merely strives towards one. It can therefore do no more than build a temple for the God, in which Sculpture, the typically Classic Art, then sets the God himself, the expression of self-conscious Spirit. The worshipping community then enter the temple, with their depth of feeling and vision to which no outward form can be equal. We pass therefore to the Romantic Arts of Painting, Music and Poetry. In Painting Art frees itself from three-dimensionality, and achieves a higher ideality in terms of coloured visibility, an abstraction compensated by an unlimited concreteness in what it may represent. In Music the mutual outsideness of existence in Space is superseded. Sounds, which are themselves alternate abandonments and reassumptions of materiality (*vide* the *Philosophy of Nature*) are used to express a range of purely spiritual attitudes. Art then passes on to Poetry, where the sounded word becomes a mere symbol for the unsounded thought or mental picture. 'Poetry', says Hegel, 'is the universal Art of the Spirit which has become free in itself, and is not bound for its realization to external sensuous material, but which merely proceeds in the interior Space and Time of picture-thoughts and sensations.'[1]

Enough will have been said to indicate both the notional framework and the rich empirical filling of Hegel's *Lectures on Aesthetics*. Together with the *Phenomenology*, they represent Hegel at his most concrete, as the philosopher who above all others has plumbed the depths and breadths of human experience. They also represent the operation of Hegelian categories at its most successful. Perhaps, indeed, Hegelianism is in its outcome an aesthetic philosophy, one whose role it is to see things variously and pregnantly, and also to combine its varied, pregnant visions into an unbelievably fine synthesis of kaleidoscopic variety and well-balanced unity.

III   THE REPRESENTATIONAL-FEELING FORM OF ABSOLUTE SPIRIT: RELIGION

The transition from Art to Religion is straightforward. In Art the Idea is expressed by the notional suffusion of a remoulded sensuous reality, a suffusion which can, however, not be complete, and which, in the striving, symbolic forms of Art is acknowledged

---

[1] *Aesth.*, I, p. 131.

to be incomplete. In Religion the Idea now receives a better expression, a so-called revelation, in the Feelings, Intuitions, Presentations and Worshipful Actions of the individual, where artistic presentations only play a subordinate part.

That Religion and Philosophy—by which Hegel means a Philosophy whose final form is his own Philosophy of Spirit—have an identical content, is something that becomes clear as the treatment proceeds. Hegel assumes that a religious term like 'God' will, when stripped of pictorial associations, reveal itself as meaning no more than the 'I' of self-consciousness, which is for Hegel also the element of universality and unity present in all thinking, which is inseparable from the finite particular self to which it may *seem* transcendent, but which uses the latter as the vehicle through which it achieves its self-consciousness. 'God', on Hegel's view, has 'created' the world of Nature and finite Spirit, but only in the sense that these are the necessary conditions of pure self-consciousness. That this is Hegel's view, comes out in passages too numerous to mention. The best brief statement is the passage in *Encyclopaedia*, § 564, where God is said to be God only in so far as He knows Himself, where this self-knowledge is said to be God's self-consciousness *in Man*, and to be *Man's* knowledge of God, which develops into Man's self-knowledge *in* God. In an atmosphere thick with theological tensions, one cannot expect Hegel to be more explicit. What is interesting for our purpose is not, however, this general Hegelian opinion, which we have dealt with on other occasions, but the specific *differentiae* of the religious mode of apprehension, in particular the meaning of the terms 'Feeling' (*Gefühl*) and 'Representation' (*Vorstellung*) of which Hegel makes so much use in discussing Religion.

Hegel's fullest account of the religious mode of presentation occurs in a section of the *Philosophy of Religion* called 'The Religious Relationship' (*Das religiöse Verhältniss*, Vol. I, pp. 114–220). Here Feeling, Intuition (*Anschauung*) and Representation (*Vorstellung*) are discussed in great detail. By 'Feeling' Hegel means, not a simple affective state like being pleased or pained, but a consciousness which can be *of* any object whatever, whether simple or complex, exalted or ignoble, valid or delusive, which may include various subjective attitudes, e.g. remorse, but which is distinct from all other ways of being conscious by its total lack of *analytic clarity*. In particular, a state of Feeling is one in which there is no clear distinction between what is subjective and what is objective. When I *feel* a hard object—Hegel does not scruple to use this example—the hardness is as much *my* determination as it is the object's. In Feeling, says Hegel, 'the foreign determination becomes fluid in my universality, and that which is other than myself I make mine (*vermeinige ich*)'.[1] The Religious Feeling-relationship is therefore one in which *God* is made mine, just as an object's hardness is made mine when I feel it. It is, however, of the nature of this Feeling-relationship to break up and analyse itself in various ways. My Feeling-consciousness of God therefore naturally develops into my *reflective* consciousness of God's universal being, on the one hand, and my own profound nullity, on the other, and also into various attitudes of wrath, fear, gratitude, compassion, etc., between us. Hegel further emphasizes that we are not more intimately in touch with God, the universal element in self-consciousness, when we feel Him than when we think of Him. Feeling may very well yield us a confused or false picture; it is only in thought that we can hope to make God satisfactorily our own, to apprehend Him validly, and as He absolutely is. The unanalysed, often delusive Feelings of Religion are therefore a mere prelude to the wholly analysed, valid thoughts of Philosophy.

'Representation' (*Vorstellung*), the other term often used in connection with Religion, is given a fairly clear meaning by Hegel. It is not exactly the same as an image or mental picture, as one might tend to suppose, but is an image 'raised to the form of universality, of thinking'. What Hegel means is that Representations are thoughts which, despite their essential differences from mental pictures, none the less have some of the properties of the latter. They take whatever notions they deal with as merely given, like the things of sense, they treat them as external to one another like existences in Space and Time, and they merely *note* the relationships among them, instead of gaining insight into their necessity.[2] By 'representational thought' Hegel, in short, means a quasi-empirical, naïvely discovering way of embarking upon notional questions, such as has been practised, for instance, by modern British Neo-Realists. In the field of Religion, thought about the *wrath* of God, about the *begetting* of God's Son, about

<hr>

[1] *Phil. of Rel.*, I, p. 138. [2] *Phil. of Rel.*, I, pp. 152–162.

the *Creation* of the World, etc. etc. all involve this representational style of picture-thought, to eliminate which would be to turn Religion into Speculative Philosophy.

Hegel now follows the historic development of Religion through various allegedly necessary phases, beginning with a magical, purely natural stage of Religion, passing through the Religions of Pantheistic Substantiality (The Chinese Religion of Measure, the Indian Religion of Fantasy and the Buddhist Religion of Interiority), through the transitional Religions of Light (Zoroastrianism), of Suffering (the Syriac), and of the Riddle (the Egyptian), to the Religions of Spiritual Individuality, where Hegel distinguishes the Religion of Sublimity (Judaism), of Beauty (Greek Religion), and of Purposiveness (Roman Religion). Finally, as in the *Phenomenology*, he passes on to Absolute or Revealed Religion, a phase of Religion that for the first time explicitly realizes the *notion* of Religion, that of being merely the self-revelation or self-communication of Absolute Spirit. This stage of Religion Hegel identifies with Christianity. Here he deals with the 'Kingdom' of the Father, where the persons of the Trinity are identified with the three moments of Universality, Particularity and Individuality in the Hegelian Notion, and with the Kingdoms of the Son and the Spirit, where the Creation, Fall, Incarnation, Resurrection, Ascension and the Pentecostal Descent of the Spirit, are all given speculative interpretations. Thus the death of death involved in the Christian Resurrection and Ascension is held to be a representational expression of the 'absolute negativity' of Spirit, the principle that Spirit can affirm itself only by first denying itself and then denying that denial.[1] All this may sound faintly absurd, but there is nothing arbitrary and external in Hegel's detailed exegeses. Very often they catch the very spirit and savour of the New Testament. They can only seem arid and false to those who see nothing mysterious and godlike in the facts of human thought.

IV THE THINKING FORM OF
ABSOLUTE SPIRIT: PHILOSOPHY
AND ITS HISTORY

Religion with its picture-thought will, however, always be involved in inconsistencies, which will afford a ready handle to

[1] *Phil. of Rel.*, II, p. 300.

rationalistic criticism. Its speculative content will not always accord with its representational, quasi-empirical mode of statement. It must therefore press onward to Philosophy, in whose abstract conceptual medium it is alone possible to make the Idea a concrete achievement. Philosophy for Hegel is, however, simply the History of Philosophy as restated in the medium of pure thought; the supreme achievement of Spirit is accordingly to recapitulate and understand its own reflective history, from Thales' identification of the 'all' with water, to Hegel's identification of it with self-conscious Spirit. At this point we may refer to Hegel's justly celebrated *Lectures on the History of Philosophy*, where he attempts to show, with an inconceivable depth of knowledge and understanding, how there has at all times only been a single philosophy necessarily possessing a number of distinct sides, and how the historical sequence of philosophical systems is not casual, but represents the necessary line of development of thinking self-knowledge. He also argues that the last philosophy of an epoch necessarily sums up all previous stages of philosophy, and is the highest phase, so far, in the self-consciousness of Spirit.

From this point of view Hegel can speak somewhat grandiloquently of his own philosophy. 'It appears', he remarks, 'that the World-Spirit has now had success in doing away with all foreign objective essence, and at last apprehending itself as Absolute Spirit, in producing out of itself whatever is to be its object, and in holding this tranquilly in its power. The struggle of the finite self-consciousness with the absolute self-consciousness, which appeared to the former as outside of itself, ceases. The finite self-consciousness has ceased to be finite, and the absolute self-consciousness, on the other hand, has gained the reality that it previously lacked. It is the whole previous world-history in general, and the history of philosophy in particular, that represents only this struggle, and which seems to have reached its term, when this absolute self-consciousness, whose picture it has had, has ceased to be anything strange, and where Spirit as Spirit is actual.'[1]

But this grandiloquent passage is shortly followed by one in which Hegel points out that we can no longer be Platonists, that one must rise wholly above the pettiness of personal opinion and personal vanity, since 'it is the *standpoint of the individual* to

[1] *Hist. of Phil.*, III, pp. 689-90.

apprehend the inner substantial Spirit: within the whole, individuals are like blind men whom the inner Spirit drives'.[1] These
words suggest that while it is right for a philosopher to apply the
word 'absolute' to his system, and to say that he *knows* its truth,
provided it represents the latest fruit of philosophical progress,
it will be just as right (though Hegel finds it unnecessary to say
so) for another later philosopher to speak of it otherwise. Hegelian
Truth is on this view a strictly contemporary affair, and Hegel
expects no more permanence for his own system than to be
preserved in such good systems as come after it. This interpretation of his statements is at least as reasonable as thinking that he
really thought the shades of night were coming down in 1830.

V APPRAISAL OF HEGEL AS A ANTI-METAPHYSICIAN, EMPIRICIST, IDEALIST AND DIALECTICIAN

We have now covered, in its main features, the doctrine of
Hegel's early *Phenomenology of Spirit* and of his later encyclopaedic
system. It is now time to seek to sum up the whole performance,
and to consider what, as a philosophy, it can say to us. We have
given certain preparatory indications of our view of the system
in our opening chapters, and have also interpreted and criticized it as we went along. It is now time to draw the threads of
this criticism together, and to attempt a comprehensive 'reaction'
to the whole system.

What one will think of Hegel's philosophy will depend largely
on what one thinks philosophy should be, in what directions
one thinks its unspecialized, detached musings may most profitably go. One's view of it will differ according as one thinks that
philosophy should dig down to a deeper level of being, perhaps
denying what are ordinarily looked on as well-established facts,
or rejecting what are ordinarily looked on as sound notions or
well-grounded assumptions, or whether one thinks, on the other
hand, that nothing that a philosopher can establish is likely to be
better founded than the broad certainties of the 'common-sense'
view of the world. It will differ according as one thinks that
philosophy should integrate the facts brought forward in the
sciences, and should range them under more comprehensive

[1] *Hist. of Phil.*, III, p. 691.

hypotheses (as some have sought to explain everything by 'evolution'), or whether one thinks that it should merely examine the relations of *abstract* types or forms of being, so as to ascertain what *may* be the case in other possible world-orders, or what *must* be the case in all possible world-orders whatever. It will differ according as one thinks that philosophy should offer us one single world-picture, dismissing others as senseless or self-contradictory, or that it should offer us a number of alternative views, leaving experience to arbitrate among them. It will differ, further, according as one thinks philosophy to be, in a broad sense, 'ontological', something that may shed light on the 'nature of things', or whether one thinks its whole task to be conceptual or linguistic, to consist, perhaps, in a mere analysis of ordinary talk and thought, perhaps in a series of 'recommendations' which seek to alter this at certain points, perhaps, lastly, in a critical purge of the abuses of ordinary modes of thought and speech which have led to a large number of spurious contradictions and puzzles. It will differ, further, according as one thinks that the modes of speech and thought to be adopted by philosophers should have some relation of more or close fit to the empirical data on which we use them. If we hold that they should, the adoption of such modes of speech and thought will involve also the tacit adoption of certain guiding assumptions regarding the things we deal with. It will differ, lastly, according as one thinks that philosophy is merely a performance of 'first review', one that merely does what ordinary thought does but more thoroughly, more reflectively or more analytically, or whether one looks on it as fundamentally a performance of 'second review', one which, while not subverting or overthrowing ordinary accounts of things, none the less adds to them something of a more removed, widely ranging, profoundly illuminating sort.

Strange as it may seem, Hegel's philosophy does much to satisfy all these conceptions of philosophy: it is unsatisfactory to any of them because it does so much justice to them all. While it analyses ordinary concepts and ways of speech, and leaves them undisturbed at their level, it also subjects them to devastating higher-level criticism. While it allows us to think in alternative ways, and grants each a limited charter of legitimacy, it also ranges them in a hierarchical order of adequacy, at the summit of which there is only one completely satisfactory mode of conception, the Absolute Idea. If it permits itself much piecemeal treatment of separate issues, it also gathers these treatments together in a concerted attack on the Absolute. And while it certainly does not tailor its notions to fit every detail of fact, and makes no attempt to set up natural or social laws, it none the less digs down further into the detail of experience than is at all usual among philosophers, nor are its general principles ever without profound relevance to the facts of history and science. And while it strongly insists on seeing its innovations as belonging to the sphere of thought and language (which are for Hegel the same) it also does not refuse to use mere ontological, realistic forms of expression. And while it often multiplies entities in a manner reminiscent of the realistic metaphysicians, it is also always ready to liquidate them in the transfigured ordinariness of the Idea. Hegel's thought being thus varied, what one says of it must be largely a matter of emphasis. This emphasis may, however, be that of the independent system-maker, who uses Hegel's ideas for his own inspiration, as has been the case in too much of the Hegelianism of the past. It may also be the emphasis of the system itself, as it reveals itself to those without any private philosophical axe to grind.

Here it may first be held that, despite much opinion to the contrary, Hegel's philosophy is one of the most anti-metaphysical of philosophical systems, one that *remains* most within the pale of ordinary experience, and which accords no place to entities or properties lying beyond that experience, or to facts undiscoverable by ordinary methods of investigation. Hegel often speaks the language of a metaphysical theology, but such language, it is plain, is a mere concession to the pictorial mode of religious expression. As a philosopher, Hegel believes in no God and no Absolute except one that is revealed and known in certain experiences of individual human beings, to whose being it is essential to be so revealed and known. This does not mean that Hegel is a mere humanist: the absolute and 'infinite' sides of human experience are for him the ultimate, and overreaching ones, for the sake of which the finite, individual ones may be held to exist. What is, however, fundamental is that it is only through the medium of individual human Spirits that his Absolute can *be* at all. Hegel has further no belief in a world-view which sums up all that finite individuals know and see, and which is *without specific standpoint*, whether in Space or Time. For Hegel there can be no absolute, infinite experience which is not also, from another point of view, limited and personal, nor can the Whole appear otherwise than in the perspective of an individual consciousness, stamped with the ineffaceable mark of the Here and the Now. Nor is it possible for the Absolute to be reached otherwise than by a temporal process, and to this process there can be no term, except that, in certain crucial experiences, Time ceases to count as such. The notion of an all-comprehensive, complete experience would for Hegel involve the fallacy of the Bad Infinite, and would eliminate the element of resistance and process essential to all Spiritual Reality.

If Hegel shows no tendency to go beyond the finite, individual, human consciousness, but merely to give depth to our idea of it, he shows just as little tendency to go beneath the world of natural things in Space and Time, or to undermine what would ordinarily be called their reality. Things in Space and Time are not put there by our conscious minds, and they existed long before there were any conscious minds at all. The only sense in which they are ideal, is that they may be arranged in an order of increasing analogy to conscious, spiritual beings, at the upper levels of which they are in fact bodily vehicles for such spiritual intelligences.

One may likewise hold that Hegel shows no tendency to overthrow or undermine the facts, assumptions or methods of the mathematical or natural sciences. To read the treatment of Knowledge at the end of the *Logic* is to be clear on this point. If he calls the methods and assumptions of such sciences 'contra-dictory' or 'untrue', these words mean no more than that they claim to interpret things adequately and that they fail to do so; it is a contradiction and untruth that presupposes that Hegelian accounts are the goal towards which all other accounts really strive. There is no doubt that Hegel believes in the complete validity of ordinary scientific methods at the level at which they are applied. His criticisms of them are a matter of 'second review', a consideration of them from a vantage-point foreign to them as scientific. Nor does the fact that he condemns scientific statements as contradictory or untrue mean that they in any way fail to square with the empirical facts, since, on Hegel's use of the terms, some of these facts are themselves contradictory and untrue.

That it is a *merit* for a system of thought to be as wholly 'immanent' as we have held Hegel's to be, is not anything we can here argue in detail. Possibly it is right to incorporate surds and unknowns into one's accounts of the world, symbols which complete one's theoretical accounts, and which satisfy profound theoretical needs, although it is neither possible nor desirable to give them a straightforward 'this-world' rendering. The kind of philosophy which Hegel has built up is, however, plainly one of the permanent types of philosophy, and plainly it is useful, even for the employer of transcendent surds, to be clear how far it is possible to do without them, and to incorporate Hegel's 'immanent' account into his own more difficult enterprise.

If Hegel's thought remains in this way in the familiar world of common sense and science, we may note, next, how deeply it digs into the texture of that world, we may stress the immense empiricism of the Hegelian philosophy. Hegel practises no transcendental suspension: his philosophy is no study of abstract relationships between meanings such as might have been exemplified in a wide range of worlds. His notions descend far into the detail of Nature and History, even to much that most philosophers would regard as quite beyond their province. No philosopher, except possibly Aristotle, has produced thought with a trifle of Hegel's empirical richness. That it is a merit to be thus rich and concrete need not be argued: most modern philosophizing seems watery by comparison. And not only are Hegel's *notions* empirical: his system may be said to operate with certain high-level hypotheses which, though not admitting of empirical verification or falsification, none the less stand in many logical relations to propositions which *are* thus verifiable or falsifiable. Hegel may be interpreted as saying in his philosophy that all or most of the things that exist will be found on reflection to have contributed *somehow* to the enrichment, to the deepening, and to the profounder interconnection of conscious experience. Such an assumption cannot be strictly verified, since it extends to *all* or *most* things, nor can it be strictly falsified since we can never disprove a statement involving a *somehow*. It also involves all the vagueness and the entanglement with valuation connected with such terms as 'enrichment', 'deepening', or 'interconnection'. It is not, however, without *some* empirical meaning, and one to which many actual facts are relevant. Hegel is not, of course, an empirical philosopher in the sense of correcting or anticipating the work of the scientist or the historian: he has nothing to say as to the precise future course of history, nor as to the precise number of elementary particles in the universe.

But though Hegel remains *within* the world of common sense and science, and does not undermine its reality, his approach to it is neither commonsensical nor scientific: he sees the facts of that world in a revolutionary manner, which is not that of any other philosopher. Hegel, as we made plain, sees things in terms of a 'principle of Idealism', which is not the principle of Berkeley, nor that of Plato, nor Kant, nor any previous thinker. It is a teleological or quasi-teleological principle, according to which things must be seen as if existing on account of, or as if tending towards, certain consummating experiences, experiences where there will cease to be a barrier between the self and other persons, or between the thinking mind and the world confronting it. This principle, we have suggested, may have certain remote, long-term empirical consequences, which we cannot precisely locate or pin down. Its meaning is not, however, exhausted by these latter, since it would remain a way of regarding the facts of experience, a peculiar conceptual slant, whatever these facts might turn out to be.

Hegel's idealism may best be recommended (as we said before) as expressing the basic 'faith' of all who pursue science, who 'hunger and thirst after righteousness', or who pursue the well-formed in Art; the faith that the obscure can be rendered intelligible, the passionate and unhappy transformed into their opposites, the merely humdrum and nondescript rendered aesthetically significant, and that the labour, sacrifice and pain of these efforts will meet with enough (and not more than enough) success to ensure their continuance. It may be said that no one can be an idealist in the ordinary sense, without also being an idealist in this special sense. It is not, however, necessary for the effective conduct of Science, Morality and Art that the serene confidence of Hegelianism should be our only or our predominant attitude. While hoping for the best, we may none the less prepare for the worst, and perhaps accept the worst in certain cases. Hegel lived in an age when the appearances perhaps justified a magisterial mood of spiritual confidence: we live in an age when the appearances perhaps justify a preparedness for the most tragic and dismal possibilities. It is perhaps enough for us, and even stimulating to our courage and resource, to temper Hegelian 'idealism' with injections of astringent 'realism'. But, however much this may be, we can still enter into Hegel's mood of serene, overriding confidence. It is the mood of all great Christian works of art—Handel, Dante, etc.—to which we, as Western men, cannot remain indifferent.

Hegel's philosophy is, moreover, not static but moving: it develops its principles and modes of interpretation out of other less developed modes and principles, and is original in making this development the *substance* rather than the mere prolegomena, to its treatment. This, the 'dialectical' side to Hegel's philosophy, is at once the source of some of its supreme merits and also of its most astounding demerits. One of its great merits lies in reminding us that we have a *choice* among ways in which we shall speak of, and conceive the world, and that while *within* a given mode of speech and conception there may be a standard of absolute truth and falsehood, and a strict application of logical procedures, there is no such standard of truth and falsehood *among* the varying possibilities of speech and thought, and that one can only say that one is better, or more inclusive or more profoundly adequate than another. And the reference of this, the problem of choice and accommodation among categories, to ourselves, the judging subjects, with our own standards of 'reasonableness', and not to the meaningless arbitrament of 'the facts', is one of Hegel's most important contributions to thought. Hegel's dialectical treatment of notions is also important in that it brings out the essential instability of our basic ideas. While we can cut off their corners, and give them an artificial fixity, they have, in their natural, living state, a perpetual tendency to pass over into other ideas, and sometimes several inconsistent directions of development which well-chosen questions may bring to light. In general, we may say that Hegel's Dialectic has made plain the profound difference between a valuable thesis in philosophy and a valuable thesis in the factual disciplines.

The supreme defect of Hegel's dialectical treatment of notions lies, however, in his view that dialectical development follows definite rules, that it can be regimented into a sequence of triads, that it constitutes a new sort of knowledge or science, having some sort of rigour of its own even if not the rigour of other scientific disciplines. If the painful analyses of this book have established anything, it is that there is no definite method called the dialectical, that Hegel's triadic arrangement of his thought-material can no more be called a method than the *terza rima* can be called the method of the *Divine Comedy*. In a rough manner the triplicity or triadicity stressed by Hegel does indicate something genuine about his thought, but in the main it is merely an expository integument, and one that often positively masks, rather than reveals, the actual course of his thinking. There are, in the welter of Hegel's statements, real reasons which mediate the passage of his thought from one stage to the next—reasons mainly of a teleological kind which lead us from something which does something imperfectly or unclearly to something else that does it clearly and well—these reasons have often to be sought for like needles in haystacks. The triadic formulation merely confuses the course of the actual thinking, and gives a false impression that its nodes are in one place, when they really are in another. The attempted use of a rigorous triadic method is plainly the source of all that is unpersuasive in Hegel's conclusions, as it is the source of all that is obscure in his language. A large number of words must be employed to suggest a necessary logical movement in a given direction, when the movement of thought in that direction is not logically necessary, and has reasons and motives other than those which Hegel chooses to stress. The triadic pseudo-method is, in fact, the source of the large element of sheer fraud and charlatanism which Hegel's critics have at all times recognized, and which his admirers must not seek to hide. But they should also point to the *source* of this element of fraud and charlatanism: Hegel's deep and reasoned belief in certain conclusions, and his sincere belief that they could be reached by the pseudo-method he uses. If the bogus element in the Dialectic has imposed on many great intelligences, there can be no doubt that it successfully imposed on Hegel himself.

The main reason why Hegel will remain worthy of study lies in his incomparable gathering together of the whole range of human experience into vital connection with what is best in that experience, and that without introducing anything transcendent, anything which lies beyond the range of what can be humanly mastered and understood. He is, without doubt, the Aristotle of our post-Renaissance world, our synoptic thinker without peer.

We may also praise him, without absurdity, as in a sense the most Christian of thinkers, for while the official defenders of Christianity have usually borrowed their logic and the cast of their thought from Aristotle or from other sources, Hegel alone among thinkers has borrowed the whole cast of his thought from Christianity. We may also praise him as the philosopher of the 'absolute negativity', the believer in nothing that does not spring from the free, uncommitted, self-committing human spirit. Despite his later verging towards reaction, he remains the philosopher of Reformation 'inwardness', of liberal Humanism, of perpetual, orderly revolution. If the shades of night are now falling upon the world of which Hegel was a noble ornament, it is not possible for us to look back on it, or him, without regret.

SUPPLEMENTARY NOTE

I wish to retract the view, stated on p. 353, that there is no such thing as a dialectical *method* to be found in Hegel. Hegel is unlike most philosophers in that one cannot go on studying him without continually discovering new depths of meaning and connection, and I now believe that the dialectic represents a fairly definite, very valuable method of higher-level comment on previously entertained notions and positions. See, e.g., my article on 'The Contemporary Relevance of Hegel' in *Language, Mind and Value* (Allen and Unwin, 1963).

APPENDIX

The following tables will enable the reader to place the topics discussed in this book in the detailed framework of Hegel's system, and will also bring out features of that framework which have been deliberately ignored or under-emphasized in the above treatment.

DIALECTICAL STRUCTURE OF THE PHENOMENOLOGY OF SPIRIT

Division A: Consciousness

Subdivision I: Sense-certainty, or the This and 'Meaning'.

Subdivision II: Perception, or the Thing and Illusion.

Subdivision III: Power and Understanding, Phenomena and the Supersensible World.

Division B: Self-consciousness

Subdivision I: Dependence and Independence of Self-consciousness, Mastery and Servitude.

Subdivision II: Freedom of Self-consciousness.

(1) Stoicism.

(2) Scepticism.

(3) The Unhappy Consciousness.

Division C: Reason

Subdivision I (AA): Certainty and Truth of Reason.

(A) Observational Reason.

(a) Observation of Nature.

(b) Observation of Self-consciousness; Logical and Psychological Laws.

(c) Observation of Self-consciousness in relation to physical immediacy; Physiognomy and Phrenology.

(B) The Realization of the Rational Self-consciousness through itself.

(a) Pleasure and Necessity.

(b) The Law of the Heart and the Frenzy of Self-Conceit.

(c) Virtue and the Way of the World.

(C) Individuality, which is real in and for itself.

(a) The Spiritual Zoo and Humbug, or the 'Cause' itself.

(b) Legislative Reason.

(c) Reason as testing Laws.

Subdivision II (BB): Spirit.

(A) *True* Spirit; Customary Morality.
(a) The Ethical World, the Human and the Divine Law, Man and Woman.
(b) Ethical Action, Human and Divine Knowledge, Guilt and Destiny.
(c) Legal Status.

(B) The Self-estranged Spirit; Culture.
I. The World of the self-estranged Spirit.
(a) Culture and its Sphere of Reality.
(b) Religious Faith and Rationalistic Insight.

II. The Enlightenment.
(a) The Struggle of Enlightenment with Superstition.
(b) The Truth of Enlightenment.

III. Absolute Freedom and Terror.

(C) Spirit assured of itself; Morality.
(a) The Moral World-view.
(b) Moral Duplicity.
(c) Conscience, the Beautiful Soul, Evil and Forgiveness.

Subdivision III (CC): Religion.

(A) Natural Religion.
(a) The Religion of Light (Zoroastrianism).
(b) Religious Plants and Animals (Indian Religion).
(c) The Artificer in Religion (Egyptian Religion).

(B) The Religion of Art (Greek Religion).
(a) The Abstract Work of Art (Sculpture, Hymns, Cultus).
(b) The Living Work of Art (Athletes).
(c) The Spiritual Work of Art (Epic, Tragic and Comic Poetry).

(C) Revealed Religion (Christianity).

Subdivision IV (DD): Absolute Knowledge (Philosophy).

DIALECTICAL STRUCTURE OF THE DOCTRINE OF BEING
(PART ONE OF THE LOGIC)

Division I: Quality

Subdivision I: Being (*Seyn*).
(A) Being.
(B) Nothing.
(C) Becoming.

Subdivision II: Being Determinate (*Daseyn*).

(A) Determinate Being as such.
(B) Finitude.
(C) Infinity (False and True).

Subdivision III: Being-for-self (*Fürsichseyn*).

(A) Being-for-self as such.
(B) Unity and Plurality.
(C) Repulsion and Attraction (Logical bases of atomism).

Division II: Quantity

Subdivision I: Quantity.

(A) Pure Quantity.
(B) Continuous and Discrete Quantity.
(C) Limitation of Quantity.

Subdivision II: Quantum.

(A) Number.
(B) Extensive and Intensive Quantum.
(C) Quantitative Infinity.

Subdivision III: Quantitative Ratio.

(A) Direct Ratio.
(B) Inverse Ratio.
(C) Ratio of Powers.

Division III: Measure

Subdivision I: Specific Quantity.
(A) Specific Quantum.
(B) Specifying Measure.
(C) Being-for-self in Measure.

Subdivision II: Real Measure.

(A) The Ratio of Independent Measures.
(B) Nodal Line of Measure Relationships.
(C) The Measureless.

Subdivision III: The Genesis of Essence.

(A) Absolute Indifference.
(B) Indifference as Inverse Ratio of its Factors.
(C) Transition to Essence.

DIALECTICAL STRUCTURE OF THE DOCTRINE OF ESSENCE
(PART TWO OF THE LOGIC)

Division I: Essence as Reflection into Self

Subdivision I: Mere Appearance (*Schein*).

(A) The Essential and the Unessential.
(B) Mere Appearance.
(C) Reflection (Positing, External and Determining Reflection).

Subdivision II: The Essentialities or Reflective Determinations.

(A) Identity (Abstract Identity and the Law of Identity).
(B) Difference.
    (1) Absolute Difference.
    (2) Diversity (Variety).
    (3) Polar Opposition.
(C) Contradiction (with Laws of Contradiction and Excluded Middle).

Subdivision III: Ground.

(A) Absolute Ground.
    (*a*) Form and Essence.
    (*b*) Form and Matter.
    (*c*) Form and Content.
(B) Determinate Ground.
    (*a*) Formal (tautological) Ground.
    (*b*) Real (non-tautological) Ground.
    (*c*) Complete Ground.
(C) The Condition.
    (*a*) The relatively Unconditioned.
    (*b*) The absolutely Unconditioned.
    (*c*) Entry into Existence of the Matter of Fact (*Sache*).

Division II: Appearance or Phenomenal Being

Subdivision I: Existence.

(A) The Thing and its Properties.
(B) The Constitution of the Thing out of 'Matters'.
(C) The Dissolution of the Thing.

Subdivision II: Phenomenal Being Proper.

(A) The Law of the Phenomenon.
(B) The Phenomenal World and the World-in-itself.
(C) The Dissolution of Phenomenal Being.

Subdivision III: The Essential Relationship.

(A) The Relationship of Whole and Parts.
(B) The Relationship of Force and its Manifestation (Expression).
(C) The Relationship of Inner and Outer.

Division III: Actuality

Subdivision I: The Absolute.

(A) The Exposition of the Absolute.
(B) The Absolute Attribute.
(C) The Mode of the Absolute.

Subdivision II: Actuality.

(A) Contingency, or Formal Actuality, Possibility and Necessity.
(B) Relative Necessity, or Real Actuality, Possibility and Necessity.
(C) Absolute Necessity.

Subdivision III: The Absolute Relationship.

(A) Relationship of Substantiality.
(B) Relationship of Causality.
(C) Reciprocal Interaction.

DIALECTICAL STRUCTURE OF THE DOCTRINE OF THE NOTION
(PART THREE OF THE LOGIC)

Division I: Subjectivity

Subdivision I: The Notion (Concept).

(A) The Universal Notion.
(B) The Specific (Particular) Notion.
(C) The Individual.

Subdivision II: The Judgement.

(A) The Judgement of Existence (Inherence).
    (a) The Positive Judgement.
    (b) The Negative Judgement.
    (c) The Infinite Judgement.
(B) The Judgement of Reflection.
    (a) The Singular Judgement.
    (b) The Particular Judgement.
    (c) The Universal Judgement.

(C) The Judgement of Necessity.
    (*a*) The Categorical Judgement.
    (*b*) The Hypothetical Judgement.
    (*c*) The Disjunctive Judgement.
(D) The Judgement of the Notion (Value).
    (*a*) The Assertoric Judgement.
    (*b*) The Problematic Judgement.
    (*c*) The Apodeictic Judgement.

Subdivision III: The Syllogism.

(A) The Syllogism of Existence. (First, Second, Third **and** Fourth Figures.)
(B) The Syllogism of Reflection.
    (*a*) The Syllogism of Allness.
    (*b*) The Inductive Syllogism.
    (*c*) The Analogical Syllogism.
(C) The Syllogism of Necessity.
    (*a*) The Categorical Syllogism.
    (*b*) The Hypothetical Syllogism.
    (*c*) The Disjunctive Syllogism.

Division II: Objectivity

Subdivision I: Mechanism.

(A) The Mechanical Object.
(B) The Mechanical Process.
(C) Absolute Mechanism.

Subdivision II: Chemism.

(A) The Chemical Object.
(B) The Chemical Process.
(C) Transition from Chemism.

Subdivision III: Teleology.

(A) The Subjective End.
(B) The Means.
(C) The Realized (Executed) End.

Division III: The Idea

Subdivision I: Life (The Immediate Idea).

(A) The Living Individual.
(B) The Life-Process.
(C) The Genus (Kind).

Subdivision II: The Idea of Knowledge.

(A) The Idea of the True.
    (*a*) Analytic Knowledge.
    (*b*) Synthetic Knowledge.
        (1) Definition.
        (2) Division.
        (3) Theorems.
(B) The Idea of the Good.

Subdivision III: The Absolute Idea.

DIALECTICAL STRUCTURE OF THE PHILOSOPHY OF NATURE

Division I: *Mechanics*

Subdivision I: Mathematical Mechanics.

(A) Space.
(B) Time.
(C) Union of Space and Time (Place, Motion, Matter).

Subdivision II: Finite Mechanics, Gravity.

(A) Inertia.
(B) Impact.
(C) Falling.

Division II: *Physics*

Subdivision I: The Physics of Universal Individuality.

(A) The free physical Bodies.
    (1) The Sun.
    (2) The Bodies of Opposition (Moons and Comets).
    (3) The Planet as the Body of Individuality.
(B) The Elements.
    (1) Air.
    (2) The Elements of Opposition (Fire and Water).
    (3) Earth.
(C) Meteorology.

Subdivision II: The Physics of Specific Individuality.

(A) Specific Gravity.
(B) Cohesion (Adhesion, Coherence and Elasticity).
(C) Sound.
(D) Warmth.

Subdivision III: The Physics of Total Individuality.

(A) Shape.
(1) Shapelessness (Powders and Fluids).
(2) Magnetism.
(3) Crystallography.

(B) The Specific Properties of Bodies.
(1) Relationship to Light.
(a) Transparency.
(b) Refraction.
(c) Theory of Colour.
(2) Properties of the Opposition.
(a) Smell as specified Airiness.
(b) Taste as specified Water.
(3) Electricity.

(C) The Chemical Process.
(1) Alloys and Mixtures.
(2) The Real (Chemical) Process (Galvanism, Combustion, Formation of Salts, Chemical Affinity).
(3) Chemical Isolation.

Division III: Organics

Subdivision I: The Terrestrial Organism.

(A) History of the Earth.
(B) Geology (Land Forms).
(C) Terrestrial Life (universal and unindividualized).

Subdivision II: The Plant.

(A) The Morphological Process.

(B) The Process of Assimilation.

(C) The Process of Reproduction.

Subdivision III: The Animal.

(A) Morphology.
(a) Organic Functions.
(b) Organic Systems (Nervous, Muscular, Circulatory, Digestive).
(c) Total Structure.
(d) The Formation of Structure.

(B) Assimilation.
(1) The Theoretical (Sensory) Process.
(2) The Practical (Instinctive and Reflex) Process.
(3) The Urge towards Construction.

(C) Reproduction.
    (1) The Relationship of the Sexes.
    (2) Zoology.
        (*a*) Worms and Molluscs.
        (*b*) Insects.
        (*c*) Vertebrates.
    (3) Veterinary Science.
        (*a*) Nosology.
        (*b*) Therapy.
        (*c*) The Death of the Individual.

DIALECTICAL STRUCTURE OF THE PHILOSOPHY OF SUBJECTIVE SPIRIT

Division I: Anthropology.

Subdivision I: The Natural Soul.

(A) Natural Qualities.
    (1) Universal (Cosmic, Sidereal, Terrestrial) Psychic life.
    (2) Specific Psychic Life of Regions and Races.
    (3) Individual Temperament, Talent, Character, Physiognomy and other Dispositions.

(B) Natural Alterations.
    (1) Infancy, Youth, Maturity, Senescence.
    (2) Sexual development, Marriage, Bringing up of a Family.
    (3) Sleeping and Waking.

(C) Sensation and its Varieties.

Subdivision II: The Feeling Soul.

(A) The Feeling Soul in its Immediacy.
    (1) The Genius.
    (2) Magnetic Somnambulism and cognate states.

(B) Self-feeling.
    (1) Normal Self-feeling.
    (2) Derangement.
        (*a*) Dullness and Mental Confusion.
        (*b*) Idiocy.
        (*c*) Insanity.

(C) Habit.

Subdivision III: The Actual Soul.

Division II: Phenomenology

Subdivision I: Consciousness.

(A) The Sensory Consciousness.

(B) Perception.

(C) Understanding.

Subdivision II: Self-consciousness.

(A) The Desiderative Self-consciousness.

(B) The Recognitive (Acknowledging) Self-consciousness.
(1) The Life and Death Struggle.
(2) Master and Slave.
(3) The Community of Need and Care.

(C) Universal Self-consciousness.

Subdivision III: Reason.

Division III: Psychology

Subdivision I: Theoretical Spirit.

(A) Intuition.
(1) Sensation.
(2) Attention.
(3) Intuition Proper.

(B) Imaginative Reproduction (*Vorstellung*).
(1) Recollection.
(2) Imagination (*Einbildungskraft*).
(3) Memory Proper (*Gedächtniss*).

(C) Thinking.
(1) The Understanding.
(2) The Judgement.
(3) Syllogistic Reason.

Subdivision II: Practical Spirit.

(A) Practical Feeling.

(B) The Passions and the Act of Choice.

(C) Happiness.

Subdivision III: Free Spirit.

DIALECTICAL STRUCTURE OF THE PHILOSOPHY OF RIGHT
(OBJECTIVE SPIRIT)

Division I: Abstract Right

Subdivision I: Property.

(A) Seizure.

(B) Use.

(C) Alienation.

Subdivision II: Contract.

(A) Gifts.

(B) Exchanges.

(C) Guarantees and Pledges.

Subdivision III: Wrongs.

(A) Civil Wrongs.

(B) Fraud.

(C) Crime and Punishment.

Division II: Morality

Subdivision I: Design and Blame.

Subdivision II: Intention and Welfare.

Subdivision III: The Good and Conscience, Pathology of Conscience.

Division III: Customary Morality (*Sittlichkeit*)

Subdivision I: The Family.

(A) Marriage.

(B) The Family Property.

(C) The Bringing up of the Children and the Dissolution of the Family.

Subdivision II: Civil Society.

(A) The System of Wants.

(1) Needs and their Satisfactions.

(2) Labour and its Varieties.

(3) The Means of Subsistence and the Social Classes.

(B) The Administration of Justice.

(1) Justice as Law.

(2) The Existence (Promulgation) of Laws.

(3) Courts of Justice.

(C) The Police and Corporations (Trade Guilds,.

Subdivision III: The State.
  (A) Constitutional Law.
      (1) The Constitution in itself.
          (a) The Princely Power.
          (b) The State Authorities.
          (c) The Legislature.
      (2) External Relations of the State, War.
  (B) International Law.
  (C) World History.

DIALECTICAL STRUCTURE OF TREATMENT OF ABSOLUTE SPIRIT

Section I: Art.

Section II: Religion.

Section III: Philosophy.

INDEX